Industry and Company Information

Illustrated Search Strategy and Sources

(Library Research Guide Series, no. 10)

by

A. Craig Hawbaker
Business Librarian
University Library
University of Arizona
Tucson, Arizona

Judith M. Nixon
Consumer & Family Sciences Librarian
Libraries of Purdue
Purdue University
West Lafayette, Indiana

The Pierian Press
Ann Arbor, Michigan
1991

DEDICATION:

This book is dedicated to all students who ever tried
to research a company or industry in their libraries.
It is also dedicated to Peggy Hawbaker and Bob Nixon, who
believed this book was needed, and Michelle and Mark
Hawbaker and Betsy Nixon, who will need it some day.

ISBN: 0-87650-287-7

The Pierian Press
Box 1808
5000 Washtenaw
Ann Arbor, MI 48106-1808
1-800-678-2435

TABLE OF CONTENTS

Preface v

Acknowledgments vii

PART I: INTRODUCTION

Chapter 1: **Introduction to Search Strategy and Topic Selection** 1

Chapter 2: **Computers and Business Research** 13

PART II: INDUSTRY RESEARCH

Chapter 3: **Industry Overviews** 33

Chapter 4: **Periodical and Newspaper Indexes** 43

Chapter 5: **Statistics** 61

Chapter 6: **Associations and Directories** 73

PART III: COMPANY RESEARCH

Chapter 7: **Private, Public, or Subsidiary Company?** 87

Chapter 8: **Private Companies** 93

Chapter 9: **Public Companies** 107

Chapter 10: **Subsidiary Companies** 127

Chapter 11: **Financial Ratios** 133

PART IV: LIBRARY SKILLS TEST AND OTHER RESOURCES

Chapter 12: **Other Resources** 141

Appendix A: **Library Skills Test** 155

Appendix B: **Additional Resource Materials: A Bibliography** 159

Index of Titles 171

PREFACE

Companies in the information age of the 1990s will be hiring employees who know the value of facts and figures. If information is power, then, indeed, you can be a more powerful and successful student, job applicant, and employee by utilizing the basic industry and company resources available in most libraries.

Imagine the job applicant who, at the appropriate time during the interview asks, "I understand that there may be a major management shuffle in your company during the next thirty days. How will this affect the company's structure?" Or the applicant might make the passing comment, "You must be pleased by your company's current dividends!" These remarks tell the interviewer that the applicant knows how to locate information. Either of these remarks might make the difference between success and failure for the job applicant.

Tomorrow's companies will also seek those individuals who can write concise and effective reports and analyses. The ability to communicate, both orally and in writing, will be paramount.

As a result of this increased emphasis on researching, writing, and communicating in the "real world," more teachers and professors are realizing the importance of these skills. More courses are emphasizing writing and communicating, and a report or term paper that demands library research is common in these courses.

IS THIS THE BOOK YOU NEED?

The answer is yes if you find yourself in one of the following situations:

1) If you are a college student majoring in business (finance, management, marketing, MBA, and so on), you will need to know how to locate appropriate library materials for term papers and other assignments. This book introduces you to the basic library sources that will provide industry and company information. It will guide you step-by-step through the most useful library reference tools available in most libraries.

v

2) If you are a college student majoring in science, humanities, fine arts, or another field, you may find yourself in the position of writing a term paper on an industry or company. This book will guide you to many useful reference sources.

3) If you are a job applicant, you might want to find company information for interview purposes or simply to make a mundane letter of application more polished. This book will give you many different alternatives for locating such information.

4) If you are an entrepreneur or business person, you may need to locate information on a particular industry or company. This book will get you started in the right direction.

5) If you are a professor who makes business assignments or a reference librarian, this book will help you advise students on how to find relevant library sources.

6) If you are a library school student who needs an introduction to the basic business resources, this book should be invaluable.

The answer is no if you find yourself in one of the following situations:

1) If you are writing a term paper on a subject such as collective bargaining or hostile takeovers or Lee Iacocca, then this book will not help. It is aimed at providing a guide to industry and company information.

2) If you need to know the general procedures for writing term papers, including notetaking, outlining, and bibliographical forms, this book will not help. Instead, use this book in conjunction with a style manual that your professor recommends, such as Kate L. Turabian's *A Manual for Writers of Term Papers, Theses and Dissertations*, 5th edition, 1987, published by University of Chicago Press. Popularly known as Turabian, you will find this style manual in almost every reference department.

ACKNOWLEDGMENTS

Many people have helped in the production of this book. Special thanks are due to Thomas G. Kirk for his assistance, patience, and help. Craig Hawbaker extends special thanks to the University of Arizona for granting a sabbatical leave, which enabled him to work on this book.

Thanks are also due to the publishers and authors listed below who granted permission to use sections of their copyrighted works as illustrations. This book would not be possible without their support.

CREDITS FOR FIGURES

Figures 2.2, 2.3 and 2.4: From *TRADE & INDUSTRY INDEX*tm, Foster City, CA: Information Access Company. Permission granted. COPYRIGHT 1989 INFORMATION ACCESS COMPANY, FOSTER CITY, CA 94404.

Figures 3.1 - 3.4: From *Industry Surveys*, New York, NY: Standard & Poor's Corporation, 1989. Reprinted With Permission of Standard & Poor's Corporation.

Figures 3.5 and 3.6: From *Value Line Investment Survey*, New York, NY: Value Line, Inc., 1989. Copyright (c) 1989 by Value Line, Inc.; used by permission.

Figures 4.1 and 4.2: From *Annals of Tourism Research*, Elmsford, NY: Pergamon Press, Inc., 1988. Reprinted With Permission from *Annals of Tourism Research*, volume 15(3), Title page and Statement of Purpose, 1988, Pergamon Press plc.

Figures 4.3, 4.4 and 4.5: From *Business Periodicals Index*, Bronx, NY: The H. W. Wilson Company, October 1988. Copyright (c) 1988 by The H. W. Wilson Company. Material reproduced with permission of the publisher.

Figure 4.6: From *INFOTRAC*tm, Foster City, CA: Information Access Company. Permission granted. COPYRIGHT 1989 INFORMATION ACCESS COMPANY, FOSTER CITY, CA 94404.

Figure 8.5: From *D-U-N-S Account Identification Service*, Parsippany, NJ: Dun's Marketing Services, Inc., 1989. Copyright 1989, Dun's Marketing Services, Inc. All Rights Reserved. Reprinted With Permission.

Figure 8.6: From *D&B - Dun's Market Identifiers*, Parsippany, NJ: Dun's Marketing Services, Inc., 1989. Copyright 1989, Dun's Marketing Services, Inc. All Rights Reserved. Reprinted With Permission.

Figure 8.7: From *INFOTRAC*™, Foster City, CA 94404: Information Access Company, Permission granted. COPYRIGHT 1989 INFORMATION ACCESS COMPANY, FOSTER CITY, CA 94404.

Figure 8.8: From *Advertising Age*, Chicago, IL: Crain Communications Inc., 1988. Reprinted With Permission from the November 14, 1988 issue of *Advertising Age*. Copyright 1988 by Crain Communications Inc.

Figure 8.9: From *Predicasts F&S Index: United States*, Cleveland, OH: Predicasts, December 1986. Reprinted With Permission from Predicasts.

Figure 8.10: From *Hotel & Motel Management*, Cleveland, OH: Business Information Services, 1986. Reprinted With Permission of *Hotel & Motel Management* (c) September 1986.

Figures 9.1 and 9.2: From *Hilton Hotels Corp.'s Annual Report*, Beverly Hills, CA: Hilton Hotels Corporation, 1988. Reproduced with permission from Cheryl L. Marsh, Corporate Secretary of the Hilton Hotels Corporation.

Figure 9.3: From *Hilton Hotels Corp.'s 10-K Report*, Beverly Hills, CA: Hilton Hotels Corporation, 1988. Reproduced with permission from Cheryl L. Marsh, Corporate Secretary of the Hilton Hotels Corporation.

Figure 9.4: From *Compact Disclosure*, Bethesda, MD: Disclosure Information Group, 1989. Reprinted With Permission from Disclosure Incorporated.

Figures 9.5 and 9.6: From *Value Line Investment Survey*, New York, NY: Value Line, Inc., April 28, 1989. Copyright (c) 1989 by Value Line, Inc.; used by permission.

Figure 9.7: From *Moody's Complete Corporate Index*, New York, NY: Moody's Investors Service, Inc., 1988. Reprinted With Permission from Moody's Investors Service.

Figures 9.8 and 9.9: From *Moody's Industrial Manual*, New York, NY: Moody's Investors Service, Inc., 1988. Reprinted With Permission from Moody's Investors Service.

Figure 9.10: From *Moody's 5000 Plus*, New York, NY: Moody's Investors Service, Inc. Reprinted With Permission from Moody's Investors Service.

Figure 9.11: From *Standard Corporation Descriptions*, New York, NY: Standard & Poor's Corporation, Reprinted With Permission of Standard & Poor's Corporation.

Figure 9.12: From *Business Periodicals Index*, Bronx, NY: The H. W. Wilson Company, April 1989. Copyright (c) 1989 by the H. W. Wilson Company. Material reproduced with permission of the publisher.

Figure 9.13: From *Predicasts F&S Index: United States*, Cleveland, OH: Predicasts, December 1987. Reprinted With Permission from Predicasts.

Figures 10.1 and 10.2: From *Directory of Corporate Affiliations*, Wilmette, IL: National Register Publishing Company, 1990. Reprinted With Permission of Macmillan Directory Division.

Figure 10.3: From *Hilton Hotels Corp.'s 10-K Report*, Beverly Hills, CA: Hilton Hotels Corporation, 1988. Reproduced with permission from Cheryl L. Marsh, Corporate Secretary of the Hilton Hotels Corporation.

Figures 11.1 and 11.2: From *Moody's Industrial Manual*, New York, NY: Moody's Investors Service, Inc., 1988. Reprinted With Permission from Moody's Investors Service, Inc.

Figure 11.3: From *Industry Surveys*, New York, NY: Standard & Poor's Corporation, March 1989. Reprinted With Permission of Standard & Poor's Corporation.

Figure 11.4: From *Industry Norms & Key Business Ratios*, Murray Hill, NJ: Dun & Bradstreet, Inc., 1989. Copyright 1989 Dun & Bradstreet, Inc. All Rights Reserved. Reprinted With Permission.

Figure 12.1: From *Encyclopedia of Business Information Sources*, 7th ed, edited by James Woy, Detroit, MI: Gale Research Inc., 1988. Copyright © 1988 Gale Research Inc. Reprinted by permission of the publisher.

Figure 12.2: From *Handbook of Business Information* by Diane Strauss, Englewood, CO: Libraries Unlimited, Inc., 1988. Reprinted With Permission from Diane Strauss, Davis Library, University of North Carolina, at Chapel Hill.

Figure 12.3: From *Hotel and Restaurant Industries* by Judith M. Nixon, Phoenix, AZ: Oryx Press, 1988. Reprinted from *Hotel and Restaurant Industries* by Judith Nixon with permission from Oryx Press, 2214 North Central at Encanto, Phoenix, AZ 85004.

Figure 12.4: From *Lodging and Restaurant Index* by Judith M. Nixon, West Lafayette, IN: Restaurant, Hotel & Institutional Management Institute, 1988. Reprinted With Permission from Restaurant, Hotel & Institutional Management Institute, Purdue University, West Lafayette, Indiana.

Figure 12.5: From *F.I.U. Hospitality Review*, Miami, FL: School of Hospitality Management, Florida International University, 1988. Reproduced with permission from N. H. Ringstrom, editor of *F.I.U. Hospitality Review*.

Figure 12.7: From *Index to Arizona News in the Arizona Daily Star* by Bonnie Hintzman, Tucson, AZ: University of Arizona Library, 1989. Reproduced with permission of W. David Laird, University Librarian, University of Arizona.

Figure 12.8: From *Arizona Daily Star*, Tucson, AZ: Arizona Daily Star, 1989. Reprinted With Permission of the publisher.

Figure APPENDIX.2: From *Business Periodicals Index*, Bronx, NY: The H. W. Wilson Company, 1987/88. Copyright (c) 1988 by the H. W. Wilson Company. Material reproduced with permission of the publisher.

CHAPTER 1

INTRODUCTION TO SEARCH STRATEGY AND TOPIC SELECTION

You may find yourself in a number of situations where you need industry or company information:

- Your professor has given you an assignment.

- You are preparing for a job interview, or you are writing a letter of application.

- Your boss has given you a project.

Locating this desired information on an industry or company can be a very frustrating experience. The information you need may be buried in an annual report to shareholders, in the text of a *Wall Street Journal* article, or in a report published by a professional association. It may be contained in a statistical chart, in a computer database, or in a government publication. As a result, this myriad of choices may leave you bewildered. And what's more, this research is going to take too much of your precious time! What can you do to make all of this a more pleasant and productive, yet less time-consuming, task? How can you find information on industries and companies efficiently and effectively?

That is the major goal of this book: to provide you with a step-by-step illustrated guide to the major industry and company research sources available in most libraries. It answers the questions students most often ask.

- Where do I begin?

- What sources should I use?

- How do I use each of the sources?

Our purpose is to show you, by example, how to do your own research by following a "search strategy." A search strategy is both a systematic and organized way to 1) locate an appropriate topic and 2) find information in the library on that topic.

CHOOSING AN APPROPRIATE INDUSTRY AND COMPANY

Choosing the industry and company is the first and most important step of your search strategy. Of course, you may be in a situation where a professor or superior provides the industry and company for you. In these situations, you have no choice.

If you can choose, however, do not perform this search strategy step in a hurried manner with little forethought. Choosing a topic that allows itself to be researched will save time and energy. Doing some checking before choosing an industry and company will yield answers to the following questions:

1) Is information available on the industry and company you have in mind?

Some industries, such as the accounting industry, are dominated by large, private companies such as Price Waterhouse and Arthur Andersen & Company. These private companies are not required to release public reports, and information on them is very sketchy or non-existent in standard reference books. Since private companies dominate the accounting industry, there is a resulting lack of industry information as well. Writing a paper on the Price Waterhouse Company and its relationship to the accounting industry might prove to be difficult.

On the other hand, the lodging industry is dominated by several publicly owned corporations, including Hilton Hotels Corporation, Holiday Corporation, and Marriott Corporation. You can locate a wealth of information on each of these companies and the lodging industry.

2) Can you choose an industry and a company that is relevant to your career aspirations?

If you are going to research an industry and company, why not make it as relevant as possible to your real-life needs! Unless you are one of the fortunate few who already has a job waiting upon graduation, at some point you will need to start the job-hunting process. Your project at hand is a good opportunity to explore an industry and company that interests you. If you have a job interview in the near future, here is a good opportunity to improve your knowledge of the company.

3) Can you choose an industry and a company that complements an assignment in another course?

Possibly you have assignments in other courses that require library research. How about that speech on a controversial topic? Is your chosen industry embroiled in some environmental or legal issue that could also be relevant for the speech? Is your company undergoing a crisis due to managerial changes? Possibly you can kill the proverbial two birds with one stone.

In summary, if you have the option, be certain to choose an industry and company for which you can locate adequate information. And, if you can choose an industry and company that relates to some aspect of your current life, all the better. A search strategy will help you with these objectives.

This book will show you how to do industry and company research by taking the examples of the lodging industry (hotels and motels) and the Hilton Hotels Corporation and Red Roof Inns specifically. We will look at the problem of overbuilding in the industry. Illustrations or excerpts from standard reference sources will show you the strategy of locating information as well as how to use the sources.

FINDING INFORMATION IN THE LIBRARY

Now that the hotel industry, Hilton Hotels Corporation, and Red Roof Inns, have been chosen as examples, you are ready to proceed with the next step in the search strategy—finding information in the library. You probably have done other library assignments in a haphazard fashion, simply by consulting books that sounded appropriate, by utilizing several encyclopedias, or by browsing through the library stacks. Although this approach might work for some topics, it will definitely not be satisfactory for industry and company research. There is a proven search strategy for locating this specialized information.

Just as an airline pilot should never take off without a destination, your research should never start without a good idea of where it will proceed and ultimately end. Should you spend hours researching the lodging industry when your primary research interest is one particular company? Probably not, but it is important to have a good overview of the industry in the beginning. That industry overview is your take-off, or starting point. Your final destination will vary, however, according to your particular assignment or research interest. You may have a direct flight that utilizes each chapter of this book. However, you may have an interrupted flight that skips several unnecessary chapters, yet still reaches your final destination.

Once you understand the search strategy in this book, you will be able to apply it to research involving any industry or company. You will have the knowledge and ability to locate information in a logical sequence of steps—a search strategy.

Each step in the search strategy will lead you to a different type of industry or company information. If your library does not have a particular source, look in Appendix B for alternate reference sources, or ask your reference librarian for a suggestion.

Now let's look at what reference sources are included in each search strategy step. The flowcharts on pages 4 and 5 provide you with an outline of the search strategy steps. The questions illustrate the importance of each step.

3

SEARCH STRATEGY FLOWCHART

INDUSTRY SEARCH

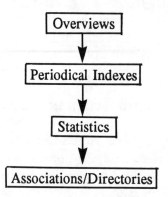

COMPANY SEARCH

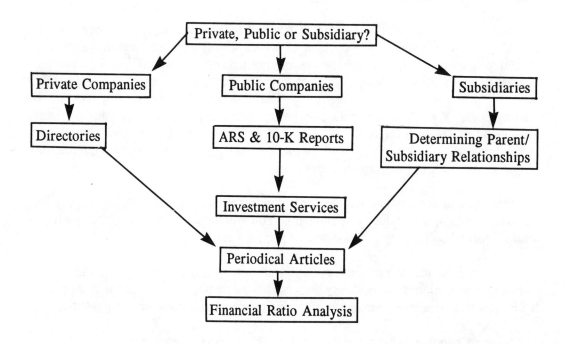

4

SEARCH STRATEGY OBJECTIVES

Overviews:

- What are the major problems facing the hotel industry?
- Is the industry overbuilt?

Periodical Articles on the Industry:

- Has anyone written an article forecasting the business conditions for the hotel industry (in newspapers and trade journals)?

Statistics on the Industry:

- Where can you find a statistical report on the lodging industry?
- Are there any industry statistics that indicate the industry is overbuilt?

Associations and Directories:

- Are there any trade associations that have very current information on the industry?
- What information can you compile on the lodging industry from a directory?

Public, Private or Subsidiary Company?:

- Is Hilton Hotels Corporation privately or publicly owned?
- Where can you find a list of the larger privately and publicly owned companies in the lodging industry?

   Private:
   - What information is available on Red Roof Inns, a private company?

   Public:
   - What information is available on Hilton Hotels Corporation, a public company?

   Subsidiary:
   - Does Hilton Hotels Corporation own any subsidiary companies?
   - How can you find information on Hilton Service Corporation?

Ratio Analysis:

- How does Hilton Hotels Corporation compare financially with other companies in the industry?

5

So far, you should understand the importance of two concepts:

1) industry and company selection, and
2) the search strategy.

With these two concepts in mind, you are now ready to see a summary of what you will be learning in the rest of this book.

COMPUTERS AND BUSINESS RESEARCH (CHAPTER 2)

What: 1) business databases,
              2) end-user online searching, and
              3) CD-ROM database searching.

Importance: Provides improved access to business information.

Computers and databases are increasingly important components of business research. They provide fast, efficient retrieval of information.

INDUSTRY OVERVIEWS (CHAPTER 3)

What: 1) *Industry Surveys*, and
              2) *Value Line Investment Survey*

Importance: Provides a list of potential industries for research and overviews of U.S. industries.

Industry overview sources supply a listing of the primary industries in the U.S. economy, along with a general assessment of each industry's trends and problems. This overview provides a framework to evaluate a company, since the future of a company depends on the health of the industry. The brighter the outlook for an industry's product or service, the better chance the company has for survival. In an industry plagued with problems, even the most efficiently managed and soundly financed company may fail.

PERIODICAL AND NEWSPAPER INDEXES (CHAPTER 4)

What: 1) *Business Periodicals Index,*
2) *Business Index/INFOTRAC*™,
3) *Predicasts F&S Index: United States,* and
4) *Wall Street Journal Index.*

Importance: Provides citations to periodical and newspaper articles about the industry.

Periodical and newspaper indexes provide an efficient way to find recent articles about an industry.

STATISTICS (CHAPTER 5)

What: 1) *Statistical Abstract of the United States,*
2) *Statistical Reference Index,* and
3) *American Statistics Index.*

Importance: Provides statistics that add reliability and substance to a report.

Professional organizations, educational institutions, businesses, and the government collect and disseminate statistics. When properly researched and cited, statistics can support opinions and issues with facts and figures.

ASSOCIATIONS AND DIRECTORIES (CHAPTER 6)

What: 1) *Encyclopedia of Associations,* and
2) *Directories in Print.*

Importance: Provides access to specialized industry information.

There are literally thousands of associations and directories. The important bond between associations and directories lies in their ability to lead to specialized sources of information both inside and outside the library.

PRIVATE, PUBLIC, OR SUBSIDIARY COMPANY? (CHAPTER 7)

What: *Million Dollar Directory.*

Importance: Provides brief information on 160,000 companies and indicates whether the company is publicly or privately owned.

    The research strategy for company information depends on whether it is a privately owned company, a publicly owned company, or a subsidiary company. Private companies are not required by law to release any information to the public, and, as a result, information on them can be scarce. On the other hand, publicly owned companies must release their financial reports, and information on them is usually plentiful. A subsidiary company is owned by another larger company, and it presents unique research problems. Before you begin looking for information on a company, the first step is to determine if it is a private, public, or subsidiary company.

PRIVATE COMPANIES (CHAPTER 8)

What: 1) *Million Dollar Directory,*
             2) *WARD'S BUSINESS DIRECTORY^{tm}*,
             3) *D-U-N-S Account Identification Service,*
             4) *Dun's Market Identifiers (online),*
             5) *Business Index/INFOTRAC^{tm}*, and
             6) *Predicasts F&S Index: United States.*

Importance: Provides information on private companies.

    While the large majority of companies in the United States is private, the amount of information on these companies is very sparse. Chapter 8 illustrates how to locate information on Red Roof Inns, a private company.

PUBLIC COMPANIES (CHAPTER 9)

What: 1) Annual Report to Shareholders (ARS),
             2) 10-K Report,
             3) *Value Line Investment Survey,*
             4) *Moody's Manuals,*
             5) *Moody's 5000,* and
             6) *Standard Corporation Descriptions.*

Importance: Provides detailed financial data and the future plans for a publicly owned company.

Due to government regulations regarding public companies, there is a large amount of information available on publicly owned companies. Chapter 9 discusses the importance of annual reports to shareholders and 10-K Reports. It also illustrates how to use three major investment services to locate information on Hilton Hotels Corporation.

SUBSIDIARY COMPANIES (CHAPTER 10)

What: *Directory of Corporate Affiliations.*

Importance: Provides a listing of parent and subsidiary companies and shows corporate family trees.

Like most other large corporations, Hilton Hotels Corporation owns other companies, which are called subsidiaries. A lot of information can be located on the parent company (Hilton), but little or no information is available for subsidiaries. Although it is important to know the difference between a parent and a subsidiary, it is equally important to know where to find information on the corporate structure.

FINANCIAL RATIOS (CHAPTER 11)

What: *Industry Norms and Key Business Ratios.*

Importance: Provides industry ratios that can be compared against company ratios.

Industry financial ratios are averages that can then be compared to a company's ratios. By comparing the lodging industry's ratios to Hilton's ratios, you gain some understanding of how the company is performing. Chapter 11 illustrates how to locate financial ratios for Hilton Hotels Corporation as well as the lodging industry.

OTHER RESOURCES (CHAPTER 12)

What: 1) business guides and bibliographies,
2) specialized indexes,
3) interlibrary loan,
4) card catalogs, and
5) local resources.

Importance: Provides additional avenues to business information.

The final chapter in this book introduces several information resources and library services that lead to additional research avenues.

540 STANDARD INDUSTRIAL CLASSIFICATION

1389	Hot oil treating of oil field tanks: on a contract basis
1389	Hot shot service: on a contract basis
3547	Hot strip mill machinery—*mfg*
3255	Hot top refractories, clay—*mfg*
3297	Hot top refractories, nonclay—*mfg*
2449	Hot tubs, coopered—*mfg*
3088	Hot tubs, plastics or fiberglass—*mfg*
5999	Hot tubs—retail
5091	Hot tubs—wholesale
3639	Hot water heaters, household: including nonelectric—*mfg*
3493	Hot wound springs, except wire springs—*mfg*
3312	Hot-rolled iron and steel products—*mfg*
1522	Hotel construction—general contractors
7389	Hotel reservation service
3262	Hotel tableware and kitchen articles, vitreous china—*mfg*
7041	Hotels operated by organizations for members only
7011	Hotels, except residential
6513	Hotels, residential: operators
7011	Hotels, seasonal
8322	Hotlines
3634	Hotplates, electric—*mfg*
3821	Hotplates, laboratory—*mfg*
1521	House construction, single-family—general contractors
5963	House delivery of purchased milk—retail
8712	House designers
1799	House moving—contractors
1721	House painting—contractors
3142	House slippers—*mfg*
7519	House trailer rental
5963	House-to-house selling of coffee, soda, beer, bottled water, or other products—retail
1521	House: shell erection, single-family—general contractors
7999	Houseboat rentals
3732	Houseboats, building and repairing—*mfg*
2384	Housecoats, except children's and infants'—mfpm—*mfg*
2369	Housecoats: girls', children's, and infants'—mfpm—*mfg*
2253	Housecoats—mitse—*mfg*
2335	Housedresses: women's, misses', and juniors'—mfpm—*mfg*
2392	Housefurnishings, except curtains and draperies—*mfg*
5722	Household appliance stores, electric or gas—retail
2842	Household bleaches, dry or liquid—*mfg*
3991	Household brooms and brushes—*mfg*
3263	Household earthenware, semivitreous—*mfg*
2512	Household furniture upholstered on wood frames, except dual-purpose sleep furniture—*mfg*
2519	Household furniture, glass and plastics—*mfg*
2511	Household furniture, wood: except upholstered—*mfg*
2519	Household furniture: rattan, reed, malacca, fiber, willow, and wicker—*mfg*
5712	Household furniture—retail
5021	Household furniture—wholesale
3069	Household gloves, rubber—*mfg*
4214	Household goods moving, local: combined with storage
4226	Household goods warehousing and storage, without local trucking
2879	Household insecticides—*mfg*
3262	Household tableware and kitchen articles, vitreous china—*mfg*
2899	Household tints and dyes—*mfg*
3365	Household utensils, cast aluminum: except die-castings—*mfg*
3469	Household utensils, porcelain enameled—*mfg*
3469	Household utensils, stamped and pressed metal—*mfg*
2499	Household woodenware—*mfg*
8811	Households, private: employing cooks, maids, chauffeurs, gardeners, etc.
7349	Housekeeping (cleaning service) on a contract or fee basis
9223	Houses of correction—government
2452	Houses, portable: prefabricated wood—except mobile homes—*mfg*
3448	Houses, prefabricated: metal—*mfg*
3792	Housetrailers, except as permanent dwellings—*mfg*
5719	Housewares stores—retail
5963	Housewares: house-to-house, telephone or party plan selling—retail
9531	Housing agencies, nonoperating—government
9531	Housing authorities, nonoperating—government
6531	Housing authorities, operating
3443	Housing cabinets for radium, metal plate—*mfg*
3272	Housing components, prefabricated: concrete—*mfg*
3444	Housings for business machines, sheet metal: except stamped—*mfg*
3469	Housings for business machines, stamped metal—*mfg*
3443	Housings, pressure—*mfg*
3489	Howitzers, more than 30 mm. (or more than 1.18 inch)—*mfg*

Figure 1.1: "Alphabetical Index" from *Standard Industrial Classification Manual*, 1987.

10

...DARD INDUSTRIAL CLASSIFICATION (SIC)

...nderstand business research and the search strategy process, ...ant concept that will resurface throughout this book. The ...Industrial Classification" or "SIC," and it is contained in a ...*Standard Industrial Classification Manual* (Washington, DC: ...rinting Office, 1987). More commonly called the *SIC Manual*, this ...sification system of paramount importance in business research. The ...a uniform classification system and definitions for all businesses and ...United States. Each manufactured product and service has its own unique ...each company in the United States can be classified under one or more ...ese numbers, called the SIC numbers, are used by the federal government ...onomic census. They are also used by authors and publishers of business directories, online databases, and periodical indexes.

Part III of the *SIC Manual* is the "Alphabetic Index" (figure 1.1). Looking up Hotels, you see that there are several entries with the word "hotel" or "hotels" in them. At this point, select the entry and number that sound most appropriate (i.e., 7011) and turn to Part I of the *SIC Manual*, which is arranged numerically according to SIC numbers. Here you find a description, or definition, of the industry assigned SIC number 7011, as shown in figure 1.2. From this description, you can confirm that SIC 7011 is the best number for the hotel/lodging industry. SIC 7011 will be used for illustrative purposes throughout this book.

SUMMARY

1) A search strategy is both a systematic and organized way to locate an appropriate topic and find information in the library on that topic.

2) Choosing an industry and company for research is a very important step. If possible choose a publicly owned company.

3) Each chapter in the book is outlined and summarized.

4) The Standard Industrial Classification is a system that classifies and defines all products and services available in the United States. It is used in the economic censuses and by many business reference sources.

Major Group 70.—HOTELS, ROOMING HOUSES, CAMPS, AND OTHER LODGING PLACES

The Major Group as a Whole

This major group includes commercial and noncommercial establishments engaged in furnishing lodging, or lodging and meals, and camping space and camping facilities.

Industry Group No.	Industry No.	
701		**HOTELS AND MOTELS**
	7011	**Hotels and Motels**

Commercial establishments, known to the public as hotels, motor hotels, motels, or tourist courts, primarily engaged in providing lodging, or lodging and meals, for the general public. Hotels which are operated by membership organizations and open to the general public are included in this industry. Hotels operated by organizations for their members only are classified in Industry 7041. Apartment hotels are classified in Real Estate, Industry 6513; rooming and boarding houses are classified in Industry 7021; and sporting and recreational camps are classified in Industry 7032.

Auto courts	Motels
Bed and breakfast inns	Recreational hotels
Cabins and cottages	Resort hotels
Casino hotels	Seasonal hotels
Hostels	Ski lodges and resorts
Hotels, except residential	Tourist cabins
Inns, furnishing food and lodging	Tourist courts

702		**ROOMING AND BOARDING HOUSES**
	7021	**Rooming and Boarding Houses**

Establishments primarily engaged in renting rooms, with or without board, on a fee basis. Rental of apartments, apartment hotels, and other housing units are classified in Real Estate, Industry Group 651. Rooming and boarding houses operated by membership organizations for their members only are classified in Industry 7041. Homes for the aged, for children, and for the handicapped that also provide additional services, other than nursing care, are classified in Industry 8361, and homes that provide nursing care are classified in Industry Group 805.

Boarding houses, except organization	Rental of furnished rooms
Dormitories, commercially operated	Rooming houses, except organization
Lodging houses, except organization	

703		**CAMPS AND RECREATIONAL VEHICLE PARKS**
	7032	**Sporting and Recreational Camps**

Establishments primarily engaged in operating sporting and recreational camps, such as boys' and girls' camps, and fishing and hunting camps. Establishments primarily engaged in operating sports instructional camps, such as baseball, basketball, football, or karate camps, and those operating day camps are classified in Industry 7999.

Boys' camps	Hunting camps
Camps, sporting and recreational	Nudist camps
Dude ranches	Summer camps, except day and sports
Fishing camps	instructional
Girls' camps	

Figure 1.2: "Titles and Descriptions of Industries" from *Standard Industrial Classification Manual*, **1987.**

CHAPTER 2

COMPUTERS AND BUSINESS RESEARCH

Computers are widely visible in today's society. Supermarkets use them to register purchases. Banks use them as automatic teller machines (ATMs). Police stations use them to track missing children. This list could go on and on. But let's not leave out one important user of computers—libraries!

Libraries use computers for many different purposes. An online catalog means that you no longer have to use the manual card catalog. A computerized circulation system means that you no longer have to complete a form before you can check out a book. And online databases and CD-ROM databases, which we will be exploring in this chapter, mean that much of the information that used to be in printed encyclopedias, directories, and indexes is now available in a faster, more efficient machine-readable, computer format.

Because many publishers of indexes, journals, encyclopedias, and other printed books are providing the same data in computer format, this technology is becoming more prominent and important in business research. In fact, more than half of the resources illustrated in this book can be searched in a computer format. Due to the importance of this trend, this chapter is placed at the front of the book.

After reading this chapter, you will have a better understanding of the databases and other computer products that are mentioned in the rest of the book. Throughout the remaining chapters, you will find examples of databases that correspond to the printed reference books being illustrated. Although there are literally hundreds of computer databases and computerized library products on the market, this book will concentrate on those that provide industry and company information.

In this chapter you will learn about:

1) business databases and online searching,

2) end-user online searching and CD-ROM database searching, and

3) developing a search query.

BUSINESS DATABASES

A database is a file of information on a particular subject. The subject may be very broad, such as a database that indexes the most popular magazines in business and industry. Or it may be very narrow, such as one that concentrates on the coffee industry or microcomputers. Indeed, there are databases on all of these subjects available to you today.

While *Coffeeline* and *Microcomputer Index* are specialty databases on one particular product or industry, *TRADE & INDUSTRY INDEX*tm and *ABI/INFORM* are general business databases that index a wide range of business and economic journals as well as trade publications and business news.

*TRADE & INDUSTRY INDEX*tm provides indexing to more than 500 trade and industry journals plus business news from area and national newspapers, while *ABI/INFORM* indexes over 650 journals.

The primary purpose of *TRADE & INDUSTRY INDEX*tm is to provide indexing to company and industry information. *ABI/INFORM*, on the other hand, strives to index literature that has more interest to management, marketing, and other business disciplines. The latter database has more of an academic slant. One other important distinction between the two databases is in the amount of information supplied on each indexed article. *TRADE & INDUSTRY INDEX*tm provides, in most cases, only a citation to the article, which includes the author, title, journal name, pages, date, and descriptors (subject headings). *ABI/INFORM*, on the other hand, includes not only the citation, but also a lengthy, descriptive abstract (summary) of the article.

There are over a hundred other databases that have business applications. A few of the more important ones are listed in Appendix B. Check with a reference librarian to find listings and descriptions of other databases.

ONLINE SEARCHING

How can you access all of these databases? Typically, a librarian searches databases for you, using a computer terminal, a telephone, and a modem to hook up to a computer in another city. Once the correct commands and passwords are entered, the librarian is "online" and can "search" any of the available databases, such as *TRADE & INDUSTRY INDEX*tm or *ABI/INFORM*. Thus, this is called an "online search."

Like any service, there are advantages and disadvantages to online searching of databases.

Advantages

1) Online searching is faster than searching printed indexes. Computers can retrieve keywords and concepts almost instantly.

2) Online searching is also more efficient. Computers can combine keywords and concepts, which is very difficult to do in printed indexes.

3) Online databases are more current than printed indexes. New citations are added to databases more frequently than printed issues are published. Once new citations are entered into the database, they are immediately accessible.

4) Some databases are only available online. *ABI/INFORM* is a good example of an online database that does not have a paper counterpart.

Disadvantages

1) Online searching costs money. Many of the business databases are expensive, sometimes costing more than $100 per hour of connect time.

2) Online databases are not available in all subject areas. However, in the business area there is a wide range of databases.

3) Online databases primarily cover only recent literature. Most business databases do not cover literature older than ten to fifteen years.

Since new databases are being created monthly, and many of them have their own search commands, it is very difficult to stay abreast of the online searching field. What's more, the cost of online searching is expensive. An online search on a business topic or company often costs more than $50. For these reasons, librarians with special computer training have traditionally performed these difficult and costly online searches.

However, in many libraries you, the end-user, can now do online searches on your own, and these may be available free of charge or for a very small fee. This is possible because of two new developments: 1) end-user online searching and 2) CD-ROM database searching.

END-USER ONLINE SEARCHING

As an end-user, you can search many of the online databases that were once primarily the exclusive territory of librarians. In fact, with proper equipment (a personal computer, modem, telephone line, a password, and communication software) and sufficient experience, you can perform online searches from your home or office. This is because the companies that offer these databases have made it easier and less expensive to search them. "Menus" now tell you what to do each step of the way, including the selection of the database that is best for your research. The online search also may be less expensive because the service is being offered during non-prime time hours, primarily during nights and weekends.

As a result of this simplification and lower cost, more libraries are offering online searching to students free, or at a nominal charge. Find out if your library offers end-user online searching—and how you can take advantage of it. For more information on end-user searching, either contact your reference librarian or consult one of the following books:

- Kesselman, Martin, and Sarah B. Watstein, eds., *End-User Searching: Services and Providers* (Chicago: American Library Association, 1988).

- Scanlan, Jean. *Business Online: The Professional's Guide to Electronic Information Sources* (New York: John Wiley & Sons, 1988).

Other helpful books on online searching are listed in Appendix B.

CD-ROM DATABASE SEARCHING

Another very exciting technological advancement, which has made computerized database searching more widely available is called CD-ROM. This stands for Compact Disk—Read Only Memory. This innovation makes it possible for an enormous amount of data to be stored on a small five-inch hard plastic disk, similar to audio CDs. The data are etched on the disk with a laser beam and then read with a laser beam by a compact disk player. Over 250,000 pages of information can be stored on one compact disk, which is equivalent to the capacity of 1,500 standard 5 1/4-inch computer diskettes. Two CD-ROMs can store all the names, addresses, ZIP codes, and telephone listings for the entire United States!

Many database producers are placing their information on compact disks and selling, or leasing, the CD-ROM database to libraries. For libraries, this means that the databases that once required mainframe computers and that were only available online can now be searched on microcomputers with a CD-ROM player. Once the library has paid for the CD-ROM database, there is no limit to the number of searches that can be done—and all without online charges!

Due to these two innovations—end-user online searching and CD-ROM database searching—many libraries are offering training sessions or workshops that teach you how to operate computer terminals, how to perform online searches and CD-ROM database searches, and how to develop a search query.

Whether you are searching an online database or a CD-ROM database, there are five basic steps that will lead to an effective, productive search.

- Step 1: State the research topic.

- Step 2: Select the database.

- Step 3: Develop key concepts.

- Step 4: Combine the key concepts.

- Step 5: Perform the search.

Step 1: State the research topic.

Before you search a database, you need to take some time and determine exactly what your research topic is. Start by writing the topic down, preferably all in one sentence. Be succinct; eliminate any unnecessary words. It may help you to put the topic in the form of a question, such as:

"WHAT EFFECT DOES OVERBUILDING HAVE ON THE LODGING INDUSTRY?"

Step 2: Select the database.

Careful choice of the database is an essential and important step. The best search query will not be effective if you are not in an appropriate database. Ask the reference librarian for a recommendation. For many topics, there may not be an appropriate database available in your library. Instead, a paper index or reference source may be more appropriate. Databases have not replaced all of the reference tools that you will be learning in this book!

Another way to choose an appropriate database is to consult the list of databases in Appendix B of this book. There are several databases that might retrieve information on our topic of "overbuilding in the lodging industry."

ABI/INFORM, *Business Periodicals Index*, *Management Contents*, and *TRADE & INDUSTRY INDEX*™ are all logical choices. Are any of these databases available in your library, either through an end-user online search service or through a CD-ROM? If not, ask a reference librarian to suggest alternative databases or printed tools that would be appropriate.

Step 3: Develop key concepts.

After stating your research topic and selecting the database, it is time to identify the most important concepts in the statement. These will serve as the basis for your entire search. Look at the research topic and circle the most important words. Write each word in a separate column on a piece of paper. In the topic statement "WHAT EFFECT DOES OVERBUILDING HAVE ON THE LODGING INDUSTRY?" there are two key concepts, as shown below:

key concept 1	key concept 2
lodging	overbuilding

Since authors frequently use different words for the same idea, it is necessary to add synonyms to the above list for each key concept. For example, synonyms for "lodging" are "hotel" and "motel;" and a possible synonym for "overbuilding" is "excess rooms." Add both singular and plural forms. There are times when you will want to use a phrase that might be written as one word or two words. "Overbuilding" is a good example. To have the computer search for "overbuilding" both as one word and as two words, you will need two separate terms in key concept 2. To have the computer search for "over building" as two words, just enter the entire phrase with one space between the words. This directs the computer to retrieve the words where they occur together. Our concepts and keyword lists now look like this:

key concept 1	key concept 2
lodging	overbuilding
hotel	over building
hotels	excess rooms
motel	
motels	

Frequently it is helpful to search both a singular and a plural form of a term. This is so commonly done that there is a simple command that permits this. This technique is called *truncation*. The symbol for truncation in the system we are demonstrating is a question mark (?). Other systems use other symbols such as a dollar sign ($). Ask the reference librarian what the truncation symbol is for the system in your library. In our example, hotel? retrieves hotel or hotels or hotelier. Be careful though; truncation can result in some strange results: hot? retrieves hotel or hotels but also hot, hotfoot, hothead, and so on. Using truncation, the concepts are:

key concept 1	key concept 2
lodging	overbuilding
hotel?	over building
motel?	excess rooms

Step 4: Combine the key concepts.

These key concepts are now ready to be structured into a logical search query. The terms are combined by using the two logical connectors OR and AND. These two logical connectors specify how the words are to be processed by the computer.

First of all, the terms in each key concept of the search query are combined with the connector OR, as shown below:

lodging OR hotel? OR motel?
overbuilding OR over building OR excess rooms

The computer will collect all citations (references to books, articles, etc.) with any one of the key words in each concept and assign the set a number. The OR connector broadens the search. The more terms you connect with OR, the more citations you will retrieve. (We have capitalized OR for emphasis here; you can enter it in upper or lower case, because the computer does not distinguish case.)

Since we have two concepts in this search, we have set 1 and set 2. Next, these two key concepts are combined using the logical connector AND: 1 AND 2. It directs the computer to retrieve only records where both concepts are present. This is an exclusive or narrowing command. The Boolean diagrams in figure 2.1 illustrate graphically how the computer processes the AND and OR logical connectors.

Figure 2.1:
Boolean
Diagrams.

lodging **OR** hotel

lodging **AND** overbuilding

Step 5: Perform the search.

Now that you have stated the search topic, selected a database, developed the key words, grouped them into concepts, and combined the key concepts using logical operators (AND and OR), you are ready to perform the search.

There are several major companies that make many of the same databases available. These companies offer end-user searching, each utilizing its own protocols and commands. As a result of these differences, it is impossible to illustrate all of the variations within this book. To avoid confusion, the authors have chosen one online end-user system called Knowledge Index, which is produced by Dialog Information Services, Inc. Knowledge Index has two levels of searching. One is for the novice and is called

Menu Mode. In Menu Mode you do not need to know any commands as the system will lead you through the search with a series of "menus." The other level is called Command Mode, which uses five basic commands to direct the computer to search a question. We will start with an illustration of the Menu Mode and then show the same search done in Command Mode. Once you see the basics of Knowledge Index, it will be easy to transfer your knowledge to another online end-user system or to a CD-ROM database.

USING MENU MODE ON KNOWLEDGE INDEX

Figure 2.2: Sample Search of Menu Mode on Dialog Information Services, Inc. of *TRADE & INDUSTRY INDEX*tm.

Figure 2.2: Screen 1: OPENING SCREEN

The system asks you to select which mode you will be using. In this illustration you choose 1, Menu Mode.

> > > >Type 1 and press ENTER.

```
                    WELCOME TO KNOWLEDGE INDEX


          Accounting starting at 14:41:18 EST
          Date:      10apr90

                    Welcome to KNOWLEDGE INDEX!
                         Main Menu

          Select one of the following options:

               1 Menu Mode
               2 Command Mode
               3 DIALMAIL
               4 Help in formulating a search
               5 Knowledge Index Bulletin
               6 General Information

          Copr. 1990 Dialog Information Services, Inc.
          All rights reserved.

          Enter option NUMBER and press ENTER to continue.
           /H = Help                      /L = Logoff

           ?1
```

Figure 2.2: Screen 2: SECTIONS SCREEN

Next you are asked to choose a section. Since we are searching for information on the hotel industry, Business is a logical choice.

> > > >Type 3 and press ENTER.

```
                         Knowledge Index
                            Sections

          1  Agriculture & Nutrition       8  Law & Government
          2  Bibliography--Books & Monographs  9  Medicine, Biosciences, & Drugs
          3  Business Information          10  News & Current Affairs
          4  Chemistry                     11  Popular Information
          5  Computers & Electronics       12  Science & Technology
          6  Directories & Reference       13  Social Sciences & Humanities
          7  Education                     14  Travel - Official Airline Guide


          Enter option NUMBER and press ENTER to continue.  Enter D for a list of
          databases in each subject category or D<option number> (e.g., D2) for
          specific section descriptions.

           /H = Help          /L = Logoff          /Nomenu = Command Mode

           ?3
```

Figure 2.2: Screen 3:
BUSINESS INFORMATION SCREEN

The business databases are then listed on the screen. (Since there are so many of them, they fill more than one screen. To see additional screens, press ENTER.) Either *TRADE & INDUSTRY INDEX*™ or *ABI/INFORM* is a logical choice for the hotel industry.

> > > >Type 11 *TRADE & INDUSTRY INDEX*™ and press ENTER.

```
                   Business Information            1 of 3
Company Information:
              1   Canadian Business and Current Affairs
              2   ICC British Company Directory
              3   Standard & Poor's News 7/85 - present
              4   Standard & Poor's News 1979 - 6/85
              5   S & P Corporate Descriptions
              6   S & P Register - Biographical
              7   S & P Register - Corporate
              8   Agribusiness U.S.A.
              9   Chemical Business Newsbase
             10   The Computer Database
             11   Trade & Industry Index
             12   ABI/Inform
General Business Information
             13   ABI/Inform
             14   Economic Literature Index
             15   Facts on File
             16   Harvard Business Review
Press ENTER to see additional databases.

Choose a file by entering the option NUMBER.  Enter D for a section
description or D<option number> (e.g., D2) for a specific database
description.
  /H = Help      /L = Logoff     /M- = Previous Menu    /MM = Main Menu

?11
```

Figure 2.2: Screen 4:
SEARCH MODE OPTIONS SCREEN

The computer then asks what type of search: subject, author, and so on.

> > > >Type 1 to choose subject search and press ENTER.

```
                   Trade & Industry Index
                     Search Mode Options

  Select one of the following options:

  1. Subject Search
  2. Author Search
  3. Journal Search
  4. Company Name Search


  Enter option NUMBER and press ENTER to continue.
  /H = Help     /L = Logoff     /M- = Previous Menu     /MM = Main Menu

  ?1
```

21

Figure 2.2: Screen 5:
ENTERING SUBJECT
CONCEPTS SCREEN

You are asked to type in the keywords from the first concept in the search strategy, separating them with OR.

> > > >Type lodging OR hotel? OR motel? and press ENTER.

```
Enter subject concept(s).  Logical OR, AND, or NOT may be used to
separate concepts (e.g., MICROCOMPUTER? OR PERSONAL COMPUTER?).

?LODGING OR HOTEL? OR MOTEL?
  Your search is being processed
```

Figure 2.2: Screen 6:
COMPUTER'S RESPONSE SCREEN

The computer found 19,623 articles and asks if you want to modify or display the search.

> > > >Type 1 to modify the search and press ENTER.

```
                    Trade & Industry Index
                    Continuation Options


   **  19623  ** records were found.

Concept 1:LODGING OR HOTEL? OR MOTEL?

           1  Modify your search
           2  Display records at your terminal (maximum is 980 records)
                 You may /SET SCROLL ON or /SET SCROLL OFF
           *  Order source documents
           4  Start a new search

Enter option NUMBER and press ENTER to continue.
  /H = Help     /L = Logoff     /M- = Previous Menu     /MM = Main Menu

?1
```

22

Figure 2.2: Screen 7:
MODIFY SEARCH MENU SCREEN

You want to combine the first concept on hotels with the second concept on overbuilding to reduce the number of citations found. To do this you need to narrow the topic by combining the concepts with the AND operator. Thus, choice 1 is the appropriate option.

>>>>Type 1 to narrow the search and press ENTER.

The keywords from the second concept can now be entered.

>>>>Type in overbuilding OR over building OR excess rooms and then press ENTER.

Figure 2.2: Screen 8:
COMPUTER'S RESPONSE SCREEN

The computer responds that 24 articles match your search.

Now you are ready to display these 24 titles.

>>>>Type 2, then press ENTER.

```
                 Trade & Industry Index
                     Modify Search

     **  19623  ** records were found.

   Concept 1:LODGING OR HOTEL? OR MOTEL?

   1. Narrow subject concepts (logical AND)
   2. Widen subject concepts (logical OR)
   3. Replace subject concepts
   4. Select limits
   5. Select author(s) (logical AND)
   6. Select journal(s) (logical AND)

   Enter option NUMBER and press ENTER to continue.
    /H = Help     /L = Logoff    /M- = Previous Menu    /MM = Main Menu

   ?1
```

```
     1: LODGING OR HOTEL? OR MOTEL?
   Enter new subject concept(s).  Logical OR, AND, or NOT may be used to
   separate concepts (e.g., MICROCOMPUTER? OR PERSONAL COMPUTER?).
   ?OVERBUILDING OR OVER BUILDING OR EXCESS ROOMS
    Your search is being processed

                 Trade & Industry Index
                   Continuation Options

     **  24  ** records were found.

   Concept 1:LODGING OR HOTEL? OR MOTEL?
   Concept 2:OVERBUILDING OR OVER BUILDING OR EXCESS ROOMS

           1  Modify your search
           2  Display records at your terminal (maximum is 980 records)
                You may /SET SCROLL ON or /SET SCROLL OFF
           *  Order source documents
           4  Start a new search

   Enter option NUMBER and press ENTER to continue.
    /H = Help     /L = Logoff     /M- = Previous Menu     /MM = Main Menu

   ?2
```

23

Figure 2.2: Screen 9:
DISPLAY OF TITLES SCREEN

The computer then lists the first 10 titles. You can choose to display any of the full records by typing the option number. (If you want to view the rest of the titles in the search, just press ENTER.)

> > > >Type 1-2 to display the full citation for the first two titles.

```
              Trade & Industry Index
            ** 24 ** records for DISPLAY
              Enter HALT to exit DISPLAY

Option                TITLE
  No. ..............................................................
  1  Trump stalled by overbuilding on Las Vegas strip. (Donald Trump)
  2  Hotel/motel: overbuilding has forced hoteliers to treat F&B as a major pr
  3  Profiles in hotel feasibility: the consequences of overbuilding.
  4  Hotels rebound from spate of overbuilding. (Houston)
  5  Many factors can contribute to overbuilding scenarios.
  6  Of black holes and dinosaurs. (Overbuilding creates deteriorating full-se
  7  Poor management, overbuilding are main hotel woes.
  8  How to discourage hotel overbuilding: a case study.
  9  Opportunities exist despite overbuilding; yields on real estate continue
 10  Segmentation, overbuilding create industry slump. (food service; 1987 Ann
Enter option number(s), HALT, /H for help, or press ENTER for next screen:

?1-2
```

Figure 2.2: Screen 10:
DISPLAY OF CITATIONS SCREEN

The computer then displays the full record (citation) for the first title.

```
 selection 1 of 1
 0804B229 DIALOG File 148: TRADE & INDUSTRY INDEX
 Trump stalled by overbuilding on Las Vegas strip. (Donald Trump)
 Lalli, Sergio
 Hotel & Motel Management  v204 p1(3) Oct 16, 1989
 SOURCE FILE: TI File 148
 Illustration; portrait; photograph
 GEOGRAPHIC CODE: NNUSWNVL
 GEOGRAPHIC LOCATION: Las Vegas, Nevada
 SIC CODE: 7011; 7993
 CAPTIONS: Donald Trump.
 NAMED PEOPLE: Trump, Donald--investment activities
 COMPANY NAME(S): Trump Nevada Inc.--management
 DESCRIPTORS:  Casinos--acquisitions and mergers; Las Vegas, Nevada--hotels and
   motels

        Copyright 1990 Information Access Company
```

Figure 2.2: Screen 11:
LOGOFF SCREEN

> > > >Type LOGOFF or /L to logoff
the system.

The computer then displays the cost of the
search.

```
?LOGOFF



Menu system v. 5.36  ends.
      10apr90 14:49:14 User085662 Session A383.21
      $1.82    0.132 Hrs FileKI
      $1.82  Estimated total session cost    0.132 Hrs.
Logoff: level 22.02.3 A  14:49:15



DIALNET: call cleared by request


Enter Service:
```

COMMAND MODE SEARCHING ON KNOWLEDGE INDEX

The Menu Mode, which was illustrated above, is very useful for novice searchers. However, there is another level of searching called Command Mode that is also designed for end-users. Instead of using menus, you use five basic commands that are quicker and more efficient than the Menu Mode. Most online systems and CD-ROMs use similar commands, although they may be called by different names. In Knowledge Index the commands are:

BEGIN,
FIND,
DISPLAY,
TYPE, and
LOGOFF.

The BEGIN command selects the database to be searched. The FIND command directs the computer to search for the key words, combining them into sets using the logical connectors that you type. The DISPLAY and TYPE commands are used to view or print the records. DISPLAY directs the computer to show them one at a time on the screen, while TYPE directs the computer to show them on the screen in a continuous scroll. LOGOFF disconnects you from the computer.

BEGIN—Selecting a database

Once connected to the computer, you will be asked which Mode, Menu or Command, you want to use. Choose #2 for Command Mode. When the computer is ready for you to begin your search, it will put a question mark in the far left column of the screen. This is called a prompt and means the computer is ready for you to give it the first command. In Command Mode the computer does not list the available databases. You will need to have chosen the database before logging on. Since the topic of "OVERBUILDING IN THE LODGING INDUSTRY" has more of an industry slant, start searching in *TRADE & INDUSTRY INDEX*tm. The abbreviation for this file is BUSI2.

To start searching in *TRADE & INDUSTRY INDEX*tm, type BEGIN BUSI2, then hit the ENTER key. The computer will respond by announcing the name of the database and the time coverage (figure 2.3).

FIND—Entering your search

As soon as the prompt (?) appears in the far left column, the computer is ready for the next command, FIND. The FIND command instructs the computer to start searching the database. Type the word FIND and follow it with the first concept, using the OR logical connector between each word or phrase. End by hitting the ENTER key (see Part A of figure 2.3).

For Example:

?FIND lodging or hotel? or motel?

The computer responds that it has found 19,623 records in *TRADE & INDUSTRY INDEX*tm that have any of these words. It assigns the number one (S1) to this set of records.

Enter the next FIND command, as shown below:

?FIND overbuilding or over building or excess rooms

The computer responds again with the number of records (97) and assigns number two (S2) to this set (see Part B of figure 2.3).

Now that you have the results for the two key concepts, you are ready to combine them using AND. Below is how you would type the command.

?FIND S1 and S2

Figure 2.3:
Sample
Search of
Command
Mode on
Dialog
Information
Services, Inc.
of *TRADE &*
INDUSTRY
***INDEX*tm.**

```
                    WELCOME TO KNOWLEDGE INDEX

        Date:        10apr90

                     Welcome to KNOWLEDGE INDEX!
                            Main Menu

        Select one of the following options:

                  1 Menu Mode
                  2 Command Mode
                  3 DIALMAIL
                  4 Help in formulating a search
                  5 Knowledge Index Bulletin
                  6 General Information

        Copr. 1990 Dialog Information Services, Inc.
        All rights reserved.

        Enter option NUMBER and press ENTER to continue.
         /H = Help                    /L = Logoff

        ?2

        ?begin busi2

        Now in BUSINESS INFORMATION (BUSI) Section (BUSI2) Database
        TRADE AND INDUSTRY INDEX 81-90/MAY
        (COPR. 1990 IAC)

        ?find lodging or hotel? or motel?
```

Figure 2.3:
Part A

```
                     635  LODGING
                   19445  HOTEL?
                   15970  MOTEL?
            S1     19623  LODGING OR HOTEL? OR MOTEL?

        ?find overbuilding or over building or excess rooms
```

Figure 2.3:
Part B

```
                      89  OVERBUILDING
                   31062  OVER
                   19376  BUILDING
                       8  OVER BUILDING
                    2178  EXCESS
                    1020  ROOMS
                       0  EXCESS ROOMS
            S2        97  OVERBUILDING OR OVER BUILDING OR EXCESS ROOMS

        ?find s1 and s2
```

Figure 2.3:
Part C

```
                   19623  S1
                      97  S2
            S3        24  S1 AND S2
```

```
?display
      Display 3/2/1


08048229  DIALOG File 148: TRADE & INDUSTRY INDEX
Trump stalled by overbuilding on Las Vegas strip. (Donald Trump)
 Lalli, Sergio
 Hotel & Motel Management  v204 p1(3) Oct 16, 1989
 SOURCE FILE: TI File 148
 illustration; portrait; photograph
 GEOGRAPHIC CODE: NNUSWNVL
 GEOGRAPHIC LOCATION: Las Vegas, Nevada
 SIC CODE: 7011; 7993
 CAPTIONS: Donald Trump.
 NAMED PEOPLE: Trump, Donald--investment activities
 COMPANY NAME(S): Trump Nevada Inc.--management
 DESCRIPTORS:  Casinos--acquisitions and mergers; Las Vegas, Nevada--hotels
      and motels

 ?d
      Display 3/2/2


07984127  DIALOG File 148: TRADE & INDUSTRY INDEX
         *Use Format 9 for FULL TEXT*
Hotel/motel:  overbuilding  has  forced  hoteliers  to treat F&B as a major
     profit center. (22nd Annual Restaurant Growth Index)
 Brennan, Denise M.
 Restaurant Business Magazine  v88 p106(2) Sept 20, 1989
 SOURCE FILE: TI File 148
 illustration; table
 AVAILABILITY: FULL TEXT Online  LINE COUNT: 00095
 SIC CODE: 7011; 5812
 CAPTIONS: Hotel/motel market: foodservice sales.
 DESCRIPTORS: Food service--growth; Hotels and motels--food service

?type s3/s/1-5

 3/S/1
08048229  DIALOG File 148: TRADE & INDUSTRY INDEX
Trump stalled by overbuilding on Las Vegas strip. (Donald Trump)

 3/S/2
07984127  DIALOG File 148: TRADE & INDUSTRY INDEX
Hotel/motel:  overbuilding  has  forced  hoteliers  to treat F&B as a major
     profit center. (22nd Annual Restaurant Growth Index)

 3/S/3
07768221  DIALOG File 148: TRADE & INDUSTRY INDEX
Profiles in hotel feasibility: the consequences of overbuilding.

 3/S/4
07763515  DIALOG File 148: TRADE & INDUSTRY INDEX
Hotels rebound from spate of overbuilding. (Houston)

 3/S/5
07509437  DIALOG File 148: TRADE & INDUSTRY INDEX
```

```
                Many factors can contribute to overbuilding scenarios.
                ?logoff

                Menu system v. 5.36  ends.
                      10apr90 15:39:11 User085662 Session A385.4
                      $0.77    0.055 Hrs FileKI
                      $0.77   Estimated total session cost   0.055 Hrs.
                Logoff: level 22.02.3 A  15:39:12



                DIALNET: call cleared by request
```

The computer combines set one and set two and looks for records that have both concepts present. It responds by indicating there are 24 records and assigns the number three (S3) to this set. You are now ready to view the citations (see Part C of figure 2.3).

DISPLAY and TYPE—Viewing the records and printing the results

To view the records, enter the command DISPLAY, as shown in Part D of figure 2.3. This command directs the computer to show the first record in your search. The computer will display all the information stored in its memory for that record. The second, third, and subsequent records can be displayed by typing another D after each record.

You can view the citations in three formats, as shown in figure 2.4. The long format includes all the information stored in the computer. The medium format includes only the author, title, and journal citation. The short format includes only the title. If you do not specify a format, the computer will display the citations in long format. If you would like to view only the titles of the records, so that you can select those that appear to be the most useful, give the DISPLAY command this way:

DISPLAY s3/s/all

Here's how this command works. It specifies which set you want displayed (set 3), which format (short), and which records (all). You may tell it a range of records (i.e., DISPLAY s3/s/1-5) or you may ask for particular records (i.e., DISPLAY s3/s/5,7,9-12). Each portion of the command is separated by a slash (/).

If you would like to have all the records scroll across the screen without a pause between them, give the command TYPE (or T). The format for the TYPE command is the same as the DISPLAY command:

TYPE s3/s/1-5

LONG FORMAT

```
07768221  DIALOG File 148: TRADE & INDUSTRY INDEX
Profiles in hotel feasibility: the consequences of overbuilding.
 Overstreet, George A., Jr.
 Cornell Hotel & Restaurant Administration Quarterly  v30 p10(9) May, 1989
 SOURCE FILE: TI File 148
 illustration; photograph; table
 GEOGRAPHIC CODE: NNUSUVA
 GEOGRAPHIC LOCATION: Virginia
 SIC CODE: 7011
 CAPTIONS:  Charlottesville lodging market changes, 1983-89.; Estimated
    financial structure - Hilton (Sheraton) (1984-1989).; Reconstructed pro
      forma,  University Hilton.;  Reconstructed pro forma, Sheraton.;
    University Hilton sensitivity analysis.; Sheraton sensitivity analysis.
    ; Reconstructed pro forma, Omni.
 DESCRIPTORS: Charlottesville, Virginia--hotels and motels; Hotel and motel
    management--case studies; Industrial capacity--case studies
```

MEDIUM FORMAT

```
07768221  DIALOG File 148: TRADE & INDUSTRY INDEX
Profiles in hotel feasibility: the consequences of overbuilding.
 Overstreet, George A., Jr.
 Cornell Hotel & Restaurant Administration Quarterly  v30 p10(9) May, 1989
 SOURCE FILE: TI File 148
```

SHORT FORMAT

```
07768221  DIALOG File 148: TRADE & INDUSTRY INDEX
Profiles in hotel feasibility: the consequences of overbuilding.
```

Figure 2.4: Sample Citations from Dialog Information Services, Inc. of *TRADE & INDUSTRY INDEX*™.

Looking at figure 2.3, Part E, you see the first 5 citations in the short format. If you were to print each of the citations in long format, you would find at least one word from key concept one and at least one word from key concept two in each record. Figure 2.4 has the keywords highlighted.

If you have a printer attached to the microcomputer, you can activate it so everything that scrolls across the screen is printed. You can also activate the microcomputer so it captures everything in its memory, and copies it onto a formatted floppy disk. This procedure is called downloading, and it has two advantages. First of all, it will speed up the search process because the computer can capture the data faster than the printer can print it. Second, it will also allow you to edit the search on a word processing system at a later date. Ask your reference librarian for more information about downloading in your library.

LOGOFF—Finishing the search and disconnecting.

A critical command to remember is LOGOFF. When you are finished searching and displaying the results, type the word LOGOFF at the next prompt (?) sign. The computer will respond with the time you have been online and the price you will be billed for the search. If you forget to logoff, the computer will drop you after a certain amount of time. However, you will have to pay for the time between when you stopped searching or displaying and when the computer finally disconnects you (see figure 2.3, Part F).

This chapter has introduced you to two of the more recent computer developments in libraries—end-user online searching and CD-ROM database searching. The future will bring more and more computer products and computer innovations into the library. Although the primary purpose of this book is to teach you a search strategy for locating industry and company information, the authors realize the increasing importance that computers will play in library research. Appendix B lists the more important business databases available. Furthermore, examples and illustrations of online and CD-ROM databases will be shown throughout this book.

SUMMARY

1) Computer databases are becoming more prevalent in libraries.

2) End-user online searching and CD-ROM database searching have made it easier and less expensive to access databases.

3) Efficient and effective database searching involves careful preparation of a search query.

4) The search query involves five steps:

    a) stating the research topic,
    b) selecting the database,
    c) developing the concepts,
    d) combining the key concepts, and
    e) performing the search.

5) Knowledge Index is one example of an end-user online searching system that has two modes: 1) Menu Mode for novice searchers and 2) Command Mode for more experienced searchers.

CHAPTER 3

INDUSTRY OVERVIEWS

As you read this book's Introduction, you gained an understanding of what a search strategy entails. It is a systematic and organized way to locate an appropriate topic and find information on it in the library. The Introduction discussed the importance of each search strategy step.

Unless it has already been determined for you, one of the most difficult search strategy steps is deciding which industry to research. Chapter 3 covers two very popular and widely available reference sources to help you with this problem. Both *Industry Surveys* (New York: Standard & Poor's Corporation, quarterly) and *Value Line Investment Survey* (New York: Value Line, Inc., weekly) provide a good overview of the U.S. industries. Although both tools have important investment and company information as well, this chapter concentrates on industry data.

A primary purpose of *Industry Surveys* is to provide information on U.S. industries, such as aerospace, computers, health care, telecommunications, and leisure-time. It is available in two different formats, either as a soft bound two-volume set or as a loose-leaf service. Whatever format your library has, the way you use it is the same.

First of all, consult the "Subject Guide" in the front of the volume. Here you will find an alphabetical list of the different industries contained in *Industry Surveys*. "Lodging" is found on pages L32-L34 (figure 3.1).

Industry Surveys provides a narrative analysis of the lodging industry, including its trends, issues, and outlook. This is called the "Basic Analysis," as the excerpts in figure 3.2 illustrate.

index to surveys

STANDARD & POOR'S INDUSTRY SURVEYS
Standard & Poor's is a subsidiary of McGraw-Hill, Inc.

APRIL 27, 1989 (Vol. 157, No. 17, Sec. 1)   Replaces Index to Surveys dated March 30, 1989

Dates of latest surveys

File issues alphabetically. Only Surveys with dates the same as or later than those listed below have reference value. Discard old Surveys as new ones arrive.

IN VOLUME 1

		Current Analysis	Basic Analysis
A	Aerospace & Air Transport	11-10-88	*4-28-88
	Autos-Auto Parts	3-23-89	11-17-88
B	Banking	1-19-89	4-7-88
	Building & Forest Products	2-9-89	10-27-88
C	Chemicals	*1-19-89	10-13-88
	Computers & Office Equipment	2-2-89	10-1-87
E	Electronics	*9-2-87	1-12-89
F	Food, Beverages & Tobacco	6-23-88	2-2-89
H	Health Care	12-15-88	6-9-88
I	Insurance & Investment	10-27-88	4-13-89
L	Leisure-Time	12-8-88	3-16-89

IN VOLUME 2

		Current Analysis	Basic Analysis
M	Media	2-23-89	11-3-88
	Metals–Nonferrous	3-30-89	7-21-88
O	Oil (w/Gas Drilling & Svs.)	1-26-89	8-18-88
R	Railroads & Trucking (incl. coal)	*1-5-89	9-22-88
	Retailing	12-22-88	4-20-89
S	Steel & Heavy Machinery	3-9-89	7-7-88
T	Telecommunications	6-16-88	12-22-88
	Textiles, Apparel & Home Furn.	4-27-89	9-8-88
U	Utilities–Electric	10-20-88	3-2-89
	Utilities–Gas	12-1-88	*5-12-88

*Tentatively scheduled for publication during May 1989.

SUBJECT GUIDE

VOLUME 1 CONTAINS PAGES A THROUGH L

A
Access charges ... T16
Acid rain ... U20
Acquisitions
  Utilities–Gas ... U93-95
Advertising ... M36-38
  Broadcast ... M15-16
  Magazine ... M34
  Newspaper ... M33
Advertising ... M36-38
Aerospace & Air Transport ... A15-50
  Aerospace financial ... A27-29
  Aerospace fundamentals ... A16-17
AFUDC ... U80
Agricultural chemicals and
  Products ... C31-34
Agricultural equip. ... S35-37
AIDS ... I-29-30
Air cargo ... A37-38
Aircraft ... A20-21
Airlines ... A31-37
Air transport financial ... A39-40
Alcoholic beverages ... F28-35
Aliphatics ... C23-24
Alloy steels ... S18, S23
Aluminum ... M75-79
Annuity products ... I-34
Apparel ... T83-91
Apparel markets ... T82
Appliances ... T98-100
Aramco ... O-17
Argon ... C23
Aromatics ... C24-25
Asset quality ... B13
Atomic energy plants ... U17-20
Auto dealers ... A79
Autos–Auto Parts ... A75-100
  Auto parts ... A85-87
  Imports & exports ... A83-84
  Sales & production ... A77-81
  Technology ... A82-83
Automobiles ... A75-84, S16

B
Bank Analyzation ... B26-30, B31
Bank regulation ... B23-24

Banking ... B15-43
  Consolidation ... B22-23
Basic chemicals ... C17-23
Batteries, automotive ... M85
Beer ... F28-31
Beverages ... F22-35
Biotechnology ... H24-25
  Products for AIDS ... H25-27
Boating ... L41-42
Book publishing ... M39-42
Brewers ... F24-27
Broadcasting ... M15-20
Brokerage firms ... I-41-50
Brokerage services ... B23-24
Building & Forest Prod. ... B75-108
Building products ... B88-89

C
Cable industry backgd ... M22
Cable television ... M20-25, L25
Cameras ... L42-43
Capacitors ... E26
Capital require. ... B30-32, U17, U90
Capital spending ... U92
Capacitors ... E35
Carbon dioxide ... C22
Carbon steel ... S18, S19, S23
Cardiovascular products ... H35-36
Carpets ... T80, T95-96
Carriers, motor ... R31-36
Case goods ... T95
Cash flow underwriting ... I-16-17
Casing & tubing ... O-82
Casino gaming ... L28-31
Cassette recordings ... L26
Casualty insurance ... I-15-24
Caustic soda ... C18-19
Cellulosic fiber ... C29
Cellular telephone svc. ... T24-27
Cement ... B88
Cereals, ready-to-eat ... F17
Chemical products ... C35-37
Chemicals ... C15-42
  World developments ... C37-39
  Financial ... C40-42
Chewing tobacco ... F37

VOLUME 2 CONTAINS PAGES M THROUGH U

Chlor-Alkalies ... C17-19
Cigarettes ... F36-39
Cigars ... F37
Clothing ... T83-91
CMOS technology ... E28-30
Coal ... R42-49, U22, 25
  Labor ... R45-47
  Productivity ... R49
Cogeneration ... U22-23
Coils & transformers ... E35
Combination stores ... R102
Commercial aerospace ... A24-27
Commercial banks ... B15-24
  Banking terminology ... B25
  Fundamentals ... B26-33
  How to analyze a bank ... B26-29
Commercial vehicles ... A80-81
Commodity cartel ... O-21
Commodities Outlook ... F20-22
Commuter airlines ... A36-37
Compact disks ... L26-27
Components, electronic ... E28-34
Computer-aided design ... E23
Computers & Office Equip ... C75-120
  Glossary of terms ... C88-89
  Large scale systems ... C77-81
  Medium scale systems ... C82-84
  Small scale systems ... C85-87
Connectors ... E35
Construction ... B75-79
  Equipment ... S16, S38-40
  Products ... S25, S27
  Spending ... S38-39
Consolidation ... B35
Consumer credit ... B38-41
Consumer price index ... M89-90
Continuous casting ... S19
Contract carriage ... R33
Copper ... M80-84
Corporate borrowing ... B20-21
Cosmetics ... H37-39, R86
Credit quality ... B18
Crude oil ... O-20, 30, 35
Custom semiconductor chips ... E23, E30-31

D
Defense electronics ... E36, E38-40
Demand
  Gas ... U82-85
Department stores ... R80, 81-82
Deregulation ... B22-23, R28-33, U28-29, U32, U92-93
Desktop computers ... C87
Detergents ... C36-37
Diagnostic tests ... H26
Diesel engines ... A81
Digital switches ... T41
Disk drives ... C104-105
Distilled spirits ... F34-35
Distributors, natural gas ... U78-79, 93
Diversification ... U33-34
Drapes & upholstery ... T91-92
DRGs ... H24-29
Drilling, oil-gas ... O-30-31
Drug retailing ... R84-89
Drugs ... H17-27, R86

E
Earthmoving mach. ... S38, S40
E-beam lithography ... E38
Educational publishing ... M39-40
Electric utilities ... U15-U57
Electrical demand ... U23-27
  Commercial ... U23, 24
  Industrial ... U23-24
  Residential ... U23, 25
Electrical supply ... U17-23
Electromedical equip. ... E38, H31
Electron tubes ... E35
Electronic banking ... B25
Electronics ... E15-41
  Capital equipment ... E37-39
  Components ... E28-34
  Distribution ... E40-41
  Industry overview ... E17-27
  Other electronics ... E35-36
Energy efficiency ... O-27
Ethical drugs ... H21-23
Excavation machinery ... S40
Exercise equip. ... L41

Figure 3.1: Part 1: "Subject Guide, an Index to Surveys from *Industry Surveys*, 27 April 1987.

VOLUME 1 CONTAINS PAGES A THROUGH L

	Page
Exploration & prod.	O-27–34, O-43–44
Exploration & prod (oil & gas)	
Canada	O-32
Alaska	O-32–33
Onshore lower 48	O-33
Gulf of Mexico	O-33
Other US offshore areas	O-33
North Sea	O-29
Exports	A17, A83–84, F34, S15, S32, S39, T79 T93

F Fabrics
Fast food
FAS #97
Farm equip
FSLIC
Ferroalloys
Fertilizers
Finance companies
Financial (Oil) O-43–45
Floor coverings T97
Food, Beverages & Tobacco .. F15–51
Foods F16–19
Fuel Use Act U79
Fungicides C34
Furniture T91–96

G Gallium arsenide E32–33
Galvanizing M88
Gaming L28–31
Gas utilities U75–107
Gas supplies U86–91
Gasification U76, 88
Gasoline O-36–37
General aviation A22–23
General merch. retailers .. R75–85
Generic drugs H23
Gold M89–92
Government electronics E36
Grocery chains R86–92
Group life insurance I-30
Gypsum B88 89

H Hand tools S34
Health & beauty aids .. R93–95
Health Care H15–49
Herbicides C34
HMOs H30–31
Homebuilding B75–79
Home computers C87
Home diagnostics H31
Home furnishings T79 80, T91 96
Home prices B75, 76, 77
Home shopping R82
Hospitals H16, 29
Hospital facilities H29–30
Hospital supplies H28–30
Household furniture T95 96
Housing activity B77–81, T93–94
Hydrogen C22 23
Hydrogen peroxide C20–21
Hypermarkets R81

I Imports A83–84, L39, S15, S16, S25 27, S32, T78, T83, T84, T99, U90–91
Industrial control equip. E38
Industrial fabrics T81
Industrial gases C21–22
Industrial markets T83
Industrial organic chemicals .. C23–25
Industrial process equip. E36
Ingot-based lower power rate M77–78
Inorganic chemicals C19–21
Inorganic pigments C21
Insecticides C34
Insurance & Investment I-15–61
Insurance terms defined .. I-39–40
Integrated circuits E20–25
Interest rates B27
International lending . B15–17, 32–33
Interstate banking B21–22
Investment banking B20–21
Iran-Iraq War O-19–20

JK Jet planes A-21–23
Kraft paper B90

L Labor costs A38, R21, 25–29, 40–41, 45–47, R95–96, S24–25, T90
Lasers (medical) H36
Lead M84–86
Leasing, truck R36–39
Legislation U28
Leisure-time L15–58
Life insurance I-25–30
Linerboard B91
Liquefied natural gas U88, 91
Liquor F34–35
Loans B16–18, B20, B32–33, B34–35, B36–41
Local telephone service T16–24
Lodging L32–34
Long-distance service T28–37
Lumber B84–86

M Machine tools S31–33
Machinery Outlook S29–31
Magazines M34–36
Magnetic resonance imaging H35
Mainframe computers C78
Major airlines A31–34
Man-made fibers C28
Manufactured housing B81–83
Market pulp B91
Marketing U82–86
Material handling equipment. .. S39
Media M15–51
Glossary of industry terms M26–29
Medical equip. H33–37
Medical facilities H27–33
Medicare .. H15–16, 19–20, 27–29
Medicines H17–24
Medium-scale computers C82
Memory devices E33–34
Men's wear R83
Merchandising R77–79, R93–94
Mergers .. I-42, I-46–50, M83–84
Metal furniture T95, T96
Metallurgical coal R44–45
Metals-nonferrous M75–108
Methanol C25
Microcomputers C87–92
Microlithography E38
Microprocessors E17, E22–23, E28–30
Military aircraft A20–21
Military contracts A20
Military electronics E36, E39
Military markets A18–21
Minicomputers C85
Mini supercomputers C81
Mining M91–92, 95
Mining equip. S40
Molybdenum M98
Mortgages B33–34
MOS memory devices ... E22–23
Motion pictures L17–21
Distribution L21
Motors, outboard L41–42
Musical recordings L26–28
Mutual funds I-43, I-48

N NASA A21, 22–23
National airlines A35
Nationwide banking B18–21
Natural gas O-31–32, U75–108
Natural Gas Policy Act U78, U80–83, U84, U90
Newspaper publishing M30–33
Newsprint B91, M32–33
Nickel M97–98
Nitrogen C22, C32
Nonautomotive products A87
Noncellulosic fibers C28–29
Nuclear power U17–19, 21
Nursing homes H32
Nursing shortage H29–30

O Oil O-45–46
Oilfield Hardware & Svs O-39–43, 44
Oil prices O-23–24

VOLUME 2 CONTAINS PAGES M THROUGH U

	Page
Optical lithography	E38
OPEC	O-15–18, 19, 23, 38
Order 436	U75–76, U77–79
Order 451	U82–U83
Original equipment (autos)	A86
Organic chemicals	C23–25
Orthopedic sales	H34–35
OTC drugs	R93, 95
Oxygen	C22

P Paints & Coatings C35–36
Paper B90–95
Paperbacks M39
Pay TV M20–25
Peak load U17–21
Personal care items H32–33
Personal computers C87
Personal loan companies .. B39–41
Industry fundamentals B40
Pesticides C33, C34
Petrochemicals O-38–39
Petroleum O-15–41
Pharmaceuticals H17–24
Photofinishing L43
Photography L42–43
Pipelines
Natural gas U77, 78, 79, 81, 95
Plastics C25–29
Platinum M95–96
Pollution controls U22
Population growth F16
Precious metals M89–98
Prerecorded music L26–28
Pres. drugs .. H20–22, R93, 95–99
Private carriage trucking .. R34–35
Private label J89
Processed foods F16–19
Property-casualty insur. .. I-15–24
Proposition 103 ...... I-17–19, I-21
Proprietary drugs H23–24
Psychiatric hospitals .... †129–30
Publishing M30–35, M39–42
Pulp B91

R Radio M22
Railroads & Trucking .. R15–50
Railroads R15–33
Contracts R29–33
Cost recovery R27
Deregulation R37–38
Labor R25–29
Rates & Regulation R15
Revenue adequacy R15
Rates & Regulation U76–79
Refining & marketing .. O-35–39
Regional airlines A35–36
Regulation U27–33, U75, 76–79
Reinsurance market I-21–22
Replacement parts (auto) A87
Residential construction .. B75–79
Resistors E38
Restaurants L34–37
Retailing R75–114
ROMs E30
Rubber fabricating A87–89

S Savings & loans B33–38
Analyzing an S&L B37
S&L fundamentals B36–38
Semiconductors E17–20, E25
Production equipment E37
Service overview T15–16
Silver M93–95
Small-scale computers C82
Smokeless tobacco F34–35
Soaps C36–37
Soda ash C19
Soft drinks F20–23
Software and services .. C93–103
Computer Services C103
Mainframe and mini .. C96–99
Micro .. C96, C99–103
Piracy C97
Space programs A21–23
Specialty foods R100–101
Specialty gases C23
Specialty retailing R80
Specialty steel S23

Sporting goods L41
Sports L41–42
Steel & Heavy Machinery .. S15–52
Strategic programs A19–20
Substitute natural gas ... U76, 81, 91
Supercomputers C80
Supermarkets R86–92
Supermini computers C87
Supermicro computers .. C86–87
Super-regional banks B20
Superstores R90–92
Supplemental sources U94–96
Surface mount technology .. E16, 35
Surfactants C22
Surgery (plastic) H37, 39
Switches T40–41
Synthetic fuels U92–93
Synthetic materials C25–30
Synthetic rubber A88, C29–30

T Tactical programs A20–21
Telecommunications T15–52
Equipment T38–45
Network diagram T21
Telephones T45
Telephone services T16–37
Reg & pricing T32–34, 35–36
Television M15–20, L23–24
Independent stations .. M17–18
Pay-per-view M24
Test & measurement equip. E38
Textbooks M39–42
College texts M40
El-hi texts M38–39
Textiles T75–83
Industry fundamentals .. T80–81
Markets T79–82
Textiles, App., Home & Furn. T73–96
Therapeutic drugs H26
Thermoplastics C26–28
Thermoset resins C28
Tight formations U91
Tire shipments A88–89
Tires A88–89
Titanium dioxide C21
Tobacco F36–39
Toiletries H32–33, R90
Towels T79, 81–82
Toys L37–40
Tractors S36–37
Trailers A80
Transportation
Airlines A31–38
Automobiles A75–84
Railroads R15–31
Trucking R36–41
Trucking R36–41
Less-than-truckload .. R36–40
Trucking labor R40–42
Trucks A83

U Universal life I-25
Upholstered furniture T96
Utilities-Electric U15–55
Utilities-Gas U75–107
Utility construction U36–37

V Vacancy rates I-39–40
Variable life I-25
Video cassettes L22–23
Video games L38–39

W Waferboard B85
Warehouse stores R83, 92–93
Whole life I-27
Wines F30–32
Wood furniture T95–96
Wood products B84–87
Wood pulp B91, 94
World developments O-15–24

X X-ray lithography E38

Z Zinc M87–88

Editor: Thomas Nugent
Associate Editor: Eileen Bossong-Martines
Copy Editor: Nicholas Boyle
Assistant to Editor: Victoria Landi

Subscriber relations: (212) 208-8768
Facsimile machine: (212) 412-0299
● 1989 by Standard & Poor's Corp.
All rights reserved. USPS No. 517-780

STANDARD & POOR'S INDUSTRY SURVEYS is published weekly. Annual subscription: $1,115 Executive and Editorial Offices: Standard & Poor's Corporation, 25 Broadway, New York, NY 10004 Officers of Standard & Poor's Corporation: Harold W. McGraw, III, President, Chief Executive Officer and Chairman; Kurt D. Steele, Senior Vice President, General Counsel and Secretary; Frank Penglase, Treasurer. Second-class postage paid at New York, 10004. POSTMASTER: Send address changes to INDUSTRY SURVEYS, attention Mail Prep, Standard & Poor's Corp. 25 Broadway, New York, NY 10004 ....ation has been obtained by INDUSTRY SURVEYS from sources believed to be reliable. However, because of the possibility of human or mechanical error by our sources, INDU......VEYS, or others, INDUSTRY SURVEYS does not guarantee the accuracy, adequacy, or completeness of any information and is not responsible f........s or omissions or for the results obtained from the use of such information.

Figure 3.1: Part 2: "Subject Guide," an Index to Surveys from *Industry Surveys*, 27 April 1987.

Higher occupancy, room rates have managers smiling

For the U.S. lodging industry, 1988 was a another year of improvement. Aided by the sixth consecutive year of economic expansion, demand for rooms increased 4.9% over 1987, according to *Lodging Outlook*, a newsletter published by Smith Travel Research. The supply of rooms rose a smaller 3.5%, enabling industry occupancy to edge higher to 62.7%. Room rates in 1988 averaged $54.13, up 3.8% from a year earlier, and total room sales rose 8.9%, significantly exceeding the 7.5% growth in U.S. gross national product. In 1988, roughly $35 billion was spent on hotel and motel rooms in the U.S. Currently about 44,500 lodging properties and 2.85 million hotel rooms are open for business in the U.S. (based on mid-1988 figures from the American Hotel and Motel Association—largely exclusive of facilities with less than 15 rooms), or about one room for every 84 Americans. According to Smith Travel, roughly 33% of all rooms are in highway locations, 31% at suburban sites, 17% in urban settings, 12% at resorts, and 7% at airports. As with restaurants, the chains are the most visible part of the hotel industry. At the end of 1988, the 10 largest hotel chain companies accounted for about 40% of U.S hotel rooms.

Further improvement possible

A slowdown in the amount of new hotel space coming on stream should be beneficial to the industry over the next several years. According to a preliminary report from the U.S. Department of Commerce, the value of new construction for hotels and motels during 1988 totaled $6.50 billion, down 11% from 1987. The pace of lodging construction has grown dramatically over the past 15 years. From 1984–88, in inflation-adjusted dollars, average annual new construction put in place was 63% above that of the prior five year period and more than triple the average annual level during 1974–78.

The recent decline in new construction is partly a consequence of the federal Tax Reform Act of 1986, which curtailed tax benefits available from new projects. Prior to the law, losses from limited partnership interests in hotels could be easily used to shelter income from other sources. For partnerships formed after passage, however, an investor's share of the losses from a so-called "passive" limited partnership can be used only to offset (shelter) income from

other passive investments, which lessens the attraction of buying into a hotel project as a tax strategy. Adding to the problem, industry oversupply may make it more difficult for developers to get financing for new projects.

Regional differences dictate results

In 1988, there were major differences between lodging markets in various parts of the country. Among 25 metropolitan areas tracked by Smith Travel, New York had the highest average room rate ($112.61), while Las Vegas had the lowest ($47.43). Honolulu had the highest occupancy level (85.0%) and Denver ranked the lowest (53.4%). The Riverside-San Bernardino area of California posted the largest rise in both room demand (16.0%) and room sales (18.6%). The greatest increase in room supply was in the Phoenix area (10.5%), where an above-average rise in demand did not keep pace with new rooms, causing occupancy to decline. The largest lodging markets are Los Angeles, Chicago, New York, Orlando, Las Vegas, and Washington, D.C., each with roughly 58,000–66,000 rooms.

According to Laventhol & Horwath, a Philadelphia-based research firm, rooms rentals accounted for 54.4% of lodging industry revenues in 1987; food and beverage contributed most of the remainder. U.S. travelers accounted for 89.2% of lodging business, and leisure traveling accounted for only 32.8% of industry demand, according to Laventhol & Horwath. Business and government travel composed 40.3% of the total; conferences represented 20%.

Fat profits in a night's sleep

Lodging companies have a huge gross profit margin on room sales. Once constructed, the cost of filling and maintaining a room are quite low. Based on a study of 650 lodging properties, Laventhol & Horwath found the median profit margin on rooms to be 74%, compared with a gross margin of only 13.7% for food and beverage sales. From 1985–87, however, Laventhol & Horwath found that median U.S. lodging property operated at a loss, as sales income failed to cover fixed charges, which include interest expense, depreciation, rent, and insurance. In 1987, the median revenue per available room was $22,685 ($62.15 per day, assuming full-year availability), but after all expenses were figured, the industry had a median per-room pretax loss of $748.

Not that the industry operated at a loss. A median calculation means that half of the sample did better and the other half did worse; results from the more profitable (and perhaps more expensive) properties could have offset those of the weaker facilities. A look at the income statements of MARRIOTT CORP., HOLIDAY CORP., and HILTON HOTELS suggests that even in a period of industry oversupply, substantial profits can be made from the hotel business. Also, a sizable portion of industry expenses are noncash items, including depreciation and amortization, which averaged 7.5% of revenues in 1987.

To own, manage, or franchise?

Participation in the lodging industry takes a variety of forms. Companies can choose to own, manage, and/or franchise properties, and some do all three. Ownership can include properties that are part of someone else's franchise

Lodging industry profile

Segment	Occupancy (%) 1987	Occupancy (%) 1988	Room Rate 1987	Room Rate 1988	% change 1988 vs 1987 Sales	% change 1988 vs 1987 Supply	% change 1988 vs 1987 Demand
U.S. industry	61.8	62.7	$52.15	$54.13	+8.9	+3.5	+4.9
Full-service							
Luxury	62.9	63.9	$75.12	$78.38	+9.6	+3.4	+5.1
Upscale	63.2	63.8	$52.62	$54.51	+7.0	+2.3	+3.3
Basic	59.7	60.2	$40.59	$41.54	+4.9	+1.6	+2.5
Limited-service							
Upper	61.9	63.3	$42.42	$43.61	+14.2	+8.6	+11.1
Moderate	63.8	64.5	$27.92	$28.86	+7.8	+3.1	+4.3
By property location							
Urban	63.4	64.4	$72.54	$75.97	+9.4	+2.9	+4.5
Suburban	61.3	62.2	$50.80	$52.51	+9.1	+3.9	+5.6
Airport	66.4	66.4	$53.79	$54.89	+7.5	+5.3	+6.3
Highway	59.7	60.6	$40.05	$41.28	+8.2	+3.4	+5.0
Resort	66.1	67.2	$75.14	$78.53	+8.7	+2.3	+4.0

Source: *Lodging Outlook*

Figure 3.2: Section on "Lodging" from *Industry Surveys*, 16 March 1989.

Industry Surveys also provides a large number of statistical tables and charts in the "Basic Analysis" of the lodging industry (figure 3.3).

Figure 3.3: Chart on "Lodging Industry Profile" from Industry Surveys, 16 March 1989.

	Occupany (%)		Room Rate		% change 1988 vs 1987		
Segment	1987	1988	1987	1988	Sales	Supply	Demand
U.S. industry	61.8	62.7	$52.15	$54.13	+8.9	+3.5	+4.9
Full-service							
Luxury	62.9	63.9	$75.12	$78.38	+9.6	+3.4	+5.1
Upscale	63.2	63.8	$52.62	$54.51	+7.0	+2.3	+3.3
Basic	59.7	60.2	$40.59	$41.54	+4.9	+1.6	+2.5
Limited-service							
Upper	61.9	63.3	$42.42	$43.61	+14.2	+8.6	+11.1
Moderate	63.8	64.5	$27.92	$28.86	+7.8	+3.1	+4.3
By property location							
Urban	63.4	64.4	$72.54	$75.97	+9.4	+2.9	+4.5
Suburban	61.3	62.2	$50.80	$52.51	+9.1	+3.9	+5.6
Airport	66.4	66.4	$53.79	$54.89	+7.5	+5.3	+5.3
Highway	59.7	60.6	$40.05	$41.28	+8.2	+3.4	+5.0
Resort	66.1	67.2	$75.14	$78.53	+8.7	+2.3	+4.0

Lodging industry profile

Source: *Lodging Outlook*

The "Basic Analysis" for the lodging industry is one of many grouped under the broad heading of "Leisure-Time." Since related industries, such as gambling and restaurants, certainly have an influence on the lodging industry, you may wish to read these other "Basic Analysis" sections. To find a list of these, browse forward until you come to the "Leisure-Time Basic Analysis" title page (figure 3.4). In addition, there will be a "Current Analysis" at the beginning of the survey, which provides the latest developments and available industry, market, and company statistics.

Another useful tool for locating industry overviews is *Value Line Investment Survey*, which is issued weekly in a loose-leaf format. Since it is one of the most well-known business reference sources in America, you will find it in most large academic and public libraries. Although its primary purpose is investment advice on public companies, *Value Line Investment Survey* should not be overlooked as a very good source of industry information.

Part I of *Value Line Investment Survey*, called "Summary & Index," is the index to the entire service. On the front page of Part I you will find the "ANALYSES OF INDUSTRIES IN ALPHABETICAL ORDER WITH PAGE NUMBER." Figure 3.5 shows an excerpt from this, with an arrow highlighting "Hotel/Gaming" and the page number. Do not confuse the page number with the number in parentheses, which is the rank for probable performance.

STANDARD&POOR'S

industry surveys

© 1989 Standard & Poor's Corporation USPS No. 517-780.

The Outlook 15

Filmed Entertainment 17

Prerecorded Music 26

Gaming 28

Lodging 32

Restaurants 34

Toys 37

Sports 41

Photography 42

Financial 43

Industry References 46

Composite Industry Data 47

Comparative Company Analysis 50

Figure 3.4: Title Page for "Leisure-Time Basic Analysis" from *Industry Surveys*, 16 March 1989.

THE VALUE LINE
Investment Survey
CONSUMER & FAMILY SCIENCES LIBRARY

Part 1
Summary & Index

File at the front of the *Ratings & Reports* binder. Last week's *Summary & Index* should be removed.

April 28, 1989

TABLE OF SUMMARY-INDEX CONTENTS

Summary-Index Page Number

Industries, in alphabetical order 1
Stocks—complete list with latest prices, Timeliness and Safety Ranks, Betas, estimated earnings, estimated
dividends, and option exchanges; also references to pages in Ratings & Reports carrying latest
full-page reports 2-23
Noteworthy Rank Changes 24-26

SCREENS

Industries, in order of Timeliness Rank 24
Timely stocks (1 & 2 for Performance) 27-29
Conservative stocks (1 & 2 for Safety) 30-31
High Yielding stocks 32
High 3- to 5-year appreciation 32
Cash generating companies 33
Best Performing stocks last 13 weeks 33
Poorest Performing stocks last 13 weeks 33
Stocks below book value 34
Low P/E stocks 35

High P/E stocks 35
High total return stocks 36
High 3- to 5-year dividend returns 36
Companies with high return on capital 37
Bargain Basement stocks 37
Untimely stocks (5 for Performance) 38
High yielding non-utility stocks 38
High growth stocks 39
Stock market averages 40

The Median of Estimated **PRICE-EARNINGS RATIOS** of all stocks with earnings	The Median of **ESTIMATED YIELDS** (next 12 months) of all dividend paying stocks under review	The Estimated Median **APPRECIATION POTENTIAL** of all 1700 stocks in the hypothesized Economic environment 3 to 5 years hence
12.4	**2.9%**	**65%**

26 Weeks Ago*	Market Low 12-23-74*	Market High 9-4-87*	26 Weeks Ago*	Market Low 12-23-74*	Market High 9-4-87*	26 Weeks Ago*	Market Low 12-23-74*	Market High 9-4-87*
11.8	4.8	16.9	3.0%	7.8%	2.3%	80%	234%	40%

*Estimated medians as published in *The Value Line Investment Survey* on the dates shown.

ANALYSES OF INDUSTRIES IN ALPHABETICAL ORDER WITH PAGE NUMBER
Numeral in parenthesis after the industry is rank for probable performance (next 12 months).

	PAGE		PAGE		PAGE		PAGE
Advertising (72)	1820	Electrical Equipment (62)	1001	Machinery (45)	1301	Real Estate (81)	664
Aerospace/Defense (79)	551	Electric Util. (Central) (90)	701	Machinery (Const&Mining) (30)	1349	R.E.I.T. (92)	1171
Air Transport (22)	251	Electric Utility (East) (89)	164	Machine Tool (47)	1337	Recreation (26)	1751
Aluminum (3)	1220	Electric Utility (West) (91)	1717	Manuf. Housing/Rec Veh (44)	1541	Restaurant (24)	300
Apparel (32)	1601	Electronics (52)	1024	Maritime (73)	282	*Retail Building Supply (5)	892
Auto & Truck (12)	101	European Diversified (10)	817	Medical Services (25)	1276	Retail (Special Lines) (29)	1672
Auto Parts (OEM) (61)	793	Financial Services (69)	2048	Medical Supplies (28)	201	Retail Store (21)	1629
Auto Parts (Replacement) (64)	113	Food Processing (40)	1451	Metal Fabricating (85)	586	Securities Brokerage (80)	1185
Bank (57)	2001	Food Wholesalers (42)	1519	Metals & Mining (Gen'l) (15)	1220	Semiconductor (86)	1061
Bank (Midwest) (58)	641	*Furn./Home Furnishings (82)	907	Metals & Mining (Ind'l) (2)	616	Shoe (6)	1660
Beverage (19)	1530	Gold/Diamond (S.A.) (—)	1212	Multiform (77)	1360	Steel (General) (16)	603
Broadcasting/Cable TV (4*)	173	Grocery (36)	1498	Natural Gas (Distrib.) (88)	465	Steel (Integrated) (1)	1413
*Building Materials (39)		Home Appliance (53)	130	Natural Gas(Diversified) (49)	444	Steel (Specialty) (7)	2104
Canadian Energy (85)		*Homebuilding (35)	880	Newspaper (63)	1807	Telecom. Equipment (76)	774
*Cement (87)		Hotel/Gaming (60)	1772	Office Equip & Supplies (59)	1118	Telecom. Services (55)	750
Chemical (Basic) (4)		Household Products (14)	968	Oilfield Services/Equip. (38)	1848	Textile (75)	1618
Chemical (Diversified)		Industrial Services (37)	331	Packaging & Container (34)	953	Thrift (84)	1151
Chemical (Specialty) (51)		Insurance (Diversified) (48)	2072	*Paper & Forest Products (9)	921	Tire & Rubber (17)	125
Coal/Alternate Energy (8)	1868	Insurance (Life) (68)	1198	Petroleum (Integrated) (46)	401	Tobacco (33)	322
Computer & Peripherals (71)	1076	Insurance(Prop/Casualty) (23)	624	Petroleum (Producing) (78)	1826	Toiletries/Cosmetics (31)	805
Computer Software & Svcs (74)	2110	Investment Co.(Domestic) (54)	2089	Precious Metals (70)	1220	Toys & School Supplies (18)	1551
Copper (13)	1220	Investment Co.(Foreign) (—)	363	Precision Instrument (66)	138	Trucking/Transp. Leasing (27)	269
Drug (11)	1253	*Investment Co. (Income) (56)	979	Publishing (83)	1789	
Drugstore (20)	785	Japanese Diversified (43)	1558	Railroad (67)	288	*Reviewed in this week's edition.

In three parts: This is Part I, the Summary & Index. Part II is Selection & Opinion. Part III is Ratings & Reports. Volume XLIV, No. 32.
Published weekly by VALUE LINE, INC. 711 Third Avenue, New York, N.Y. 10017
For the confidential use of subscribers. Reprint by permission only. Copyright 1989 by Value Line, Inc.

Figure 3.5: "Analyses of Industries in Alphabetical Order with Page Number" from *Value Line Investment Survey*, 28 April 1989.

This group continues to log healthy earnings gains despite only a small recent improvement in the chronically sagging domestic hotel market. On the gaming front, an era passes with Drexel's forced exit from Atlantic City, but changes in casino financing are probably only just beginning.

COMPOSITE STATISTICS: HOTEL/GAMING INDUSTRY							
1984	1985	1986	1987	1988	1989	© VALUE LINE, INC.	91-93E
10061	11090	12483	14067	15150	16800	Sales ($mill)	23350
17.0%	18.0%	17.3%	17.2%	17.5%	17.0%	Operating Margin	16.5%
549.9	614.8	709.6	699.4	715	790	Depreciation ($mill)	1050
423.9	518.2	548.3	661.0	745	830	Net Profit ($mill)	1450
43.3%	42.5%	41.0%	40.9%	37.0%	37.5%	Income Tax Rate	37.5%
4.2%	4.7%	4.4%	4.7%	4.9%	4.9%	Net Profit Margin	6.2%
302.0	215.8	204.2	388.6	450	475	Working Cap'l ($mill)	1100
4696.0	5487.6	6829.1	8675.8	10400	10200	Long-Term Debt ($mill)	9800
3937.9	3908.2	4542.5	3337.2	2950	3350	Net Worth ($mill)	6600
8.0%	9.2%	7.8%	9.2%	9.5%	10.0%	% Earned Total Cap'l	12.0%
10.8%	13.3%	12.1%	19.8%	25.5%	25.0%	% Earned Net Worth	22.0%
8.1%	10.8%	9.8%	17.8%	22.0%	22.0%	% Retained to Comm Eq	20.0%
24%	19%	19%	11%	13%	12%	% All Div'ds to Net Prof	10%
16.9	15.8	20.8	17.9	*Bold figures are*		Avg Ann'l P/E Ratio	14.0
1.57	1.28	1.41	1.20	*Value Line*		Relative P/E Ratio	1.15
1.5%	1.2%	.9%	13.9%	*estimates*		Avg Ann'l Div'd Yield	.7%

The Domestic Lodging Industry Is Still Overbuilt ...

New hotel construction, spurred by favorable tax laws, mushroomed throughout most of the current business expansion. As a result, average occupancy rates never really recovered from their recession levels. And competition in the lodging industry, which normally just tracks GNP, has been unusually fierce. Only strong demand from business and leisure travelers has saved U.S. hotel operators from a major calamity.

The building boom came to an abrupt halt with the passage of the 1986 tax reform law. Average occupancy rates have finally begun to edge higher – a point or so in 1987 and 1988. Room rental rates, meanwhile, are rising in line with inflation – even pulling ahead in strong markets.

Real improvement, however, is probably years away. The national chains, for their part, continue to expand aggressively. Better conditions should ultimately arrive, but only slowly, and at the expense of hundreds of independent operators and small chains, who will go under or be absorbed in coming years by their larger counterparts.

... But Earnings Are Rising At A Healthy Pace.

Bottom-line growth lately logged by the companies under review here has been a good deal better than what might be supposed, given the aforementioned lackluster conditions. The national chains have learned to cope and even thrive at occupancy rate levels considered disastrous a decade ago. Aftertax profits probably rose 10%–15% in 1988, a good deal faster than revenues, according to our calculations.

Most of the earnings growth wasn't due to dramatic operating improvements, although operating margins may well have widened modestly. Last year's gains were significantly boosted by falling tax rates. And in some cases (most notably that of *Holiday Corp.*, which carries a large weighting in our composite statistics), accelerated property sale gains imparted added zip to earnings. Finally, gaming operations had an excellent year, and likely contributed importantly to the group's momentum.

The lodging industry probably won't see great change in these fundamentals in the year ahead. Continued modest improvement in the hotel sector is the most likely scenario, as demand growth more than holds its

own against the influx of new properties. The economic slowdown we forecast for the end of this year probably won't have a discernible effect on these companies. Typically, the hotel/gaming industry lags the business cycle by around six months. Fuel costs and the dollar remain at low levels, and that's good for operators, particularly at the onset of the summer travel season. In all, double-digit top- and bottom-line gains appear to be on tap for this group in 1989.

Drexel Has Been Shown The Door In Atlantic City

The New Jersey Casino Control Commission suspended investment banker Drexel Burnham Lambert from doing businesses with Atlantic City casinos until federal charges against the firm are resolved. If it hadn't been for Drexel and the financing it made available to Atlantic City casino operators, in the form of high-yield ("junk") bonds, the New Jersey gaming market almost certainly would be a fraction of its current size, a decade after its birth. Drexel underwrote about $2.5 billion worth of financing in Atlantic City, around 70% of the capital raised there by all securities firms.

... *Manufacturing* would quite likely have been af... Drexel's troubles. But it dropped plans to spin ... no operations – plans that originally called ... 400 million worth of debt to be raised by ... when the Casino Control Commission ex... oncern about excessive leverage.

...ough Drexel's suspension perhaps marks the passing of an age, even that firm's permanent exile from Atlantic City would probably have little effect on financing activity there. Competitors following in Drexel's footsteps are now willing and quite able to take up the slack.

The financing of gaming assets is still in its infancy, as a matter of fact. Although hotel operators have moved away from owning hotel properties for years now (they sell new units to investors, instead making money on development, management, and franchising activities), casinos are almost always owned by their operators. *Holiday*, and very likely others, are currently exploring ways to free up capital invested in casino real estate, in much the same way that has been accomplished in the hotel industry. We wouldn't be surprised to see casino sale transactions in coming years, even if Drexel isn't a player.

Meanwhile, gaming operations will most likely enjoy continued prosperity in the year ahead. Both Atlantic City and Las Vegas are registering double-digit revenue growth. Major supply additions will eventually cause dislocations, but probably not much before late 1990.

(Continued on page 1905)

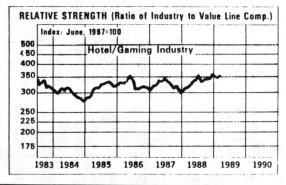

RELATIVE STRENGTH (Ratio of Industry to Value Line Comp.)

Index: June, 1967=100

Hotel/Gaming Industry

Figure 3.6: "Hotel/Gaming Industry" Section from *Value Line Investment Survey*, 10 March 1989.

Note that *Value Line Investment Survey* chooses to call its relevant section "Hotel/Gaming" rather than "Lodging." Since reference sources do not have uniform names for industries, always be prepared to search for alternate titles, such as: lodging, hotel/gaming, hotels and motels, or hospitality.

Now that you know the page number is 1772, turn to that page in Part III, which is called "Ratings & Reports." This part of *Value Line Investment Survey* contains the essence of the service—one-page reports on industries and companies (figure 3.6). Although the information is not as detailed or extensive as that in *Industry Surveys*, it does provide a good overview of the industry. Note the section titled "The Domestic Lodging Industry is Still Overbuilt."

You may have noticed that both *Industry Surveys* and *Value Line Investment Survey* mention the problem of "overbuilding or excess rooms" in regard to the lodging industry. In addition to providing an overview of the lodging industry, these two industry overview sources supplied a viable research topic: "Is the lodging industry overbuilt and is there an excess supply of rooms?" Many times industry overviews will mention industry issues and problems that lend themselves to research. This is one of the primary reasons for using the industry overviews—*Industry Surveys* and *Value Line Investment Survey*.

With a basic understanding of the lodging industry plus a research topic in mind, you are ready to explore other reference resources. The next step in our search strategy illustrates the best periodical indexes for industry research.

SUMMARY

1) *Industry Surveys* and *Value Line Investment Survey* are two sources that provide industry overviews.

2) Industry overviews provide basic information and data on industries. They identify and address issues and problems in the industry that may lead to ideas for research topics.

3) Using *Industry Surveys* and *Value Line Investment Survey*, we have identified a research topic for the hotel industry: "Is the lodging industry overbuilt and is there an excess supply of rooms?"

CHAPTER 4

PERIODICAL AND NEWSPAPER INDEXES

Business trends and financial situations change every day. A company alters its marketing strategy, the Dow-Jones average fluctuates, a major strike affects an industry. These changes affect not only our economy, but also our daily lives. A strike by a major airline may not only affect your personal vacation plans, but it also affects the lodging industry on a broader scale. How can you keep track of these current events in a particular industry such as lodging?

So far, we have discussed the importance of industry overviews. These overviews briefly cover what is happening in the lodging industry. But in order to conduct more thorough research on the lodging industry, you will want to supplement these overviews with very current information.

You might be able to find a recent book about the lodging industry that addresses all of the issues, problems, and trends. However, even if it's a new book, the information in it will be too old to be useful. The author and publisher may take one to five years to write and publish a book. Information that old will not be impressive to a teacher, boss, or interviewer.

Magazines and newspapers, on the other hand, have a shorter publication time lag. There may be only a few weeks or months from the time a magazine article leaves an author's desk until it is published. For a newspaper article, the time lag is only a day or two. For this reason, magazine and newspaper articles are an essential source of current information about any industry.

"Periodicals" is a rather broad term encompassing any publication that comes out regularly (e.g., daily, weekly, monthly, or semi-annually) and that is published on a continuing basis. Periodicals include everything from the school newspaper to the most prestigious scholarly journal. Between these two extremes, there are several different kinds of periodicals. First, there are newspapers and magazines that are written for the general public. Second, there are trade journals or periodicals aimed at the practical side of business. Finally, there are scholarly research journals. The word "journal" usually

ANNALS OF TOURISM RESEARCH
A SOCIAL SCIENCES JOURNAL

1988

Volume 15, Number 3

CONTENTS

Articles

Pamela J. Riley	313	Road Culture of International Long-Term Budget Travelers
Victor B. Teye	329	Coup d'Etat and African Tourism: A Study of Ghana
Karl Raitz / Meftah Dakhil	357	Recreational Choices and Environmental Preference
Erik Cohen	371	Authenticity and Commoditization in Tourism
Roger J. Calantone / Anthony di Benedetto / David C. Bojanic	387	Multimethod Forecasts for Tourism Analysis
Jafar Jafari / Dean Aaser	407	Tourism as the Subject of Doctoral Dissertations

Research Notes and Reports

Sarah L. Richardson / John Crompton	430	Vacation Patterns of French and English Canadians
Richard L. Dukes / Jill Brickner / Lori Meyer / Robert Mullins / Tony Perry / Shawna Rooney / Sharlyn Whigham	436	Semester at Sea: Research Note for 1982 Voyage

(Continued)

INDEXED IN Current Contents/Social & Behavioral Sciences, Social Sciences Citation Index, Communications Abstracts, Sociological Abstracts, Abstracts in Anthropology, Public Affairs Information Service Bulletin, Leisure Recreation and Tourism Abstracts, Geo Abstracts, Journal of Travel Research, Touristic Analysis Review, Documentation Touristique, and Sociology of Leisure and Sports Abstracts.

ISSN 0160-7383

(689)

Figure 4.1: Title Page from *Annals of Tourism Research* 15:3 (1988).

44

ANNALS OF TOURISM RESEARCH

STATEMENT OF PURPOSE

Annals of Tourism Research is a social sciences journal focusing upon the academic perspectives on tourism. While striving for a balance of theory and application, *Annals* is ultimately dedicated to developing theoretical constructs. Its strategies are to invite and encourage offerings from various disciplines; to serve as a forum through which these may interact; and thus to expand frontiers of knowledge in and contribute to the literature on tourism social science. In this role, *Annals* both structures and is structured by research efforts of a multidisciplinary community of scholars.

Annals of Tourism Research est un journal des sciences sociales consacré aux perspectives académiques sur le tourisme. Tout en visant à un équilibre entre la théorie et l'application, *Annals* est voué en dernière analyse au développement de modèles théoriques. Ses stratégies sont d'encourager des contributions de diverses disciplines, de servir de tribune par laquelle celles-ci peuvent agir réciproquement, et ainsi d'agrandir le champs des connaissances de la science sociale du tourisme. *Annals* structure et est structuré par les recherches d'une communauté pluridisciplinaire de savants.

Manuscripts: All parts of manuscripts must be typed double space, with ample margins provided. Forward the original manuscripts, along with four complete photocopies, addressed to the Editor of *Annals*. For additional information, please read *Style* published in each issue of the journal.

Article Evaluation Process: *Annals* is a refereed journal. All articles are evaluated by at least three referees. The evaluation is done anonymously (double-blind system).

Second Language of Annals: The editorial pages and abstracts of the feature articles also appear in French.

Editorial Office: J. Jafari, Editor-in-Chief, *Annals of Tourism Research*, Dept of Habitational Resources, University of Wisconsin-Stout, Menomonie. WI 54751, USA. Telephone (715) 232-2339.

Publishing, Subscription and Advertising Offices: Pergamon Press, Inc., Fairview Park, Elmsford, NY 10523, USA: and Pergamon Press plc, Headington Hill Hall, Oxford OX3 0BW, England.

Published Quarterly. *Annual institutional subscription rate* (1988): DM255.00; *Two-year institutional subscription rate* (1988/89): DM484.50. *Professional subscription rate* (1988): DM93.00. Prices are subject to change without notice. Notify 8 weeks in advance of address change with a copy of the subscription mailing label. *Microform subscriptions:* Back issues of all previously published volumes are available direct from Pergamon Press. Back issues of Pergamon journals in microform can be obtained from UMI, 300 North Zeeb Road, Ann Arbor, MI 48106, USA.

The views expressed in this journal are those of the authors and contributors and not necessarily endorsed by the editors or publisher.

Figure 4.2: "Statement of Purpose" from *Annals of Tourism Research* 15:3 (1988).

means that the periodical is aimed at the practitioner or professional, while the word "magazine" implies that the periodical is oriented toward the general public. Being able to distinguish a magazine from a trade and research journal is essential for research purposes. If you have never done this before, here are some clues that can help.

Popular magazines are aimed at the general public. You will recognize them as the ones you frequently see at newsstands. They have colorful, glossy covers, many advertisements, and articles written for the general reader.

Trade journals look very much like popular magazines, since they frequently have full-color covers and extensive advertising. However, they differ from magazines in that the articles will be of interest only to business people or professionals in the industry.

Scholarly journals are more extensively researched than trade journals. Since many articles in scholarly journals are written by professors or researchers, a good clue to a scholarly journal is the university affiliation listed after the author's or editor's name (figure 4.1). Another clue is that scholarly journals frequently have a statement of purpose that identifies their goal as furthering research (figure 4.2). And the last and final clue is to look for a statement that the journal is "refereed" (figure 4.2). A refereed journal article is evaluated and critiqued by one or more scholars in the field before it is accepted for publication.

Since your task is to find some current information on the industry, you will want to bypass the popular magazines because they will not have much in-depth information to help you evaluate the industry. However, trade periodicals and scholarly journals will be very valuable. In them you will find current information on an industry. However, keeping track of all the current business and financial news printed in newspapers and journals is a daunting task! Reading *The Wall Street Journal* and *Business Week* may keep you abreast of the general business world, but what about the information contained in those specialized industry periodicals such as *Lodging* and *Hotel & Motel Management*? It's in these trade journals that you will really be able to find information on the problems in the hotel industry, such as overbuilding.

Although it is impossible to read all of these specialized publications, there is an easy way to track what is being published. That is by using periodical indexes. Because there are literally thousands of periodicals published, one index could never list all the articles! Instead, indexes specialize in defined subject fields. To find current business articles, you need to find the indexes that cover the business periodicals. Then, you must learn how to use them. That is the purpose of this chapter—to identify business indexes and to explain how to use them.

The first part of this chapter illustrates how to use four periodical indexes. The second part explains how you can find periodicals and trade journals in a library. And the third part explains several methods for finding a list of journals on an industry.

USING PERIODICAL INDEXES

In the past you may have used *Readers' Guide to Periodical Literature* to find articles for other papers you have had to write. It is the most well-known periodical index and includes references to popular magazines like *Time* and *Newsweek*. However, it does not index very many business journals. If you used *Readers' Guide* to research "overbuilding in the lodging industry," you would find very few articles. Furthermore, they would be inappropriate for college-level papers. However, there are several indexes that specialize in the business area. The most widely available ones are:

1) *Business Periodicals Index*,
2) *Business Index/INFOTRAC™*,
3) *Predicasts F&S Index: United States*, and
4) *Wall Street Journal Index*.

Business Periodicals Index....What Is It?

In the business field one of the most well-known indexes is *Business Periodicals Index* (New York: H. W. Wilson Company, 1958-), which is published by the same company that publishes *Readers' Guide*. Large public libraries and most academic libraries with business programs have this publication, which indexes articles from over three hundred English-language business periodicals, such as *Hotel and Motel Management*. *Business Periodicals Index* is available in three formats: as a printed index, as an online file, and as a CD-ROM database. Most libraries will have it in printed format. Since that is the most readily available format, we will explain in detail how to use the printed version.

The printed version of *Business Periodicals Index* is published monthly. Every third issue cumulates the references for three months. At the end of the year, an annual cumulation is compiled. To start your search, we recommend that you use the most recent annual cumulation, then go on to the monthly and quarterly cumulations for the current year. If more information is needed, look in the older annual cumulations.

Each article in *Business Periodicals Index* is listed under the subject terms that best describe its contents. In other words, someone has already done the scanning of all those periodicals and has listed the articles under subject headings arranged alphabetically. Use the subject heading "Hotels and Motels" (figure 4.3). Before the list of articles, there is a list of "See also" subject headings, which are related to the hotel and motel industry, and a list of company names. You can look under any of these topics or companies for additional articles. These "See also" cross-references are put in the index to guide you to the most appropriate headings for your research question.

Since there are many articles on the topic of "Hotels and Motels," they have been subdivided. These subdivisions, such as "Acquisitions and mergers," are printed in bold

Hostages
See also
    Kidnapping
    When in doubt, grab a hostage. tab *Economist* 306:37 F 6 '88

Hostile antitakeover measures *See* Corporate acquisitions and mergers—Antitakeover measures

Hostility (Psychology)
    Hostility towards homosexuals at work. R. Upton and R. Furness. *Pers Manage* 20:25-6 Ap '88

Hot air heating *See* Warm air heating

Hot rock energy *See* Geothermal energy

Hotel administration *See* Hotel management

Hotel management
    It's management's fault if customers get poor service. R. Sherer. *Hotel Motel Manage* 203:20+ Ap 18 '88
    Managing your hotel's fitness facility. R. Shaw. *Hotel Motel Manage* 203:20+ Mr 28 '88
    Rodeway seeking stable ground: chain progressing in turnaround task. G. Taninecz. *Hotel Motel Manage* 203:1+ Ap 18 '88
    Surviving a start-up with sleeves rolled up [starting a bed and breakfast inn teaches perils of small business] R. Hotch. *Nations Bus* 76:4 Ap '88
    Turnaround efforts must be well-planned, goal-oriented. C. Brewton. *Hotel Motel Manage* 203:42-3 Mr 28 '88

Study and teaching
See also
    Hotel management schools

Hotel management companies
See also
    Lodging Unlimited, Inc.

Hotel management schools
    Cornell students help homeless via new course. *Hotel Motel Manage* 203:156 Ap 18 '88

Hotel protection *See* Hotels and motels—Security measures

Hotels and motels
See also
    Airport hotels
    Hotels and motels as an investment
    Resorts
    See also the following corporate names
    Allegis Corporation
    Best Inns
    Budgetel Inns
    Caesars World, Inc.
    Chattanooga Choo-Choo Co.
    Chicago Hotel Women (Organization)
    Consort North America
    Country Hospitality Inns Inc.
    Days Inns Corp.
    Doubletree, Inc.
    Embassy Suites Hotels
    Hampton Inns (Firm)
    Hilton Hotels Corp.
    Hilton International Co.
    Holiday Corp.
    Holiday Inns, Inc.
    La Costa Hotel and Spa
    Marriott Corporation
    Neighborhood Inn
    Ramada Inc.
    Resorts International Inc.
    Rodeway Inns International, Inc.
    Sofitel-North America (Firm)
    Stouffer Restaurant & Hotel Divisions
    Trump's Castle Hotel and Casino
    Surviving a start-up with sleeves rolled up [starting a bed and breakfast inn teaches perils of small business] R. Hotch. *Nations Bus* 76:4 Ap '88

Acquisitions and mergers
See also
    Hotels and motels—Sales transactions
    Canadian National sells hotel interests. M. Fisher. *Hotel Motel Manage* 203:2+ Mr 28 '88

All-suite hotels
All-suite breakfast concept receives mixed reviews [free cooked-to-order breakfasts] P. M. LaHue. *Hotel Motel Manage* 203:32+ My 9 '88
Extended stay: DeBoer starting chain with 30-day minimum [Neighborhood Inn] M. Fisher. *Hotel Motel Manage* 203:1+ Ap 18 '88
Hilton sets construction plans for all-suite in Chicago area. S. M. Bard. il *Hotel Motel Manage* 203:3+ Mr 28 '88
HoJo hits all-suite double. M. DeLuca. il *Hotel Motel Manage* 203:1+ Mr 7 '88
Holiday unveils Homewood: past experience, customer preferences bring return to extended-stay market. M. DeLuca. il *Hotel Motel Manage* 203:1+ My 9 '88

More growth key message for all-suites [third annual All-Suite Hotel Conference] R. A. Nozar. *Hotel Motel Manage* 203:2+ Ap 18 '88

Beverage service
See also
    Hotels and motels—Liquor service

Chain and franchise operations
Best Inns dedicated to consistency. P. M. LaHue. il tab *Hotel Motel Manage* 203.3+ Mr 28 '88
Clubcourt chains forecast substantial expansion; homey style finding market niche. D. W. Daniele. il tab *Hotel Motel Manage* 203:46-52 Mr 7 '88
Consort U.K. set to cross Atlantic. H. Chipkin. *Hotel Motel Manage* 203:1+ Mr 28 '88
Country Hospitality aiming full-speed for 300 properties. K. Seal. *Hotel Motel Manage* 203:1+ Ap 18 '88
Days Inns leadership forecasts sunny days [Days Inns Franchise Conference, New Orleans] B. Gillette. *Hotel Motel Manage* 203:1+ Mr 7 '88
Extended stay: DeBoer starting chain with 30-day minimum [Neighborhood Inn] M. Fisher. *Hotel Motel Manage* 203:1+ Ap 18 '88
HoJo hits all-suite double. M. DeLuca. il *Hotel Motel Manage* 203:1+ Mr 7 '88
Holiday Inns registers big expansion year. *Hotel Motel Manage* 203:24 Ap 18 '88
Investor outlook: top 50 economy/limited-service lodging chains [special report] *Hotel Motel Manage* 203:56-80 Ap 18 '88
Limited service doesn't have to mean limited food [Clubhouse Inns] R. Becker. *Hotel Motel Manage* 203:41 Mr 28 '88
Reality governs Budgetel growth. G. Taninecz. tab *Hotel Motel Manage* 203:3+ My 9 '88
Rodeway seeking stable ground: chain progressing in turnaround task. G. Taninecz. *Hotel Motel Manage* 203:1+ Ap 18 '88
Ruffer takes Marriott into economy hotels [Fairfield Inn] J. Meyers. por *Advert Age* 59:80 Ap 18 '88
Sofitel announces plans to increase U.S. hotels. H. Chipkin. *Hotel Motel Manage* 203:2+ Ap 18 '88

Communication systems
RIMSNET on the road. B. Somerville. il *Risk Manage* 35:32-3+ Ap '88

Competition
See also
    Market share—Hotels and motels
Competition heats up in Atlanta's Buckhead. R. Shaw. *Hotel Motel Manage* 203:1+ Ap 18 '88

Data processing
See also
    Hotels and motels—Reservation systems—Data processing
Conditions and consequences of hotel automation. V. Chandrasekar. *Hotel Motel Manage* 203:132+ Ap 18 '88
Lodging automation continues to advance. G. Taninecz. *Hotel Motel Manage* 203:132+ Ap 18 '88

Design and construction
Building boom alters skyline in Las Vegas. S. Lalli. *Hotel Motel Manage* 203:2+ Mr 28 '88
Casino, nine hotels anchor Vegas project [Southstar project] S. Lalli. *Hotel Motel Manage* 203:2+ Mr 7 '88
Convention complex unveiled at Walt Disney World Epcot Center [Walt Disney World Dolphin Hotel and Convention Center] il *Buildings* 82:36 Ap '88
Disney World maps out convention/resort hotels. M. Fisher. il *Hotel Motel Manage* 203:1+ Mr 7 '88
Effective meeting-space design puts focus on comfort. R. Baraban. *Hotel Motel Manage* 203:92-4 Ap 18 '88
Hilton sets construction plans for all-suite in Chicago area. S. M. Bard. il *Hotel Motel Manage* 203:3+ Mr 28 '88
Hotel development in transition, say industry execs. M. DeLuca. *Hotel Motel Manage* 203:51 Mr 7 '88
Loss control keeps heads above water [accident scenario of collapsed hotel swimming pool] *Bus Insur* 22:24 Mr 28 '88
Prefab gains edge in commercial market. A. Nydele. il *Buildings* 82:104-6+ Ap '88
Ramada planning to grow by 1,700 rooms in Northcentral region [through new construction or conversions] S. M. Bard. *Hotel Motel Manage* 203:2+ Ap 18 '88
Santa Monica gets popular with builders. K. Seal. *Hotel Motel Manage* 203:3+ Mr 28 '88
Taunts help kill hotel proposal [Rochester, Mich.] K. Burgess. *Hotel Motel Manage* 203:2+ Ap 18 '88

Figure 4.3: Subject Section from *Business Periodicals Index*, October 1988.

For Ind — Forest Industries
Forbes — Forbes
Fortune — Fortune
Frozen Food Dig — Frozen Food Digest
Fueloil Oil Heat — Fueloil & Oil Heat
Futures — Futures (Cedar Falls, Iowa)

G

Global Trade — Global Trade
Global Trade Exec — Global Trade Executive
Gov Finance Rev — Government Finance Review
Graph Arts Mon Print Ind — Graphic Arts Monthly and the Printing Industry

H

Handl Shipp Manage — Handling & Shipping Management
Harv Bus Rev — Harvard Business Review
Health Care Manage Rev — Health Care Management Review
Healthcare Financ Manage — Healthcare Financial Management
Hotel Motel Manage — Hotel & Motel Management
Hum Resour Manage — Human Resource Management
Hum Resour Plann — Human Resource Planning

I

I/S Anal — I/S Analyzer
IEEE Trans Eng Manage — IEEE Transactions on Engineering Management
Inc — Inc.
Ind Dev — Industrial Development
Ind Distrib — Industrial Distribution
Ind Labor Relat Rev — Industrial and Labor Relations Review
Ind Manage Data Syst — Industrial Management & Data Systems
Ind Mark Manage — Industrial Marketing Management
Ind Relat — Industrial Relations
Ind Week — Industry Week
Infosystems — Infosystems
Inquiry — Inquiry
Inst Investor — Institutional Investor
Int Labour Rev — International Labour Review
Int Manage — International Management (Europe edition)
Int Monet Fund Staff Pap — International Monetary Fund Staff Papers
Int Trade Forum — International Trade Forum
Interavia — Interavia
Interfaces — Interfaces
Intern Audit — The Internal Auditor
Iron Age — Iron Age
Iron Age Met Prod — Iron Age Metals Producer
Issues Bank Regul — Issues in Bank Regulation

J

J Account — Journal of Accountancy
J Account Audit Finance — Journal of Accounting, Auditing & Finance
J Account Res — Journal of Accounting Research
J Advert — Journal of Advertising
J Advert Res — Journal of Advertising Research
J Am Real Estate Urban Econ Assoc — Journal of the American Real Estate and Urban Economics Association
J Am Soc CLU ChFC — Journal of the American Society of CLU & ChFC
J Bank Finance — Journal of Banking and Finance
J Bus — The Journal of Business (Chicago, Ill.)
J Bus Commun — Journal of Business Communication
J Bus Res — Journal of Business Research
J Bus Strategy — Journal of Business Strategy
J Commer Bank Lending — The Journal of Commercial Bank Lending
J Common Mark Stud — Journal of Common Market Studies
J Consum Aff — The Journal of Consumer Affairs
J Consum Res — The Journal of Consumer Research
J Dev Areas — The Journal of Developing Areas
J Econ Bus — Journal of Economics and Business
J Econ Issues — Journal of Economic Issues
J Financ Quant Anal — Journal of Financial and Quantitative Analysis
J Finance — The Journal of Finance
J Int Bus Stud — Journal of International Business Studies
J Manage — Journal of Management

J Manage Stud — Journal of Management Studies (Oxford, England)
J Mark — Journal of Marketing
J Mark Res — Journal of Marketing Research
J Money Credit Bank — Journal of Money, Credit and Banking
J Oper Res Soc — Journal of the Operational Research Society
J Portf Manage — Journal of Portfolio Management
J Prop Manage — Journal of Property Management
J Purch Mater Manage — Journal of Purchasing and Materials Management
J Retail — Journal of Retailing
J Retail Bank — Journal of Retail Banking
J Risk Insur — The Journal of Risk and Insurance
J Small Bus Manage — Journal of Small Business Management
J Syst Manage — Journal of Systems Management
J Tax — The Journal of Taxation
J Urban Econ — Journal of Urban Economics

L

Labor Law J — Labor Law Journal
Land Econ — Land Economics
Long Range Plann — Long Range Planning

M

Madison Ave — Madison Avenue
Mag Bank Adm — Magazine of Bank Administration
Manage Account — Management Accounting (New York, N.Y.)
Manage Decis — Management Decision
Manage Int Rev — Management International Review
Manage Rev — Management Review
Manage Sci — Management Science
Manage Solut — Management Solutions
Manage Today — Management Today
Manage World — Management World
Mark Commun — Marketing Communications
Mark Media Decis — Marketing & Media Decisions
Mark News — Marketing News
Mass Transit — Mass Transit
McKinsey Q — McKinsey Quarterly
Mergers Acquis — Mergers & Acquisitions
Milbank Q — Milbank Quarterly
Mini-Micro Syst — Mini-Micro Systems
Mod Off Technol — Modern Office Technology
Mod Power Syst — Modern Power Systems
Mon Labor Rev — Monthly Labor Review
Money — Money
Mortg Bank — Mortgage Banking

N

Nations Bus — Nation's Business
Natl Food Rev — National Food Review
Natl Inst Econ Rev — National Institute Economic Review
Natl Pet News — National Petroleum News
Natl Real Estate Investor — National Real Estate Investor
Natl Saf Health News — National Safety and Health News
Natl Tax J — National Tax Journal
Natl Underwrit (Life Health Financ Serv Ed) — National Underwriter (Life & Health/Financial Services Edition)
Natl Underwrit (Prop Casualty Employee Benefits Ed) — National Underwriter (Property & Casualty/Employee Benefits Edition)
Nurs Homes Sr Citizen Care — Nursing Homes and Senior Citizen Care

O

OECD Obs — The OECD Observer
Office — The Office
Oil Gas J — Oil & Gas Journal
Online — Online (Weston, Conn.)
Oper Res — Operations Research
Organ Behav Hum Decis Processes — Organizational Behavior and Human Decision Processes
Organ Dyn — Organizational Dynamics

P

Pap Trade J — Paper Trade Journal
Pension World — Pension World

Figure 4.4: "Abbreviations of Periodicals Indexed" from *Business Periodicals Index*, October 1988.

Figure 4.5: Sample Citation from *Business Periodicals Index*, **October 1988.**

```
┌─────────────────────────────────────────────────────────────┐
│                        Forecasting                            │
│   Ten  key  trends  will  shape  hospitality  industry's  future. │
│      R. C. Hazard, Jr. Hotel Motel Manage 203:22+ Mr          │
│      7 '88                                                    │
│           ↑                    ↑                  ↑       ↑    │
│          Date             Journal Name        Volume    Page  │
└─────────────────────────────────────────────────────────────┘
```

type and centered in the middle of the columns (figure 4.3). Scan the subtopics and select those that are most appropriate to overbuilding. The article entitled "Ten key trends will shape hospitality industry's future" under "Forecasting" looks promising (figure 4.5).

The name of the journal in which this article appears—"*Hotel Motel Manage*"—is abbreviated and in italics. The full names of the journals are given in a chart called "Abbreviations of Periodicals Indexed," which is in the front of the volume (figure 4.4). Here you will find that the full title is *Hotel & Motel Management*. The journal title is followed by the volume number, the page numbers, and the date of the issue (figure 4.5). With the full name of the periodical and the other information supplied in the citation, you are ready to locate this article in the library.

Your library may also provide access to *Business Periodicals Index*ᵗᵐ on CD-ROM or as an online file. If it does, read chapter 2 of this book for an explanation of computer searching or ask a reference librarian how to use the machine-readable versions of this publication.

*Business Index/INFOTRAC*ᵗᵐ...What Is It?

Your library also may carry either *Business Index*ᵗᵐ (Foster City, CA: Information Access Company, 1981-) or *INFOTRAC*ᵗᵐ (Foster City, CA: Information Access Company, 1981-). Both products index the same business journals, but they are produced in two different formats. While *Business Index*ᵗᵐ is on microfilm and accessible via a microfilm reader, *INFOTRAC*ᵗᵐ is on compact disk and available via a microcomputer. Find out if your library has either of these indexes.

Whichever format your library has, there are two advantages to this reference tool over *Business Periodicals Index*, which we discussed previously.

1)   It indexes more journals, and

2)   It is usually more current.

Each month the library receives a new edition of the microfilm *Business Index*™ or the compact disk *INFOTRAC*™. Not only does this new edition include the most current citations, but it also includes all of the older citations from the last several years. Therefore, you have all the citations in one index and no need for monthly supplements as you do with the paper index of *Business Periodicals Index*.

How would you look for journal articles using *INFOTRAC*™?

Type the subject "Hotels" on the keyboard. You will see that the subject "Hotels and Motels" has over twenty subdivisions, including:

- art,
- designs and plans,
- economic aspects,
- forecasts,
- management,
- marketing,
- statistics, and
- supply and demand.

This last subdivision is most appropriate to the topic of overbuilding. However, "forecasts" and "statistics" may also be useful. Figure 4.6 is an excerpt from a printout of the citations from *INFOTRAC*™.

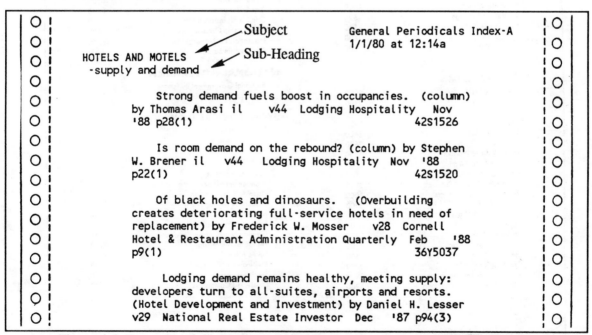

Figure 4.6: Examples of Citations Resulting from a Sample Search of *INFOTRAC*™.

51

Predicasts F&S INDEX UNITED STATES

TABLE OF CONTENTS

User's Guide.. Section A

Alphabetical Guide to the SIC Codes.................................... Section B

Source Pages .... Section C

INDUSTRY & PRODUCT BY SIC... Section 1

ECONOMIC INFORMATION

Population & Vital Statistics	E100
Labor Force & Employment	E200
National Income & Expenditure	E300
Production & Business Activity	E400
Financial Transactions & BOP	E500
Regional & Local Economic Data	E600

AGRICULTURE, MINING, CONSTRUCTION

Grains	0110
Field Crops ex Grains	0130
Fruits & Vegetables	0160
Dairy, Poultry & Livestock Farms	0200
Forestry, Fishing, Hunting	0800
Mining & Extractive Industries	1000
Coal	1100
Crude Petroleum & Natural Gas	1300
Nonmetal Mining	1400
Residential Buildings	1520
Nonresidential Buildings	1540
Nonbuilding Construction	1600
Construction Trades	1700

MANUFACTURING

Food Products	2000
Tobacco Products	2100
Textiles	2200
Apparel	2300
Wood Products	2400
Furniture	2500
Paper & Allied Products	2600
Printing & Publishing	2700
Chemicals & Allied Products	2800
Petroleum & Energy Products	2900
Rubber & Plastic Products	3000
Leather Products	3100
Stone, Clay & Glass	3200
Metals	3300
Metal Products	3400
Machinery ex Electric	3500
Electrical & Electronic Equip	3600
Transport Equipment	3700
Instruments & Related Prods	3800
Miscellaneous Manufacturing	3900

TRANSPORT & UTILITIES

Rail, Truck, Water & Air Transport	4000
Communications, Broadcasting	4800
Electric Utilities	4910
Gas Utilities	4920
Pollution Control	4950

TRADE & SERVICES

Wholesale & Retail Trade	5000
Financial Services	6000
Lodging, Personal Services	7010
Business Services	7300
Movies, Recreation	7800

OTHER ORGANIZATIONS & SERVICES

Medical & Health Services	8000
Education	8200
Social Services	8300
Arts & Humanities	8400
Science, Research & Development	8500
Membership Organizations	8600
Households & Nonprofit Insts	8800
Professional Services NEC	8900

NATIONAL GOVERNMENT

National Government by Function	9100
National Government Agencies	9110

STATE & LOCAL GOVERNMENT

State Government	9210
Local Government	9300

BUSINESS

Business Methods	9910
Management Theory & Techniques	9911
Planning & Information	9912
Production Management	9913
Marketing	9914
Finance & Stockholder Relations	9915
General Management Services	9916
Personnel Administration	9918
Public Affairs	9919
Multinational Corporations	9920
Small Business	9970
Diversified Companies	9980

COMPANIES – Alphabetical... Section 2

Figure 4.7: "Table of Contents" from *Predicasts F&S Index: United States,* June 1987.

*Predicasts F&S Index: United States...*What Is It?

The third index—and possibly the most important index for industry research—is *Predicasts F & S Index: United States* (Cleveland, OH: Predicasts, 1964-). This index specializes in industry, product, and company information. It is divided into two major sections. Section one (printed on colored paper) is on products and industries (figure 4.7). Section two (printed on white paper) is on companies and will be discussed more fully in chapters 8 and 9.

Section one is not arranged alphabetically by subject as *Business Periodicals Index* and *Business Index/INFOTRAC*™ are. Instead, it uses a numbering arrangement based on the Standard Industrial Classification (SIC) system. (*The Standard Industrial Classification Manual* was explained and illustrated in chapter 1.) By using SIC numbers, articles about similar products and industries are grouped together. For example, the following chart shows how the Service Industries are subdivided:

Service Industries	7000000
Lodging & Tourist Services	7010000
Hotels & Motels	7011000
Hotel Management	7011100
.	
.	
.	
Personnel Services	7200000

These numbers work as if there is a decimal point in front of the "7." Zeros at the end of the numbers may be dropped or ignored without changing the sorting order.

In order to find the most appropriate SIC number, use the "Alphabetical Index to SIC Numbers" in the front of each issue of the index. The SIC number for "Hotels & Motels" is 7011000 (figure 4.8).

Now turn to this number in the "Industries & Products by SIC" section (figure 4.9).

The citations in this index are very brief and include:

1) A one-sentence summary of the article instead of a title (i.e., "Hotel room building will fall to 50,000-55,000 in 1987 vs 91,000 new rooms built in 1986").

2) Abbreviated name of the journal (i.e., WSJ). Full titles are listed in the front of each issue.

3) Date and page number (i.e., 04-01-87 p31).

SIC ALPHA GUIDE **B-9** **Infrared Countermeasures**

Gross Domestic Investment	E31 200
Gross Domestic Product	E31 030
Gross Domestic Product-see also GDP	E31 030
Gross Fixed Domestic Invest	E31 203
Gross National Product	E31 000
Gross National Product Deflator	E44 100
Gross National Product-see also GNP	E31 000
Gross Private Domestic Invest	E31 201
Ground-Based Instrument Radar	366 2558
Ground-Based Intercontinental Missiles	376 1112
Ground Based Tracking Radar	366 2554
Ground Forces RDT&E Support Svces	891 1912
Ground Mobile & Base Transceivers	366 2162
Ground Mobile Radio Systems	366 2152
Ground Navigation Equipment	366 2410
Ground Stations, Comsat	366 2135
Ground Traffic Control Systems	357 3044
Ground Water Treatment Chemicals	289 9594
Ground or Treated Minerals	329 5000
Groundnuts	013 9300
Groundwood Paper, Coated	262 1310
Groundwood Paper, Uncoated	262 1210
Group Dynamics	991 1200
Guard Services	739 3100
Guidance & Auxiliary Rocket Eng	376 4550
Guided Vehicles, Industrial Automatic	353 7040
Gum & Wood Chemicals	286 1000
Gum, Chewing	206 7000
Gum ex Dietetic, Chewing	206 7012
Gums, Vegetable	207 6400
Guns & Howitzers, 30-75mm	348 9111
Guns, Mortars & Accessories	348 9100
Guns, Small Arms	348 4000
Gynecological R&D	800 0292
Gypsum Lath & Wallboard	327 5120
Gypsum Products	327 5000
Gyroscopes, Aeronautical	381 1120

H

Hair Care Equip, Electric	363 4510
Hair Colorings	284 4350
Hair Colorings, Home	284 4353
Hair Conditioners	284 4318
Hair Dryers, Electric	363 4511
Hair Preparations	284 4300
Hair Rinses	284 4365
Hair Setters, Electric	363 4512
Hair Sprays & Rinses	284 4360
Hair Sprays, Aerosol	284 4363
Hair Sprays ex Aerosol	284 4364
Hair Wigs	399 9921
Halogenated Hydrocarbons	286 8100
Hamburger & Wiener Rolls	205 1233
Hamburger Restaurants, Fast Food	581 2022
Hand & Edge Tools	342 3000
Hand-Held Cameras, Professional	386 1131
Hand-Held Language Translators	357 3083
Hand Lotions	284 4518
Hand Tools, Pneumatic	354 6240
Hard Candy	206 5351
Hard Coal	110 0100
Hardboard & Hardboard Panel Products	249 9600
Hardness Testers	382 9232
Hardware	342 9000
Hardware & Plumbing Whsle	507 0000
Hardware, Metal	342 9000
Hardware Stores	525 1000
Hardware Wholesale	507 2000
Hardwood Lumber	242 1100
Hari Care Products, Consumer	284 4302
Harrows, Disc	352 3411
Harrows, Rollers & Pulverizers	352 3400
Harvesting Machinery	352 3500
Hats & Caps, Males'	235 2210
Hats, Caps & Millinery	235 0000
Hay	013 9908
Hay Balers	352 3650
Hay Mowers & Mower Conditioners	352 3610
Haying Machines	352 3600
Hazardous Waste, Trucking of	421 3910
Hazelnuts	017 3041
HDPE	282 1411
Head-Up Displays	366 2447
Headlights, Vehicle	364 7030
Health & Beauty Aids Whsle	512 2300
Health & Education EDP Use	357 3080
Health & Human Services, Dept of	912 4000
Health & Science Software (ex Micro)	737 2360
Health & Science Software Pkgs (Micro)	737 2460
Health, Education & Welfare	800 0000
Health, Educatn & Welfare-Natl	910 5000
Health Aides	804 7300
Health Care	800 0100
Health Care, Home	809 6000
Health Care, Public	800 0120
Health Centers, Mental	806 3000
Health Clinics, Occupational	808 9080
Health Clubs & Spas	799 7300
Health Computer Systems	357 3081
Health Food Stores	549 9100
Health Foods	200 1000
Health Industry DP Services	737 4350
Health Insurance	632 0000
Health Maintenance Organizations	800 0130
Health Plans, Preferred Provider	800 0151
Health Problems	991 8670
Health Problems Prevention	800 0140
Health Research Programs	910 5220
Health Service, Public	912 4200
Health Services Administration	912 4250
Health Subsidies & Grants	910 5217
Health Supplies, Home	384 2020
Heart & Cardiovascular R&D	800 0251
Heart Shields	283 1924
Heart Valves, Biosynthetic	283 1924
Heat Exchangers	344 3110
Heat Pumps ex Industrial	358 5268
Heat Seeking Fire Control Eqp	366 2534
Heat Sensitive Photocopy Paper	386 1732
Heat Transfer Fluids	286 9685
Heaters, Electric	363 4800
Heaters, Kerosine	343 3734
Heaters, Portable Electric	363 4810
Heaters, Unit	343 3730
Heating Equip, Solar	343 3600
Heating Equipment, Induction	356 7410
Heating Furnaces & Parts	343 3700
Heating Furnaces, Warm Air	358 5810
Heating Oil	291 1410
Heating Pads, Electric	363 4402
Heavy & Medium Transport Aircraft	372 1152
Heavy Cream, Packaged	202 6232
Heavy Electrical Equipment	360 2000
Heavy Equipment Repair	755 0000
Helicopter Rotor Control Actuators	372 8163
Helicopters, Attack	372 1141
Helicopters, Civil	372 1014
Helicopters, Commercial	372 1370
Helicopters, General	372 1240
Helicopters, Military	372 1140
Helicopters, Military Transport & Utility	372 1142
Helicopters, Reconnaissance	372 1146
Helicopters, Rescue	372 1146
Helicopters, Training	372 1147
Helicopters, Turbine-Powered Civil	372 1242
Helmets	384 2352
Hematinic Preparations	283 4750
Hematological Agents, Bulk	283 3430
Hematology & Intravenous Eqp	384 1550
Hematology Equipment	384 1310
Hemostats, Collagen	283 1911
Heparin Preparations	283 4313
Herbicides	287 9600
Hex Head Bolts	345 2412
Hides & Skins	201 1910
High Altitude Research Balloons	372 1254
Highways & Streets Constructn	161 1000
Highways & Streets Repair	161 1020
Hinges & Butts	342 9450
Hispanic Americans	E12 340
Hobby & Model Kits	394 4240
Hobby, Toy & Games Stores	594 5000
Hobby Periodicals	272 1521
Hog Farm Equipment	352 3820
Hogs	021 3000
Holding Companies, Bank	602 0001
Holding Companies, Financial	671 0000
Holding Companies, Investment	671 2000
Holography, Lasers for	383 2834
Home Banking Svcs, Videotex	481 1523
Home Center Stores	521 1010
Home Dialysis Therapy	809 6120
Home Electronic Air Cleaners	363 4710
Home Furnishings, Retail	571 0000
Home Furnishings (Textile)	239 0100
Home Gardening	019 0000
Home Hair Colorings	284 4353
Home Health Care	809 6000
Home Health Supplies	384 2020
Home Intravenous Therapy	809 6140
Home Nutritional Therapy	809 6110
Home Permanents	284 4336
Home Power Humidifiers	358 5872
Home Satellite Antennas	367 9631
Home Shopping via CATV	483 4251
Home Video Games	365 1921
Homes, Motor	371 6000
Homes-see also Housing, Residential	152 0020
Honey, Raw	027 9161
Honey, Refined	209 9920
Hormonal Insecticides	287 9580
Hormone Preparations	283 4101
Hormones, Bulk	283 3201
Hormones, Menopausal Treatment	283 4131
Hormones, Veterinary Growth	283 4911
Horticultural Specialties	018 0000
Hose, Rubber	304 1020
Hosiery, Full-Fashioned	225 1400
Hosiery, Panty Hose	225 1350
Hosiery, Women's	225 1000
Hospital Beds	259 9020
Hospital-Health Facilities	154 2240
Hospital Insurance, Natl	910 5211
Hospital Supplies	384 2010
Hospital Supplies, Disposable	384 2011
Hospital Workers	801 0000
Hospitals	806 0000
Hospitals, Acute Care	806 2010
Hospitals, Community	806 0030
Hospitals, General Medical	806 2000
Hospitals, Psychiatric	806 3000
Hospitals, Specialty	806 9000
Hot Cereals	204 3050
Hot Closed Die Forgings	346 2500
Hot Melt Adhesives	289 1006
Hot Plates, Electric	363 4331
Hot Plates, Toasters & Cookers	363 4330
Hot Rolled Mill Products	331 2400
Hot Rolled Reinforcing Bar	331 2451
Hot Rolled Sheet	331 2410
Hot Rolled Steel Bar	331 2450
Hot Rolled Strip	331 2420
Hot Rolling Mill Machinery	354 7100
Hot Tubs & Jacuzzis	394 9594
Hotel & Motel Buildings	152 4040
Hotel Management	701 1100
Hotel Reservation Services	737 5932
Hotels & Motels	701 1000
Hotels-see also Casinos	776 1000
Household & Industrial Pesticides	287 9900
Household Appliance Stores	572 2000
Household Appliances	363 0000
Household Bleach	284 2200
Household Cooking Equip	363 1000
Household Detergents & Cleansers	284 1200
Household Food Preparatn Eqp	363 4300
Household Furnishings Wholesale	513 8000
Household Furniture & Bedding	251 0000
Household Goods Moving	421 4000
Household Heads	E14 130
Household Income	E33 150
Household Laundry Equip	363 3000
Household Liquid Bleach	284 2240
Household Property Income	E32 200
Household Repair-Consumer Exp	882 2244
Household Scouring Cleansers	284 1250
Household Soaps	284 1300
Household Vacuums, Mobile	363 5030
Households & Household Services	880 0000
Households by Number of Individuals	E14 120
Housewares, Electric	363 4000
Housewares ex Fans, Electric	363 4050
Housing, High Rise	152 3200
Housing, Private	152 0100
Housing, Public	152 0200
Housing, Public Assisted	152 0210
Housing Developers	655 2100
Housing, 1-Family	152 1000
Housing ex Mobile Homes	152 0020
Howitzers, 30-75mm	348 9111
Humidifiers, Home Power	358 5872
Humidifiers, Room	363 4720
Humidity Instruments (Process)	382 3600
Hunting & Trapping	097 0000
Hybrid Circuits	367 4170
Hybrid Circuits, Digital	367 4170
Hybrid Circuits, Passive	367 4175
Hybridomas	283 1232
Hydrants, Fire (Cast Iron)	332 1901
Hydraulic Cement	324 1000
Hydraulic Cranes	353 1420
Hydraulic Cylinders	359 9210
Hydraulic Equipment, Industrial	356 0100
Hydraulic Fluids, Synthetic	286 9682
Hydraulic Presses	354 2250
Hydraulic Pressure & Flow Valves	349 4230
Hydraulic Pressure Control Valves	349 4233
Hydraulic Servo Valves	349 4237
Hydrocarbons, Aliphatic	286 4000
Hydrocarbons, C2	286 4100
Hydrocarbons, C4	286 4300
Hydrocarbons, Halogenated	286 8100
Hydrocarbons,C3	286 4200
Hydrocracking	291 0210
Hydroelectric, Conventional	491 1720
Hydroelectric, Pumped Storage	491 1710
Hydroelectric Generators	361 7200
Hydroelectric Power	491 1700
Hydrofluoric Acid	281 9461
Hydrogen	281 3720
Hydrogen Fluoride	281 9461
Hydrogen Fuel	281 3721
Hydrogen Peroxide	281 9939
Hydrogen Processes, Refinery	291 0200
Hydrophilic Resins	282 1040
Hydrotreating	291 0220
Hypermarkets	532 1000
Hypodermic Syringes & Related Eqp	384 1160

I

Ibuprofen Pain Relievers	283 4223
IC Memory Chips	367 4126
IC Test Equip	382 5246
IC Voltage Multipliers & Regulators	367 4156
ICs, Gate Array	367 4112
ICs, Microwave	367 4530
ICs, Radiation-Hardened	367 4101
ICs, Random Access Memory	367 4125
ICs, VLSI	367 4103
ICs by Function	367 4180
ICs-see also Integrated Circuits	367 4100
ICBMs	376 1111
Ice Cream	202 4010
Ice Cream & Frozen Custard Stands	581 2060
Ice Cream & Frozen Desserts	202 4000
Ice Cream Freezers, Electric	363 4391
Ice Cream Novelty Forms	202 4016
Icing Stabilizers	286 9243
Identification Card Equip, Access	357 9910
Illicit Activities	775 0000
Illicit Drugs	775 4000
Ilmenite	109 3203
Image Digitizers	366 2652
Image Generators	366 2651
Image Processing Equip	366 2650
Image Processors, Video (Computerized)	366 2655
Image Recorder-Printers, Computer	357 3258
Image Sensing Arrays, Photodiode	367 4433
Imitation Jellies, Jams & Preserves	203 3830
Immigrants	E19 845
Immuno Re...nts, Enzymes for Human Use	283 1240
Imm... Assay Tests	384 1327
Ir... ers & Tests	384 1320
	283 4160
..., Anticancer	283 4147
	283 1330
Ir.	283 1334
Imp...	357 3261
Impellers, Turbine	351 1282
Implant Equip, Semiconductor	355 9581
Implantable Contact Lenses	385 1650
Implanted Drug Infusion Systems	384 1557
Implants, Biosynthetic Vascular	283 1922
Implants, Surgical & Radioactive	384 2134
Import Bans & Embargos	910 3283
Importers, General Goods	500 1010
Imports of Goods & Services	E31 320
Imports of Merchandise ( )	E57 112
Impoundment (Budgets)	910 0044
In-Feed Equip, Printing Press	355 5915
Incinerators, Refuse	356 9271
Income, Disposable Personal	E33 140
Income, Household Property	E32 200
Income, National	E32 000
Income Loss Insurance	632 3000
Income per Capita	E33 210
Income per Capita, Dispbl	E33 230
Income-see also Personal Income	E33 000
Incontinent Pads, Disposable	384 2173
Independent Insurance Agents	641 1100
Indian Health Service	912 4253
Indicators, Auto Turn	369 4696
Induction Furnaces & Heating Eqp	356 7410
Industrial & Scientific X-Ray	369 3130
Industrial Adhesives	289 1040
Industrial Advertising	731 0200
Industrial Bldgs & Warehouses	154 1000
Industrial Bleach	281 9263
Industrial Blenders	356 9987
Industrial Buildings	154 1100
Industrial Capacitors	362 9100
Industrial Chemicals	280 0400
Industrial Communications Eqp	366 2010
Industrial Controls	362 2000
Industrial Diamonds	149 7100
Industrial Dispersers	356 9984
Industrial Electric Equip	362 0000
Industrial Electronics	360 1020
Industrial Energy	290 0103
Industrial Engineers	852 7040
Industrial Equipment, Nuclear	366 2710
Industrial Equipment Fans	356 4310
Industrial Flowmeters	382 4254
Industrial Gases	281 3000
Industrial Gases Whsle	516 1300
Industrial Goggles	385 1340
Industrial Hydraulic Equipment	356 0100
Industrial Inorganics Whsle	516 1900
Industrial Lasers	383 2830
Industrial Locks incl Electronic	342 9820
Industrial Lube Additives	286 9640
Industrial Machinery Vibration Control E	356 9943
Industrial Machinery Whsle	508 4000
Industrial Mixing Equip	356 9980
Industrial Molasses	206 0700
Industrial Molds	354 4200
Industrial Nonbldg Constructn	162 9200
Industrial Noncellulosic Fibers	282 4040
Industrial Painting Contractors	172 1300
Industrial Plastic Products	307 5000
Industrial Power Boilers	344 3301
Industrial Power Supplies ex Computer	362 9240
Industrial Pressed Wool Felts	229 1011
Industrial Process Eqp, Digital	382 3230
Industrial Process Equip	382 0000
Industrial Product Finishes	285 2000
Industrial Production	E41 000
Industrial Production, Mfg	E41 100
Industrial Radiators	344 3157
Industrial Real Estate Developers	655 2600
Industrial Robots	356 9400
Industrial Robots, Inspection	356 9440
Industrial Robots, Mfg & Assembly	356 9450
Industrial Robots, Welding	356 9420
Industrial Safety Devices	384 2300
Industrial Spray Equip	356 3500
Industrial Spray Equip ex Paint	356 3590
Industrial Textiles	229 9400
Industrial Truck & Tractor Parts	353 7190
Industrial Trucks & Tractors	353 7000
Industrial Tubing, Rubber	304 1650
Industrial Water Pollution	495 1010
Industrial Water Treat Equip	356 9211
Industrl Electrnc Air Cleaners	356 4541
Infants' Toiletries	284 4502
Infants Formulas, Dry	202 3121
Infertility Treatments	283 4125
Inflation	E44 000
Inflight Refueling Devices	372 8193
Information Systems	991 2610
Information Systems & Theory	991 2600
Information Systems, Marketing	357 3022
Information Systems, Mgmt	357 3021
Infrared Countermeasures	366 2525

Figure 4.8: "SIC Alpha Guide" from *Predicasts F&S Index: United States*, March 1989.

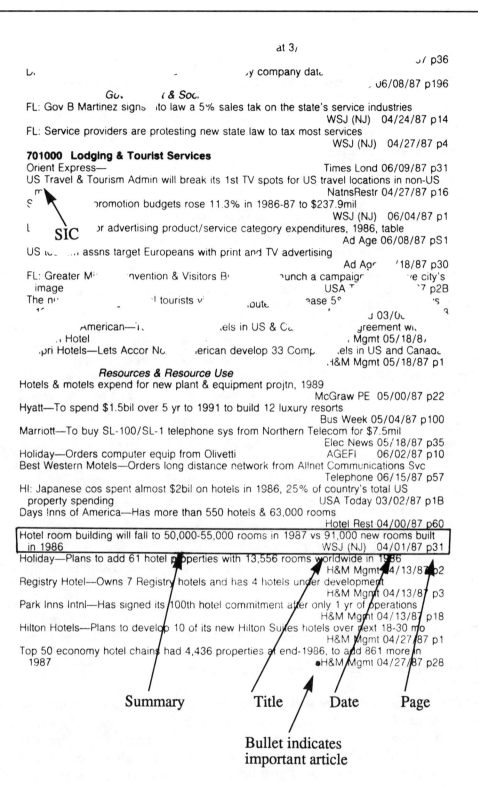

at 3,

⌐/ p36

L.   ,y company date.

⌐ 06/08/87 p196

Gov... ι & Soc.

FL: Gov B Martinez signs ιto law a 5% sales tak on the state's service industries

WSJ (NJ)   04/24/87 p14

FL: Service providers are protesting new state law to tax most services

WSJ (NJ)   04/27/87 p4

701000 Lodging & Tourist Services

Orient Express—   Times Lond 06/09/87 p31

US Travel & Tourism Admin will break its 1st TV spots for US travel locations in non-US

ιm   NatnsRestr 04/27/87 p16

S   ⌐romotion budgets rose 11.3% in 1986-87 to $237.9mil

WSJ (NJ)   06/04/87 p1

L.   ⌐r advertising product/service category expenditures, 1986, table

Ad Age 06/08/87 pS1

SIC

US ιc_ ... assns target Europeans with print and TV advertising

Ad Agr   '18/87 p30

FL: Greater M'   nvention & Visitors B'   ιunch a campaig'   e city's

image   USA T   ⌐7 p2B

The n'   ⌐ tourists v'   ιoute.   ιase 5°   's

1'   _   J 03/0ι   ι

American—ι,   ιels in US & Cι   ⌐greement wι.

ι Hotel   ι Mgmt 05/18/8ι

⌐ri Hotels—Lets Accor Nι ιerican develop 33 Comμ ιels in US and Canadι

.1&M Mgmt 05/18/87 p1

Resources & Resource Use

Hotels & motels expend for new plant & equipment projtn, 1989

McGraw PE 05/00/87 p22

Hyatt—To spend $1.5bil over 5 yr to 1991 to build 12 luxury resorts

Bus Week 05/04/87 p100

Marriott—To buy SL-100/SL-1 telephone sys from Northern Telecom for $7.5mil

Elec News 05/18/87 p35

Holiday—Orders computer equip from Olivetti   AGEFI   06/02/87 p10

Best Western Motels—Orders long distance network from Allnet Communications Svc

Telephone 06/15/87 p57

HI: Japanese cos spent almost $2bil on hotels in 1986, 25% of country's total US

property spending   USA Today 03/02/87 p1B

Days Inns of America—Has more than 550 hotels & 63,000 rooms

Hotel Rest 04/00/87 p60

Hotel room building will fall to 50,000-55,000 rooms in 1987 vs 91,000 new rooms built

in 1986   WSJ (NJ)   04/01/87 p31

Holiday—Plans to add 61 hotel properties with 13,556 rooms worldwide in 1986

H&M Mgmt 04/13/87 p2

Registry Hotel—Owns 7 Registry hotels and has 4 hotels under development

H&M Mgmt 04/13/87 p3

Park Inns Intnl—Has signed its 100th hotel commitment after only 1 yr of operations

H&M Mgmt 04/13/87 p18

Hilton Hotels—Plans to develop 10 of its new Hilton Suites hotels over next 18-30 mo

H&M Mgmt 04/27/87 p1

Top 50 economy hotel chains had 4,436 properties at end-1986, to add 861 more in

1987   ●H&M Mgmt 04/27/87 p28

Summary   Title   Date   Page

Bullet indicates
important article

Figure 4.9: "Section 1: Industries & Products by SIC" from *Predicasts F&S Index: United States*, **June 1987.**

This is the "bare bones" of what you need to locate the journal in the library. You may notice that some citations have a black dot or "bullet" before the name of the periodical (figure 4.9). This bullet indicates that the article is lengthy and that the indexer felt it was an important article. Issues of the index published after 1987 do not use the bullet to indicate key articles.

The Wall Street Journal Index...What Is It?

The Wall Street Journal Index (New York: Dow Jones, 1957-) is another very useful reference source that is available in most large public and academic libraries. It indexes all the articles in the preeminent business newspaper, *The Wall Street Journal*. Like *Predicasts F&S Index*, it is divided into two sections. The first section is called "Corporate News." For industry information look in the second section called "General News" (figure 4.10). You would logically try "Hotels and Motels" since this is the heading used in the other indexes. The actual subject in this instance, however, is "Hotels." Headings vary from index to index. If your first idea is not successful, try various synonyms. Since all references are to *The Wall Street Journal*, the name of the newspaper is omitted from the citation (figure 4.10). Only the date, page, and column numbers are listed. All citations are to the east coast edition of *The Wall Street Journal*.

By utilizing these four periodical indexes, you can locate citations to journals, trade publications, and newspapers on almost any business topic. However, very few libraries can afford to subscribe to all the periodicals included in these indexes. Your next step is to determine which periodicals are available in your library. Where do you begin?

FINDING TRADE JOURNALS AND PERIODICALS IN A LIBRARY

Each library will have a listing of its periodicals. Usually this is an alphabetical listing by title. It may be available on paper, on microforms, on cards, or on computer. Check with a reference librarian for the listing in your library and become familiar with it. You will need it for almost every research paper you write. This list will give you a call number or some other designation as to where that title will be shelved in the library.

Finding the Periodicals You Need in the Library

Libraries do not have one standard way of shelving periodicals. In many libraries the current issues of periodicals and journals are kept in a separate room. In other libraries the current issues are kept with the older bound volumes. Some libraries shelve periodicals by title, while other libraries shelve them by call number. Due to these variations, you will want to stop at your library's reference desk and ask how periodicals are shelved.

HOROWITZ, MICHAEL (Cont.)
displayed in vetoing the Pledge of Allegiance bill contrast sharply with his signing of a bill in 1987 that redistricted the Massachusetts House of Representatives; was declared unconstitutional by a federal court. 9/12-18:3

HORSE RACING
Edward DeBartolo Sr. could be facing a long shot in bid to launch a thoroughbred track in Oklahoma. 9/30-29:3

HORTICULTURE
(see Flowers, Gardening, Plants)

HOSPITALS
The NLRB proposed regulations allowing hospital employees to organize into eight bargaining units; regula- tions ...uld lead to significant increase in union me ...rested parties have 45 days to comment. 9/...

Subject →

p... edpan may be unnecessary for many ...ctors' orders, say nursing researchers at Un... ...xas Southwestern Medical Center in Dalla... ...tes) 9/22-41:1

HOTELS
Marriott Corp. plans to invest $1 billion in the next five years to more than double its stake in the hottest area of the hotel industry--extended-stay hotels. 9/8-4:2

Lawmakers are planning to propose a bill requiring federal employees who want reimbursement for trips to stay at hotels with fire sprinklers. (Tracking Travel) 9/15-33:2

McDonald's victory turns out lights for 'McSleep Inn'; Manor Care unit of Quality Inns International Inc. will rename low-priced hotel chain after trademark ruling; new name will be Sleep Inn. 9/19-42:3

New Battleground: How hotels in Japan and the U.S. compare in the services game; Japan still excels in the field, fast becoming globalized, but gap may be closing; discusses Goro Yamazaki, executive manager of the Okura, and Julian Abio, general manager at the Helmsley; a failure to wipe all the dust. 9/21-1:1

Takeover of Resorts International by Griffin is looking less and less like a sure thing. (Heard on the Street)

> The number of troubled hotels and motels is rising; some estimate that as many as 700 to 1,000 properties could end up in foreclosure by 1990; one measure of industry's difficulties is number of hotels seeking help to improve financial performance. (Real Estate) 9/23-21:1

Date · **Page** · **Column**

In a move to solidify pending sale ...tiona... national Inc., Merv Griffin and Donald ...heir ...rump's ...ffin's agreement to include $25 million own money and a total of $29 mill ...from Mr. Trump. 9/23-31:2

HOUSE OF REPRESENTATIVES
Home Team Shutout: Editorial sa... ...house in- cumbents will be re-elected in November because House is now controlled by Democratic political team holding de facto lifetime contracts. 9/6-30:1

sion to require a seven-day waiting period for handgun purchases; the vote, which knocked out the so-called Brady amendment for James Brady, was considered a gun-lobby victory. 9/16-48:5

...As another race illustrates flow of special interest money; Thomas Ward, Democratic House candidate for Indiana district, raises almost twice as much money from PACs as his challenger, Rep. John Hiler. (Campaign '88) 9/19-60:1

House leaders decided against insisting on a conference with the Senate on the textile bill, setting the stage for a possible veto-override battle with President Reagan just weeks before Election Day. 9/20-4:1

House passed a bill that would require all railroad workers in jobs that could affect safety to undergo random testing for drugs and alcohol use; legislation now goes to Senate. 9/21-21:3

The House passed slimmed-down pesticide bill that would require the EPA to re-examine more than 600 ingredients used in pesticides for health and environmental effects; bill was passed by voice vote and sent to Senate. 9/21-30:5

Jim Wright's Intelligence: Editorial criticizes House Speaker Jim Wright's statement that the CIA deliberately provoked an overreaction by the Nicaraguan government; Sen. Boren has spent the past year trying to restore Congress's credibility in handling U.S. intelligence infor- mation after several leaks from Capitol Hill; Speaker Wright's statement is an act of gross irresponsibility. 9/22-38:1

The House overwhelmingly approved a tough anti- drug bill that includes penalties for drug-related crimes ranging from loss of federal benefits to execution. 9/23-44:1

Comparable Worth: A Bad Idea That Won't Die: Editorial-page article by Dick Armey criticizes bill that House is considering that sets up a study comparing wage levels in federal jobs predominantly held by women with those predominantly held by men; only the free market can set wages and prices that efficiently allocate resources. 9/26-26:3

The House approved legislation that would impose limited sanctions against Iraq for its alleged use of poison gas against Kurdish rebels. 9/28-4:4

Last Chance on Legal Services: Editorial says House vote for $308 million to fund the Legal Services Corp. shows that some now think corrupt agency, which uses public funds to lobby for social issues, is beyond reform; the good news is that 231 to 175 vote is not enough to override a presidential veto. 9/28-24:1

U.S. Customs Service Commissioner William Von Raab, testifying before House Ways and Means subcom- mittee hearing, acknowledged that inconsistencies and other problems within agency contribute to trade industry problems, and said efforts are being made to resolve problems. 9/28-50:6

The House cleared more spending bills as lawmakers forged ahead in their effort to pass all appropriations

Energy and Commerce Committee, endorsed the idea of barring bank affiliates from underwriting mutual funds and corporate debt. 9/16-16:3

The House Energy and Commerce Committee, compli- cating prospects for bank legislation, approved a bill that would curb the growth of banks' securities underwriting and restrict their insurance activities. 9/23-4:1

A Northrop Corp. director told House panel that directors were unaware when they approved firm's $6.3 million investment in Korea in 1984 that the deal had already been completed. 9/29-10:1

HOUSE OF REPRESENTATIVES—Ethics Committee
Silence prevails at House Ethics Committee regarding Rhode Island Rep. St. Germain, as he faces a tough primary Sept. 14; panel was asked to look into allegations that the House Banking Committee chairman accepted tens of thousands of dollars in meals and drinks from a lobbyist. (Washington Wire) 9/9-1:5

Double Whooper: Editorial on House Speaker Wright's remarks insinuating that Ethics Committee inves- tigation of his business dealings is a partisan political vendetta against him; a partisan political vendetta in Washington? how about those the speaker has smeared? 9/30-26:1

HOUSE OF REPRESENTATIVES—Foreign Affairs Committee
The House Foreign Affairs Committee passed a limited sanctions bill against Iraq for allegedly using poison gas against Kurdish rebels. 9/23-3:3

HOUSE OF REPRESENTATIVES—Ways & Means Committee
Phillip Moseley was named minority staff chief of House Ways & Means Republicans; he succeeds Arthur Singleton, who will be a consultant to Washington law firm Webster, Chamberlain & Bean. (Tax Report) 9/14-1:5

HOUSING
Housing starts in Japan fell 1.9% in July, to 151,617 unit, from a year earlier, the first such decline in 27 months. 9/1-16:3

In a divorce case, where first-refusal right was awarded to an ex-husband, he exercised it and bought a house from his ex-wife; IRS private ruling 8833018 notes that his right was established by divorce decree and concludes that his purchase of the home was incident to the divorce; as a result, any gain that the ex-wife realized from selling the home isn't taxable. (Tax Report) 9/7-1:5

A couple employed by their corporation rent part of their home to it as its sole business place; but the 1986 tax act bars deduction of business costs for a home office rented to an employer; so, says IRS private ruling 8824026, the couple may deduct only property taxes and mortgage interest for the office--and no business costs. (Tax Report) 9/7-1:5

Yonkers City Council reversed itself early Sept. 10 and approved a court-ordered housing desegregation plan; move came as fines against the New York City suburb hit $1 million a day and hundreds of workers faced layoffs; a federal judge is to meet with the parties in the case to discuss modifications to the plan. 9/12-1:3

Figure 4.10: Sample Page from "General News" Section of *The Wall Street Journal Index*, September 1988.

It is important to note that very few libraries can afford to subscribe to all indexed periodicals. It is not uncommon to locate a citation that sounds perfect for your paper, only later to discover that the library does not carry that periodical. When this happens, there is an alternative or two! Other libraries in your city or region might carry this journal. Libraries in many regions of the country have prepared "union" lists, which indicate the journals held by two or more libraries. A union list may be available for libraries in your community. If not, it may be possible for your library's interlibrary loan service to obtain a photocopy of the article. This service is discussed more thoroughly in chapter 12.

FINDING TRADE JOURNALS ON AN INDUSTRY

There may be times when you want to scan many of the library's trade and scholarly journals on a particular industry. Scanning the current issues of journals in the field will put you in touch with the issues facing the industry today, while regular reading of these journals is the best way to keep informed about current trends and problems.

Scanning journals on a particular industry may be difficult, however, due to their arrangement in a library. Here are several possibilities for locating a list of periodicals on your industry.

1) Locate the appropriate subject heading for your industry in your library's catalog. The subject heading for the lodging industry is "Hotels, taverns, etc." Under this subject heading is a sub-heading called "Periodicals" (figure 4.11). Here you will find a listing of periodicals on the lodging industry.

Figure 4.11:
Catalog Card for
Lodging.

```
        Subject                                          Sub-Heading
        Heading▶ HOTELS, TAVERNS, ETC.--PERIODICALS◀
        SERIAL
        647.9405 Lodging. v. 1-    Sept. 1975-        [New
        L821        York, American Hotel & Motel
                    Association]
        1 CFS           v. ill. 28 cm.
                    monthly (except Aug. and Dec.).
                    "Official publication of the American
        Hotel & Motel Association."
                    L74394
                    Key title: Lodging, ISSN 0360-9235


                    1. Hotels, taverns, etc.--
                Periodicals. 2. Motels--Periodicals.
                I. American Hotel & Motel Association.


        InLP    07 MAY 81    2245158   IPLSxc        75-650010
```

58

2) Check in *Ulrich's International Periodicals Directory* (New York: Bowker, 1932-). This is a directory of current foreign and U.S. periodicals arranged by subject. Look under the heading "Hotels and Restaurants." This is a very comprehensive list of periodicals; it includes popular, trade, and professional journals.

3) Consult a professional in the field, such as a professor who teaches hotel management or an actual hotel manager in your community. These people often have the inside track on what are the most well-respected trade publications, and they will also be aware of any new journals in the field.

4) Professional associations, which will be discussed in chapter 6, may be able to supply a list of industry publications.

5) Ask the reference librarian for other ideas. It is possible that your library might have an easy way of solving this problem, such as a list of periodicals that is broken down into subject areas.

SUMMARY

1) The best source for current information on any industry is trade and scholarly journals.

2) *Business Periodicals Index, Business Index/INFOTRAC™, Predicasts F&S Index*, and *The Wall Street Journal Index* are reference sources that index and identify articles in the business field. They list periodical and newspaper articles by subject.

3) All libraries do not shelve their journals in the same way. Some interfile them by call number with their books. Others keep them in a separate area and shelve them by call number or by title. Check at the reference desk to see how journals are arranged in your library.

4) To find the names of periodicals in an industry, look in your library's catalog. Other sources for lists of periodicals in an industry are *Ulrich's International Periodical Directory*, your professors, local professionals in the industry, or trade associations.

CHAPTER 5

STATISTICS

Numbers are a part of our lives. Your blood pressure is 120/70. Your boss is giving all employees a 5 percent year-end bonus. The television show you enjoyed several nights ago had a 26 Nielsen rating. The unemployment rate is expected to be 10 percent by the end of the year. Individually, as well as collectively, we are a nation of people very interested in numbers or as they are more commonly referred to—statistics. Based upon these statistics, you sometimes must make a decision. For example, if your boss has given you only a 1 percent year-end bonus for the last two years, you must decide if that is enough to stay with the company or if it is time to look for a new job.

Why are statistics important? Business people must make decisions based upon available data. At some point, you will be in the position of decision maker. If you can locate statistics that relate to a pending problem or issue, you can make a more informed decision. By using statistics, you can replace personal judgments and generalizations with documented knowledge acquired through surveys, experiments, and other research methods. Statistics are an important step in the search strategy because they provide data to support your particular thesis or position. Is there an area in your research paper that is particularly weak? Do you have opinions or personal viewpoints that are not backed by facts or figures? Do you make broad generalizations? If so, you may wish to locate statistics that give these areas a more concrete, factual foundation. For example, consider the following two statements. Which one would you rather have in your paper? If you were reading the two statements in a newspaper, which one would have the most impact?

- The number of new hotels in the city has risen dramatically over the last few years.

- Based on a study by the chamber of commerce, there has been a 10 percent increase in the number of new hotels in the city during each of the last five years.

Obviously, the second statement will have more of an impact on the reader because it is backed by statistics. Not only that, but the statistics were generated by a credible source—the chamber of commerce.

61

There are many published statistics available on the hotel industry, such as how many hotels there are in the country, how many new hotels are under construction, and the average room rate and occupancy rate of hotels. You already found some of these statistics through utilization of industry overviews and periodical indexes. There may be situations, however, when you need more statistics than those found through overviews and periodicals. This chapter will introduce you to a one-volume source of industry statistics as well as teach you how to use a statistical index.

Before you learn how to use these statistical publications, however, you need to be aware of several factors regarding published statistics.

1) Always look at the original source of the statistics. Is it someone who could benefit by skewing or altering the statistics? Is the collector of the statistics an impartial research organization or association? Be wary of statistics that do not cite the source.

2) Can you find statistics that really prove your point? Whenever you search for statistics, it is important to remember that you may not find data that exactly meet your criteria. "Stretching" statistics so far that they are not relevant is pointless. Readers will be able to see through this, and you will be discredited. Entire books have been written on this concept of "how to lie with statistics." You should avoid stretching the meaning and intent of statistics.

3) Is the statistic current? Data that are more than a few years old are probably not worthwhile—unless you are doing historical research. As a general rule, you must try to locate the most recent statistics.

4) You may track down a reference to an industry report that sounds as if it will have the desired data in it, but this publication may not be available in your library—or any library for that matter. Some industry reports are available for purchase from the market research firm that collected the data, but with price tags ranging from several hundred dollars to more than $20,000! Obviously, libraries cannot afford to buy these specialized publications. The primary customers for these reports are larger companies in the industry.

Now that you understand the importance of published statistics, as well as some limitations, you are ready to learn how to use library resources to track down statistics on every imaginable topic.

The U.S. federal government is a major collector and publisher of statistics. Many federal agencies, bureaus, and offices collect statistics, which are then published in hundreds of different publications. One of the most popular government publications is *Statistical Abstract of the United States* (Washington, DC: U.S. Department of Commerce, 1878-), which serves as an excellent starting point when looking for U.S. social, political, and economic statistics. Although published by the government, the statistics come from a variety of sources, including private organizations as well as gov-

Table

Law enforcement, Federal courts, and prisons—Continued
  Police protection—Continued
    Payroll 287
    Prison sentences, by offense 308
    Prisoners under sentence of death 309, 310, 312
    Prisons and prisoners 306, 307
    Probation 306
    Public officials, prosecutions 285
    Wiretaps 284
Lawnmowers, shipments and retail value 1356
Lawyers 288, 289
  Employment 657
    Projections 656
Lead and zinc ores, mining industry 1209
Lead, summary 1209, 1210, 1215, 1216, 1218, 1240
  Air quality 332–334
  Foreign trade 1218, 1240
  Mining industry 1209
  Prices, New York and London 780, 1215, 1240
  Production and supply 1210, 1240
  Water quality 329
  World production 1216, 1240
Leases, permits and licenses, public lands 520
Leather and leather products (*see also* Hides and leather
  products *and* Footwear):
  Foreign trade 1320, 1321, 1409, 1411
  Manufacture 1304
    Employees 672, 1304, 1318
      Earnings 672
      Injury rates 697
    Expenditures for plant and equipment, new 1304
    Production indexes 1311
  Producer price indexes 769
Lebanon. *See* Foreign countries.
Legal services:
  Advertising expenditures 930
  Employees 1358
  Gross National Product 1357
  Receipts ....
Legislative service (Federal):
  Budget authority and outlays ....
  Expenditures ....
Legislatures, State, composition ....
Leisure activities. *See* Recreation.
Lemons ....
Lend-lease, grants and credits 386
Leprosy 163
Lesotho. *See* Foreign countries.
Lettuce 782, 1158
  Consumption 179
Liberia. *See* Foreign countries.
Libraries 368
  By type 257
  College expenditures for 243
  Elementary and secondary schools; media centers 216
  Employees 477
    City governments 477
    Payrolls 477
  Patron use of computers 258
Libya. *See* Foreign countries.
Licensed drivers, by age groups 1030
Licenses, permits, etc.:
  Drivers licenses, by States 1020
  Fishing and hunting 379
  Public lands 520
  Taxes 446
Life expectancy 105–108
  Foreign countries 1436, 1439
  States 107
Life insurance 842–846
  Assets, earning rate, liabilities, etc 793–796, 842, 843
  Companies 794, 822, 842, 843
    Acquisition of investments 843
  Flow of funds 793–796
  Mortgage loans outstanding 822
  Ownership by households and adults 845
  Reserves 793, 795, 796, 842
Life sciences 990, 993, 994
  Degrees conferred 253
  Employment 986
  Research, U.S. Government obligations for 976
Light and power. *See* Electric lights, etc.
Lighting equipment, manufacture 1304
Lime, summary 780, 1210, 1237
  Production and value 1210
Limes 1159
Liquefied petroleum gases 1231
Liquors and beverages (*see also* Malt liquors) 1322, 1323
  Advertising expenditures 927–929
  Alcoholic beverages 718

Table

Liquors and beverages (*see also* Malt liquors)—Continued
  Consumer expenditures 718–721
  Consumption 174, 181
  Imports 1409
    Prices 771
  Retail sales 1361, 1363, 1367, 1369
    Inventories 1363
  Retail trade summary 1369
  Revenue, State and local governments 445
  Stores, Government finances 431, 438, 446, 461
  Taxes 497
    Government finances 431
    Governmental revenue 429, 446
  Wholesale trade 1377
    Sales inventories 1375
    Summary 1377
Livestock. *See* Animals, domestic, *and individual classes.*
Living cost. *See* Consumer price indexes *and* Prices.
Loans and mortgages (*see also* Debt):
  Banks 807, 808, 820, 821
  Construction loans 820
  Credit market, flow of funds 793, 795, 796
  Credit unions 819
  Farm. *See* Farm mortgage loans.
  Federal government loans 491, 893
  Federal Housing Administration 821
  Foreign countries 814
  Held by financial institutions 820, 824
  Home mortgage loans 820, 1274
  Insurance companies 921, 842
  Interest rates 825
  Land loans 820
  Minority-operated small businesses 893
  Mortgages, nonfarm homes 821, 822, 833
  Personal loans 824
  Savings and loan institutions 815, 817, 818
  Veterans 572, 821
Lobsters 1189, 1195, 1198, 1200, 1205
Local government. *See* individual governmental units and
  State and local government.
Locomotives (railroad) 1048
Lodging industries, summary 1299, 1381
Logging camps and contractors, earnings ....
Lotteries ....
Loudspeakers ....
Louisiana. *See* State data.
Louisiana Purchase ....
Luggage, manufacture ....
Lumber and allied products:
  Consumption ....
  Employees 1175
    Earnings 1175
  Foreign trade 1176, 1180, 1187, 1320, 1321, 1409, 1411
    Waterborne commerce 1077
  Manufacture 1304
    Consumption 1176, 1180
    Employees 672, 1304, 1318
      Earnings 672
      Injury rates 697
    Expenditures, new plant and equipment 1304
    Production 1176, 1180–1182, 1311
      Indexes 1311
      World 1432
    Stocks 1180
    Prices 1178, 1179
      Import 771
      Producer indexes 769, 1178, 1260
    Railroad car loadings of 1051, 1052
    Retail sales 1361, 1367
    Wholesale trade 1375, 1377
      Sales inventories 1375
      Summary 1377

M

Macadamia nuts 1159
Macao, population and area 1437
Machine tools 1339, 1408
  Orders and shipments 1339
Machinery (*see also* individual classes):
  Earnings per share 892
  Exports, U.S. as compared to world 1315
  Farm, expenditures for and number on 1133
  Farm input indexes 1131, 1133
  Foreign trade 1320, 1321, 1405, 1407–1409, 1411
  Manufacture 1304
    Capital appropriations and expenditures 1314
    Corporation sales, profits, and dividends 885, 892
    Employees 672, 1304

Figure 5.1: "Index" Section from *Statistical Abstract of the United States, 1987.*

No. **1381.** THE LODGING INDUSTRY, BY TYPE OF ESTABLISHMENT—SUMMARY: 1984 AND 1985

[An economy lodging establishment offers clean, standard-sized, fully-furnished modern rooms at usually $10.00 to $20.00 per night below the rate of typical full-service motor hotels. Their customers do not need food facilities, banquet rooms or meeting facilities, indoor recreation areas, or entertainment. An All-suite hotel doesn't have rooms, only suites. A suite differs from a hotel room by several characteristics. Generally, there is a separate bedroom, and guest amenities often include "extras" such as a wet bar or microwave, and in some cases a full kitchen. A resort hotel is a lodging facility providing an environment conducive to leisure and recreation and an ambiance of isolation/destination while providing a full range of leisure oriented amenities. Based on Annual Surveys of Lodging Establishments. Covers approximately 600 full-service, 300 economy, 50 all suite, and 125 resort establishments in 1985]

ITEM	FULL-SERVICE		ECONOMY		ALL-SUITE		RESORT	
	1984	**1985**	**1984**	**1985**	**1984**	**1985**	**1984**	**1985**
Room occupancy rate	67.9	65.5	63.7	66.7	76.1	69.3	68.4	66.1
Average room rate (dol.)	52.15	53.81	26.19	29.09	65.04	72.44	63.39	67.62
Sales per available room (dol.)	20,877	20,118	6,282	7,096	30,062	22,045	23,338	26,959
Payroll and related expenses per available room (dol.)	7,099	6,433	1,227	1,487	(NA)	6,376	10,408	11,881
Ratio of net income before income tax to sales	2.6	−.6	12.4	5.7	(NA)	(NA)	9.8	−3.9
Employees [1] per 100 available rooms	56.0	53.2	(NA)	(NA)	(NA)	38.9	(NA)	87.4
Sales per employee [1] (dol.)	35,906	35,757	(NA)	(NA)	(NA)	43,134	(NA)	29,759
Composition of market—(percent)								
Business travelers/government officials	46.8	44.1	46.5	53.3	(NA)	57.8		
Tourists	24.7	29.6	44.9	39.3	(NA)	26.7		
Conference participants	19.2	18.5	2.5	2.8	(NA)	12.8		
Percent advanced reservations	66.3	68.3	47.2	40.1	(NA)	80.8		

NA Not available.   [1] Full-time equivalent employees.

Source: Laventhol & Horwath, Philadelphia, PA, *U.S. Lodging Industry*, annual; and *U.S. Economy Lodging Industry*, annual.

Citation to
Source of
Data

Figure 5.2: Table No. 1381: "The Lodging Industry, by Type of Establishment"
from *Statistical Abstract of the United States*, 1987.

ernmental agencies. In addition to serving as a convenient, one-volume reference tool, *Statistical Abstract of the United States* also functions as a guide to other, more detailed, statistical publications. Will it provide you with statistical data on the topic of overbuilding or excess rooms?

In the back of *Statistical Abstract of the United States* is an index. Look under the heading of "Lodging industries, summary" (figure 5.1). The index leads you to two tables—not page numbers. Table 1381, as illustrated in figure 5.2, contains data on "room occupancy rate" for full service, economy, all-suite, and resort hotels.

You may wonder why we are looking under the heading "room occupancy rate" rather than "overbuilding." Statistics on overbuilding are not collected because overbuilding cannot be measured in statistical terms. Room occupancy rate, however, is a statistic that indicates the relationship of rented rooms to the total number of rooms available. A low room occupancy rate is an indication of overbuilding. If too many new hotels have been built for the amount of business available, there will be a low room occupancy rate. Since room occupancy rate is a readily available statistic, it will be valuable in your research on overbuilding.

In addition to the statistics on room occupancy rates, Table 1381 provides another piece of very valuable information—the complete citation to the source of the statistics is given below the table (figure 5.2). In this case, the statistics were taken from the publication *U.S. Lodging Industry*, which was prepared by the research firm, Laventhol and Horwath. You can check to see if your library has this publication.

Other than the federal government, there are thousands of associations, organizations, companies (such as Laventhol and Horwath), and educational institutions that collect and disseminate a wide variety of statistics. A particular agency or organization may focus on the lodging industry as a whole, or it may concentrate on one particular aspect of the industry, such as management or construction. Where and how, then, can you find statistics emanating from all these sources? Indeed, it used to be very difficult to pinpoint such publications. Now it is much easier due to two statistical indexes:

- *American Statistics Index* or *ASI*. (Washington, DC: Congressional Information Service, 1973-).

- *Statistical Reference Index* or *SRI*. (Washington, DC: Congressional Information Service, 1980-).

ASI and *SRI* have helped address this problem by indexing thousands of statistical publications issued by the federal government, state governments, research institutions, and professional and trade associations.

American Statistics Index's primary purpose is to index and abstract all statistical publications of the U.S. government—the largest publisher in the world. Although it may not achieve this goal, it does cover most U.S. government publications.

Statistical Reference Index, on the other hand, provides an index with abstracts to the large body of business, financial, economic, and social statistical data emanating from private organizations and state governments.

Although *ASI* and *SRI* cover different publications, the way to utilize them is very similar. Because they are so similar, *Statistical Reference Index* is illustrated in this chapter. It is published monthly and cumulated on a quarterly and annual basis. The illustrations here are taken from an annual cumulation.

SRI is divided into three parts:

- the index,
- the abstracts, and
- a microfiche collection.

Your search strategy will begin with the index volume, move on to the abstracts volume, and end with the microfiche collection.

California property tax exemptions, by type and county, FY87, annual rpt, S0835–1.2

Colorado statistical abstract, general data, 1987 biennial rpt, U6430–4.1, U6430–4.17

DC statistical profile, general data, 1987 annual rpt, S1535–3.5

Florida medical assistance recipients and payments, by type and service, and recipient age, sex, and race, FY86, annual rpt, S1745–4.2

Florida public and instn libraries, finances, holdings, staff, and capacity, by system, location, and instn, FY85, annual rpt, S1800–2

Florida statistical abstract, general data, 1986 annual rpt, U6660–1.20

Georgia community hospital beds and occupancy rates, with comparisons to US, 1984, article, U6730–2.804

Georgia county guide, general data, 1987 annual rpt, U6750–1

Georgia socioeconomic data, 1986 annual rpt, S1920–3.3, S1920–3.5

Georgia statistical abstract, general data, 1986-87 biennial rpt, U6730–1.1

Hawaii data book, general data, 1986 annual rpt, S2090–1.2

Hawaii hospital bed capacity, by type of care and instn, by county, 1986, annual rpt, S2065–1.3

Iowa statistical profile, general data, 1987 annual rpt, S2780–1.5

Kansas statistical abstract, general data, 1985/86 annual rpt, U7095–2.1

Kentucky Medicaid recipients and payments, by program, county, and type of medical service, monthly rpt, S3140–5

Maryland hospital and nursing home deaths, by race and location, 1983, annual rpt, S3635–1.3

Maryland local govt financial condition, including revenues by source, expenditures by function, and debt obligations, FY86, annual rpt, S3618–1.1

Maryland medical assistance payments and recipients, by program, type of service, location, demographic characteristics, and facility, FY86, annual rpt, S3635–3

Massachusetts hospital employment, by detailed occupation, 1983, triennial rpt, S3808–2.3

Michigan live births, by infant race-ethnicity, place of delivery, and type of attendant, 1984, annual rpt, S4000–3.1

Michigan medical assistance recipi⁻ payments, by county and typ⁻ monthly rpt, S4010–1

Michigan statistical abstract, ⸗ 1986 annual rpt, U9660–1.

Mississippi statistical abstract, ⸗ 1986 annual rpt, U3255–4.2

Montana private health care facility capacity, utilization, and finances, by instn, 1985, annual rpt, S4690–2

Nebraska public welfare cases, recipients, and payments, by program and county, FY86 and trends, annual rpt, S4957–1

Nebraska statistical handbook, general data, 1986-87 biennial rpt, S4855–1.11

Nevada statistical abstract, general data, 1986 biennial rpt, S5065–1.7

New Hampshire births and infant deaths, by hospital, 1985, annual rpt, S5215–1.1

New Jersey abortions by type of facility, procedure, county, and recipient characteristics, 1984, annual rpt, S5405–1.6

New Mexico institutional library holdings, services, and finances, by instn, FY86, annual rpt, S5627–1

New York State medical assistance expenditures, by State area and type of care, 1985, annual rpt, S5800–2.2

North Carolina socioeconomic statistics for counties, MSAs, and State regions, 1970-84, recurring rpt, S5930–7

Ohio public, academic, and other library finances, holdings, and staff, by library and location, 1986 and trends, annual rpt, S6320–1

Oklahoma statistical abstract, general data, 1986 biennial rpt, U8130–2.10

Oklahoma welfare and social service program recipients and payments, and recipient characteristics, by county and type of service, FY86 and trends, annual rpt, S6455–1.2

Rhode Island community hospital cost and occupancy data, with comparisons to US and other New England States, 1982, recurring rpt, S6995–2

South Dakota hospital income, and Medicare vs non-Medicare admissions and length of stay, various years 1980-85, article, U8595–1.802

South Dakota medical assistance recipients and payments, by type of service, program, and county, FY86, annual rpt, S7385–1

Tennessee statistical abstract, general data, 1987 annual rpt, U8710–2.17

Utah live births, and infant and fetal deaths, by instn, and city and/or county of occurrence, 1984, annual rpt, S7835–1.3

Vermont births and deaths by location, including individual instns, 1985, annual rpt, S8054–1

West Virginia statistical profile, general data, 1987 recurring rpt, A9370–1.5

see also Clinics
see also Emergency medical service
see also Health facilities administration
see also Health maintenance organizations
see also Hospitalization
see also Mental health facilities and services
see also Military hospitals
see also Nurses and nursing
see also Nursing homes
see also State funding for health and hospitals
see also Veterans health facilities and services

Hotels and motels

All-suite lodging financial and operating data, by region, establishment characteristics, and type of location, 1985, annual rpt, B5050–13

Business trends for lodging industry, with occupancy rates and finances, by region, location, size, and type, monthly survey, B5050–4

Casino hotel financial and operating data, by corporation, 1984-85, annual rpt, B5050–6

Cities, top 10 ranked by conventions held, with number of hotel rooms within 30-minute drive of downtown, 1986, article, C2710–1.826

Economy lodging financial and operating data, by region, establishment characteristics, and type of location, 1985 and trends, annual rpt, B5050–12

Employee union wage rates for 17 occupations, and benefits, by city, various years 1983-88, recurring rpt, A1875–3

Energy and water use, by property size, State, region, and individual facility (not named), 1985 and trends, annual rpt, A1875–2

Financial and operating data for hotel industry worldwide, by country and world region, 1985 and trends, annual rpt, B7100–1

Financial and operating data for lodging industry, by region, establishment characteristics, and type of location, 1985-86, annual rpt, B5050–2

Financial and operating data for lodging industry, by region, establishment type and size, and rate group, 1985, annual rpt, B7100–2

Financial and operating data for top 400 hotel and lodging facilities in 5 market categories, 1987 annual feature, C7000–5

Food service executive salaries in lodging industry, by position, 1986, annual article, C5150–5.803

Food service industry sales and outlets, by market segment, 1984-87, annual feature, C1850–3.804

Food service industry sales and units by market segment, for top 400 organizations, 1986, annual feature, C1850–3.813, C1850–3.814

Food service industry sales, purchases, and outlets, by market segment, 1984-85, annual article, A8200–1.808

Food service industry sales trends and forecast, by market segment, 1984-87, annual feature, A8200–1.802

Food service revenues, 1983-87, article, C5150–5.801

Food service sales, purchases, and establishments, by market segment, 1985-86, with sales projection for 1991, annual feature, C1200–5.817

Industrial distributors overnight business trips, and lodging preferences and expenditures, 1987 survey article, C1850–4.803

Industrial/commercial activity detailed indicators, by SIC 4-digit industry, county, and State, 1986, annual survey, C1200–1.808

Intl hotel financial and operating performance, including data for selected depts, by world region, 1986, annual rpt, B5050–1

Latin America statistical abstract, general data by country, 1987 annual rpt, U6250–1.14

Operating and financial composite ratios for corporations, with establishments and receipts, for approx 200 SIC 2- to 4-digit industries, by asset size, FY84, annual rpt, C7800–1

Operating data by world region, and establishments and rooms for top 50 chains, 1987 annual rpt, C2140–1

Pacific area hotel rooms and occupancy rates, by country, 1984-90, annual rpt, A8670–1

Subject

Figure 5.3: "Index by Subjects and Names" from *Statistical Reference Index*, 1987.

66

I.9. Composition of sales [percent from rooms, food, beverages, telephone, minor operated depts, and rentals/other]. (p. 49)

I.10. Minor operated depts and other income [and expenses] median amounts per room and ratios to total sales. (p. 50)

I.11. Food and beverage statistics [sales, shown variously per room, per seat, and per guest; with detail by type of facility and for room service, selected ratios, average check size, and covers served per seat]. (p. 51-52)

I.12. Employment statistics [including sales per employee, productivity index, and FTE employees per 100 available rooms by dept]. (p. 53)

I.13. Analysis of undistributed operating expenses [amounts and ratios to sales, for administrative/general, marketing, energy, and property operation/maintenance, with comparative ratios for 1985]. (p. 54)

I.14. Energy costs per occupied room per day [by energy source; credit for energy sales; and net energy costs, 1985-86]. (p. 55)

I.15. Method of payment for hotel services [percent from cash, credit card, and other credit]. (p. 55)

I.16. Credit card commission annual cost per occupied room [and ratio to sales]. (p. 55)

I.17. Credit card sales [distribution] by type of card [4 major companies and all others]. (p. 55)

I.18. Fixed charges [leased equipment, rent, property taxes, insurance, interest, and depreciation/amortization], median amounts per room and [aggregate] ratio to total sales [with comparative ratios for 1985]. (p. 56)

I.19. [Statement of income and expenses] per available room. (p. 57)

I.20. Ratio to total sales [for each income and expense item]. (p. 58)

ASIA AND AUSTRALASIA

II.1-II.20. [Tables I.1-I.20 are repeated for Asia/Australasia, with detail for Asia, Pacific Basin/Far East, and Australia.] (p. 60-75)

NORTH AMERICA

III.1-III.20. [Tables I.1-I.20 are repeated for North America, with detail for Canada and U.S.] (p. 76-90)

EUROPE

IV.1-IV.20. [Tables I.1-I.20 are repeated for ▯ ~ith detail for Continental Europe, and UK.] (p. 91-105)

Accession ▯/CARIBBEAN
Number   ▯les I.1-I.20 are repeated for La-
          with detail for South America
↓   ▯an.] (p. 106-120)

B5050-2   U.S. LODGING INDUSTRY, 1987 EDITION: 55th Annual Report on Hotel and Motor Hotel Operations
Annual. 1987. 71 p.
ISSN 0361-2198.
LC 76-640984.
SRI/MF/complete, current & ◄ Availability
previous year reports   Note

Annual report on median operating results of the U.S. lodging industry, by selected establishment characteristics, 1986, with comparisons to 1985. Most data are based on 764 responses to a Laventhol and Horwath survey.

Contains contents listing and foreword (p. 1-3), and the following:

a. Articles on lodging topics, with 3 tables and 4 charts showing the following: number of rooms and properties, for 10 largest international lodging chains, 1986; selected travel growth indicator trends from 1940; hotel payroll, employees per room, and average hourly earnings, selected years 1933-82; and percent of lodging facilities with various types of automated systems, in-room entertainment systems, telephone services, and other services (no date). (p. 4-14)

b. Industry overview, with narrative and 4 tables (p. 15-22); regional profiles, with highlights and 8 tables (p. 23-38); and detailed survey findings, with 1 chart and 20 tables (p. 39-67). All tables are listed below.

c. Explanation of terms, worksheet, and Laventhol and Horwath contacts and office addresses. (p. 68-71)

Previous report, for 1985, was also reviewed in SRI during 1987 and is also available on SRI microfiche under B5050-2 [Annual. 1986. 61 p. $65.00].

Previous report differs from the current report in the following respects: article tables present data on lodging demand sources, profitability, and advertised room rates and discounts; statistical section format differs (although data topics are similar); and a table showing 10-year trends in occupancy rates, room rates, and net income per room is included.

Availability: Laventhol and Horwath, Publications, 1845 Walnut St., Philadelphia PA 19103, $65.00; SRI/MF/complete.

TABLES:
[Data are shown for 1986, unless otherwise noted. Most data are shown as medians or means.
Data are shown by selected establishment characteristics, variously including number of rooms, average room rate, occupancy rate, type of location, affiliation, restaurant operation, and region.]

B5050-2.1: General and Sales Data

INDUSTRY OVERVIEW

1. Profile of contributors [also includes percent operating at profit and loss]. (p. 19)

2. Market data [percent domestic, foreign, and repeat business; distribution of leisure, business/government, conference, and other sources of business; and percent advance reservations, and distribution by type]. (p. 20)

3. General statistics [ratio of income before fixed charges to room and total sales, 1985-86]. (p. 21)

4. Occupancy, guests per room, and average room rate [1985-86]. (p. 22)

REGIONAL ANALYSIS

5-12. [Data from tables 2 and 4 are repeated ~ ~ns]. (p. 25-38)

▯EPARTMENTAL DATA

▯pt [revenue and expense] ratios ▯. (p. 40-41)

▯ion of sales [percent cash, credit ▯ other credit sales; share of cash sales generated by travel agents/tour operators; and distribution of credit card sales, by 6 major credit cards]. (p. 40)

15. Sales per guest day [by dept]. (p. 41)

16. Ratios of total food and beverage sales [for sales cost and dept expense items]. (p. 42-43)

17. Food and beverage statistics [including sales per available room and per seat, average check, and covers served per seat, with detail as applicable for dining room, room service, banquet, and bar/lounge depts]. (p. 44-47)

18. Ratios to telephone dept expenses [cost of calls, equipment rental, and payroll/related and other expenses; and net dept income]. (p. 48)

19. Minor operated depts and other income, amounts per available room and ratios to total sales. (p. 49)

20. Analysis of administrative and general expenses: ratios to total sales. (p. 50)

MARKETING, MANAGEMENT FEES, ENERGY COSTS, AND FIXED CHARGES

21. How the marketing dollar was allocated [including advertising expenses by media]. (p. 50-51)

22. Management fees, amount per room and ratio to total sales. (p. 51)

23. Energy and property operation/maintenance depts, amounts per available room [including fuel, electricity, water, and steam costs, and energy credits]. (p. 52)

24. Fixed charges, amounts per available room and ratio to total sales. (p. 53)

SUMMARY

[25-32.] Amounts per available room, and ratios to total sales [summary data for revenue, expense, and profit items]. (p. 54-67)

B5050-3   CALIFORNIA RESTAURANT OPERATIONS, 1986 EDITION: 11th Annual Report on Restaurant Operations in California
Annual. 1986. 34 p.
SRI/MF/complete

Annual report presenting financial and operating data for the California restaurant industry, by establishment characteristics, 1986, with comparisons to 1984-85. Includes data on income and expenses by item, profits, average check, sales per square foot, full- and part-time employment, seat turnover, and labor productivity, with selected summary comparisons to U.S.

Data are shown as industry medians and, for most topics, upper and lower quartiles; income and expense items often are shown per seat and as ratios to sales.

Establishment characteristics include age, menu type (full and limited table service and other), sales size, types of beverages served (full liquor service, wine and/or beer only, and no alcohol), menu theme (steak/seafood, American, ethnic, and sandwich/hamburger), location (urban, suburban, and rural), and profitability (net profit vs. net loss).

California data are based on responses of 142 restaurants to a Laventhol and Horwath survey. U.S. data are from National Restaurant Assn's *Restaurant Industry Operations Report '86,* described in SRI 1986 Annual under A8200-3.

Contains contents listing (1 p.); introductory comments from local areas (p. 3-4); data explanation, with 2 tables (p. 5-6); narrative analysis, with 7 charts and 23 tables (p. 7-31); and worksheet and definitions (p. 32-34).

Figure 5.4: Entry B5050-2: "U.S. Lodging Industry" from *Statistical Reference Index*, 1987.

The index volume contains references to topics, places, people, and things. The most important part of the index volume is the alphabetically arranged "Index by Subjects and Names," which comprises most of the volume. Under "Hotels and motels" are short descriptions of statistical publications on the industry (figure 5.3).

The publication might be a book, a state document, a periodical article, or another type of publication that contains statistical data. There are several potentially useful references for your topic in figure 5.3. However, the reference marked in figure 5.3 looks like the best bet for statistical data on the oversupply of rooms. To follow through with the use of *SRI* you need to note the number after this entry: B5050-2. This *SRI* accession number leads you to the abstracts volume, which is arranged according to accession numbers (figure 5.4).

The B5050-2 abstract is a very detailed description and list of tables in the publication *U. S. Lodging Industry*. The mention of "occupancy" in the abstract is indicated in figure 5.4. This publication is worth pursuing, especially since it is the same publication found in *Statistical Abstract of the United States*.

There are two possible ways to find this publication. You need to determine if:

1) Your library subscribes to the *SRI* microfiche collection, or

2) Your library has the report.

If your library subscribes to the *SRI* microfiche service, you will have access to over 90 percent of the indexed publications. How can you tell whether *U.S. Lodging Industry* is one of the microfiche publications?

Each publication indexed in *SRI* has three levels of availability.

1) The entire publication is microfilmed, indicated by the statement: "SRI/MF/complete."

2) Only statistical portions of the publication are microfilmed, indicated by "SRI/MF/excerpts."

3) None of the publication is microfilmed, indicated by "SRI/MF/not filmed."

A complete copy of *U.S. Lodging Industry* is available through the *SRI* microfiche collection, which is indicated by "SRI/MF/complete" (figure 5.4).

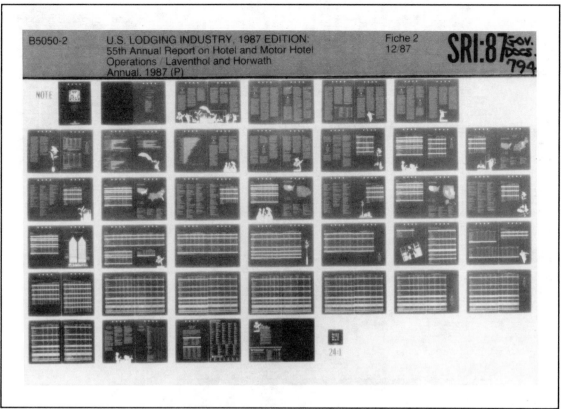

Figure 5.5: Photocopy of *U.S. Lodging Industry* **on microfiche from**
*Statistical Reference Index Microfiche Collection***, 1987.**

Now that you know the publication is on microfiche, several other pieces of data are needed to find the correct microfiche in your library:

1)   The year of *SRI* that you are using—1987.

2)   The abstract number—B5050-2.

3)   The date of the publication—1987 edition, 55th Annual Report.

Locate the *SRI* microfiche collection in your library. They are arranged first according to year and then by abstract number. The microfiche is shown in figure 5.5.

Once you have located the *SRI* microfiche collection in your library and retrieved the appropriate microfiche, it can be read and/or printed on a microfiche reader or reader/printer. Excerpts of pages 15, 16, and 22 from *U.S. Lodging Industry* are shown in figures 5.6 and 5.7.

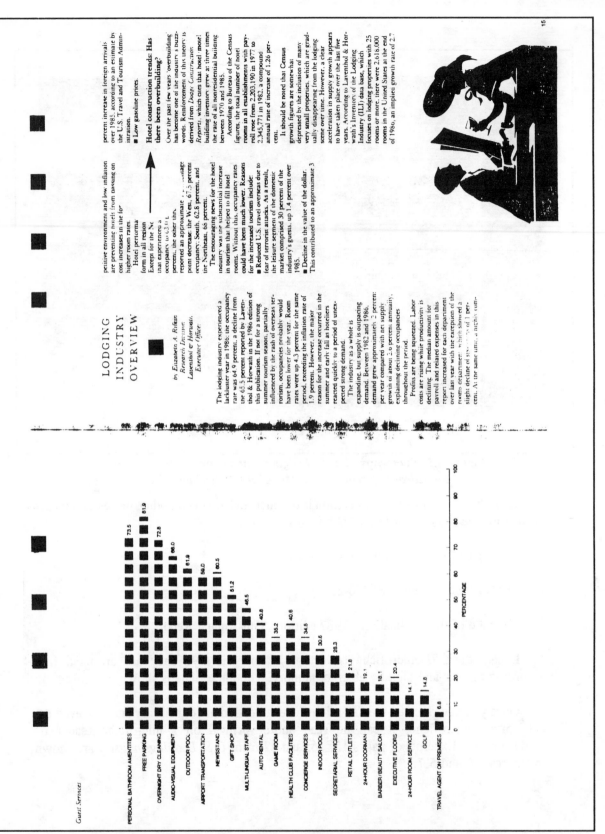

Figure 5.6: "Lodging Industry Overview" Excerpt from *U.S. Lodging Industry,* **as Included in the Statistical Reference Index Microfiche Collection, 1987.**

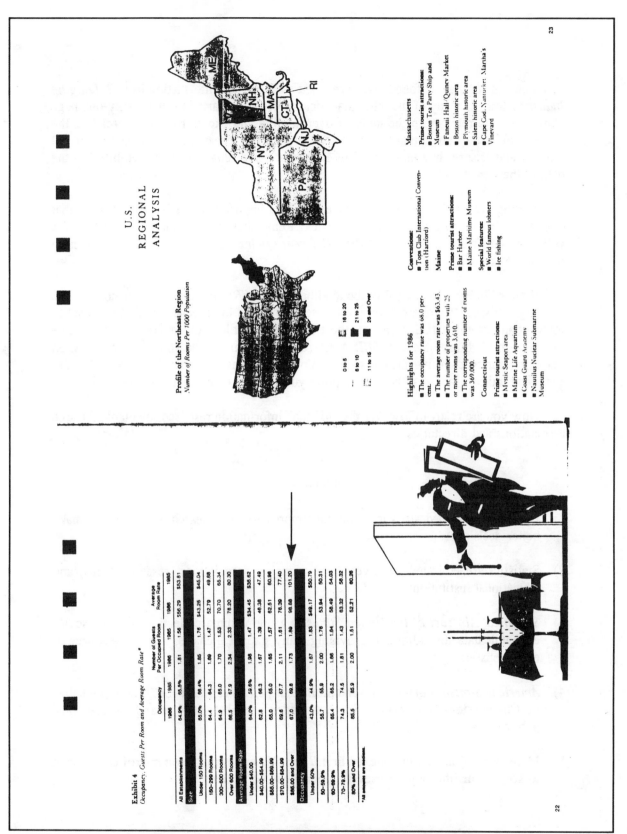

**Figure 5.7: Statistical Table from *U.S. Lodging Industry*,
as Included in the Statistical Reference Index Microfiche Collection, 1987.**

You can see that we found highly relevant statistics and information in *U.S. Lodging Industry*. In fact, many of the other statistical tables and charts in this seventy-one page publication are relevant to the topic of overbuilding and excess rooms. By reading the report, you also discover that Laventhol & Horwath is a research firm specializing in the lodging and leisure-time industry. This fact adds more reliability and credibility to the data in the report.

Through utilization of *SRI*, you have retrieved important statistical information that would be difficult to locate without an index. Remember that *American Statistics Index* will lead to different data than *Statistical Reference Index*, so check both when conducting thorough research.

If your library does not subscribe to either *ASI* or *SRI*, you may wonder how to find relevant statistics. There are several other sources listed in Appendix B that can lead to relevant and useful statistics. In fact, these sources might lead to statistics that cannot be retrieved through use of *ASI* or *SRI*. A reference librarian can be your best friend when searching for that elusive fact or figure. Your librarians also may be aware of other statistical indexes, and may be able to point you to local or unusual sources of data.

Now you are ready to discover the "hidden" information resources available through associations and directories.

SUMMARY

1) By using published statistics, you can improve your research and you can make better decisions.

2) Statistics are collected by government agencies, associations, research firms, and educational institutions.

3) *Statistical Abstract of the United States* is a one-volume collection of U.S. socio-economic data. In addition to providing many statistical charts, it lists the source of each statistic.

4) *American Statistics Index (ASI)* and *Statistical Reference Index (SRI)*, both published by Congressional Information Services, index and abstract thousands of statistical publications.

5) Many of the publications indexed in *ASI* and *SRI* are available on microfiche. Check to see if your library purchases the microfiche collections.

CHAPTER 6

ASSOCIATIONS AND DIRECTORIES

So far, your search strategy has progressed through industry overviews, periodical and newspaper indexes, and statistical indexes to find information on the topic: "Is the lodging industry overbuilt and is there an excess supply of rooms?" You have found relevant information in each of these resources.

However, now you are ready to ask more specific questions, such as:

1) Has the occupancy rate in Tucson, Arizona, increased or decreased in the last year?

2) How many rooms are there in the Tucson area?

More than likely, these questions cannot be answered by using industry overviews, periodical and newspaper indexes, and statistical indexes. More specialized resources will be necessary for these topics. This chapter will illustrate how to use associations and directories to locate information that is "hidden" or not readily available in most libraries.

The library has many books that list sources of "hidden" information. These sources include industry experts, government agencies, entrepreneurs, and companies that collect and publish statistics, specialized lists, directories, and other valuable information. Although these sources of information may not be physically located in the library, their addresses and telephone numbers are. These sources might be able to supply you with information that is otherwise unavailable.

One important source of "hidden" information is trade associations. An association is a group joined together by a common interest or purpose. Trade associations specialize in one particular business or industry area. For example, the National Bed and Breakfast Association collects and disseminates information on a specialized segment of the lodging industry. Associations are an excellent "hidden" information source. Although there are several places to look for information regarding associations, the most well-known reference source is *Encyclopedia of Associations* (Detroit, MI: Gale Research, 1956-).

The second important source of "hidden" information is directories. Directories list names and addresses of companies or people that have a common link. Probably the most commonplace directory is the telephone book, which lists people and businesses in a specific city. Entries in a business directory are linked by what they do, such as a directory of bed and breakfast houses. Finding a directory that is related to your research topic may lead to information that is unavailable elsewhere. *Directories in Print* (Detroit, MI: Gale Research, 1989-) is an excellent reference tool for locating specialized directories.

Now that you know where to locate a list of associations and directories, you need to know how to use *Encyclopedia of Associations* and *Directories in Print*. First of all, however, let's examine several issues related to writing associations to request information.

Caveat 1) It takes time to send a letter and receive information back from an association. Give yourself at least four weeks before you expect to receive a reply.

Caveat 2) The association that sounds like it will definitely have the desired information may not—or it may not be willing to provide it. Some associations expect to be paid for the information they provide. Send the request to several associations that look like possibilities, and one may respond with useful information. If an association has a library or an information center, send your request to its attention.

Caveat 3) Don't expect your library to have all the directories that you find listed in *Directories in Print*. Some directories are very expensive, and most libraries can only afford to acquire a representative selection of high-demand directories. If your library does not have the directory you need, you may be able to find it at some other library or company in town. Or the directory information you need may be available via an online computer search. Ask a reference librarian for help.

Now that you know what sources to use and are aware of these caveats, you are ready to learn how to use these two sources of "hidden" information.

Living — ENCYCLOPEDIA OF ASSOCIATIONS, 23rd Edition - 1989 — 2458

Living Theatre; Coun. of the - Defunct.
Living Tree Centre ... 5811
Living With Cancer - Defunct.
Livres de la CEE; Groupe des Editeurs de ... ★EA Int
Livres de Jeunesse; Union Internationale pour les ... ★EA Int
Livsmedel; Nordisk Metodikkommitte for ... ★EA Int
Livsmedelsfragor; Permanenta Nordiska Utskottet for ... ★EA Int
Liza Minnelli Fan Club ... 21010
Lizard; Military Order of the ... ★17899
Llama Assn.; Intl. ... 3953
Llano Estacado Center for Advanced Professional Studies and Research ... RCD
(Llewelyn Powys), Powys Soc. ... EA Int
(Lloyd), Borgward Owners' Club ... 18128
Lloyd Shaw Found. ... 7267
Lloyd Wood Fan Club ... 21283
Lloyd's Maritime Data Network ... EISS
Loading Dock Equipment Mfrs. Assn. ... 2057
Loading Ramp Inst.; Industrial Lift and - Defunct.
Loan Administrators; Assn. of Small ... ★4958
Loan Advisory Coun.; Federal Saving and ... FYB
Loan Advisory Coun.; Federal Savings and ... GM
Loan Advisory Coun.; Federal Savings and ... EGAO
Loan Assn.; Jewish Free ... 17205
Loan Associations; Amer. Coun. of Independent Savings and - Defunct.
Loan Bd.; Federal Farm ... EGAO
Loan Business; Advisory Comm. on Govt. Securities of the Savings and ... EGAO
Loan Controllers; Soc. of Savings and ... ★1437
Loan Cooperatives; Latin Amer. Confed. of Savings and ... EA Int
Loan and Credit Officers; Robert Morris Associates - Natl. Assn. of Bank ... 520
Loan Dealers Assn.; Govt. Guaranteed ... ★3484
Loan Found.; Savings and ... ★500
Loan Fund; Jewish ... ★17205
Loan Fund; Valentine ... ★9439
Loan Guarantee Programs in Health Advisory Comm. ... EGAO
Loan Guaranty Fund; Mutual Aid and ... ★EA Int
Loan; Hebrew Free ... ★17205
Loan Inst.; Amer. Savings and ... ★502
Loan Institutions for Construction; European Fed. of Savings and ... ★EA Int
Loan Insurance Corp. Industry Advisory Comm.; Federal Savings and ... EGAO
Loan League; Amer. Savings and ... ★483
Loan League; Natl. Savings and ... ★514
Loan League; U.S. Savings and ... ★522
Loan Marketing Assn.; Student ... EGAO
Loan Plans; Natl. Conf. of Executives of Higher Education ... ★7434
Loan Policy Bd. ... EGAO
Loan Program; Advisory Comm. on Administrative Costs for the Natl. Defense Student ... EGAO
Loan Programs; Natl. Coun. of Higher Education ... 7434
Loan Stock Companies; Coun. of Savings and - Defunct.
Loan Supervisors; Natl. Assn. of Small ... ★4958
Loan Supervisors; Natl. Assn. of State Savings and ... ★482
Loans Program; Rural - Defunct.
Loans to South Africa; Campaign to Oppose Bank - Defunct.
Loans to Students; Advisory Coun. on Insured ... EGAO
Loans to Vocational Students; Advisory Coun. on Insured ... EGAO
Lobby; Natl. Student ... ★8078
Lobby Political Action Comm.; Solar ... ★6812
Lobbyists; Amer. League of ... 15344
Lobbyists and Lawyers for Campaign Finance Reform ... 15365
Lobster Assn.; Atlantic Offshore Fish and ... ★5044
Lobster Assn.; South African Rock - Defunct.
Lobster Dealers Assn.; Maine Wholesale - Defunct.
Lobster Fishermen's Assn.; Maine - Address unknown since 1964.
Lobstermen's Assn.; Maine ... 3442
Local Administrators of Vocational Education and Practical Arts; Natl. Coun. of ... 8167
Local Air Pollution Control Officials; Assn. of ... 6663
Local Airlines; Conf. of - Inactive.
Local Arts Agencies; Natl. Assembly of ... 8378
Local Authorities; Intl. Union of ... EA Int

Local Authority Employers Associations; European Union of ... EA Int
Local Cable Programmers; Natl. Fed. of ... 13901
Local Cartage Natl. Conf. ... ★3808
Local Cartage Natl. Conf.; Heavy Specialized Carriers Sect. - ... ★3813
Local Credit; Intl. Centre for ... EA Int
Local Development; Intl. Coun. for ... EA Int
Local Elected Officials of America ... ★15435
Local Elected Officials; Natl. Black Caucus of ... 5351
Local Elected Officials Project of the Center for Innovative Diplomacy ... 15435
Local Elected Officials for Social Responsibility ... ★15435
Local Environmental Health Administrators; Conf. of ... ★13357
Local Environmental Health Administrators; Natl. Conf. of ... 13357
Local Financial Project; State and ... RCD
Local Govt.; Acad. for State and ... 15477
Local Govt. Administration; Center for ... RCD
Local Govt. Administration and Rural Development; Inst. for ... RCD
Local Govt. Advisory Comm.; Natl. State and ... EGAO
Local Govt. Advisory Committees; Regional State and ... EGAO
Local Govt. Center ... 5349
Local Govt.; Center for State and ... RCD
Local Govt. Cooperation; Comm. on State and ... EGAO
Local Govt. Energy Policy Advisory Comm. ... EGAO
Local Govt. Information Network ... EISS
Local Govt.; Inst. of ... RCD
Local Govt. Public Facilities Coun.; State and ... ★5985
Local Govt.; Rose Inst. of State and ... RCD
Local Govt. Studies Center ... RCD
Local Govt. Technology; Center for ... RCD
Local Governments on Hazardous Wastes; Natl. Assn. of ... 6917
Local Growth Management Clearinghouse Project ... ★11128
Local Health Officers; U.S. Conf. of ... 5453
Local Health Services; Assn. of State and Territorial Directors of - Defunct.
Local History; Amer. Assn. for State and ... 8887
Local Housing Finance Agencies; Assn. of ... 5086
Local Initiatives Support Corp. ... 14079
Local, and Intergovernmental Center; State, ... RCD
Local Issues; Center for the Study of ... RCD
Local Legal Center; State and ... ★15477
Local Officials; Amer. Soc. of - Defunct.
Local Officials; Hispanic Elected ... 5346
Local Officials for Soviet Jews; State and ... 14884
Local Policies; Conf. on Alternative State and ... ★15494
Local Post Collectors Soc. ... 19197
Local; Project - Defunct.
Local Public Policies; Conf. on Alternative State and ... ★15494
Local Public Welfare Administrators; Natl. Coun. of ... 11157
Local and Regional Authorities of Europe; Standing Conf. of ... ★EA Int
Local Self-Reliance; Inst. for ... 10330
Local and Short Haul Carriers Natl. Conf. ... ★3808
Local and State Govt.; Center for ... RCD
Local Tax Research; Center for ... 5508
Local Transportation; Natl. Conf. on ... ★2903
Locals Collectors; U.S. ... 19273
Locals Study Group ... ★19229
Location Analysts and Negotiators; Natl. Assn. of ... ★3279
Locaux; Union Internationale des Villes et Pouvoirs ... ★EA Int
Loch Ness Investigation Bur. - Inactive.
Lock and Builders' Hardware Mfrs.; European Fed. of Associations of ... EA Int
Lock Collectors Assn.; Amer ... 18486
Lock Museum of America ... 8700
Locke, Jr., Computer Center; John L. ... RCD
Locker Assn.; Natl. Frozen Food ... ★2614
Locker and Freezer Provisioners; Natl. Inst. of ... ★2614
Locker Inst.; Frozen Food ... ★2614
Locker Inst.; Natl. Frozen Food ... ★2614
Locksmith Security Assn. ... 3502
Locksmith Suppliers Assn.; Natl. ... 1921
Locksmiths of America; Associated ... 1909
Locksmiths Assn.; Natl. - Inactive.
Locksmiths and Safemen of America; Insured - Defunct.

Locomotion Studies; Center for ... RCD
Locomotive Engineers; Grand Intl. Brotherhood of ... ★20418
Locomotive Engineers; Intl. Brotherhood of ... 20418
Locomotive Firemen; Assn. of Railway Trainmen and - Address unknown since 1964.
Locomotive Firemen and Enginemen; Brotherhood of ... ★20421
Locomotive Historical Soc. - Pennsylvania; Lancaster Railway and ... ★9686
Locomotive Historical Soc.; Railway and ... 9692
Locomotive Maintenance Officers' Assn. ... 3240
Locomotives; European Mfrs. of Thermal and Electric ... EA Int
Locomotives Thermiques et Electriques; Constructeurs Europeens de ... ★EA Int
Locust Control Comm.; FAO Desert ... EA Int
Locust Control Orgn. for Central and Southern Africa; Intl. Red ... EA Int
Locust Control Orgn. for Eastern Africa; Desert ... EA Int
Locust Control Service; Intl. Red ... ★EA Int
Locust in the Eastern Region of Its Distribution in South West Asia; Commn. for Controlling the Desert ... EA Int
Locust in the Near East; Commn. for Controlling the Desert ... EA Int
Locust in North-West Africa; Commn. for Controlling the Desert ... EA Int
Locust Orgn.; Intl. African Migratory ... EA Int
Locust Research and Control Coordination Sect.; FAO Northwest African Desert ... ★EA Int
Lodge Center for Intl. Studies; John Davis ... ★15493
Lodgers; Mexborough ... ★9730
Lodgers; Mrs. Hudson's ... ★9730
Lodgers; Veiled ... ★9730
(Lodging), Hotel Sales and Marketing Assn. Intl. - European Office ... EA Int
Lodging Inst.; Foodservice and ... 1516
Lodging and Travel Research Found.; Hospitality ... 2415
(Lodgings), Amer. Bed and Breakfast Assn. ... 2410
(Lodgings), Amer. Hotel & Motel Assn. ... 2411 ←
(Lodgings), Amer. Travel Inns ... 2412
(Lodgings), Bed and Breakfast League ... 2413
(Lodgings), Caribbean Hotel Assn. ... 2414
(Lodgings), European Hotel Managers Assn. ... EA Int
(Lodgings), European Motel Fed. ... EA Int
(Lodgings), Hospitality Lodging and Travel Research Found. ... 2415
(Lodgings), Hotel Employees and Restaurant Employees Intl. Union ... 20362
(Lodgings), Hotel-Motel Greeters Intl. ... 2416
(Lodgings), Hotel Sales and Marketing Assn. Intl. ... 2417
(Lodgings), Independent Innkeepers Assn. ... 2418
(Lodgings), Intl. Assn. of Holiday Inns ... 2419
(Lodgings), Intl. Hotel Assn. ... EA Int
(Lodgings), Intl. Orgn. of Hotel and Restaurant Associations ... EA Int
(Lodgings), Intl. Soc. of Hotel Assn. Executives ... 2420
(Lodgings), Natl. Assn. of Black Hospitality Professionals ... 2421
(Lodgings), Natl. Bed-and-Breakfast Assn. ... 2422
(Lodgings), Preferred Hotels Assn. ... 2423
(Lodgings), Tourist House Assn. of America ... 2424
Lodi District Vintners Assn. ... 4833
Lodzer Young Men's Benevolent Soc. ... 16330
Log Analysts; Soc. of Professional Well ... 6605
Log Exporting Industries; Coun. of Pacific Northwest - Address unknown since 1970.
Log Homes Coun. ... ★739
Log Homes Coun.; North Amer. ... 739
Log House Assn. of North America ... ★1010
Log House Builder's Assn. of North America ... 1010
Log Rolling Assn.; Intl. - Address unknown since 1966.
Logement; Federation Europeenne d'Epargne et de Credit pour le ... ★EA Int
Loggers Assn.; Helicopter ... 1701
Loggers Assn.; Northeastern ... 1716
Loggers Assn.; Pacific Northwest - Address unknown since 1964.
Loggers; Portland Western Assn. of Lumbermen and ... ★1740
Logging Assn.; Northern Woods ... 1719
Logging Conf.; Redwood Region ... 4377
Logging Cong.; Lake States ... ★1735
Logging Cong.; Pacific ... 1722
Logic; Assn. for Symbolic ... 6418
Logic for Automatic Teaching Operations; Project on Programmed ... RCD

Figure 6.1: "Alphabetical Index to Organization Names and Keywords" from *Encyclopedia of Associations*, 23d ed., 1989.

Encyclopedia of Associations is a multi-volume directory of over 20,000 national and international organizations. The first two volumes contain the descriptions of all the associations. The third volume contains the index to the first two volumes.

Begin your search with the "Alphabetical Index to Organizations," which is found in the third volume and is illustrated in figure 6.1. This index lists the associations by every important keyword in the name. For example, the American Hotel & Motel Association is listed under "American," "Hotel," and "Motel." In addition, keywords such as "Lodging," which are not in the name, are also added to the index. As a result, all associations related to lodging, such as the American Hotel & Motel Association, also are listed under the keyword "Lodging."

Following the American Hotel & Motel Association's listing is the number 2411. This entry number leads you to the description of the American Hotel & Motel Association, which is found in the first volume of the set (figure 6.2). In addition to the address and telephone number, which is all you really need to contact the association, *Encyclopedia of Associations* provides other valuable data that helps pinpoint appropriate associations. You learn that the American Hotel & Motel Association (AH&MA) is a federation of fifty state and regional hotel associations with a combined membership of 8,900. In addition, it conducts research and compiles statistics.

Since the American Hotel & Motel Association is one of the most prominent associations in the lodging industry, a request was made to them for information on occupancy rates in Tucson, Arizona. Although it took over two months to receive the information, the AH&MA did supply relevant data, including Pannell Kerr Forster's *Arizona Lodging Forecast 1989* (figures 6.3 and 6.4).

Arizona Lodging Forecast 1989 is compiled by Pannell Kerr Forster, a well-known and reputable public accounting firm serving the lodging industry. As such, this publication contains statistical data on Tucson and other cities in Arizona that would be difficult to find anywhere else. The data and information in figure 6.4 show the percentage of occupancy from 1985 to 1988 and includes forecast data for 1989. This information has answered one of the questions at the start of this chapter: Has the occupancy rate in Tucson increased or decreased in the last year?

Before we leave *Encyclopedia of Associations*, look back at figure 6.1. Notice that several organizations do not have an entry number, but instead the notation "EA Int." If you look in the front of the volume, you will find that *Encyclopedia of Associations* provides references to associations listed in more than ten other directories. "EA Int" stands for *Encyclopedia of Associations: International Edition* (figure 6.5).

Publications: (1) Lightrays, bimonthly; (2) Transportation Notes, quarterly; also publishes Lighting Your Life. **Convention/Meeting:** annual conference, with workshop - always fall. 1988 Oct. 4-6, Reno, NV; 1989 Sept. 17-19, Washington, DC; 1990 Sept. 16-18, Scottsdale, AZ.

★2402★   CERTIFIED BALLAST MANUFACTURERS ASSOCIATION
(Lighting) (CBM)
Hanna Bldg., #772
1422 Euclid Ave.   Phone: (216) 241-0711
Cleveland, OH 44115   M. C. Davies, Sec.-Treas.
Founded: 1939. **Members:** 7. **Staff:** 5. Manufacturers of fluorescent lamp ballasts who participate in a certification program requiring independent laboratory examination and certification and whose sample ballasts meet specifications of American National Standards Institute (see separate entry). **Committees:** Ad Hoc; Advertising; Technical. **Publications:** News, quarterly. **Convention/Meeting:** annual.

★2403★   INDUSTRIAL LIGHTING DISTRIBUTORS OF AMERICA (ILDA)
20457 Valley Blvd.   Phone: (714) 594-3101
Walnut, CA 91789   Bob Small, Pres.
Founded: 1985. **Members:** 20. Distributors of lamps and lighting products. Seeks to improve the industry through the exchange of information on products and technological developments. Holds seminars. **Committees:** Ethics. **Convention/Meeting:** semiannual.

★2404★   INTERNATIONAL ASSOCIATION OF LIGHTING MANAGEMENT
COMPANIES (NALMCO)
2017 Walnut St.   Phone: (215) 569-3650
Philadelphia, PA 19103   Robert H. Ecker, Exec.Dir.
Founded: 1953. **Members:** 100. **Staff:** 4. Independent lighting management contractors that manage, clean, repair, re-lamp, and retrofit commercial and industrial lighting installations on a contract basis. Individual members usually operate within 50 to 100 miles of their offices. Compiles statistics; conducts specialized education and seminars. **Committees:** Certification. **Publications:** Main-Lighter (newsletter), 8/year. **Formerly:** (1978) National Association of Lighting Maintenance Contractors; (1987) International Association of Lighting Maintenance. **Convention/Meeting:** 2-3/year.

★2405★   MANUFACTURERS OF ILLUMINATION PRODUCTS (Lighting)
(MIP)
158-11 Jewel Ave., Rm. 307   Phone: (718) 591-1100
Flushing, NY 11365   Hy Greenblatt, Exec.Sec.
Founded: 1944. **Members:** 25. Manufacturers of lighting equipment; negotiates labor agreements with unions.

★2406★   NATIONAL ASSOCIATION OF LIGHTING REPRESENTATIVES
(NALR)
P.O. Box 214   Phone: (201) 974-1900
Sea Girt, NJ 08750   Paul Saunders, Exec.Dir.
Founded: 1980. **Members:** 600. **Staff:** 3. Manufacturers, importers, and representatives who sell residential lighting fixtures and accessories. Presents industry awards. **Telecommunications Services:** Fax, (201)974-1900. **Committees:** Ethics; Industrial Relations. **Publications:** (1) Lantern, monthly (members only); (2) Profile Directory of Sales Representative Members, annual. **Convention/Meeting:** annual National Lighting Fair (with exhibits). Also holds annual business meeting and periodic regional lighting show.

★2407★   NATIONAL LIGHTING BUREAU (NLB)
2101 L St., N.W., Suite 300   Phone: (202) 457-8437
Washington, DC 20037   Richard Geissler, Exec.Dir.
Founded: 1976. **Staff:** 3. Trade associations involved in electrical manufacturing, distribution, and installation; companies involved in the lighting industry. To promote the concept of lighting energy management. Focuses on all aspects of lighting energy management, which includes productivity to lumen output. Does not promote any specific form of lighting or brand name component. Presents annual Lighting Awards Program. **Publications:** (1) Newsreleases, 20/year; (2) Directory, periodic; also publishes trade magazine articles and handbooks.

★2408★   NATIONAL ORNAMENT AND ELECTRIC LIGHTS CHRISTMAS
ASSOCIATION (Lighting) (NOEL)
230 Fifth Ave., Suite 1611   Phone: (212) 889-8343
New York, NY 10001   Phyllis Southad, Exec.Sec.
Founded: 1975. **Members:** 47. Manufacturers or importers of Christmas lights and decorations; associate members are sales representatives specializing in this field and retailers selling decorations. Seeks to promote safety, positive public relations, and to enable the industry to deal as a unit with various governmental regulatory agencies. Provides a credit service. **Committees:** Credit. **Publications:** (1) Membership Directory, periodic; (2) News Bulletin, periodic. **Supersedes:** Christmas Decorations Association; Decorative Lighting Guild of America. **Convention/Meeting:** None.

★2409★   SOCIETY OF GAS LIGHTING (SGL)
c/o Philadelphia Electric Co.
2301 Market St.
S20-1   Phone: (215) 841-4950
Philadelphia, PA 19101   Philip Mulligan, Pres.
Founded: 1875. **Members:** 150. **Budget:** $28,000. Persons whose relation to the gas industry "qualifies them to aid in its advancement." Publishes membership listing. **Convention/Meeting:** annual - always December, New York City. 1988 Dec. 8; 1989 Dec. 14.

LIGHTING
Also See Index

LOCKSMITHS
See Index

★2410★   AMERICAN BED AND BREAKFAST ASSOCIATION (Lodgings)
(ABBA)
16 Village Green, Suite 203   Phone: (301) 261-0180
Crofton, MD 21114   Sarah Sonke, Dir.
Founded: 1982. **Members:** 10,000. **Staff:** 3. **Budget:** $50,000. Reservation service agencies and bed and breakfast innkeepers; bed and breakfast visitors. (Bed and breakfast accommodations are residential lodgings where breakfast is provided; such arrangements are less expensive than hotel accommodations.) Serves as trade association for those who provide bed and breakfast services; acts as information clearinghouse on bed and breakfast accommodations throughout North America. Sponsors Evergreen Bed and Breakfast Club, which offers special accomodations rates for members over 50. Maintains speakers' bureau; compiles statistics. **Computerized Services:** Data base of bed and breakfast lodgings in North America with rates and descriptions. **Publications:** (1) B & B Shoptalk, monthly; (2) B & B Travel Club, bimonthly; (3) B & B Hostlist, semiannual; (4) A Treasury of Bed and Breakfast (directory), annual; also publishes special interest guides. **Convention/Meeting:** biennial conference.

★2411★   AMERICAN HOTEL & MOTEL ASSOCIATION (Lodgings)
(AH&MA)
888 Seventh Ave.   Phone: (212) 265-4506
New York, NY 10106   Kenneth F. Hine, Exec.V.Pres.
Founded: 1910. **Members:** 8900. Federation of 50 state and regional hotel associations, representing over 1.3 million hotel and motel rooms. Promotes business of hotels and motels through publicity and promotion programs. Works to improve operating methods through dissemination of information on industry methods. Conducts educational institute for training at all levels, through home study, adult education, and colleges. Provides guidance on member and labor relations. Reviews proposed legislation affecting hotels. Sponsors seminars and study group programs. Maintains speakers' bureau; conducts research; compiles statistics; sponsors competitions and presents awards. **Committees:** AH&MA/ISHAE Liaison; American Express Advisory; American Hotel and Motel Political Action; Communications; Condominium; Convention Liaison; Copyright Music; Employee Relations; Energy Task Force; Executive Engineers; Financial Management; Food and Beverage; Governmental Affairs; Human Resources; Industry Real Estate Financing Advisory Council; International Travel; Marketing; Quality Assurance; Quality Environment; Research; Resort; Safety and Fire Protection; Security; Smaller Hotels and Motels; Telecommunications; Travel Related Organizations. **Divisions:** American Hotel Foundation; General Agency. **Publications:** (1) Construction and Modernization Report, monthly; (2) Lodging, monthly; (3) Directory of Hotel and Motel Systems, annual; also publishes Who's Who in the Lodging Industry and reprints of articles and makes available hotel information kits. **Formerly:** (1917) American Hotel Protective Association; (1962) American Hotel Association. **Convention/Meeting:** annual (with exhibits) - 1989 Apr. 6-9, Boston, MA. Also holds annual midyear meeting - always fall, New York City.

★2412★   AMERICAN TRAVEL INNS (Lodgings) (ATI)
640 W. North Temple   Phone: (801) 521-0732
Salt Lake City, UT 84116   Wesley Sine, Pres.
Founded: 1958. **Members:** 35. **Staff:** 4. Hotel/motel recommending service. Offers recognized brand-name identity without loss of individuality through national advertising program. Sponsors reservations through member-to-member referrals and group marketing. Offers reduced costs for credit card business. Sponsors training and management techniques and specific market research information to assist with individual marketing needs. Maintains strong quality control. **Publications:** Travel Guide Directory, semiannual. **Formerly:** (1977) American Travel Association. **Convention/Meeting:** annual.

★2413★   BED AND BREAKFAST LEAGUE (Lodgings) (BBL)
3639 Van Ness St., N.W.   Phone: (202) 363-7767
Washington, DC 20008   Millie Groobey, Dir.
Founded: 1976. **For-Profit.** A reservation service for a network of private homeowners in Washington, DC, and its suburbs who welcome "selected travelers into their homes." Traditionally, in a bed and breakfast (B and B) es-

Figure 6.2: Entry 2411 on American Hotel & Motel Association
from *Encyclopedia of Associations*, 23d ed., 1989.

METROPOLITAN TUCSON MARKET
DISTRIBUTION OF DEMAND
1988 VERSUS FORECASTED 1989

Market Segment	1988 Percent Distribution	Forecasted 1989 Percent Distribution
Commercial	35%	35%
Group	29	29
Tourist	28	27
Other	8	9
Total	100%	100%

Source: Pannell Kerr Forster

Occupancy Performance

From 1985 through 1987, occupancy levels in Metropolitan Tucson declined from 61 percent in 1985 to 58 percent in 1987.   In 1988, however, occupancy levels increased to 60 percent.   In 1989, we forecast that because of the limited addition of new rooms in the market, coupled with moderate growth in demand, market occupancies will increase one percentage point over 1988 levels to 61 percent.   The actual increase, if not for rounding to the nearest whole number, would be be 1.8 percentage points.

Average Room Rate

Average room rates in Metropolitan Tucson have been growing at 5.6 percent annually on an average since 1985. In 1989, we anticipate a 3.3 percent (or a $2.00) increase in average rate over 1988 levels and forecast an overall average rate of $62.00 in the Tucson Metropolitan Area.

Summary of Market Performance

In the table which follows, we present a summary of the historic 1985 through 1988 market performance of the Metropolitan Tucson lodging industry, as well as our forecast for 1989.

Figure 6.3: "Metropolitan Tucson Market Distribution of Demand 1988 Versus Forecasted 1989" from *Arizona Lodging Forecast 1989*.

TOTAL METROPOLITAN TUCSON MARKET
METROPOLITAN TUCSON, ARIZONA
SUMMARY OF MARKET PERFORMANCE
1985 THROUGH FORECASTED 1989

	1985	1986	1987	1988	FORECASTED 1989	PERCENT CHANGE 1985-1989	ACTUAL CHANGE 1985-1989	COMPOUND ANNUAL GROWTH PERCENTAGE 1985-1988	1985-1989
SUPPLY									
Average Number Of Daily Rooms	6,163	7,423	8,446	8,491	8,602	39.6%	2,439	11.3%	8.7%
Percent Change From Prior Year		20.4%	13.8%	0.5%	1.3%				
Actual Change From Prior Year		1,260	1,023	45	111				
DEMAND									
COMMERCIAL Demand	502,500	537,100	602,900	642,500	677,200	34.8%	174,700	8.5%	7.7%
Percent Change From Prior Year		6.9%	12.3%	6.6%	5.4%				
Actual Change From Prior Year		34,600	65,800	39,600	34,700				
GROUP Demand	337,100	419,000	506,200	532,800	555,900	64.9%	218,800	16.5%	13.3%
Percent Change From Prior Year		24.3%	20.8%	5.3%	4.3%				
Actual Change From Prior Year		81,900	87,200	26,600	23,100				
TOURIST Demand	418,200	457,300	524,700	516,000	525,500	25.7%	107,300	7.3%	5.9%
Percent Change From Prior Year		9.3%	14.7%	-1.7%	1.8%				
Actual Change From Prior Year		39,100	67,400	(8,700)	9,500				
OTHER Demand	118,000	125,400	155,000	158,100	167,000	41.5%	49,000	10.2%	9.1%
Percent Change From Prior Year		6.3%	23.6%	2.0%	5.6%				
Actual Change From Prior Year		7,400	29,600	3,100	8,900				
TOTAL Demand	1,375,800	1,538,800	1,788,800	1,849,400	1,925,600	40.0%	549,800	10.4%	8.8%
Percent Change From Prior Year		11.8%	16.2%	3.4%	4.1%				
Actual Change From Prior Year		163,000	250,000	60,600	76,200				
OCCUPANCY									
Annual Occupancy Percentage	61%	57%	58%	60%	61%	---	0.2%	---	---
Change In Occupancy Points From Prior Year		-4%	1%	2%	2%				
AVERAGE ROOM RATE									
Annual Average Room Rate	$51	$55	$58	$60	$62	21.6%	$11.00	5.6%	5.0%
Percent Change From Prior Year		7.8%	5.5%	3.4%	3.3%				
Actual Change From Prior Year		$4	$3	$2	$2				

Note: Totals may not add due to rounding.

SOURCE: PANNELL KERR FORSTER

Figure 6.4: "Total Metropolitan Tucson Market, Metropolitan Tucson, Arizona Summary of Market Performance" from *Arizona Lodging Forecast 1989.*

79

If an organization appears in the Index with a star (★) before the entry number, it is not listed separately in the *Encyclopedia* but is mentioned within the description of the entry indicated by the number.

For example, the sample entry on page xiv would have the following listings in the index:

```
Amer. Earth......................................................................................................... *4420
Amer. Soc. of Earth Sciences ................................................................................4420
Earth; Amer............................................................................................................ *4420
Earth Sciences; Amer. Soc. of ..............................................................................4420
Earth Sciences Coun. ........................................................................................ *4420
Geological Inst.; Natl. ....................................................................................... *4420
(Geology), Amer. Soc. of Earth Sciences ...........................................................4420
Geology Soc.; Natl. ............................................................................................ *4420
Natl. Geological Inst. .......................................................................................... *4420
Natl. Geology Soc. .............................................................................................. *4420
Sciences; Amer. Soc. of Earth ..............................................,.............................4420
Sciences Coun.; Earth ........................................................................................ *4420
```

► References to organizations from *International Organizations* and the other thirteen directories are interfiled in the index with Volume 1 listings and are identified by a book title acronym rather than an entry number. For example:

```
Amer. Justice Inst ...........................................................................................CCOD
Amer. Language Inst .......................................................................................... RCD
Amer. Medals Comm.; Young ...........................................................................EGAO
```

Following are acronyms and bibliographic information for the directories cited in this edition's Name and Keyword Index:

CCOD=*Consultants and Consulting Organizations Directory*, Eighth Edition. Edited by Janice McLean. Detroit: Gale Research Inc., 1987. Supplement *New Consultants* 1988.

CD=*Congressional Directory*, 1987-88. Washington, D.C.: U.S. Government Printing Office, 1987.

CYB=*Congressional Yellow Book*. Washington, D.C.: Washington, Monitor Inc., 1984. Updates.

➤ **EA Int**=*Encyclopedia of Associations: International Organizations*, 1988. Edited by Karin E. Koek. Detroit: Gale Research Inc., 1988. Supplement 1988.

EAR=*Encyclopedia of American Religions*, Second Edition. Edited by J. Gordon Melton. Detroit: Gale Research Inc., 1986. Supplement 1987.

EGAO=*Encyclopedia of Governmental Advisory Organizations*, Sixth Edition. Edited by Denise M. Allard and Donna Batten. Detroit: Gale Research Inc., 1987. Supplement *New Governmental Advisory Organizations*, 1988.

EISS=*Encyclopedia of Information Systems and Services*, Eighth Edition. Edited by Amy Lucas and Annette Novallo. Detroit: Gale Research Inc., 1987. Supplement *New Information Systems and Services* 1988.

EOP=*Encyclopedia of Occultism and Parapsychology*, Second Edition. Edited by Leslie A. Shepard. Detroit: Gale Research Inc., 1985. Supplement *Occultism Update* 1987.

FD=*Foundation Directory*, Eleventh Edition. Edited by Loren Renz. New York: Foundation Center, 1987.

FYB=*Federal Yellow Book*. Edited by Betsy Kinnas Cook. Washington, D.C.: Monitor Publishing Co., 1988.

Figure 6.5: List of Acronyms from *Encyclopedia of Associations*, 23d ed., 1989.

Although it is relatively easy to see how an association might supply specialized information, it may be more difficult to imagine how a directory might help with a research problem. Consider the problem again: What is the outlook for the hotel industry in Tucson, Arizona? It would be helpful to know the number of hotels and hotel rooms in the city. A directory of Tucson hotels would answer this, but where can you start looking for such a directory?

Directories in Print is a two-volume reference tool that provides descriptions of thousands of different directories (figure 6.6). It has a subject index in the back of volume 2. There is a heading "Hotel and motel industry." Scanning the list of directory titles in figure 6.6, you see *Hotel & Travel Index*, which is entry number 1822.

With the entry number, you can now proceed to volume 1 and look up 1822 in numerical order. Here you find a complete description of the *Hotel & Travel Index* (figure 6.7).

This description of *Hotel & Travel Index* mentions a geographical arrangement as well as the number of rooms in each hotel, so it is worth pursuing further for this research project. Check to see if your library has a copy; if not, you can purchase it from the address listed in *Directories in Print*. Figure 6.8 illustrates a page from *Hotel & Travel Index*, which does list all Tucson hotels and includes the number of rooms in each hotel. *Directories in Print* has led us to an information source that would have been very difficult to locate otherwise. It has provided us with a resource that answers one of the questions posed at the beginning of this chapter: How many rooms are there in the Tucson area?

By utilizing *Encyclopedia of Associations* and *Directories in Print*, you have located "hidden" information sources that provided added facts and figures for the research topic.

You have now covered the basic sources for industry information. These include:

- industry overviews (Chapter 3),
- periodical indexes (Chapter 4),
- statistics sources (Chapter 5), and
- associations and directories (Chapter 6).

Now you are ready to explore the vast arena of company information. The second half of this book explores important reference tools for locating facts, figures, and insights on companies.

Directory of American Baptist Retirement Homes, Hospitals, Nursing Homes, Children's Homes & Special Services 9038

Directory of Catholic Special Facilities and Programs in the United States for Handicapped Children and Adults 8531

Directory of Child Life Activity Programs in North America [Hospital care] 8534

Directory of Episcopal Facilities for the Elderly 8544

Directory of Facilities Obligated to Provide Uncompensated Services [Hospitals and health care facilities] 8545

Directory of Health and Welfare Ministries 8550

Directory of Investor-Owned Hospitals, Hospital Management Companies, and Health Systems 8561

Directory of Jewish Health and Welfare Agencies 9046

Directory of Student Placements in Health Care Settings in North America [Care of children in hospitals] 8592

Directory of Veterans Administration Facilities 9200

Electronic Yellow Pages: Professionals Directory [Database] 211

Encyclopedia of Medical Organizations and Agencies 8619

Federal Benefits for Veterans and Dependents 9207

Guide to Biomedical Standards 5551

Health Resources Directory 8668

Healthcare Foodservice Who's Who 8671

Hospital Market Atlas 8687

Hospital Phone Book 8688

Hospitals Directory 8690

International Business Travel and Relocation Directory 1935

International Halfway House Association—Directory of Residential Treatment Centers 8712

Masonic Homes, Hospitals, and Charity Foundations 9106

Mental Health Directory 8771

National Association of Private Psychiatric Hospitals— Hospital Directory 8791

National Directory of Addresses and Telephone Numbers 439

Nursing Career Directory 8833

Nursingworld Journal Professional Career Guide 8836

Source Book [Hospitals and suppliers] 8928

Texas Hospital Association—Directory 8945

330-Funded Community Health Centers Directory 8946

Uniformed Services Medical/Dental Facilities in the U.S.A. 5099

U.S. Medical Directory 8953

U.S. Medicine—Directory of Major Federal Government Medical Treatment Facilities Issue 8954

Yellow Book of Funeral Directors and Services

Hospitals and clinics—Data processing

Directory of Hospital Information System Products 8556

Hospital Software Sourcebook 8689

Hospitals and clinics—Design and construction

Directory of Planning and Design Professionals for Health Facilities 8582

Hospitals and clinics—Equipment, supplies, and services. See Medical and hospital equipment, supplies, and services

Hospitals and clinics—Management

Allied Health Education Directory 8326

American Academy of Medical Directors—Directory of Members 8336

American College of Healthcare Executives— Directory 8390

American Society for Hospital Marketing and Public Relations—Membership Directory 8420

American Society for Hospital Materials Management— Roster 8421

College of Osteopathic Healthcare Executives— Directory 8494

Directory of Health Care Group Purchasing Organizations 8552

Directory of Hospital Personnel 8557

Directory of Investor-Owned Hospitals, Hospital Management Companies, and Health Systems 8561

Health Care Material Management Society— Membership Directory 8650

Medical Group Management Association— Directory 8753

Multi-Hospital Systems and Group Purchasing Organizations Directory 8781

Hospitals and clinics—Management, study and teaching of

Medical and Health Information Directory 8744

Hostels

American Youth Hostels International Handbook 9323

Australia in 22 Days 9345

China in 22 Days 9410

Cyclists' Yellow Pages 10002

Germany, Austria & Switzerland in 22 Days 9536

Great Britain in 22 Days 9543

Handbook, A Directory of Hostels in the U.S. 9566

India in 22 Days 9599

Japan in 22 Days 9628

Mexico in 22 Days 9658

New Zealand in 22 Days 9706

Norway, Denmark & Sweden in 22 Days 9718

Sleep Cheap Guide to North America 9796

Spain and Portugal in 22 Days 9809

22 Days in Europe 9869

West Indies in 22 Days 9892

Hot springs

Common Ground: Resources for Personal Transformation 7700

Great Hot Springs of the West 9546

Hot Springs Gazette 9583

Hot tubs. See Hot water bathing equipment industry

Hot water bathing equipment industry

Hot Tubs and Spas-Retail 1820

Pool & Spa News—Directory Issue 10202

Spa and Sauna—Buyer's Guide Issue 10242

Swimming Pool Age and Spa Merchandiser—Data and Reference Annual 10256

Hotel and motel guidebooks

American Urban Guidenotes: The Newsletter of Guidebooks 9321

Hotel and Motel Guides [Information note] 9584

Hotel and motel Industry (See also subheading Business and agriculture under state names; Tourist homes and inns)

Airport Lodging and Meeting Facilities 698

American Bus Association Motorcoach Marketer: Complete Directory of the Intercity Bus & Travel/ Tourism Industry 9303

Best Places to Stay in America's Cities 9371

Best Places to Stay in New England 9372

Budget Vacationers Guidebook—Western U.S. 9386

Figure 6.6: Part 1: "Subject Index" from *Directories in Print*, 6th ed., 1989.

Business Organizations, Agencies, and Publications Directory 1052
Catalog of Nonsmoking Hotel Rooms 9398
Corporate Travel—Directory of Corporate Travel Issue 9434
Directory of Hotel & Motel Systems 1369
Directory of Hotel Lenders 3436
Discount Guide for Travelers over 55 9474
Eastern Travel Sales Guide 1484
Endless Vacation—World Directory of Resorts Issue 9490
Explore Minnesota Resort Guide 9501
Florida Hotel & Motel Journal—Buyer's Guide Issue 1614
Footloose in the Swiss Alps: A Hiker's Guide to the Mountain Inns and Trails of Switzerland 9525
France on Backroads: The Motorist's Guide to the French Countryside 9529
Golf Digest—Places to Meet Guide Issue 10049
Guide to the Small and Historic Lodgings of Florida 9561
Handbook, A Directory of Hostels in the U.S. 9566
Hotel & Motel Management—D   Hotel/Motel Management Companies
Hotel & Travel Index 1822 ◄
Hotels & Motels Directory [A   ss Directories Series] 1823
Incentive Marketing—Travel Buye.   .ctory Issue 1869
Insurance Conference Planner—Conference Facilities Guide Issue 1914
Lodging Hospitality—400 Top Performers Issue 2069
Meetings and Conventions—Gavel International Directory Issue 2160
Monthly Resort Real Estate Property Index 3608
Music & Booking Source Directory 7364
National Directory of Addresses and Telephone Numbers 439
National Directory of Budget Motels 2285
New York City Tour Package Directory 9705
North Carolina Accommodations Directory 9712
OAG Travel Planner Hotel & Motel Redbook (European Edition) 2372
OAG Travel Planner Hotel & Motel Redbook (North American Edition) 2373
Official Hotel & Resort Guide 2393
Official Meeting Facilities Guide 2396
Resorts Directory 9775
Restaurants & Institutions—Annual 400 Issues 2684
Southwest Hotel-Motel Review—Buyers Guide Issue 2860
State by State Guide to Budget Motels 9817
Successful Meetings—[Year] Sourcebook 2894
Tennis—Fall Travel Guide Issue 10263
Touring with Towser 9835
Travel Agent—Group Travel Reference Guide: USA and Canada Issue 9847
Travel Industry Personnel Directory 3025
Travel Trade—Personnel Sales Guide Issue 3026
Traveler's Fitness/Health Directory 9858
Washington, D.C. Destination Planning Guide 9886
Western Association News—Hotel/Facilities Directory Issues 3152
Western Travel Sales Guide 3159
Where to Stay USA (From $3 to $30 a Night) 9896
Who's Who in the Lodging Industry 3206
Woodside Directory of Hotel Corporate Rates 3235

Hotel and motel industry—Equipment, supplies, and services
Directory of Chain Restaurant Operators 1321
Hotels & Restaurants International—Buyers' Guide Issue 1824
Lodging Magazine—Buyers Guide for Hotels and Motels Issue 2070
Motor Hotel Development Guide 2228
Rental Equipment Register—Product Directory & Buyer's Guide Issue 2666
Resorts & Parks Purchasing Guide 2679
Southwest Hotel-Motel Review—Buyers Guide Issue 2860
Who's Who in the Lodging Industry 3206
Hotels and motels (general national and international guides) (See also Tourist homes and inns)
All Suite Hotels 9300
American Express Pocket Guides: Paris 9306
American Express Pocket Guides to England & Wales 9307
American Express Pocket Guides to Mexico 9308
American Express Pocket Guides to Spain 9309
American Express Pocket Guides to Venice 9310
Australia in 22 Days 9345
"Best of" Guides 9370
Britain for the Very Good Years [Senior citizens discounts] 9383
Castle Hotels of Europe: Official Guide to Europe's Most Unusual Accommodations 9396
Chile and Easter Island: A Travel Survival Kit 9409
China in 22 Days 9410
Elegant Small Hotels 9488
Germany, Austria & Switzerland in 22 Days 9536
Golf World—Resort Guide Issue 10055
Great Britain in 22 Days 9543
Great Castle Hotels of Europe 9544
Ian Keown's European Hideaways 9593
India in 22 Days 9599
Japan in 22 Days 9628
Long Walks in France 9646
Mexico in 22 Days 9658
Michelin Red Guides 9660
New Zealand in 22 Days 9706
Norway, Denmark & Sweden in 22 Days 9718
OAG Travel Planner Hotel & Motel Redbook (European Edition) 2372
Passport to Europe's Small Hotels and Inns 9736
Peru: A Travel Survival Kit 9742
Premier Hotels of Great Britain 9762
Rough Guides 9781
Senior Citizen's Guide to Budget Travel in Europe 9784
Sleep Cheap Guide to North America 9796
Spain and Portugal in 22 Days 9809
22 Days in Europe 9869
Weekend Cycling: A Selection of Fully Planned Scenic Routes [Great Britain] 9890
West Indies in 22 Days 9892
Hotels and motels—Management, study and teaching of
Directory of Hospitality Educators 1368
Guide to Hospitality and Tourism Education: A Directory of CHRIE Member Colleges and Universities 1764
Hotel & Motel Management—Directory of Hotel/Motel Management Companies 1821

1517

Figure 6.6: Part 2: "Subject Index" from *Directories in Print*, 6th ed., 1989.

83

cooperation with "Body Fashions/Intimate Apparel Magazine." Formerly published by Harcourt Brace Jovanovich, Inc..

★1819★
HOSPITALITY SCENE—BUYERS GUIDE ISSUE
Bolger Publications, Inc.
3301 Como Avenue, S. E.
Minneapolis, MN 55414   Phone: (612)645-6311
Publication includes: List of over 600 food and food service equipment suppliers, including manufacturers, distributors, and dealers, and their representatives. **Entries include:** Company name, address, phone. **Arrangement:** Alphabetical for manufacturers and others; individual representative listings follow principal's. **Indexes:** Product. **Frequency:** Annual, June/July. **Price:** Free (ISSN 0279-3814).

★1820★
HOT TUBS AND SPAS-RETAIL
American Business Directories, Inc., Division
American Business Lists, Inc.
5707 S. 86th Circle
Omaha, NE 68127   Phone: (402)331-7169
Number of listings: 6,020. **Entries include:** Name, address, phone (including area code), size of advertisement, year first in "Yellow Pages." **Arrangement:** Geographical. **Frequency:** Annual. **Price:** $120.00, payment with order. Significant discounts offered for standing orders. **Online through:** Publisher under title "Instant Yellow Page Service." **Other Information:** Compiled from telephone company "Yellow Pages," nationwide. **Computer readable formats:** Magnetic tape; diskette. **Other formats:** Mailing labels; 3x5 cards.

Hotel & Motel Management—Calendar Section *See* Hotel & Motel Management—Directory of Hotel/Motel Management Companies (1821)

★1821★
HOTEL & MOTEL MANAGEMENT—DIRECTORY OF HOTEL/MOTEL MANAGEMENT COMPANIES
Edgell Communications, Inc.
7500 Old Oak Boulevard
Cleveland, OH 44130   Phone: (216)243-8100
Covers: Approximately 1,000 companies specializing in hotel/motel management services. **Entries include:** Company name, address, phone, principal officers, year founded, types of properties managed, fees, and special services. **Arrangement:** Alphabetical. **Frequency:** Annual, July. **Editor:** Mike DeLuca. **Advertising accepted. Former title(s):** Hotel and Motel ManagementCalendar Section. **Price:** $15.00, plus $3.00 shipping. **Send orders to:** Edgell Communications, Inc., One E. First Street, Duluth, MN 55802 (218-723-9200). **Other Information:** Formerly published by Harcourt Brace Jovanovich, Inc..

★1822★   ←
HOTEL & TRAVEL INDEX
Murdoch Magazines, Division
News Group Publications, Inc.
One Park Avenue
New York, NY 10016   Phone: (212)503-5600
Covers: Over 36,000 hotels, motels, resorts, inns, and guest houses, worldwide; hotel and motel systems; hotel representatives and reservations services. **Entries include:** All entries show company name, address, phone; hotel listings show rates, manager's name, hotel representative, telex, toll-free number, automated CRT access codes, travel agency commission. **Arrangement:** Geographical, alphabetical. **Pages (approx.):** 3,000. **Frequency:** Quarterly, late February, May, August, November. **Editor:** Jerry Preece. **Advertising**

accepted. Circulation 60,000. **Price:** $35.00 per copy; $70.00 per year.

★1823★
HOTELS & MOTELS DIRECTORY [American Business Directories Series]
American Business Directories, Inc., Division
American Business Lists, Inc.
5707 S. 86th Circle
Omaha, NE 68127   Phone: (402)331-7169
Number of listings: 73,070. **Entries include:** Name, address, phone (including area code), size of advertisement, year first in "Yellow Pages," coding indicates brands carried, specialties, or franchises held. **Arrangement:** Geographical. **Frequency:** Annual. **Price:** $450.00, payment with order. Significant discounts offered for standing orders. **Online through:** Publisher under title "Instant Yellow Page Service." **Other Information:** Regional editions available: Eastern, $300.00; Western, $280.00. Compiled from telephone company "Yellow Pages," nationwide. **Computer readable formats:** Magnetic tape; diskette. **Other formats:** Mailing labels; 3x5 cards.

★1824★
HOTELS & RESTAURANTS INTERNATIONAL—BUYERS' GUIDE ISSUE
Cahners Publishing Company
1350 E. Touhy Avenue
Des Plaines, IL 60018   Phone: (312)635-8800
Publication includes: List of manufacturers of equipment, suppliers of services, and their restaurant, hotel, and institutional markets; international coverage. **Entries include:** Company name, address, phone, telex, cable, parent company, products and services, trade names, and regional and local distributors. **Arrangement:** Alphabetical. **Indexes:** Product/service. **Frequency:** Annual, December. **Editor:** Mary Scoviak. **Advertising accepted.** Circulation 40,000. **Former title(s):** Service World International; Hotels & Restaurants International - Directory Issue (1986). **Price:** $25.00.

Hotels & Restaurants International—Directory Issue *See* Hotels & Restaurants International—Buyers' Guide Issue (1824)

★1825★
HOUSE BEAUTIFUL'S DIRECTORY OF HARD-TO-FIND SHOPS AND SERVICES
House Beautiful
Hearst Corporation
1700 Broadway
New York, NY 10019   Phone: (212)903-5000
Covers: About 140 firms which specialize in the restoration of antiques; metal, china, and glass repair; silver plating; furniture and hardware; and other specialty services and shops. **Entries include:** Shop or firm name, address, phone, description of specialty, services offered, preferred method for contact. **Arrangement:** Classified by area of service or material. **Pages (approx.):** 5. **Frequency:** Revised every two years. **Editor:** Sylvia Sunderlin. **Price:** $1.50.

★1826★
HOUSE BEAUTIFUL'S DIRECTORY OF MATCHING SERVICES FOR CHINA, SILVER, AND GLASS
House Beautiful
Hearst Corporation
1700 Broadway
New York, NY 10019   Phone: (212)903-5000
Covers: Sources for securing matching pieces of fine china, quality earthenware, sterling, silver plate, stainless steel, American pressed and cut glass, and European crystal. **Frequency:** Annual. **Price:** $1.50.

Figure 6.7: Entry 1822 on *"Hotel & Travel Index"* from *Directories in Print*, 6th ed., 1989.

Figure 6.8: Sample Page on Tucson, Arizona, from *Hotel & Travel Index*, Spring 1989.

SUMMARY

1) An association is a group joined together by a common interest or purpose. Trade associations specialize in one particular business or industry area.

2) A directory lists names and addresses of companies or people that have a common link.

3) Both associations and directories can be useful resources for finding "hidden" information in the library.

4) *Encyclopedia of Associations* leads to appropriate trade associations that may be willing to supply useful facts and figures.

5) *Directories in Print* leads to directories that contain specialized information.

CHAPTER 7

PRIVATE, PUBLIC, OR SUBSIDIARY COMPANY?

Chapters 3 through 6 of this book explained how to search for information on an industry—in this example, the hotel industry. You learned how to find overviews and journal articles containing the latest information, how to find statistics to document specific points, and how to identify associations and directories that could supply additional information. However, most students and researchers are more interested in learning how to find information about a particular company. As a matter of fact, you may have skipped, or quickly skimmed over, the first six chapters in this book. If you have, we strongly recommend that you take a few minutes to read at least chapter 3 on "Industry Overviews." Before you research a company, it is essential to have an understanding of the industry's trends and problems. With this groundwork laid, researching a particular company will be more meaningful because you will see the company in the context of the industry and its problems.

In chapters 7 though 11 of this book we will explain how to find information on a particular company. Three companies will serve as our examples:

1) Red Roof Inns, Inc., a privately owned company;

2) Hilton Hotels Corporation, a publicly owned company; and

3) Hilton Service Corporation, a subsidiary of Hilton Hotels Corporation.

Red Roof Inns, Inc., like most companies in the hotel industry, is privately owned. This means that their financial position does not have to be disclosed to the public. You can generally assume that if a company doesn't have to release information, it's not going to do so! You will not find detailed financial data such as sales, receipts, expenditures, and debts for most private companies. And our example—Red Roof Inns, Inc.—does not publish an annual report either. Sometimes the only information that can be found on a private company is its address and telephone number. However, you may find some additional information from directories and periodical articles. Chapter 8 illustrates how to research a privately owned company.

On the other hand, Hilton Hotels Corporation is a publicly owned company. That means that the public can buy stock in the company. Because publicly owned companies must keep their stockholders and the general business world informed about their financial position, they publish annual reports for shareholders and 10-K Reports for the United States Securities and Exchange Commission. In addition, there are usually many newspaper and journal articles available on publicly owned companies. Chapter 9 illustrates the search strategy for finding these reports and articles—as well as investment services analyses.

Different again is Hilton Service Corporation, a subsidiary of Hilton Hotels Corporation. This presents a different research problem, because subsidiaries, like private companies, do not publish annual reports or 10-K Reports. The most successful search method is to look for journal articles. It is sometimes necessary and desirable to first determine who the parent is and then research the parent company. Researching a subsidiary company is the focus of chapter 10.

Whatever company you select, one question you must answer should now be apparent! Is the entity a publicly owned company, a private company, or a subsidiary company? Needless to say, the easiest type of company to research is the publicly owned company. If you haven't already selected a company or been assigned a particular company, it is wise to select a publicly owned one. Here you might also ask another question. Where can I find a list of publicly owned companies in a particular industry? Both of the above questions can be answered by one source—*The Million Dollar Directory* (Parsippany, NJ: Dun's Marketing Service, 1959-). Similar alternate sources are listed in Appendix B, or you may wish to ask the reference librarian for advice.

THE MILLION DOLLAR DIRECTORY

The Million Dollar Directory, a multi-volume set, lists over 160,000 of the larger U.S. companies. While a large majority (140,000) of the companies are private, publicly owned companies are also represented and indicated by a triangle (▲) before the company's name. Companies are listed alphabetically and each entry in the white pages includes the company's address, telephone number, number of employees, names of corporate officers, annual sales, primary business, and SIC code. Stock exchange and ticker symbol are included for publicly owned companies. Check directly under a publicly owned company's name to see if it is a subsidiary (figure 7.1).

If your company appears in *The Million Dollar Directory*, the first question is answered. You now know if you are looking for information on a private, public, or subsidiary company. If the company does not appear in *The Million Dollar Directory*, you may wish to read chapters 8, 9, and 10 before consulting a reference librarian. These three chapters will give you further leads to locating and identifying your company.

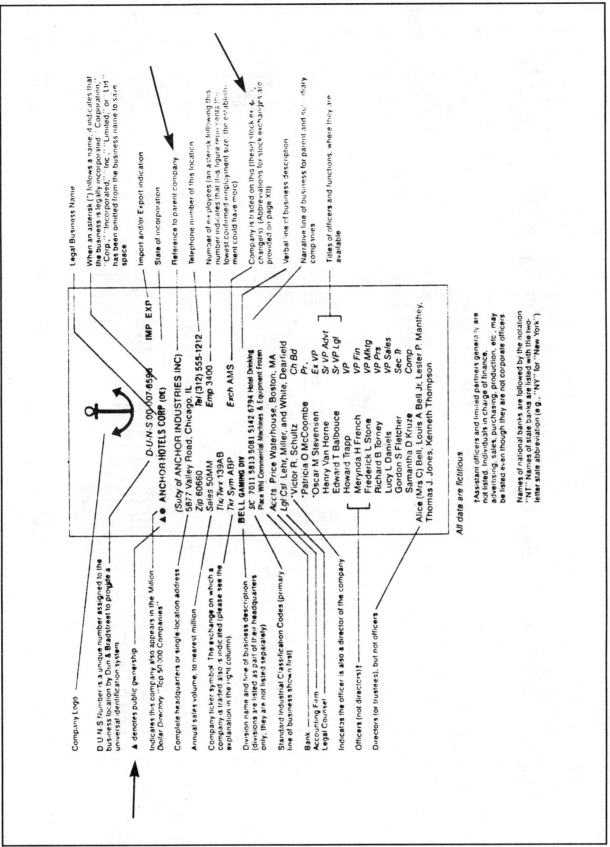

Legal Business Name

When an asterisk (*) follows a name, it indicates that the business is legally incorporated. "Corporation," "Corp.," "Incorporated," "Inc.," "Limited," or "Ltd." has been omitted from the business name to save space

Import and/or Export indication

State of incorporation

Reference to parent company

Telephone number of this location

Number of employees (an asterisk following this number indicates that this figure represents the lowest confirmed employment size; the establishment could have more)

Company is traded on this (these) stock exchange(s) (Abbreviations for stock exchanges are provided on page XII)

Verbal line of business description

Narrative line of business for parent and subsidiary companies

Titles of officers and functions, where they are available

Company Logo

D-U-N-S Number is a unique number assigned to the business location by Dun & Bradstreet to provide a universal identification system

▲ denotes public ownership

Indicates this company also appears in the *Million Dollar Directory* "Top 50,000 Companies"

Complete headquarters or single-location address

Annual sales volume, to nearest million

Company ticker symbol. The exchange on which a company is traded also is indicated (please see the explanation in the right column)

Division name and line of business description (divisions are listed as part of their headquarters only; they are not listed separately)

Standard Industrial Classification Codes (primary line of business shown first)

Indicates the officer is also a director of the company

Officers (not directors)†

Directors (or trustees), but not officers

Bank
Accounting Firm
Legal Counsel

All data are fictitious

†Assistant officers and limited partners generally are not listed. Individuals in charge of finance, advertising, sales, purchasing, production, etc., may be listed even though they are not corporate officers

Names of national banks are followed by the notation "NT." Names of state banks are listed with the two-letter state abbreviation (e.g., "NY" for "New York").

Figure 7.1: Mock Up Entry for Anchor Hotels Corp. from *The Million Dollar Directory*, 1989.

89

B D R INVESTMENT CORP   P 388   SIC 6799
N 3014 Flora Rd
Spokane, WA 99216
Tel (509) 928 1765

BROWN SAMUEL H   P 713   SIC 6799
702 A St
Tacoma, WA 98402
Tel (206) 272-8367

SAV MART INC   P 4458   SIC 6799
1729 N Wenatchee Ave
Wenatchee, WA 98801
Tel (509) 663 1671

NORTH SHORE BLDG CO   P 3689   SIC 6513
13424 175th St
Woodinville, WA 98072
Tel (206) 483-8286

SPRING BOE FINANCL COMPANIES*   P 4763   SIC 6531
16655 W Bluemound Rd #270
Brookfield, WI 53005
Tel (414) 786-8200

PETRETTI FRANK & CORINNE   P 3960   SIC 6513
1805 Birch Rd
Kenosha, WI 53140
Tel (414) 551-7255

MAYFAIR INVESTMENTS INC   P 3250   SIC 6799
1109 N Mayfair Rd Rm #205
Milwaukee, WI 53226
Tel (414) 257-4050

S C J MKTG INC   P 4405   SIC 6799
4041 N Main St
Racine, WI 53402
Tel (414) 631-4042

SCHUETTE BLDG CENTERS INC   P 4488   SIC 6512
901 N Cherry St
Wausau, WI 54401
Tel (715) 675-9428

FRIEDBERG JACK & ASSOC FIN   P 1963   SIC 6799
414 W 7th Ave
Cheyenne, WY 82003
Tel (307) 634-1530

TUTTLE INVESTMENTS   P 5170   SIC 6799
520 E 18th St
Cheyenne, WY 82003
Tel (307) 634-7924

COULTER DARREL R & CO   P 1223   SIC 6799
2608 Meadow Ln
Gillette, WY 82716
Tel (307) 686-1933

7011   HOTELS MOTELS & TOURIST COURTS

← SIC 7011 Arranged by State

EDMONDS HUGH DISCOUNT CO   P 1578   SIC 6411
423 Walnut
Centreville, AL 35042
Tel (205) 926-4846

TOURWAY INNS OF AMERICA INC   P 5088   SIC 7011
2230 Chisholm Rd
Florence, AL 35630
Tel (205) 766-2030

GILBREATH JOHN   P 2083   SIC 5251
2310 Gault Ave
Fort Payne, AL 35967
Tel (205) 845-2969

J & J MOTEL INC   P 2635   SIC 7011
1828 N Gault
Fort Payne, AL 35967
Tel (205) 845-0481

TRAVEL INN MOTEL   P 5114   SIC 7011
Hwy 43 N
Grove Hill, AL 36451
Tel (205) 275-3215

KINGS INN   P 2830   SIC 7011
11245 S Memorial Pky
Huntsville, AL 35815
Tel (205) 881-1250

JASFER MOTEL CORP INC   P 2670   SIC 7011
1400 Hwy 78 By-Pass
Jasper, AL 35501
Tel (205) 387-1421

MC CAIG MOTEL   P 3258   SIC 7011
Talladega Hwy 77
Lincoln, AL 35096
Tel (205) 763-7731

K A & ASSOCS   P 2740   SIC 7011
1100 W South Blvd
Montgomery, AL 36105
Tel (205) 281-1660

MONTGOMERY 76 AUTO TRCK PLZ*   P 3482   SIC 5541
980 W South Blvd
Montgomery, AL 36105
Tel (205) 288-3700

BRISTOL BAY NATIVE CORP   P 689   SIC 7011
445 E 5th Ave
Anchorage, AK 99501
Tel (907) 278-3602

BRISTOL CORP   P 689   SIC 7011
500 W 3rd
Anchorage, AK 99501
Tel (907) 272-7411

CALISTA CORP   P 812   SIC 1542
516 Denali St
Anchorage, AK 99501
Tel (907) 279-5516

EGEMO ROD   P 1585   SIC 4469
13320 Old Seward Hwy
Anchorage, AK 99509
Tel (907) 562-1606

PLAZA INN HOTELS INC   P 4022   SIC 7011
321 E 5th Ave
Anchorage, AK 99501
Tel (907) 276-7226

WESTMARK HOTELS INC   P 5479   SIC 7011
880 H St Ste 101
Anchorage, AK 99510
Tel (907) 272-9403

ARCTIC SLOPE REGIONAL CORP   P 283   SIC 1629
Main St
Barrow, AK 99723
Tel (907) 852-8633

RUTH ANNS RESTAURANT   P 4392   SIC 5812
Main St
Craig, AK 99921
Tel (907) 826-3377

SHAAN-SEET INC   P 4557   SIC 7011
Front St
Craig, AK 99921
Tel (907) 826-3251

KANTISHNA WILDERNESS TRAILS   P 2759   SIC 7011
Kantishna
Denali Park, AK 99755
Tel (907) 345-1160

CHOGGIUNG LTD   P 998   SIC 1521
Rur Rd
Dillingham, AK 99576
Tel (907) 842-5218

GOLDEN HORN LODGE INC   P 2115   SIC 7011
55 Miles N
Dillingham, AK 99576
Tel (907) 243-1455

CLEARY SUMMIT INC   P 1049   SIC 5941
719 2nd Ave
Fairbanks, AK 99701
Tel (907) 456-5520

GWITCHYAA ZHEE CORP   P 2224   SIC 4521
3rd St
Fort Yukon, AK 99740
Tel (907) 827-4221

BEST WESTERN BIDARKA INN   P 551   SIC 7011
Sterling Hwy
Homer, AK 99603
Tel (907) 235-8148

COUNTRY LANE INC   P 1225   SIC 7011
9300 Glacier Hwy
Juneau, AK 99801
Tel (907) 789-5005

SILVERBOW INN   P 4618   SIC 7011
120 2nd St
Juneau, AK 99801
Tel (907) 586-4146

CAPE FOX CORP   P 838   SIC 7011

  P 5486   SIC 7011

Kotzebue, AK 99752
Tel (907) 442-3301   P 3568   SIC 7011

POLARIS ENTERPRISES INC   P 4034   SIC 7011
Main St
Nome, AK 99762
Tel (907) 443-5102

SALLAK INC   P 4427   SIC 5812
918 S Colony Way
Palmer, AK 99645
Tel (907) 745-6771

TANADGUSIX CORP   P 4960   SIC 7011
Main St
St Paul Is, AK 99660
Tel (907) 546-2312

SHEE ATIKA INC   P 4573   SIC 7011
330 Seward St Rm 207
Sitka, AK 99835
Tel (907) 747-3534

BUNK HOUSE INN   P 745   SIC 7011
44701 Sterling Hwy
Soldotna, AK 99669
Tel (907) 262-7654

LAKE LUCILLE INN INC   P 2916   SIC 7011
1300 W Lucile Ln
Wasilla, AK 99687
Tel (907) 373-1776

H & H CAFE & LODGE   P 2226   SIC 7011
HC 89 Box 616
Willow, AK 99688
Tel (907) 733-2415

ROADHOUSE LODGE   P 4304   SIC 7011
Mile 4 Zimovia Hwy
Wrangell, AK 99929
Tel (907) 874-2335

FALCC INC   P 1715   SIC 7011
Main St
Yakutat, AK 99689
Tel (907) 784-3232

OASIS PARK MOTEL/APTS   P 3740   SIC 7011
126 Lee Ave
Bullhead City, AZ 86430
Tel (602) 754-2826

RIVER QUEEN CORP   P 4297   SIC 7011
7th St & Long
Bullhead City, AZ 86430
Tel (602) 754-3214

CAREFREE INN RESORT INC   P 857   SIC 7011
Mule Train Rd
Carefree, AZ 85377
Tel (602) 944-2673

HUMBLE S L CORP   P 2496   SIC 7011
Sunland Gin Rd & I-10
Casa Grande, AZ 85222
Tel (602) 836-5000

DROSOS ARTHUR   P 1500   SIC 1521
401 N Alma School Rd #6
Chandler, AZ 85224
Tel (602) 899-5551

▲AMFAC RESORTS INC   P 227   SIC 7011
5200 E Cortland Ste A-16
Flagstaff, AZ 86004
Tel (602) 527-2100

▲FAIRFIELD SNOW BOWL INC   P 1712   SIC 7011
1900 Country Club Dr
Flagstaff, AZ 86002
Tel (602) 779-6126

H & L ENTERPRISES INC   P 2229   SIC 7011
1560 E Santa Fe
Flagstaff, AZ 86001
Tel (602) 774-7186

CIRCLE G RANCHES   P 1014   SIC 7011
1600 E Lakeside

Indicates Public Ownership →

Tel (602) 638-2673
SQUIRE MOTOR INNS INC   P 4769   SIC 7011
Hwy 64
Grand Canyon, AZ 86023
Tel (206) 827-4221

BLUE DANUBE ENTERPRISES AZ*   P 603   SIC 7011
2176 Birch Sq
Lk Havasu Cy, AZ 86403
Tel (602) 855-5566

EVERGREEN AIR CENTER INC   P 1683   SIC 4582
Pinal Air Pk
Marana, AZ 85238
Tel (602) 682-4181

WHITING BROS OIL CO*   P 5502   SIC 5541
2130 E Brown Rd
Mesa, AZ 85203
Tel (602) 461-8535

HANESSIAN MERCANTILE CO*   P 2273   SIC 5712
1381 N Morley Ave
Nogales, AZ 85621
Tel (602) 287-3211

NOGALES SVC CENTER INC   P 3669   SIC 5541
3010 Tucson Hwy
Nogales, AZ 85621
Tel (602) 281-0865

TIME MOTEL   P 5061   SIC 7011
1200 Grand Ave
Nogales, AZ 85621
Tel (602) 287-4627

EL RANCHO PARKER MOTEL   P 1592   SIC 7011
709 California Ave
Parker, AZ 85344
Tel (602) 669-6186

DINOSAUR CAVERNS INC   P 1445   SIC 7999
PO Box 108
Peach Springs, AZ 86434
Tel (602) 422-3223

A W RENTALS INC   P 20   SIC 5812
2225 W Mtn View Ste A
Phoenix, AZ 85021
Tel (602) 943-1515

AIRPORT INN OF TUCSON INC   P 98   SIC 7011
342 W Campbell Ave
Phoenix, AZ 85013
Tel (602) 274-5885

ASSOCIATED HOTELS INC   P 323   SIC 7011
1312 N 1st St
Phoenix, AZ 85004
Tel (602) 253-4463

▲CRESCENT HOTEL GROUP*   P 1253   SIC 7011
2735 E Camelback Rd
Phoenix, AZ 85016
Tel (602) 955-8833

D S H INC   P 1310   SIC 7011
1325 Grand Ave
Phoenix, AZ 85007
Tel (602) 258-8971

DOUBLETREE INC   P 1484   SIC 7011
6225 N 24th St
Phoenix, AZ 85016
Tel (602) 955-6666

▲GLACIER PARK INC   P 2092   SIC 7011
3800 N Central Ave
Phoenix, AZ 85012
Tel (602) 248-2600

GOSNELL DEV CORP   P 2133   SIC 1542
2728 N 24th St
Phoenix, AZ 85008
Tel (602) 956-4300

HOTEL PNCHTRAIN LTD PRTNERSHIP   P 2467   SIC 7011
2735 E Camelback
Phoenix, AZ 85016
Tel (602) 954-0084

INNSUITES INTL INNS & RESORTS   P 2575   SIC 6531
7204 N 16th St
Phoenix, AZ 85020
Tel (602) 944-1500

INTERNATIONAL LEISURE HOSTS*   P 2599   SIC 7011
4530 N Central Ave
Phoenix, AZ 85012
Tel (602) 274-7558

J P K INC   P 2646   SIC 1721
10651 N 21st Ave
Phoenix, AZ 85068
Tel (602) 944-4441

KITCHELL CORP   P 2839   SIC 1541
1006 S 24th St
Phoenix, AZ 85034
Tel (602) 275-7541

PARAGON HOTELS CORP   P 3869   SIC 7011
5333 N 7th St
Phoenix, AZ 85014
Tel (602) 248-0811

PHOENIX RESORT CORP   P 3980   SIC 7011
2735 E Camelback Rd
Phoenix, AZ 85016
Tel (602) 957-7170

▲PINNACLE WEST CAPITAL CORP   P 4000   SIC 4911
2828 N Centl Ave Ste 800
Phoenix, AZ 85072
Tel (602) 250-1000

POINTE RESORTS INC   P 4032   SIC 7011
7677 N 16th St
Phoenix, AZ 85020
Tel (602) 997-2626

▲RAMADA HOTEL OPERATING CO*   P 4184   SIC 7011
3838 E Van Buren St
Phoenix, AZ 85008
Tel (602) 273-4000

▲RAMADA INC   P 4184   SIC 7011
2390 E Camelback Rd
Phoenix, AZ 85016
Tel (602) 273-4000

ROMCO FINANCIAL CORP   P 4342   SIC 7011
5333 N 7th St
Phoenix, AZ 85014
Tel (602) 248-0811

ROSTLAND AMERICA INC   P 4359   SIC 1531
2701 E Arizona Bltmr Cir
Phoenix, AZ 85016
Tel (602) 956-5335

ROSTLAND AZ INC   P 4360   SIC 7011
2701 E Arizona Bltmr Cir
Phoenix, AZ 85016
Tel (602) 956-5335

SCOTTSDALE HOSPITALITY   P 4505   SIC 7011
7204 N 16th St
Phoenix, AZ 85020
Tel (602) 944-1500

TUCSON DOUBLETREE PLZ INC   P 5160   SIC 7011
6225 N 24th St Ste 200
Phoenix, AZ 85016
Tel (602) 955-6666

▲WAHWEAP LODGE & MARINA INC   P 5360   SIC 4469
3800 N Centl Ave 15th Fl
Phoenix, AZ 85038
Tel (602) 264-8011

▲WEBB DEL E CORP   P 5416   SIC 6552
3800 N Central Ave
Phoenix, AZ 85012
Tel (602) 264-8011

HOLIDAY T M INC   P 2427   SIC 5812
409 S Montezuma
Prescott, AZ 86301
Tel (602) 445-2050

WHITING BROS INV CO*   P 5502   SIC 5502
75 E Commercial
St Johns, AZ 85936
Tel (602) 337-4544

CHAPARRAL ASSOCS INC   P 958   SIC 7011
5001 N Scottsdale Rd
Scottsdale, AZ 85253
Tel (602) 949-1414

FIRST AMERICAN HOTEL CORP   P 1812   SIC 7011
7400 E Mc Cormick
Scottsdale, AZ 85258
Tel (602) 951-7400

TENNIS RANCH ON CAMELBACK MTN   P 5001   SIC 7011
5700 E Mc Donald Dr
Scottsdale, AZ 85253
Tel (602) 948-2100

7200 NORTH SCOTTSDALE ROAD   P 5655   SIC 7011
7400 E Mc Cormick Ste B200
Scottsdale, AZ 85258
Tel (602) 951-7400

LAUBERGE LTD PARTNERSHIP   P 2954   SIC 7011
301 Little Ln
Sedona, AZ 86336
Tel (602) 282-1661

POCO DIABLO RESORT LTD   P 4030   SIC 7011
1752 W Hwy 89A
Sedona, AZ 86336
Tel (602) 282-7333

MAXWELLS MOTELS & ENTRPRS INC   P 3247   SIC 7011
480 W Deuce of Clubs Ave
Show Low, AZ 85901
Tel (602) 537-4356

PIONEER MOTEL & RESTAURANT   P 4004   SIC 7011
141 E Hwy 70
Thatcher, AZ 85552
Tel (602) 428-0733

ARIZONA INN CO*   P 289   SIC 7011
2200 F Elm
Tucson, AZ 85719
Tel (602) 325-1541

ARIZONA SUNSHINE RANCHES*   P 290   SIC 7011
Rur Rt 8 Box 66
Tucson, AZ 85710
Tel (602) 296-6275

KAI MOTELS INC   P 2748   SIC 7011
2305 W Rothraul Rd
Tucson, AZ 85705
Tel (602) 682-3377

ROCK ROAD CONSTRUCTION CO*   P 4323   SIC 1629
2727 W Club Dr
Tucson, AZ 85741
Tel (602) 297-2271

SABINO HEALTH & FITNESS RESORT   P 4413   SIC 7011
8600 E Rockcliff Rd
Tucson, AZ 85715
Tel (602) 749-9000

TUCSON INN   P 5160   SIC 7011
127 W Drachman
Tucson, AZ 85705
Tel (602) 624-8531

Figure 7.2: "Businesses by Industry Classification" from *The Million Dollar Directory*, 1989.

But how can this reference tool answer the second question? Where can I find a list of companies in the hotel industry? In addition to identifying key facts about a particular company, *The Million Dollar Directory* can lead you to a list of companies in a particular industry.

Use the "Businesses by Industry Classification" volume of *The Million Dollar Directory*, which is printed on blue paper and is arranged by Standard Industrial Classification codes. (*The Standard Industrial Classification Manual* was discussed in chapter 1 and illustrated in figures 1.1 and 1.2.) Turn to SIC 7011 in the blue pages of *The Million Dollar Directory* (figure 7.2). Publicly owned companies are indicated by a triangle (▲). This list is sub-arranged alphabetically by state and city. To the right of each company name is the page number where you can find the full entry in the main volumes (the white pages) of *The Million Dollar Directory*.

The Million Dollar Directory has answered your two questions. Is the company private, public, or subsidiary? And what are some other big companies in the industry? It has also provided some important facts about your company. But chances are you need more information, such as: How is the company doing financially? How does it rank with other companies in the industry? How is it dealing with the overbuilt industry? Chapters 8 through 11 will teach you how to find more information on a company than that contained in directories.

SUMMARY

1) Companies may be privately or publicly owned; or a company may be a subsidiary of another company.

2) Most publicly owned companies must file a 10-K Report. In addition, most publicly owned companies also publish an annual report to shareholders. Private companies generally do not release this type of information.

3) The search strategy for company information will differ depending on the company's ownership. The first step in company research is to determine if it is a public, private, or subsidiary company. *The Million Dollar Directory* identifies over 160,000 companies and indicates their ownership status.

4) *The Million Dollar Directory* can also be used to find a list of the larger companies in an industry.

CHAPTER 8

PRIVATE COMPANIES

Red Roof Inns, Inc. is a privately owned company.

* It does not have any shareholders.

* It does not publish an annual report to shareholders.

* It is not required to file a 10-K Report with the U. S. Securities and Exchange Commission.

* It is not profiled in *Value Line Investment Survey, Moody's Manuals*, or other investment services.

As a matter of fact, Red Roof Inns' financial situation is its own affair. You will not find very much information on this private company or most other private companies! The information you will find on private companies generally will come from two sources: directories and periodicals.

Company directories include information on all kinds of businesses—private, public, and subsidiary. Dun & Bradstreet, the largest collector of company information in the world, publishes *The Million Dollar Directory*. This directory, which you learned to use in chapter 7, contains information on Red Roof Inns, Inc. (figure 8.1). In addition to address, telephone number, and names of executives, note that the directory includes total sales and number of employees. These last two figures are an indication of the size of the company.

In addition to *The Million Dollar Directory*, there are many other directories that can be consulted for company information. One of the most useful is *WARD'S BUSINESS DIRECTORY*™ (Detroit, MI: Gale Research, Inc., 1989-)which covers 85,000 private and public companies. Volume 1 and 2 provide an alphabetical listing of all companies including address; phone number; limited financial information; fiscal year end; number

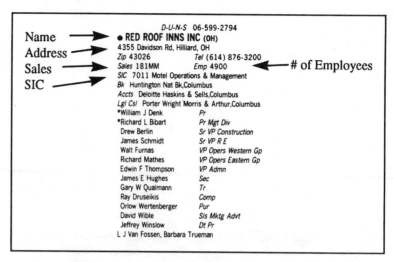

Figure 8.1: Entry for Red Roof Inns, Inc. from *The Million Dollar Directory*, 1989.

of employees; types of company, ticker symbol and exchange, if public; year founded; import/export designation, if applicable; immediate parent; SIC codes; and officers (figure 8.2).

Volume 3 of *WARD'S BUSINESS DIRECTORY*™ provides a listing of all companies arranged by zip code within each state. This feature can be very useful for sales targeting and job searching.

Volume 4 of *WARD'S BUSINESS DIRECTORY*™ is arranged according to SIC codes, and ranks companies by sales within each SIC code. Since you already know that the SIC code for the hotel industry is 7011, you can turn directly to it. However, if you do not know the SIC code for an industry, there are indexes in the front of volume 4 (figure 8.3). Figure 8.4 illustrates the ranking for SIC code 7011 on Hotels & Motels. Red Roof is ranked 39 in this list. From this list you can see which hotel companies are larger or smaller. You can also tell what *type* of company each is: R=Private, P=Public, S=Subsidiary, D=Division, J=Joint Venture, and A=Affiliate.

Although *The Million Dollar Directory* and *WARD'S BUSINESS DIRECTORY*™ both contain very similar information on Red Roof Inns, it is a good idea to check both for a particular company. In many cases a company will be listed in one directory but not the other. If your library does not have either of these two directories, there are other similar sources that might be available in your library. Check Appendix B for other titles or ask your reference librarian for other company directories available in your library.

But what are you going to do if the company you are researching is not included in any of these directories? Both *The Million Dollar Directory* and *WARD'S BUSINESS DIRECTORY*™ limit their entries to larger private companies and most small companies do not meet this criterion. Where do you look for information on these millions of smaller private companies?

Red Gold Inc.
P.O. Box 83   (317)754-7527
Elwood, IN 46036
Sales: $50.0 million
Employees: 400   **Type:** Private
Founded: 1944
SIC(s): 2033 Canned Fruits & Vegetables.
Officer(s): E.A. Reichart, *President*; Robert Savage,
Controller; C. Frazier, *Dir of Mktg.*

W.S. Red Hancock Inc.
P.O. Box 207   (601)755-2931
Bentonia, MS 39040
Operating Revenues: $6.0 million
Employees: 200   **Type:** Private
Founded: 1943
SIC(s): 1629 Heavy Construction Nec; 1389 Oil & Gas Field
Svcs Nec.
Officer(s): WR Hancock, *President*; George Kirtley, *CFO*;
Roy Hancock, *Genl Mgr.*

Red Hill Grinding Wheel Corp.
P.O. Box 150   (215)679-7964
Pennsburg, PA 18073
Sales: $2.5 million
Employees: 40   **Type:** Private
Founded: 1948
SIC(s): 3291 Abrasive Prdts.
Officer(s): RT Caserta, *President.*

Red-Kap Sales Inc.
Erie Blvd.   (518)377-6431
Schenectady, NY 12308
Sales: $20.0 million
Employees: 25   **Type:** Private
Founded: 1933
SIC(s): 5172 Petroleum Prdts Nec; 5013 Motor Vehicle
Supplies & New Parts.
Officer(s): FR Kaplan, *President*; HR Kaplan, *Chm Bd &
Treas*; Anthony Famiano, *Dir of Mktg.*

Red L Foods Inc.
15 Commerce Dr.   (203)268-8633
Monroe, CT 06468
Sales: $11.7 million   **Fiscal Year End:** 10-01
Employees: 90   **Type:** Private
Founded: 1971   **Import/Export**
SIC(s): 2051 Bread, Cake & Related Prdts.
Officer(s): S Patrice, *President*; Margaret Dragone, *Vice
President.*

Red Lake Electric Cooperative Inc.
South Side   (218)253-2168
Red Lake Falls, MN 56750
Total Assets: $5.0 million
Employees: 25   **Type:** Private
Founded: 1938
SIC(s): 4911 Electric Svcs.
Officer(s): V Arveson, *President.*

Red Lake Fisheries Assn.
P.O. Box 56   (218)679-3813
Redby, MN 56670
Sales: $1.0 million
Employees: 24   **Type:** Private
Founded: 1929
SIC(s): 2092 Fresh or Frozen Prepared Fish.
Officer(s): JB Eisenrich, *Genl Mgr.*

Red Lake Forest Products
P.O. Box 68   (218)679-3346
Redby, MN 56670
Sales: $5.0 million
Employees: 15   **Type:** Private
Founded: 1924
SIC(s): 2421 Sawmills & Planing Mills—Genl.
Officer(s): R Barrett, *Mgr*; Richard Barrett, *Dir of Mktg.*

Red Level Fashions Inc.
P.O. Box 186   (205)469-5317
Red Level, AL 36474
Sales: $13.4* million
Employees: 200   **Type:** Subsidiary
Founded: 1970
Immediate Parent: Judy Bond Inc.
SIC(s): 2331 Women/Misses/Juniors' Blouses & Shirts.
Officer(s): R Parrott, *Mgr.*

Red Lion Controls Inc.
Willow Springs Circle   (717)767-6511
York, PA 17402
Sales: $15.0 million
Employees: 100   **Type:** Private
Founded: Not available   **Export**
SIC(s): 3824 Fluid Meters & Counting Devices.
Officer(s): Lester Goodman, *CEO*; Peter Anzalone, *Mktg Mgr.*

Red Lion Hotels & Inns
4001 Main St.   (206)696-0001
Vancouver, WA 98663
Sales: $350.0 million   **Fiscal Year End:** 12-31
Employees: Not available   **Type:** Private
Founded: 1959
SIC(s): 7011 Hotels & Motels.
Description: Services: Hotel chain with food service.
Officer(s): Jerry Best, *CEO & Pres*; Raymond Bingham,
CFO; Steve Giblin, *Exec VP of Mktg*; Cliff Barry, *Dir of
Data Processing*; Steve Hubbard, *Dir of Human Resources.*

Red Lion Inns. Bellevue Center
818 112th N.E.   (206)455-1515
Bellevue, WA 98004
Sales: $4.5 million
Employees: 100   **Type:** Division
Founded: 1962
Immediate Parent: Red Lion Hotels & Inns
SIC(s): 7011 Hotels & Motels; 5812 Eatin
Drinking Places.
Officer(s): Mark McElrath, *Genl Mgr*; In
Controller; Charles Hamby, *Dir of Mki*

Red Lion Inns. Red Lion Mot
3280 Gateway St.   ,1
Springfield, OR 97477
Sales: $7.0 million
Employees: 125   **Type:** Division
Founded: 1981
Immediate Parent: Red Lion Hotels & Inns
SIC(s): 7011 Hotels & Motels; 5812 Eating Places.
Officer(s): John Erickson, *CEO*; Michael Ruell, *CFO*; Jeanne
Brunner, *Dir of Sales.*

Red McDevitt Inc.
2610 Erie Blvd. E.   (315)446-7590
Syracuse, NY 13224
Sales: $4.0 million
Employees: 15   **Type:** Private
Founded: 1956
SIC(s): 5083 Farm & Garden Machinery; 5084 Industrial
Machinery & Equip.
Officer(s): Charles H. McDevitt, *Pres & Treas*; R Cuddihe,
VP of Mktg.

Red Owl Stores Inc.
215 E. Excelsior Ave.   (612)932-2132
Hopkins, MN 55343
Sales: $800.0* million
Employees: 2,500   **Type:** Private
Founded: 1928
SIC(s): 5141 Groceries—Genl Line; 5411 Grocery Stores;
2051 Bread, Cake & Related Prdts.
Officer(s): C. Patrick Schulke, *CEO & Pres*; Charles Bidwell,
VP of Fin; John Stubstad, *Dir of Systems.*

Red Panther Chemical Co.
P.O. Box 550   (601)627-4731
Clarksdale, MS 38614
Sales: $15.0 million
Employees: 100   **Type:** Subsidiary
Founded: Not available
Immediate Parent: MFC Services
SIC(s): 2879 Agricultural Chems Nec.
Officer(s): J Duff, *President.*

Red-Ray Mfg. Co. Inc.
318 Cliff Ln.   (201)943-1000
Cliffside Park, NJ 07010
Sales: $1.0 million
Employees: 10   **Type:** Private
Founded: 1940   **Import/Export**
SIC(s): 3567 Industrial Furnaces & Ovens.
Officer(s): Mark J. O'Friel, *President*; James D. O'Neal, *Vice
President.*

Red River Implements Co.
Hwy. 75 S.   (218)643-2601
Breckenridge, MN 56520
Sales: $7.0* million
Employees: 15   **Type:** Private
Founded: 1969
SIC(s): 5083 Farm & Garden Machinery.
Officer(s): Ronald Offutt, *President.*

Red River Marine Inc.
2001 Hwy. 25 N.   (501)362-3171
Heber Springs, AR 72543
Sales: $7.0* million
Employees: 30   **Type:** Private
Founded: 1960
SIC(s): 5551 Boat Dealers.
Officer(s): Bernard Hargrove, *CEO.*

Red River Motor Co.
P.O. Box 5696   (318)742-3411
Bossier City, LA 71171
Sales: $25.0 million
Employees: 93   **Type:** Private
Founded: 1931
SIC(s): 5511 New & Used Car Dealers; 5531 Auto & Home
Supply Stores.
Officer(s): JN Fritze, *CEO*; GP Fritze, *Genl Mgr.*

Red River Valley Cooperative Power Assn.
P.O. Box 358   (218)456-2139
Halstad, MN 56548
Total Assets: $3.0 million
Employees: 25   **Type:** Private
Founded: 1937
SIC(s): 4911 Electric Svcs.
Officer(s): Ernest Oberg, *President*; Michael P. McMahon,
Genl Mgr; Sandra Haddeland, *Dir of Mktg.*

Red Rock Feeding Co.
P.O. Box 1039   (602)682-3448
Red Rock, AZ 85245
Sales: $16.0 million
Employees: 35   **Type:** Private
Founded: 1965
SIC(s): 0211 Beef Cattle Feedlots.
Officer(s): CG Stevenson, *President.*

Red Roof Inns Inc.
4355 Davidson Rd.   (614)876-3200
Hilliard, OH 43026
Sales: $170.0 million
Employees: 6,000   **Type:** Private
Founded: 1973
SIC(s): 7011 Hotels & Motels.
Officer(s): B Trueman, *Chairman of the Board*; G.
Qualmann, *Finance Officer*; David Wible, *Dir of Mktg*; Jeff
Winslow, *Dir of Systems.*

Red Seal Snack Co.
Box 7125   (303)399-2333
Denver, CO 80207
Sales: $33.0* million
Employees: 335   **Type:** Subsidiary
Founded: 1911
Immediate Parent: Borden Inc. Snacks & Intl. Consumer
Prdts. Div.
SIC(s): 2096 Potato Chips & Similar Snacks.
Description: Manufacturing: Snack chips.
Officer(s): Joe Strasser, *Mgr*; G. Bennett, *Controller*; P.
Mayer, *VP of Mktg.*

Red Spot Paint Varnish Co.
P.O. Box 418   (812)428-9100
Evansville, IN 47703
Sales: $56.0 million
Employees: 390   **Type:** Private
Founded: 1903   **Export**
SIC(s): 2851 Paints & Allied Prdts; 5198 Paints, Varnishes &
Supplies.
Officer(s): CD Storms, *President*; Steve Halling, *CFO*; M
Rhiver, *Dir of Mktg*; Larry Shoptau, *Dir of Systems*; Don
Johnson, *Dir of Human Resources.*

Red Spot Westland Inc.
550 S. Edwin   (313)729-7400
Westland, MI 48185
Sales: $16.8* million
Employees: 70   **Type:** Subsidiary
Founded: 1937
Immediate Parent: Red Spot Paint Varnish Co.
SIC(s): 2851 Paints & Allied Prdts.
Officer(s): Norman Rice, *Genl Mgr.*

Red Stick Services Inc.
205 N. 19th St.   (504)383-5267
Baton Rouge, LA 70806
Sales: $25.0* million
Employees: 575   **Type:** Subsidiary
Founded: 1930
Immediate Parent: Cintas Corp.
SIC(s): 7218 Industrial Launderers.
Description: Services: Industrial uniform rental.
Officer(s): John Kean III, *President*; Bob Buck, *Controller*; T.
Debenetto, *VP of Mktg.*

Red Tiger Drilling Co.
1720 Kan. State Bank   (316)263-2371
Wichita, KS 67202
Sales: $12.0 million
Employees: 200   **Type:** Private
Founded: 1954
SIC(s): 1381 Drilling Oil & Gas Wells.
Officer(s): GA Angle, *Owner.*

Red Top Sedan Service Inc.
P.O. Box 59207   (305)871-2370
Miami, FL 33159
Operating Revenues: $5.0 million
Employees: 300   **Type:** Private
Founded: 1929
SIC(s): 4119 Local Passenger Tranport Nec.
Officer(s): J Nudelman, *President.*

Red-White Valve Corp.
22527 S. Wilmington   (213)549-1010
Carson, CA 90745
Sales: $10.0 million
Employees: 13   **Type:** Private
Founded: 1971   **Import/Export**
SIC(s): 3494 Valves & Pipe Fittings Nec.
Officer(s): S Kitazawa, *President*; S Kitazawa, *CFO*; Mike
Lanzit, *VP of Mktg.*

Figure 8.2: Entry for Red Roof Inns, Inc. from *WARD'S BUSINESS DIRECTORY*, 1990.

Heavy Construction Equip Rental	7353	Laminated Plastics Plate & Sheet	3083
Heavy Construction Nec	1629	Landscape Counseling & Planning	0781
Help Supply Svcs	7363	Laundry & Garment Svcs Nec	7219
Highway & Street Construction	1611	Lawn & Garden Equip	3524
Hobby, Toy & Game Shops	5945	Lawn & Garden Svcs	0782
Hogs	0213	Lead & Zinc Ores	1031
Hoists, Cranes & Monorails	3536	Lead Pencils & Art Goods	3952
Holding Companies Nec	6719	Leather & Sheep-Lined Clothing	2386
Home Health Care Svcs	8082	Leather Gloves & Mittens	3151
Homefurnishings	5023	Leather Goods Nec	3199
Horses & Other Equines	0272	Leather Tanning & Finishing	3111
Hosiery Nec	2252	Legal Svcs	8111
Hospital & Medical Svc Plans	6324	Libraries	8231
Hotels & Motels	7011	Life Insurance	6311
House Slippers	3142	Lighting Equip Nec	3648
Housefurnishings Nec	2392	Lime	3274
Household Appliance Stores	5722	Linen Supply	7213
Household Appliances Nec	3639	Liquefied Petroleum Gas Dealers	5984
Household Audio & Video Equip	3651	Liquor Stores	5921
Household Cooking Equip	3631	Livestock	5154
Household Furniture Nec	2519	Livestock Svcs Exc Veterinary	0751
Household Laundry Equip	3633	Loan Brokers	6163
Household Refrigerators & Freezers	3632	Local & Suburban Transit	4111
Household Vacuum Cleaners	3635	Local Bus Charter Svc	4141
Hunting, Trapping & Game Propagation	0971	Local Passenger Tranport Nec	4119
Ice Cream & Frozen Desserts	2024	Local Trucking with Storage	4214
Individual & Family Svcs	8322	Local Trucking Without Storage	4212
Industrial & Personal Svc Paper	5113	Logging	2411
Industrial Bldgs & Warehouses	1541	Lubricating Oils & Greases	2992
Industrial Furnaces & Ovens	3567	Luggage	3161
Industrial Gases	2813	Luggage & Leather Goods Stores	5948
Industrial Inorganic Chems Nec	2819	Lumber & Other Bldg Materials	5211
Industrial Launderers	7218	Lumber, Plywood & Millwork	5031
Industrial Machinery & Equip	5084	Macaroni & Spaghetti	2098
Industrial Machinery Nec	3599	Machine Tool Accessories	3545
Industrial Organic Chems Nec	2869	Machine Tools—Metal Cutting Types	3541
Industrial Patterns	3543	Machine Tools—Metal Forming Types	3542
Industrial Sand	1446	Magnetic & Optical Recording Media	3695
Industrial Supplies	5085	Malleable Iron Foundries	3322
Industrial Trucks & Tractors	3537	Malt	2083
Industrial Valves	3491	Malt Beverages	2082
Information Retrieval Svcs	7375	Management Investment—Open-end	6722
Inorganic Pigments	2816	Manifold Bus Forms	2761
Inspection & Fixed Facilities	4785	Manufactured Ice	2097
Installation Bldg Equip Nec	1796	Marinas	4493
Instruments to Measure Electricity	3825	Marine Cargo Handling	4491
Insurance & Diversified Financial Cos	6341	Marking Devices	3953
Insurance Agents, Brokers & Svc	6411	Masonry & Other Stonework	1741
Insurance Carriers Nec	6399	Mattresses & Bedsprings	2515
Intercity & Rural Bus Transport	4131	Measuring & Controlling Devices Nec	3829
Intermediate Care Facilities	8052	Measuring & Dispensing Pumps	3586
Internal Combustion Engines Nec	3519	Meat & Fish Markets	5421
Investment Advice	6282	Meat Packing Plants	2011
Investment Offices Nec	6726	Meats & Meat Prdts	5147
Investors Nec	6799	Mechanical Rubber Goods	3061
Irish Potatoes	0134	Medical & Hospital Equip	5047
Iron & Steel Forgings	3462	Medical Equip Rental	7352
Iron Ores	1011	Medical Laboratories	8071
Irrigation Systems	4971	Medicinals & Botanicals	2833
Jewelers' Materials & Lapidary Work	3915	Membership Sports & Recreation Clubs	7997
Jewelry & Precious Metal	3911	Membership-Basis Orgn Hotels	7041
Jewelry & Precious Stones	5094	Men's Footwear Exc Athletic	3143
Jewelry Stores	5944	Men/Boys' Clothing	5136
Job Training & Related Svcs	8331	Men/Boys' Clothing Nec	2329
Junior Colleges	8222	Men/Boys' Clothing Stores	5611
Kaolin & Ball Clay	1455	Men/Boys' Neckwear	2323
Kidney Dialysis Centers	8092	Men/Boys' Shirts	2321
Knit Outerwear Mills	2253	Men/Boys' Suits & Coats	2311
Knit Underwear Mills	2254	Men/Boys' Trousers & Slacks	2325
Knitting Mills Nec	2259	Men/Boys' Underwear & Nightwear	2322
Laboratory Apparatus & Furniture	3821	Men/Boys' Work Clothing	2326
Lace & Warp Knit Fabric Mills	2258	Merchandising Machine Operators	5962

**Figure 8.3: "Index of Standard Industrial Classifications (S.I.C.s)—Alphabetical Listings,"
WARD'S BUSINESS DIRECTORY, 1990.**

Rank Company Name	Address	City	St	Zip	Phone	Type	Sales	Empls
6 Hilton Hotels Corp.	9336 Civic Center Dr.	Beverly Hills	CA	90209	213-278-4321	P	915	38.0
7 Hilton Intl. Co.	605 Third Ave.	New York	NY	10158	212-973-2200	S	897	40.0
8 Caesars World Inc.	1801 Century Pk. E., 2	Los Angeles	CA	90067	213-552-2711	S	776	10.0
9 Sheraton Corp.	60 State St.	Boston	MA	02109	617-367-3600	S	773	N/A
10 Radisson Hotels Intl. Inc.	P.O. Box 59159	Minneapolis	MN	55459	612-540-5526	S	760	20.0
11 Omni Hotels Corp.	500 Lafayette Rd.	Hampton	NH	03842	603-926-8911	S	500	9.0
12 Westin Hotel Co.	Westin Bldg.	Seattle	WA	98121	206-443-5248	S	500*	26.5
13 Ramada Inc.	2390 E. Camelback Rd.	Phoenix	AZ	85016	602-273-4000	P	477	20.2
14 Red Lion Hotels & Inns	4001 Main St.	Vancouver	WA	98663	206-696-0001	R	350	N/A
15 Motel 6 L.P.	14651 Dallas Pkwy.	Dallas	TX	75240	214-386-6161	P	338	9.6
16 Caesars Palace Inc.	3570 Las Vegas Blvd. S.	Las Vegas	NV	89109	702-731-7110	S	333	4.0
Caesars World Inc.								
17 Caesars New Jersey Inc.	1801 Century Pk. E., #	Los Angeles	CA	90067	213-552-2711	P	330	3.4
Caesars World Inc.								
18 Loew's Hotels Inc.	667 Madison Ave.	New York	NY	10021	212-545-2000	S	314	4.5
19 Showboat Inc.	2800 E. Fremont St.	Las Vegas	NV	89104	702-385-9123	P	295	5.1
20 Boyd Group	3000 Las Vegas Blvd. S.	Las Vegas	NV	89109	702-732-6501	R	290*	7.5
21 California Hotel & Casino Inc.	3000 Las Vegas Blvd. S.	Las Vegas	NV	89109	702-732-6111	R	287	7.2
22 Prime Motor Inns Inc.	700 Rt. 46 E.	Fairfield	NJ	07006	201-882-1010	P	277	8.5
23 Doubletree Inc.	410 N. 44th St., 700	Phoenix	AZ	85008	602-220-6666	S	275	10.0
24 Bally's Park Place Inc.	Park Pl. at Boardwalk	Atlantic City	NJ	08401	609-340-2000	S	265*	3.8
25 Mark Hemstreet Property Development Co.	11600 S.W. Barnes Rd.	Portland	OR	97225	503-641-6565	R	260	3.0
26 Stouffer Hotel Co.	29800 Bainbridge Rd.	Solon	OH	44139	216-248-3600	S	260*	11.6
27 Bally's Grand Hotel Casino	P.O. Box 1737	Atlantic City	NJ	08404	609-347-7111	S	250*	3.0
28 Kyo-Ya Co. Ltd.	255 Kalakaua Ave., 2ND	Honolulu	HI	96815	808-922-4422	R	250	4.1
29 Pratt Hotel Corp.	2 Galleria Tower	Dallas	TX	75240	214-386-9777	P	242	3.5
30 Showboat Inc. Atlantic City	801 Boardwalk	Atlantic City	NJ	08401	609-343-4000	S	241	3.8
Showboat Inc.								
31 Las Vegas Hilton	3000 Paradise Rd.	Las Vegas	NV	89109	702-732-5111	S	230	4.0
Hilton Hotels Corp.								
32 Greate Bay Casino Corp.	P.O. Box 627	Atlantic City	NJ	08404	609-441-4000	S	220*	3.0
Pratt Hotel Corp.								
33 MGM Grand Inc.	9744 Wilshire Blvd., St	Beverly Hills	CA	90212	213-271-3793	P	208	4.0
34 JMB Realty Corp. Arvida Co.	P.O. Box 100	Boca Raton	FL	33429	407-479-1100	D	200*	2.4
35 Servico Inc.	1601 Belvedere Rd.	West Palm Beach	FL	33406	407-689-9970	P	195	9.2
36 Fairmont Hotel Co.	950 Mason St.	San Francisco	CA	94108	415-772-5000	R	190*	5.0
37 Trusthouse Forte Inc.	1973 Friendship Dr.	El Cajon	CA	92020	619-448-1884	S	180*	2.0
38 La Quinta Motor Inns Inc.	10010 San Pedro	San Antonio	TX	78216	512-366-6000	P	174	6.3
→ 39 Red Roof Inns Inc.	4355 Davidson Rd.	Hilliard	OH	43026	614-876-3200	R	170	6.0
40 Larken Inc.	P.O. Box 1808	Cedar Rapids	IA	52406	319-366-8201	R	168	N/A
41 Holiday Corp. Holiday Inn-Holiday Casino	3475 Las Vegas Blvd. S.	Las Vegas	NV	89109	702-369-5000	D	165	2.4
Holiday Corp.								
42 Bally's Grand Inc.	Boston Ave at Pacific	Atlantic City	NJ	08401	609-347-7111	S	160*	7.5
43 Desert Inn Hotel & Casino	3145 Las Vegas Blvd. S.	Las Vegas	NV	89109	702-733-4444	S	150	4.0
MGM Grand Inc.								
44 Harley Hotels Inc.	1310 Terminal Tower	Cleveland	OH	44113	216-623-3900	S	150	2.6
45 Ramada Inc. Tropicana Resort & Casino	3801 Las Vegas Blvd. S.	Las Vegas	NV	89109	702-739-2222	D	150	2.7
Ramada Inc.								
46 Shilo Inns	11600 S.W. Barnes Rd.	Portland	OR	97225	503-641-6565	R	150	2.5
47 United Inns Inc.	5100 Poplar Ave., 2300	Memphis	TN	38137	901-767-2880	R	143	3.3
48 Imperial Palace Inc.	3535 Las Vegas Blvd. S.	Las Vegas	NV	89109	702-731-3311	R	140	2.0
49 Riviera Hotel & Casino	2901 Las Vegas Blvd. S.	Las Vegas	NV	89109	702-734-5110	R	140	1.5
50 El Rancho Hotel	2755 Las Vegas Blvd. S.	Las Vegas	NV	89109	702-796-2222	R	135	.6
51 Amfac Resorts Inc.	5200 E. Cortland Blvd.	Flagstaff	AZ	86004	602-527-2100	S	134	2.5
52 Days Inns Corp.	2751 N.E. Buford Hwy.	Atlanta	GA	30324	404-329-7466	S	128	5.3
53 Hilton Hawaiian Village	2005 Kalia Rd.	Honolulu	HI	96815	808-949-4321	J	125	2.0
54 Hotel Operating Co. of Hawaii Ltd.	2375 Kuhio Ave.	Honolulu	HI	96815	808-921-6601	R	125	2.4
55 United Inns Inc. Hotel Div.	5100 Poplar Ave.	Memphis	TN	38137	901-767-2880	D	124	N/A
United Inns Inc.								
56 Hershey Entertainment & Resort Co.	300 Park Blvd.	Hershey	PA	17033	717-534-3131	R	120	3.0
57 Del Webb Corp.	2231 E. Camelback Rd.	Phoenix	AZ	85016	602-468-6800	S	107	2.1
58 Stardust Hotel & Casino	3000 Las Vegas Blvd. S.	Las Vegas	NV	89109	702-732-6111	S	105	2.2
Boyd Group								
59 Colonial Williamsburg Foundation	P.O. Drawer C	Williamsburg	VA	23185	804-229-1000	R	100	3.6
60 Jack Tar Villages Resorts	1314 Wood St.	Dallas	TX	75202	214-670-9800	S	100*	3.5
61 Union Plaza Hotel & Casino Inc.	P.O. Box 760	Las Vegas	NV	89125	702-386-2110	S	99	1.6
62 Sahara Resorts	2535 Las Vegas Blvd. S.	Las Vegas	NV	89109	702-737-2111	P	94	1.6
63 Elsinore Corp.	202 E. Fremont St.	Las Vegas	NV	89101	702-385-4011	P	93	1.1
64 Integra-A Hotel & Restaurant Co.	4441 W. Airport Fwy.	Irving	TX	75015	214-258-8500	P	87	3.2
65 Bally's Grand Inc. Bally's Casino Resort-Las Vegas	3645 Las Vegas Blvd. S.	Las Vegas	NV	89109	702-739-4401	D	85	4.0
Bally's Grand Inc.								
66 El Pomar Foundation	P.O. Box 158	Colorado Springs	CO	80901	719-633-7733	R	85*	1.3
67 Days Inns of America Inc.	2751 Buford Hwy. N.E.	Atlanta	GA	30324	404-329-7466	S	80*	4.0
Days Inns Corp.								
68 S-K-I Ltd.	Killington Rd.	Killington	VT	05751	802-422-3333	P	76	N/A
69 Quality Inns Intl. Inc.	10750 Columbia Pike	Silver Spring	MD	20901	301-593-5600	S	76	2.0
70 Atlas Hotels Inc.	P.O. Box 80098	San Diego	CA	92138	619-291-2232	R	75	2.9
71 Bally's Grand Inc. Bally's Reno	2500 E. Second St.	Reno	NV	89595	702-789-2000	S	75	3.5
Bally's Grand Inc.								
72 El Cortez Hotel & Casino	600 E. Fremont	Las Vegas	NV	89101	702-385-5200	R	72*	1.2
73 Steamboat Ski Corp.	2305 Mount Werner Cir.	Steamboat Springs	CO	80487	303-879-6111	R	70	1.2
74 Yosemite Park & Curry Co.	P.O. Box 578	Yosemite National	CA	95389	209-372-1000	S	70	1.7
75 Super 8 Motels Inc.	1910 Eighth Ave. N.E.	Aberdeen	SD	57401	605-225-2272	S	68	.3
76 Killington Ltd.	Killington Rd.	Killington	VT	05751	802-422-3333	R	66	1.6
S-K-I Ltd.								
77 Broadmoor Hotel Inc.	1 Lake Circle	Colorado Springs	CO	80906	719-633-7733	S	65	1.1
78 TraveLodge Intl. Inc.	1973 Friendship Dr.	El Cajon	CA	92020	619-448-1884	S	63*	1.4
79 Aspen Skiing Co.	P.O. Box 1248	Aspen	CO	81612	303-925-1220	R	60*	1.6
80 Exber Inc.	107 N. Sixth St.	Las Vegas	NV	89101	702-385-1664	R	60	1.5
81 Hagadon Corp.	P.O. Box 1178	Coeur D'Alene	ID	83814	208-667-3431	R	60	1.6
82 Orient-Express Hotels Inc.	1155 Ave. of the Amer.	New York	NY	10036	212-302-5055	P	60	.5
83 Sonesta Intl. Hotels Corp.	200 Clarendon St.	Boston	MA	02116	617-421-5400	P	58	1.7
84 Palace Station Inc.	P.O. Box 26448	Las Vegas	NV	89126	702-367-2411	P	58*	1.5
85 Golf Host Resorts Inc.	P.O. Box 3131	Durango	CO	81302	303-259-2000	S	56	N/A
86 Breakers Palm Beach Inc.	P.O. Box 910	Palm Beach	FL	33480	407-655-6611	S	55	1.2
87 Maxim Hotel & Casino	160 E. Flamingo Rd.	Las Vegas	NV	89109	702-731-4300	R	55	1.1
88 Laughlin Recreational Enterprises Inc.	2525 W. Charleston Blvd	Las Vegas	NV	89102	702-877-0007	P	54	N/A
89 Aircoa Hotel Partners L.P.	4600 S. Ulster St. Pkwy	Denver	CO	80237	303-220-2000	P	53	1.3
90 Kahler Corp.	20 2nd Ave. S.W.	Rochester	MN	55902	507-282-2581	P	52	2.2

Figure 8.4: Red Roof Inns Ranked in Respective S.I.C. Industries from *WARDS BUSINESS DIRECTORY*, 1990.

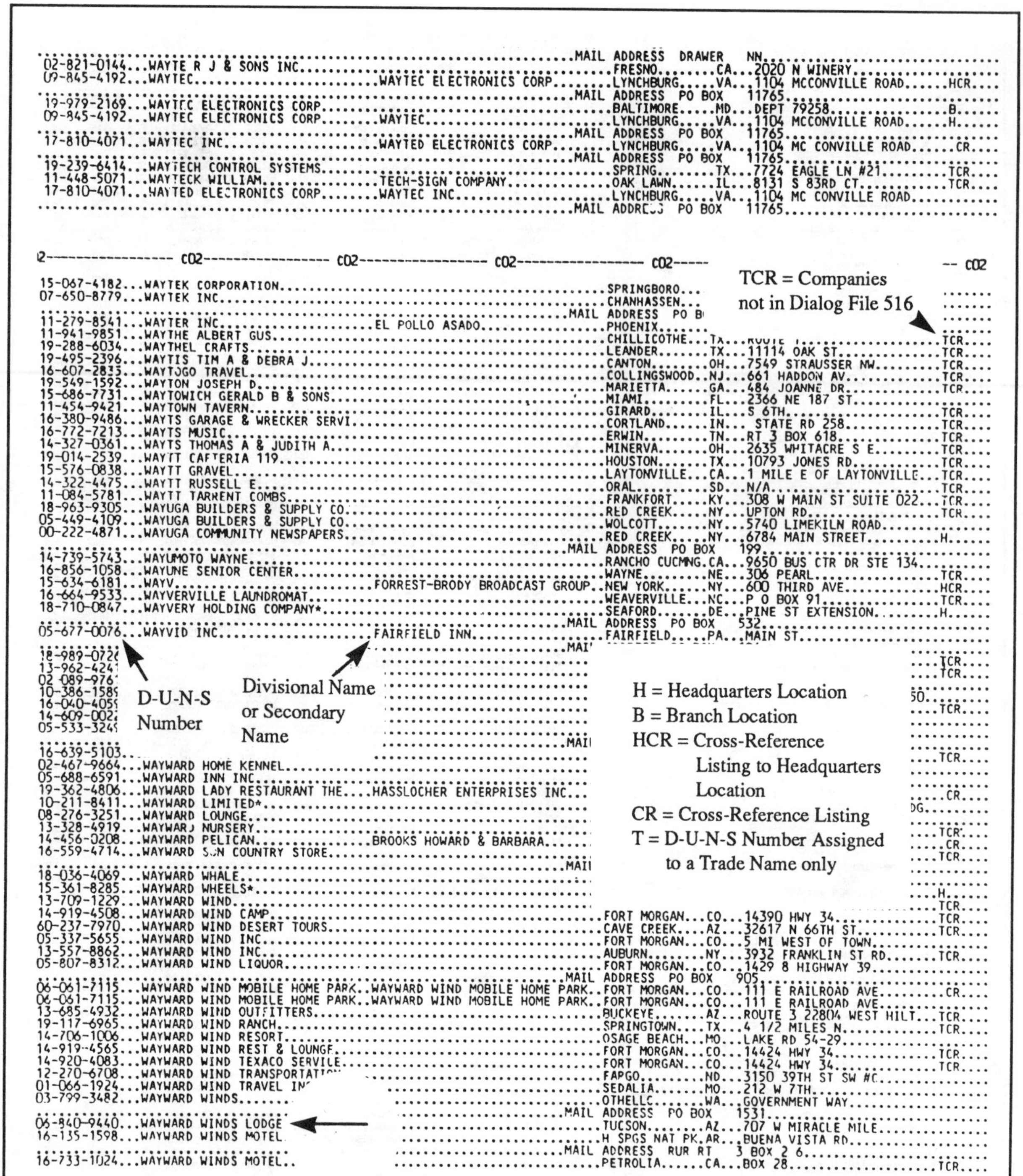

```
02-821-0144...WAYTE R J & SONS INC................................................MAIL ADDRESS DRAWER  NN...............
09-845-4192...WAYTEC.........................WAYTEC ELECTRONICS CORP...FRESNO.........CA..2020 N WINERY..............
19-979-2169...WAYTEC ELECTRONICS CORP.........................................LYNCHBURG..VA..1104 MCCONVILLE ROAD.....HCR...
                                                                    MAIL ADDRESS PO BOX  11765
09-845-4192...WAYTEC ELECTRONICS CORP.........WAYTEC.............BALTIMORE....MD..DEPT 79258.................B....
                                                                    LYNCHBURG..VA..1104 MCCONVILLE ROAD......H..
17-810-4071...WAYTEC INC....................WAYTED ELECTRONICS CORP...LYNCHBURG..VA..1104 MC CONVILLE ROAD.....CR..
                                                                    MAIL ADDRESS PO BOX  11765
19-239-6414...WAYTECH CONTROL SYSTEMS..............................SPRING.......TX..7724 EAGLE LN #21......TCR...
11-448-5071...WAYTECK WILLIAM................TECH-SIGN COMPANY......OAK LAWN....IL..8131 S 83RD CT........TCR...
17-810-4071...WAYTED ELECTRONICS CORP........WAYTEC INC.............LYNCHBURG..VA..1104 MC CONVILLE ROAD.....CR..
                                                                    MAIL ADDRESS PO BOX  11765
```

```
12----------------C02----------------C02----------------C02----------------C02-----                    -- C02
15-067-4182...WAYTEK CORPORATION..............................................SPRINGBORO...
07-650-8779...WAYTEK INC......................................................CHANHASSEN...
11-279-8541...WAYTER INC...................EL POLLO ASADO.......MAIL ADDRESS PO B
11-941-9851...WAYTHE ALBERT GUS...............................PHOENIX......                          TCR...
19-288-6034...WAYTHEL CRAFTS..................................CHILLICOTHE.TX..ROUTE 7............TCR...
19-495-2396...WAYTIS TIM A & DEBRA J.........................LEANDER....TX..11114 OAK ST......TCR...
16-607-2835...WAYTOGO TRAVEL.................................CANTON.....OH..7549 STRAUSSER NW....TCR...
19-549-1592...WAYTON JOSEPH D................................COLLINGSWOOD.NJ..661 HADDON AV......TCR...
15-686-7731...WAYTOWICH GERALD B & SONS......................MARIETTA...GA..484 JOANNE DR.......TCR...
11-454-9421...WAYTOWN TAVERN.................................MIAMI......FL..2366 NE 187 ST......TCR...
16-380-9486...WAYTS GARAGE & WRECKER SERVI...................GIRARD.....IL..S 6TH..............TCR...
16-772-7213...WAYTS MUSIC....................................CORTLAND...IN..STATE RD 258.......TCR...
14-327-0361...WAYTS THOMAS A & JUDITH A......................ERWIN......TN..RT 3 BOX 618.......TCR...
19-014-2539...WAYTT CAFTERIA 119.............................MINERVA....OH..2635 WHITACRE S E...TCR...
15-576-0838...WAYTT GRAVEL...................................HOUSTON....TX..10793 JONES RD.....TCR...
14-322-4475...WAYTT RUSSELL E................................LAYTONVILLE.CA..1 MILE E OF LAYTONVILLE..TCR...
11-084-5781...WAYTT TARRENT COMBS............................ORAL.......SD..N/A..............TCR...
18-963-9305...WAYUGA BUILDERS & SUPPLY CO.....................FRANKFORT..KY..308 W MAIN ST SUITE 022..TCR...
05-449-4109...WAYUGA BUILDERS & SUPPLY CO.....................RED CREEK..NY..UPTON RD...........TCR...
00-222-4871...WAYUGA COMMUNITY NEWSPAPERS.....................WOLCOTT....NY..5740 LIMEKILN ROAD...H..
                                                             RED CREEK..NY..6784 MAIN STREET....H..
                                                             MAIL ADDRESS PO BOX  199
14-739-5743...WAYUMOTO WAYNE..................................RANCHO CUCMNG.CA..9650 BUS CTR DR STE 134.
16-856-1058...WAYUNE SENIOR CENTER............................WAYNE......NE..306 PEARL.........TCR...
15-634-6181...WAYV.......................FORREST-BRODY BROADCAST GROUP...NEW YORK...NY..600 THIRD AVE......HCR...
16-664-9533...WAYVERVILLE LAUNDROMAT..........................WEAVERVILLE.CA..P O BOX 91.......TCR...
18-710-0847...WAYVERY HOLDING COMPANY*........................SEAFORD....DE..PINE ST EXTENSION...H..
                                                             MAIL ADDRESS PO BOX  532
05-677-0078...WAYVID INC.................FAIRFIELD INN.........FAIRFIELD..PA..MAIN ST.
```

```
18-989-0720                                                                           TCR...
13-962-4241                                                                           TCR...
02-089-976                                                                           .......
10-386-1589                                                                           .......
16-040-4059                                                                           50....
14-609-0021                                                                           TCR...
05-533-3249                                                                           .......
16-639-5103.                                                                          .......
02-467-9664...WAYWARD HOME KENNEL.............................                        .......
05-688-6591...WAYWARD INN INC.................................                        .......
19-362-4806...WAYWARD LADY RESTAURANT THE...HASSLOCHER ENTERPRISES INC.........       CR...
10-211-8411...WAYWARD LIMITED*................................                        .......
08-276-3251...WAYWARD LOUNGE..................................                        DG....
13-328-4919...WAYWARJ NURSERY.................................                        .......
14-456-0208...WAYWARD PELICAN.................................                        TCR...
16-559-4714...WAYWARD SUN COUNTRY STORE....BROOKS HOWARD & BARBARA......             CR...
18-036-4069...WAYWARD WHALE...................................                        .......
15-361-8285...WAYWARD WHEELS*.................................                        H...
13-709-1229...WAYWARD WIND....................................                        TCR...
14-919-4508...WAYWARD WIND CAMP.............................FORT MORGAN...CO..14390 HWY 34.........TCR...
60-237-7970...WAYWARD WIND DESERT TOURS.....................CAVE CREEK...AZ..32617 N 66TH ST.......TCR...
05-337-5655...WAYWARD WIND INC..............................FORT MORGAN...CO..5 MI WEST OF TOWN......
13-557-8862...WAYWARD WIND INC..............................AUBURN......NY..3932 FRANKLIN ST RD...TCR...
05-807-8312...WAYWARD WIND LIQUOR...........................FORT MORGAN...CO..1429 8 HIGHWAY 39...
                                                           MAIL ADDRESS PO BOX  905
06-061-7115...WAYWARD WIND MOBILE HOME PARK..WAYWARD WIND MOBILE HOME PARK..FORT MORGAN...CO..111 E RAILROAD AVE.....CR..
06-061-7115...WAYWARD WIND MOBILE HOME PARK..WAYWARD WIND MOBILE HOME PARK..FORT MORGAN...CO..111 E RAILROAD AVE........
13-685-4932...WAYWARD WIND OUTFITTERS.......................BUCKEYE....AZ..ROUTE 3 22804 WEST HILT..TCR...
19-117-6965...WAYWARD WIND RANCH............................SPRINGTOWN..TX..4 1/2 MILES N........
14-706-1006...WAYWARD WIND RESORT...........................OSAGE BEACH.MO..LAKE RD 54-29..........
14-919-4565...WAYWARD WIND REST & LOUNGE....................FORT MORGAN...CO..14424 HWY 34.......TCR...
14-920-4083...WAYWARD WIND TEXACO SERVILE....................FORT MORGAN...CO..14424 HWY 34........
12-270-6708...WAYWARD WIND TRANSPORTATION...................FARGO......ND..3150 39TH ST SW #C...
01-066-1924...WAYWARD WIND TRAVEL INC.......................SEDALIA....MO..212 W 7TH...........
03-799-3482...WAYWARD WINDS.................................OTHELLO....WA..GOVERNMENT WAY.....
                                                           MAIL ADDRESS PO BOX  1531
06-840-9440...WAYWARD WINDS LODGE      ←                    TUCSON.....AZ..707 W MIRACLE MILE...
16-135-1598...WAYWARD WINDS MOTEL...........................H SPGS NAT PK.AR..BUENA VISTA RD......
                                                           MAIL ADDRESS RUR RT  3 BOX 2 6
16-733-1024...WAYWARD WINDS MOTEL...........................PETROLIA...CA..BOX 28...........TCR...
```

Annotations within the figure:

- **D-U-N-S Number** (pointing to left column of numbers)
- **Divisional Name or Secondary Name** (pointing to the middle column)
- TCR = Companies not in Dialog File 516
- H = Headquarters Location
- B = Branch Location
- HCR = Cross-Reference Listing to Headquarters Location
- CR = Cross-Reference Listing
- T = D-U-N-S Number Assigned to a Trade Name only

```
!----------------D02----------------D02----------------D02----------------D02----------------D02-----------D02
15-188-8930...WAYWARD WINDS MOTEL..........SUNRISE PROPERTIES INC.........MYRTLE BEACH..SC..2609 SOUTH OCEAN BLVD.....CR....
                                                                    MAIL ADDRESS PO BOX  2297
16-519-9647...WAYWARD YOUTH CENTER............................LONG BEACH..CA..694 CERRITOS AV........TCR...
13-820-8061...WAYWEST ENTERPRISES INC........................WASILLA....AK..PO BOX 87-2012.......TCR...
13-780-5610...WAYWEST ENTERPRISES INC........................BILLINGS...MT..PO BOX 31612.........TCR...
14-597-4895...WAYWEST ENTERPRISES INC........................BOZEMAN....MT..1122 E MAIN STREET....TCR...
X1-780-2838...WAYWEST HEATING & COOLING*.....................WOOD DALE..IL..445 N MAPLE..........
X5-097-5208...WAYWICK CORPORATION............................DETROIT....MI..1480 SEMINOLE.......H..
11-426-8759...WAYWOOD BEVERAGE CO INC........................KENNETT SQ..PA..704 E BALTIMORE PIKE...
```

Figure 8.5: Entry for Wayward Winds Lodge, Tucson, AZ from *D-U-N-S Account Identification Service*, 1990.

You could look in the telephone directory, but this will work only if you already know the company's location. Besides, the telephone directory supplies only the address and telephone number. No financial information is included, of course! The most comprehensive list of companies in the United States is *D-U-N-S Account Identification Service* (Parsippany, NJ: Dun's Marketing Services, Inc., microfiche). But only large public and academic libraries will have this tool, which is a microfiche listing of over 7,000,000 U.S. companies, including very small mom-and-pop businesses. As a matter of fact, Dun & Bradstreet attempts to list every business in the United States. For example, Wayward Winds Lodge is a very small, independently owned motel in Tucson, Arizona (figure 8.5). For each company, the name, address, and Dun's number is listed. An address is not much information, but it is more than you had at the start of your research.

The Dun's number, to the left of each company name in figure 8.5, is a unique number assigned to each individual company by Dun & Bradstreet. For many (but not all!) of the companies listed in the *D-U-N-S Account Identification Service* there is more information available in an online database called *D & B—Duns Market Identifiers* (Parsippany, NJ: Dun's Marketing Services, Inc.). Figure 8.6 shows the complete record for Wayward Winds Lodge in Tucson. This database can be searched by company name, DUNS number, city, SIC code, size, and so on. This is the most complete information available in the library on very small privately owned companies. Ask your librarian if your library can access this online database. Be aware that the average online charge is $5 per company, and your library may expect you to pay this fee.

So far you have found very little information on Red Roof Inns, which is quite normal when researching a private company. A *D & B—Duns Market Identifiers* search could be done on Red Roof Inns, Inc. but it would simply duplicate the information already found in *The Million Dollar Directory*. Where can you find more information? There is another online file from Dun & Bradstreet's Credit Services called *D & B Dun's Financial Records Plus* (Murray Hill, NJ: Dun & Bradstreet Credit Services). It includes additional information such as annual sales, history of the company, who are the major owners and biographical information about them, lists of related companies, and operation information. This file has extensive information that is difficult to locate in any other source. However, the online charges are steep—ranging from $22 to $89 per record.

One of the only other ways to find information on private companies is periodical articles. If the company is large, or has done something important within the industry, there may be articles about it in business newspapers or trade journals. To find these articles you need to use periodical indexes. The best indexes to use for private company research are *Business Index/INFOTRAC*™ and *Predicasts F&S Index: United States*, which

```
0838462
Wayward Winds Lodge
707 W Miracle Mile
Tucson, AZ  85705-3706

TELEPHONE: 602-791-7526
COUNTY: Pima      SMSA: 607  (Tucson,Arizona)

BUSINESS: Motel

PRIMARY SIC:
 7011       Hotels and motels, nsk
  70110100   Motel, nsk

LATEST YEAR ORGANIZED:  1981   OWNER CHANGE DATE:        NA
ANNUAL SALES REVISION DATE: 11/06/1989

                         LATEST           TREND           BASE
                          YEAR            YEAR            YEAR
                                         (1987)          (1984)

SALES          $      240,000  $          NA  $          NA
EMPLOYEES TOTAL:          11               NA              NA
EMPLOYEES HERE:          11               NA              NA

  SALES GROWTH:  NA %  NET WORTH: $       670,052
  EMPLOYMENT GROWTH:  NA %

SQUARE FOOTAGE: NA  OWNED
NUMBER OF ACCOUNTS: NA
BANK: First Interstate Bank

THIS IS:

   A  SINGLE LOCATION
   A  PROPRIETORSHIP

DUNS NUMBER:            06-840-9440

OWNER:                 Boydstun, John  /Owner
```

Figure 8.6: Sample Online Search on Dialog Information Services, Inc. of *D&B—Dun's Market Identifiers*, 1989.

```
 O |                                     General Periodicals Index-A
 O |                                         1/1/80 at 12:05a
 O |       RED ROOF INNS INC.
 O |               Budget motels take to humor ads.  by Christy Fisher
 O |       and Ira Teinowitz il    v59 Advertising Age  Nov 14
 O |       '88 p65(1)                                 41V5480
 O |
 O |               VSAT supplies corporate-wide communications,
 O |       control.  (Vertical Small Aperture Terminals) by
 O |       Richard Taggs     v202 Hotel & Motel Management  Dec
 O |       14  '87  p48(2)
 O |
 O |               Trueman's legacy lives on at Red Roof Inns Inc.
 O |       (James R. Trueman) by Matthew Hall il    v11   Ohio
 O |       Business   June  '87  p11(2)                 34P3876
 O |
 O |               Red Roof revamps operations; but amidst big
 O |       changes, chain won't alter successful formula.  by Bill
 O |       Gillette il    v 201  Hotel & Motel Management  Sept 22
 O |       '86  p1(2)
 O |
 O |               Red Roof has confidence to keep growing.  (plans
 O |       150 motels by end of year) by Cheryl Eberhart    v200
 O |       Hotel & Motel Management  Aug   '85  p3(2)
 O |
```

Figure 8.7: Sample Search on Red Roof Inns from *INFOTRAC*tm.

were both covered in detail in chapter 4. Both of these publications index a large number of business newspapers and trade journals, which are likely to cover stories on smaller companies.

*Business Index/INFOTRAC*tm were discussed more fully in chapter 4 (figure 4.6). Company names are used as subject headings and are interfiled with all other subjects in both publications. In *INFOTRAC*tm simply type "Red Roof Inns Inc." as the subject of the search. Figure 8.7 shows the results of a search on *INFOTRAC*tm.

Looking at the articles listed in the *INFOTRAC*tm printout, you may eliminate the second one as irrelevant to research for information on the financial situation and success of Red Roof. However, the rest of the articles might be useful. Notice that they are listed in reverse chronological order, with the most current article at the top of the list. The first article might be the best one to pursue, since it is very recent and since advertising is one way a company can compete for business in the overbuilt industry. Figure 8.8 is a reprint of the article. In addition to describing the advertising, the article does include some information on the size of the economy segment and cites rapid growth and increased competition as the reason why the economy chains are increasing their advertising.

Advertising Age, November 14, 1988

Budget motels take to humor ads

By CHRISTY FISHER and IRA TEINOWITZ

Motel 6's Tom Bodett was first. Then came Red Roof Inns' Martin Mull. Now, Econo Lodges of America is humoring radio listeners with Tim Conway.

Econo Lodges, the No. 5 economy lodging chain, is airing radio spots featuring Mr. Conway as part of its $2 million "Amazing America" campaign.

Mr. Conway acts as a tour guide leading listeners to some of the nation's most off-beat tourist spots. FCB/Leber Katz Partners, New York, is Econo Lodges' agency.

To capture a bigger slice of the growing $11.7 billion economy lodging industry, hotel chains have turned on the advertising budgets.

"Advertising has become very important to the industry," said Joan Ganje-Fischer, chairwoman of the Economy Lodging Council of the American Hotel and Motel Association.

"All the major chains, especially the top 10 or 12, have media campaigns, where they have not had them previously," she said.

Rapid growth and increased competition are the two primary reasons budget chains have taken to the airwaves, Ms. Ganje-Fischer said.

There are now 82 economy lodging chains with a total of 5,042 properties and 598,000 rooms, which makes up 20% of the total lodging market. In 1985, there were

Tim Conway for Econo Lodges

"Hi, I'm Tim Conway and I'm probing Amazing America for Econo Lodges. Tonight, I'm talking to you from the cavity of a 2-ton molar in a health education museum in Cleveland. When I'm done here, I'm going to put the bite on high prices by staying in Econo Lodges, the premier economy motel where you spend a night, not a fortune.

In fact, 40,000 people will sleep tight in Econo Lodges tonight.... Uh, not all in the same one, of course. So, for reservations, call ... 1-800-55-ECONO. And, uh, don't forget to floss!"

— T. Conway

256,000 rooms.

It's not that the budget lodging industry had been totally void of advertising, Ms. Ganje-Fischer said. Outdoor boards and directories have been the primary medium.

But when No. 2 Motel 6 teamed up with the Richards Group, Dallas, and aired the successful Tom Bodett radio campaign two years

Tom Bodett for Motel 6

"Hi, Tom Bodett here for Motel 6, with a comparison. You know, in some ways, a Motel 6 reminds me of one of those big, fancy hotels. They've got beds; we've got beds. They've got sinks and showers; by golly we've got 'em, too.

There are differences, though. You can't get a hot facial mudpack at Motel 6 like at those fancy joints.

And you won't find French-milled soap or avocado body balm. You will, however, find a clean, comfortable room and the lowest rates nationwide. Under 21 bucks in most places...."

— T. Bodett

ago, the rest of the industry took notice.

"As the saying goes—success breeds envy and envy breeds emulation," said Dan Daniele, who follows the economy lodging industry for accounting firm Laventhol & Horwath.

Motel 6 will spend about $7.7 million on radio advertising this year, up 20% from last year.

The spots feature Mr. Bodett's folksy no-nonsense deadpan delivery and his signature, "We'll leave the light on for you."

No. 10-ranked Red Roof Inns continues to use Mr. Mull for its $5 million TV campaign. Mr. Mull glibly and sarcastically tells people what they won't get and won't pay

Martin Mull for Red Roof Inns

"What do $60-a-night motel chains offer you that you can't get at Red Roof Inns?

Let's add them up and see. This handy shower cap, 59¢; shampooette, 25¢; $2.

Ah, dental floss, always a plus.

Ooh, we're still spending $27 a night more than at Red Roof Inns.

Huh, wait a minute, I forgot the mint.

(Voice-over: Don't pay too much, hit the roof, Red Roof Inns. Call 1-800-THE ROOF.)

It's a good mint.

It's not worth $27, but it's good...."

— M. Mull

for at Red Roof Inns. W.B. Doner & Co., Southfield, Mich., created the effort.

No. 1 Days Inns of America has considered using humor, but discarded the idea because it couldn't agree on an approach, a spokesman said.

Instead, it continued the $6 million slice-of-life campaign via Babbit & Reiman, Atlanta.

No. 3 Comfort Inn uses light humor in its campaign from Smith Burke & Azzam, Baltimore, with spokesmen such as Pat Boone, Eva Gabor, Joe Frazier and comedian Jim Meskimen.

Each pops out of a suitcase to deliver his or her message.

The ad campaign is part of parent company Quality International's $6 million effort for all three of its hotels, Comfort, Quality and Clarion. #

TBWA

'Gee, we had to become international, so therefore we sold our agency.' The only reason we would sell is greed. So far, that has been something '...ve been able to avoi⌐ ..' #

Francisco, New England, Texas, Minnesota and Seattle, he said.

The trend toward regional marketing suppor⌐ 'hat expensive, m''· along with ⌐s has

lion investment.

He said the company has been offered that much to sell out. But Mr. Tragos, one of the agency's 43 shareholders, isn't ready to cash in.

"... We don't have the excuse,

(Continued from Page 1?)
dind; Zurich; an⌐ ⌐'
⌐ds, th⌐

65

Predicasts F&S Index: United States is another periodical index that was illustrated in detail in chapter 4 (figures 4.7—4.9). It is available online, on CD-ROM, and as a printed index. Companies are listed in the white pages, which is the second half of each issue. Use the company name as the subject heading (figure 8.9). Instead of the title of the article, a brief statement of content is listed in the index. In the right column the name of the journal is abbreviated with the date and beginning page number. Although the article listed here is somewhat dated, it might be worth pursuing, especially since it is also listed on the *INFOTRAC*™ search. In fact, this article (figure 8.10) turns out to be the most complete information available on Red Roof Inns. It lists the company's gross revenue and occupancy rate. It also discusses their expansion plans.

This covers the general sources of information on private companies. However, don't hesitate to ask your librarian if there are any other specialized or regional sources you might consult on your particular company and/or topic. Your library may have some of the specialized industry directories such as *Directory of Hotel Systems* (Washington, DC: American Hotel & Motel Association, 1962-), which might include additional information. And the reference librarian may also be aware of sources of information on local private companies.

This sample search for information on Red Roof Inns, Inc. has been, comparatively speaking, very successful for a private company. Do not expect to routinely find even this much information on most private companies. It is just not available. Private really means private in the business world. But if Red Roof Inns, Inc. decides to "go public," the amount of information available will change dramatically. The next chapter illustrates how to search for information on a publicly owned company.

..nd 08/17/86 p17

Acquires Durkee Famou... ..., ..ood co
AGEFI   11/05/86 p10
Acquires Durkee Famous Foods from Hanson Industries
Grocer 11/08/86 p17
Sells Airkem to Economics Lab for $16mil
S&C Spec 09/00/86 p19

Recognition Equipment
Will boost capital spending to $8mil in FY86 vs $6mil in
FY85   WSJ (NJ)   12/04/86 p20
Will not vye for $250mil US Postal Svc letter-sorting equip
contract   Elec News 11/24/86 p2
Reports FY86 net of $10.54mil or $1.06/shr vs FY85's
$4.32mil income   WSJ (NJ)   12/05/86 p36
Financial analysis   Value Line 09/26/86 p165

Recordati Ind Chimica
To acquire 58.3% of Technogenetics, biochemicals co
AGEFI   11/22/86 p7
To acquire 58% of Technogenetics, biochemistry co
Chimie Act 12/01/86 p19
Acquires 58.3% of Technogenetics, biotechnology and
diagnostics co   IMSPharm N 12/01/86 p3
Acquires 58.3% of Technogenetics, biotech & diagnostics
co   SCRIP   12/03/86 p15

Recticel Foam
Has begun building a polyurethane foam plant in LeRoy, NJ
R&P News 10/20/86 p20
Nears completion of plastic foam unit in LeRoy, NY
Urethane 11/00/86 p5

Red Apple Supermarket
Will have volume of $600mil in 1987
Prog Groc 12/00/86 p39

Red Lobster Inns
Launches new program targeting bus tour groups with
lunch, dinner pkgs   NatnsRestr 10/20/86 p15
Launches national ad campaign focusing on snow crab leg
dinners   NatnsRestr 11/24/86 p15

Red Owl Stores
Claims 3% of Minneapolis market in 1986, MN
●Super News 09/22/86 pS15
Sales for FY86 will rise 8% vs FY85, with a 20% earnings
increase   ●Super News 11/17/86 p1

Red River Gas Pipeline
Gas transmission pipeline shipments data, 1985
P&G Jour 08/00/86 p39
Operating revenues and net income data, 1985
P&G Jour 08/00/86 p39
Financial ranking data, 1985   P&G Jour 08/00/86 p39
Gas transmission pipeline asset value data, 1985
P&G Jour 08/00/86 p39

Red Roof Inns
Officials announce reorganization to position company for
continued growth   H&M Mgmt 09/22/86 p1

Red's Group
Albert

Albert
$9.5

One sentence   Journal   Date
note on contents   Abbreviation   Page

Redco...
Opens 120,000 sq ft corporate headqtrs & telecom equip
facility, NY   Office Sys 10/00/86 p24

Rediffusion Computer
Buys GTI's Computer Graphics Div, computer image
generation system mfr   Aerosp Dly 12/15/86 p400

Redken Laboratories
Reports FY86 net income of $1.96mil vs $8.38mil in FY85
WSJ (NJ)   10/02/86 p38
Financial analysis   Value Line 10/24/86 p822

Redland

Cor...,
Ftwr New..
German court upholds Puma ban on Reebok a..
Ftwr News 10/0..
Executive compensation data, 1986
Ftwr News 11/0
Narrowed agency review for its $10mil budget a..
to 5 finalists   Ad Age 11
This athletic shoe mfr begins trading on NYSE
symbol RBK   WSJ (NJ)
Expects 1986 earnings to exceed Wall Stree
Ftwr New..
Financial analysis of this athletic footwear mak
Value Line 12/0

Reece
Financial analysis   Value Line 11/21..

Reed & Barton
Has acquired Herco Art Mfg, lamp company
HFD   09/29/..

Reed Intnl
To buy 20 trade-professional mags from Dun & Bradstr..
for $250mil   FT London 09/10/86 p
To buy 20 magazines from Dun & Bradstreet for $250mil
Inv Chron 09/18/86 p97
Acquires Caldwell Paint Mfg, paint co
Farbe&Lack 03/00/86 p2..

Reed Plastic
Introduces blue PET bottle colorant for plastics
ModPlstInt 11/00/86

Reed Plastics
Jtly develops color concentrates for ABS resins
Mod Plast 11/00/..
New R&D facility includes analytical, processing & p
testing equip, MA   Mod Plast 11/00/..
Opens extensive R&D lab with $1mil in equip, MA
Plast Wrld 11/0

Reeves Bros
Moves part of Cornelius, NC, automotive trim pl..
Auburn, IN   Textil Wld 11

Reeves Communications
Shares outstanding data, 1986
OTC Review 09/0..
Market value data, 1986   OTC Review 09/0..
Sales data, 1986   OTC Review 09/00
Financial ranking data, 1986   OTC Review 09/00..
Financial analysis   Value Line 12/12/86
Financial assets data, 1986   OTC Review 09/00/8..

Reference Technology
Its jtly developed CD-ROM follows High Sierra Grou..
format   Computrwld 09/22/86 ..

Regal Mfg
Electric food processors share of market data, 1985
Appliance 09/00/86 p6

Regal Rugs
Focuses on the upper end of mkt by emphasizing high
fashion & quality   ●HFD   11/10/86 p80

Regency Electronics
Financial analysis   Value Line 11/07/86 p1053

Regernative Environmental
Mfrs thermal incineratn equip for emissions of solvent
coating plant   PFF Convrt 11/00/86 p..

Regina
Vacuum cleaners share of market data, 1985
Appliance 09/00/86 ..
Floor polishers share of market data, 1985
Appliance 09/00/86

Regis
Financial analysis   Value Line 12/05/86 ..

Figure 8.9: Citations on Red Roof Inns from *Predicasts F&S Index: United States*, December 1986.

Hotel & Motel Management

CONSUMER & FAMILY SCIENCES LIBRARY

Replacement Issue

INTERNATIONAL MARKET PAGE 4

An (HBJ) PUBLICATION   The newspaper for the lodging industry   September 22, 1986, Volume 201, Number 13

All-Suite Chain Sets Fall Debut

By Bill Gillette
H&MM Associate Editor

EDEN PRAIRIE, MINN.-—A new chain of all suite, courtyard style hotels is springing up in this suburb southwest of Minneapolis.

La Corté Inns Inc., based here, plans to have its first hotel in the ground by late fall, said John Kahler, La Corté's executive vice president and c.e.o.

"We've had inquiries from many parts of the country," Kahler told H&MM, "but our prefer-
continued on page 6

Red Roof Revamps Operations

But Amidst Big Changes, Chain Won't Alter Successful Formula

By Bill Gillette
H&MM Associate Editor

HILLIARD, OHIO—Red Roof Inns, the 14-year-old budget chain based in this Columbus suburb, has experienced significant changes of late.

But sometimes, as the saying goes, "The more things change, the more they remain the same."

In June, James R. Trueman, the chain's founder and a nationally known auto-racing figure, died after a lengthy battle with cancer. Later that month, Red Roof officials announced a reorganization geared to accommodate the company's steady growth.

And Bill Denk, who had been serving as president of Red Roof Development Co., was named to fill the charismatic Trueman's shoes as president of Red Roof Inns Inc.

Denk has been with Red Roof since its inception in 1972, so he's seen the chain grow from its first property in Columbus – opened in February 1973 – to its present roster of 165 hotels either open or under construction in 30 states.

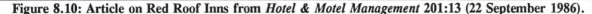

"Jim Trueman was a good leader," Denk told H&MM in a recent interview. "My challenge is to keep the product as good as Jim did."

To do that, Denk said he plans to abide by another saying: "If **Bill Denk** it ain't broke, don't fix it."

Red Roof Inns certainly "ain't broke." In 1985, the chain increased its
continued on page 31

Red Roof Inns Revamps

continued from page 1
gross revenues to a company-record $122 million. It also reported an 87.2-percent chain-wide occupancy rate, built 19 new hotels, and entered four new markets (Texas, Louisiana, New Hampshire and Mississippi).

And so far, the only "fixing" going on is the corporate restructuring.

Basically, the company has been divided into two groups: the eastern and the western. Walter Furnas, formerly a vice president of operations, will oversee the nearly 70 hotels in the western group; Richard Mathes, also a former v.p./operations, takes charge of the eastern

group's 88 properties.

Denk said the reorganization did not come about as a result of Trueman's death ("It would have happened anyway"). Rather, it was needed to maintain strict control over the chain's ever-increasing number of properties. "As we grow," said Denk, "we won't change our hands-on management style, which gives us a clean room at an exceptional price-value, a consistent product, and satisfied guests."

Another thing that won't change is Red Roof's no franchise philosophy. All its inns are company-owned and -operated – it's the largest such budget chain in the country – and, Denk said, that's one reason the chain will continue to operate and expand within roughly the same geographical boundries as it has since 1973.

"We are into Texas now," he said, "but mainly we'll stay east of Kansas City. We don't talk about going into Canada or abroad, and we don't talk about California. It's too hard to put out fires that far away."

Denk said the chain will continue its steady expansion rate of 25 to 30 properties a year, aiming at highway-visible metropolitan sites close to commercial activity. "We won't change our site personality," he said. "We are looking for new markets – much like McDonald's found the freeways and downtown areas – but

we haven't found anything yet."

The auto-racing sidelight that Jim Trueman fostered, both personally and corporately, is yet another part of the Red Roof story that won't change. "Jim's involvement in racing brought us a lot of recognition," Denk said. "It's part of our personality, and I'm committed to it."

This year's Indianapolis 500 was won by Bobby Rahal, a long-time Trueman protégé, in a car bearing the Red Roof Inns logo. Rahal's reputation as one of the more competitive drivers on the Indy-car circuit exemplifies what Denk said Red Roof Inns has been – and will be – all about: "Our goal is always to maintain our competitiveness with the best of the competition." ∎

Figure 8.10: Article on Red Roof Inns from *Hotel & Motel Management* 201:13 (22 September 1986).

105

SUMMARY

1) Finding information on private companies can be very difficult. Larger private companies will appear in directories such as *The Million Dollar Directory* and *WARD'S BUSINESS DIRECTORY*tm. Both sources provide address, telephone number, owner or chief executive officer, and a sales figure.

2) Smaller private companies frequently can be located in *D-U-N-S Account Identification Service*, a microfiche service that provides only the address and Dun's number for over seven million U.S. companies.

3) More information may be found on larger private companies in the online database, *D & B—Duns Market Identifiers*.

4) Periodical indexes, such as *Business Index/INFOTRAC*tm and *Predicasts F&S Index: United States*, are the best sources for additional information on private companies.

5) Ask your librarian about any specialized directories or local information sources.

CHAPTER 9

PUBLIC COMPANIES

Hilton Hotels Corporation is a publicly owned company.

• It must file a 10-K Report with the U. S. Securities and Exchange Commission.

• It publishes an annual report to shareholders.

• Investment firms are constantly evaluating it and assessing its value as an investment.

Although publicly owned companies constitute only a small percentage of the companies in the United States, they are responsible for a major portion of the nation's business. A "public company" is any company that sells stock to the general public. Federal law requires that any company that trades stock on one of the national exchanges or in more than one state must *disclose* (or make available) their financial situation. Because of these disclosure laws and because it is a publicly owned company, there is a great deal of information available on Hilton Hotels Corporation. This chapter, which uses Hilton Hotels as an example, will show you how to find financial and managerial information on a publicly owned company. In particular, we will look at how Hilton is addressing the problems caused by overbuilding.

In order to protect investors from purchasing stock in mismanaged or faulting companies, the Securities and Exchange Act of 1934 requires that publicly owned companies disclose their financial position by publishing certain financial records. The public has the legal right to know anything that would affect the financial decision of an investor. For this reason you can find financial data such as sales volume, expenses, profits, assets, and liabilities of a publicly owned company. You can also find out if the company is involved in any legal questions, who its top executives are, and how much they are paid.

Our renovation and expansion efforts have been rewarded by increases in our occupancy and average room rates. Our system-wide growth in average rate has been nearly double that of inflation in the past three years, while at the same time hotel occupancy grew from 65 percent in 1986 to 70 percent this year. Hotel income contribution in 1988 increased by 14 percent over 1987 and 38 percent over the 1986 level.

Focused marketing programs have complemented our improved facilities by targeting key market segments. Special efforts targeted at the leisure market through our "Golden Summer of $59" program and to the business/leisure traveler in our spring and fall "WeekEnder" programs were highly successful.

Our HHonors frequent traveler program was introduced in mid-1987. By the end of 1988 the program membership and room night activity were advancing strongly, and enhancements for 1989 promise to make HHonors even more attractive to its targeted member base.

Our gaming operations continue to be a major source of earnings growth. In 1988, gaming income contribution increased 19 percent and accounted for 53 percent of operating income. The Las Vegas Hilton and Flamingo Hilton recorded sharp gains for the year, while the Reno Hilton reversed a loss in 1987 and produced a profit for 1988. Income from the Gold Coast Conrad International Hotel & Jupiters Casino in Queensland, Australia, also improved significantly in 1988.

In 1989-90 we will spend more than $300 million expanding and refurbishing our Nevada operations, including the construction of a new hotel-casino, the Flamingo Hilton-Laughlin, in Laughlin, Nevada. These and other hotel, gaming and international expansion programs for 1989 and 1990 are discussed in detail later in this report. Following their completion these projects are expected to significantly enhance our future earnings.

Asset Value

The fundamental job of management is to build stockholder value. We believe that the way to accomplish this is to invest in properties with above average earning potential and to provide quality service to our guests. Over four decades we have patiently built a portfolio of assets that has produced a large, secure and growing stream of income and cash flow. Consequently, the value of our Company has sharply increased.

There are several ways to define value. We provide three measures in this report. The first, "stockholders' equity per share," gives the book or historical accounting basis of our assets. At the end of 1988 our stockholders' equity per share was $17.03, which represented an eight percent increase from the equity per share of $15.80 in 1987.

The deficiencies of stockholders' equity per share are apparent. For a hotel such as the Waldorf-Astoria that was acquired many years ago, the historical accounting basis bears little relationship to its value today. Therefore, since

HILTON HOTELS CORPORATION • 1988 ANNUAL REPORT

HILTON HAWAIIAN VILLAGE
Honolulu, Hawaii

Figure 9.1: Cover and Excerpts from Hilton Hotels Corporation Annual Report, 1988.

108

One of the most important financial records required is the annual report to shareholders (ARS). It is mailed out to all shareholders at the end of the company's fiscal year. Since it is readily available and relatively easy to understand, it is usually the first place to begin research on a publicly owned company (figure 9.1). The ARS is usually enhanced with glossy pictures and graphs. The company tries to portray a very upbeat, positive image. Because of this tone many people feel the ARS is nothing more than a publicity brochure. However, there is a great deal of important information in it.

Start with the letter from the chairman of the board, which reviews the past year's accomplishments and outlines the future management plan and goals. Keep in mind that the chairman is attempting to impress the stockholders (figure 9.1). Second, read the independent auditor's report in the back of the report; look to see if the auditor has given an unqualified (or clean) opinion on the financial statements. If not, something might be wrong. Third, examine the financial statement that follows the chairman's letter. It usually includes balance sheet, income statement, statement of changes in financial position, and data comparing several past years (figure 9.2). And last, read the management's discussion and analysis section where you will find management's explanation of the underlying causes and economic influences affecting the financial reports.

Hilton's Annual Report (figure 9.1) cites increased occupancy rates due to an extensive renovation and expansion program. Their marketing efforts have been targeted at specific segments and the frequent travelers program. Even though overbuilding of the industry is not cited in the ARS, much information on how Hilton is advertising and marketing to retain its successful position in the industry is available.

Besides the ARS, the company must file a 10-K Form with the Securities and Exchange Commission. Because of the name of the form, this report is commonly called the 10-K Report (figure 9.3). It is the most exhaustive financial disclosure available. In the 10-K Report, companies must answer a set of specific questions in a stated order. Because of this required format, the 10-K Reports from several companies can be easily compared. The 10-K does not include photographs or illustrations. It is a straight forward financial report divided into two sections: financial information and supporting data. It includes information on products, markets (and market share), a list of subsidiaries, and information on foreign operations and legal proceedings. For example, Hilton's expansion program is outlined in greater detail in the 10-K Report than in the ARS (figure 9.3). Hilton is expanding internationally and is also entering the all-suite segment domestically.

Sometimes the data in the 10-K Report are very similar to that contained in the ARS. In fact, some companies issue their 10-K as their ARS. However, in most cases the 10-K will be a more detailed financial report. Since the 10-K Report does not include the chairman's letter, you should read both reports to get a full picture of the company. The chart on page 112 titled "Information in the Annual Report to Stockholders and 10-K Report" indicates which information typically is available in the respective reports.

Hilton Hotels Corporation and Subsidiaries — TEN YEAR SUMMARY

	Dollars in millions except per share amounts	1988	1987	1986	1985	1984	1983	1982	1981	1980	1979	Ten-Year Compound Growth Rate
Operating Data For Years Ended December 31	Revenue											
	Hotels [1]	$1,395.2	1,279.4	1,228.3	1,138.8	1,086.3	975.0	909.0	892.0	532.7	770.1	7.4%
	Management fees	33.3	31.3	28.8	28.2	25.4	20.5	17.7	17.1	15.9	14.0	10.9
	Franchise fees	33.5	31.9	30.7	28.2	26.2	23.1	19.5	17.5	14.3	10.9	15.0
	Total hotels	1,462.0	1,342.6	1,287.8	1,195.2	1,137.9	1,021.6	940.2	926.6	562.9	795.0	7.6
	Gaming [1]	695.3	589.7	483.7	366.7	341.0	323.8	291.4	269.1	251.6	230.8	14.3
	Total	2,157.3	1,932.3	1,771.5	1,561.9	1,478.9	1,345.4	1,237.6	1,195.7	1,114.5	1,025.8	9.3
	Less non-consolidated managed	1,241.9	1,116.9	1,052.5	877.5	831.6	696.1	638.1	610.5	560.2	511.9	10.9
	Total revenue from consolidated operations	$ 915.4	815.4	719.0	684.4	647.3	649.3	599.5	585.2	554.3	513.9	7.5
	Income contribution [2]											
	Hotels	$ 115.1	100.7	83.6	90.5	107.8	101.0	92.6	113.8	114.5	105.3	2.6
	Gaming	128.6	107.7	88.1	76.4	69.7	68.6	52.2	79.1	80.0	69.9	9.6
	Total	243.7	208.4	171.7	166.9	177.5	169.6	144.8	192.9	194.5	175.2	5.7
	Net interest and dividend income (expense) [2]	(38.1)	(22.0)	(22.1)	(11.7)	(3.2)	(8.0)	3.9	12.6	8.6	(3.2)	
	Corporate expense	(20.8)	(18.3)	(17.6)	(15.0)	(10.7)	(10.5)	(10.0)	(9.0)	(7.8)	(6.1)	14.2
	Property transactions	—	43.8	(2.5)	3.1	27.9	37.6	2.8	—	—	14.7	
	Provision for income taxes	(53.9)	(72.0)	(31.7)	(43.1)	(77.5)	(76.1)	(58.1)	(83.9)	(89.2)	(81.3)	
	Net income	$ 130.9	139.9	97.8	100.2	114.0	112.6	83.4	112.6	106.1	99.3	6.8
	Funds provided from operations [3]	207.0	219.6	160.0	155.1	148.6	164.9	134.4	141.9	132.1	120.9	
	Depreciation [2]	89.5	80.5	71.3	65.4	58.9	56.7	51.1	40.2	36.1	33.8	
	Capital expenditures [2]	386.8	205.6	240.7	293.1	261.4	99.5	131.9	178.7	92.8	57.1	
Stockholder Data	Net income per share	$ 2.72	2.80	1.96	2.01	2.16	2.10	1.56	2.11	2.00	1.88	7.6
	Average common and equivalent shares	48.1	50.0	49.9	49.8	52.7	53.7	53.5	53.4	53.1	52.9	
	Stockholders' equity	$ 814.1	772.8	707.3	651.4	592.8	634.3	568.5	532.6	458.9	386.3	
	Stockholders' equity per share	17.03	15.80	14.23	13.16	12.00	11.87	10.66	9.99	8.70	7.42	
	Return on average stockholders' equity	16.5%	18.9	14.4	16.1	18.6	18.7	15.1	22.7	25.1	29.3	19.5*
	Dividends per share	$ .95	.90	.90	.90	.90	.90	.90	.83	.71	.55	9.9
	Market price — high/low	55/34	46/28	40/30	37/28	29/23	30/20	26/14	26/17	24/13	18/11	
Financial Position at Year End	Working capital	$ 279.5	206.9	173.4	259.3	125.7	165.7	99.7	109.1	132.1	98.6	
	Assets	1,892.5	1,423.6	1,302.3	1,225.6	1,163.8	1,099.2	938.3	816.5	696.8	636.1	
	Long-term debt	568.5	283.7	280.9	284.3	275.6	242.2	179.6	119.5	120.6	125.4	
	Ratio of long-term debt to total capital [4]	.36	.22	.24	.26	.27	.24	.21	.17	.19	.23	
General Information	Percentage of occupancy [1]											
	Hotels	70	68	65	64	64	60	61	65	69	71	
	Gaming	87	84	84	86	84	80	72	81	81	86	
	Number of properties at year end											
	Wholly owned or leased	9	8	8	11	11	13	14	14	15	15	
	Partially owned	12	13	14	14	13	13	14	15	14	14	
	Managed	21	22	22	23	22	23	19	16	15	17	
	Franchised	225	224	223	218	204	194	188	171	163	145	
	Gaming	4	4	4	4	3	3	3	3	2	2	
	Total	271	271	271	270	253	246	238	219	209	193	
	Available rooms at year end											
	Wholly owned or leased	6,494	6,027	6,085	7,399	7,580	10,464	10,909	11,072	11,737	11,878	
	Partially owned	13,409	13,528	14,350	14,123	12,904	13,430	14,152	13,235	12,887	12,894	
	Managed	13,383	14,183	13,425	13,692	13,258	12,031	8,852	7,977	7,454	8,052	
	Franchised	54,876	55,641	55,602	54,285	49,543	46,914	44,877	39,630	36,877	31,855	
	Gaming	7,326	7,318	7,318	6,602	6,025	6,025	6,025	5,523	4,539	3,997	
	Total	95,488	96,697	96,780	96,101	89,310	88,864	84,815	77,437	73,494	68,676	

(1) Includes properties owned or managed.
(2) Includes Hiltons proportionate share of unconsolidated affiliates.
(3) Net income plus depreciation, net deferred income taxes from operations and distributions from affiliates in excess of (less than) earnings.
(4) Total capital represents total assets less current liabilities.
* Average annual return.

Figure 9.2: Ten-Year Summary from Hilton Hotels Corporation's Annual Report, 1988.

Franchised Hotels

Pursuant to franchises granted by the Company, franchised hotels are operated under the "Hilton" or "CrestHil by Hilton" names. Those hotels operated under the "Hilton" name are generally smaller than hotels owned, leased or managed by "Hilton" and average approximately 250 rooms in size, while hotels bearing the "CrestHil by Hilton" name utilize a 156-room modular design and are constructed around a courtyard containing an indoor or outdoor swimming pool. In each instance, Hilton approves the plans for, and the location of, franchised hotels and assists in their design.

In general, each franchisee pays Hilton an initial fee based on the number of rooms in a franchised hotel and a continuing fee based on a percentage of the facility's room revenues. Although Hilton does not directly participate in the management or operation of franchised hotels, it does periodically inspect those facilities to ensure that Hilton's standards are maintained and renders advice with respect to hotel operations.

Hilton has entered into a limited number of agreements with persons who have loaned funds to certain franchisees to manage particular franchised properties should the franchisee default under the loan agreement. In those cases, Hilton will enter into a management contract, under which it will not be required to make an investment in or furnish funds for the operation of those properties.

On February 1, 1989, there were 222 hotels operated by others under the "Hilton" name. Eight new hotels are under construction, all of which are expected to be open by February 1, 1990. Of these hotels, seven will be operated under the "Hilton" name, while the remaining hotel will be operated under the "CrestHil by Hilton" name.

Expansion Program

A significant number of construction projects are either underway or scheduled to commence during the remainder of 1989, both in the United States and abroad. Other opportunities are being explored, although no assurances can be given that the negotiations will be successfully concluded or that the new hotels contemplated will be constructed. Hilton intends to expand its operation of hotels primarily through its management and franchise programs, and the Company will only invest if these facilities meet the Company's return on investment criteria.

The most significant new domestic hotel projects are identified below. Hotels under construction abroad are described under "International Hotel Operations—Expansion Program".

Hilton will mark its entry into the all-suites market in 1989, with the scheduled opening of three properties: the 230-suite Hilton Suites in Orange, California, the 212-suite Hilton Suites in Oakbrook, Illinois, just outside of Chicago, and the 199-suite Hilton Suites in the Nashville, Tennessee suburb of Brentwood. Each Hilton Suites property will feature fitness facilities, meeting facilities, a business center, a deli, convenience store and guest lounge.

The Company has also entered into, or is in advanced stages of negotiation for, management agreements to operate the following hotels, the anticipated completion dates of which are indicated parenthetically: the 400-room Brooklyn Hilton, Brooklyn, New York (winter, 1990), the 390-room Westbury Hilton on Long Island, New York (fall, 1990) and the 424-room Long Beach Hilton, Long Beach, California (winter, 1990). Except for the possible acquisition of an equity interest in the Westbury Hilton, the Company will not have any investment in, or make advances to, the owners of these hotels.

Hilton has entered into various agreements which restrict its right to operate hotels in various areas, including those hereafter described which, in management's opinion, represent the most significant restrictions to which the Company is subject. In addition, pursuant to an agreement entered into at the time of Hilton's distribution on December 1, 1964 to its stockholders of all the issued and outstanding capital stock of Hilton International Co. Hilton may not operate any facilities outside the United States identified as Hilton hotels.

6

Figure 9.3: Cover and Excerpts from Hilton Hotels Corporation's 10-K Report, 1988.

INFORMATION IN THE ANNUAL REPORT TO STOCKHOLDERS AND 10-K REPORT

Type of Information	Type of Report ARS	10-K
Auditor Name	A	A
Opinion	A	A
Compensation Plans		
Equity		S
Monetary		S
Company Information		
Nature of Business	S	A
History	S	F
Organization & Change	S	F
Debt Structure	A	A
Depreciation & Other Schedules		A
Directors, Officers, Insiders		
Identification	S	F
Background	S	S
Holdings		S
Compensation		S
Earnings Per Share	A	A
Financial Information		
Annual Audited	A	A
Foreign Operations	S	A
Legal Agreements		F
Loan Agreements		F
Plants & Properties	S	A
Product-Line Breakout	S	A
Securities Structure		A
Subsidiaries	S	A

Legend:

    A: Always included if it occurred or is significant
    F: Frequently included
    S: Special circumstances

Source: The information in this chart is condensed from *A Guide to SEC Corporate Filings* (Bethesda, MD: Disclosure, 1986), 12-13.

How can you get a copy of the ARS and the 10-K Report for Hilton Hotels Corporation? Many academic libraries and some public libraries collect these reports for companies on the New York Stock Exchange and the American Stock Exchange. Libraries that support large business programs also collect these reports for other publicly owned companies (i.e., those traded on other exchanges or over-the-counter). Some libraries request paper copies of these reports from the companies, while other libraries purchase them on microfiche. Ask at the reference desk to see if your library has these important sources of company information. If your library does not have 10-K and ARS Reports for the company you are researching, you can usually obtain them by writing to or calling the corporate headquarters and requesting copies. Another way to get the financial information published in the ARS and the 10-K report is to use *Compact Disclosure* (on CD-ROM) or Disclosure's online file, *Disclosure Database* (Bethesda, MD: Disclosure, Inc.). The Disclosure, Inc. company stores much of the financial data from the top publicly owned companies' reports in computer format. Your library may have *Compact Disclosure*, the CD-ROM version, or be able to access the Disclosure files online through Dialog or Dow Jones. Figure 9.4 shows an excerpt from part of the Hilton Hotels Corporation entry on *Compact Disclosure*. The information included, while in the typeface of a computer printer, is word-for-word the same information that appears in the company's annual report and 10-K Report.

INVESTMENT SERVICES

If the annual reports to shareholders and 10-K Reports are not readily available there are other sources that include much of this information. These sources are called investment services. Much of the information in investment services is generated from the ARS and 10-K Reports. The services' main purpose is to provide information on publicly owned companies and to advise investors on wise purchases. One of the most readily available investment services is *Value Line Investment Survey*, the same source used to find an industry overview in chapter 2.

Value Line Investment Survey

Value Line Investment Survey is a weekly, loose-leaf service that is filed in two notebooks. In Part 1, "Summary & Index," there is an alphabetical index of company names (figure 9.5). This leads you to Hilton Hotels on page 1777 of Part III, which is called "Ratings and Reports."

Figure 9.6 shows this analysis on Hilton, which includes charts of Hilton's past performance and a written summary of Hilton's prospective performance as an investment. According to this report, Hilton is "outstripping its peers and its historical record," occupancy rates are up, and Hilton is betting on its gaming hotels for future success. Overbuilding of the industry does not seem to be affecting Hilton's bottom line! In addition to this financial analysis, there is a short description of the company's major

```
HILTON HOTELS CORP

PRESIDENT'S LETTER:
(FROM ANNUAL REPORT TO SHAREHOLDERS)
    TO OUR STOCKHOLDERS
    We are pleased to report that your Company achieved record and earnings
from operations for the second consecutive year, continuing its positive
momentum both financially and operationally.  Both lodging and gaming made
significantly improved contributions to earnings.
    Net income for the year totaled $130.9 million, or $2.72 per share, compared
with $112.7 million, or $2.25 per share from operations for 1987. Inclusive of
property transactions, your Company earned $139.9 million, or $2.80 per share
in 1987.  There were no property transactions in 1988.
    The Company also continued to achieve significant cash flow from operations
(income before interest, depreciation and income taxes), reaching $312 million
1988 as compared to $271 million in 1987 and $225 million in 1986. This allows
us to continue the growth of our businesses and capitalize more readily on
opportunities while continuing our policy of distributing significant annual
dividends to our stockholders.
    Other highlights for 1988 include an increase in the quarterly cash dividend
rate and a 2-for-1 stock split in the form of a 100% stock distribution.  The
balance of this message is devoted to the factors which contributed to the most
successful operating year in the history of Hilton Hotels Corporation.
    Reputation and Industry Leadership The Hilton name is           the most
highly respected in t           According to recent ind                Hilton
is the ninth mo                  rican brand names,
global bra                            official spo
and                 and the                       ble
            ackground provides                    nt expansion.  Toda,
    ..c segments being served by h.              diversified with the
introduction of Hilton Suites, our mo       y-priced CrestHil by Hilton Program
and the expansion of our worldwide operations through Conrad International
Hotels.  With a strategic domestic and international expansion program built on
a solid foundation of 269 hotels in the U.S., we will continue to maintain our
preeminent position in the lodging industry.
    In a related development, Hilton will acquire a 32.5% interest in CONFIRM, a
joint venture developing an integrated travel reservations system using state
of the art computer technology.  The design and development of this system is
expected to take several years.  Upon completion, CONFIRM will be used by
Hilton and its partners, American Airlines, Marriott and Budget Rent-A-Car, and
will be marketed to others in the airline, car rental and lodging industries.
    Dividend Increased In recognition of the earnings progress of the Company,
the Board of Directors in June increased the annual cash dividend rate by 11
percent to $1.00 per share from $.90 per share.  Our stated dividend policy is
to pay out as cash dividends to stockholders approximately 40 percent of our
operating earnings and the Directors' action is in keeping with that policy.
    Also in June the Board authorized a 2-for-1 stock split in the form of a
100% stock distribution.  The stock split serves the purpose of making your
Company's stock more accessible to a broader market.
    Growth Factors Our 1988 performance is directly attributable to our
investment in our product, our heightened commitment to service through a
creative new employee training program, and an extensive quality assurance
program.  It reflects as well the results of an insightful, innovative
marketing strategy.
    Outstanding performances were achieved in 1988 by many of our most recently
renovated or expanded hotels, including the Waldorf-Astoria in New York, the
Capital Hilton in Washington, D.C., the Chicago Hilton & Towers, the San
Francisco Hilton on Hilton Square, the Hilton Hawaiian Village in Honolulu, and
the Las Vegas Hilton and Flamingo Hilton in Las Vegas.  Our expansion and
renovation program gave us first-class facilities at a fraction of the cost
that would have been required to build comparable properties today.
    Our renovation and expansion efforts have been rewarded by increases in our
occupancy and average room rates.  Our system-wide growth in average rate has
been nearly double that of inflation in the past three years, while at the same
time hotel occupancy grew from 65 percent in 1986 to 70 percent this year.
Hotel income contribution in 1988 increased by 14 percent over 1987 and 38
percent over the 1986 level.
    Focused marketing programs have complemented our improved facilities by
targeting key market segments.  Special efforts targeted at the leisure market
```

Figure 9.4: Excerpts from Computer Search on Hilton Hotels Corporation from *Compact Disclosure*, 1989.

PAGE NUMBERS Bold type refers to Ratings & Reports; *italics to Selection & Opinion*

NAME OF STOCK	Ticker Symbol	Timeliness		Rank For Safety	Beta	Recent Price	Estimated Range of 3-5 yr. average prices 1991-93	Current P/E Ratio 12mos.	Est'd Yield Next 12mos.	Est'd Earns. 12 mos. to 9-30-89	(f) Est'd Div'd next 12 mos.	Industry Rank	Qtr. Ended	Earns. Per.sh.	Year Ago	Technical Rank	Qtr. Ended	Latest Div'd	Year Ago	Where Options Trade
2059 Grubb & Ellis	GBE	3⅞	3	3	1.05		11- 16	(180-310%)	24.4	NIL	.16	NIL	69	12/31	.06	.02		3/31	NIL	NIL	4
564 Grumman	GQ	21	3	3	1.00		35- 50	(65-140%)	9.0	5.1%	2.34	1.08	79	12/31	.89	d.53		3/31	.25	.025	3 CBO
1824 Guilford Mills	GFD	30	4	3	.90		30- 45	(0- 50%)	12.9	2.7%	2.33	.80	75	12/31	.35	.46		6/30	.20	.20	2
432 Gulf Canada Res. (ASE)	GOU	13	–	3	NMF		17- 25	(30- 90%)	NMF	2.6%	d.28	.34-.17(h)	85	12/31	d.13(b)	.09(b)		6/30	.10 (b)	.10 (b)	–
1833 Gulf Resources & Chem.	GRE	11	4	3	1.00		10- 20	(N- 80%)	NMF	NIL	d.69	NIL	78	12/31	d.14	d 16		3/31	NIL	NIL	4
714 Gulf States Util	GSU	9⅝	3	5	.85		8- 16	(N- 65%)	10.1	NIL	.95	NIL	90	12/31	.05	31		3/31	NIL	NIL	2
840 1377 Gulf & Western	GW	53	3	3	1.10		55- 85	(5- 60%)	19.3	1.3%	2.75	.70	77	1/31	.58	54		6/30	.175	.175	3 CBO
2094 H&Q Healthcare Inv.	HQH	7¼	–	3	NMF		10- 15	(35-105%)	NMF	0.4%	NMF	.03	54	9/30	8.04(q)	9 45(q)		3/31	.02	NIL	–
2140 1176 HRE Properties	HRE	25	–	2	.60		25- 35	(0- 40%)	22.9	7.2%	1.09	1.80-1.65	92	1/31	.23	35		6/30	.45	.45	–
453 Hadson Corp.	HAD	3½	5	5	1.35		5- 10	(45-185%)	20.6	NIL	.17	NIL	48	12/31	.05	03		3/31	NIL	NIL	4
2083 Hall (Frank B.) & Co.	FBH	3¾	4	5	1.05		5- 10	(30-165%)	NMF	NIL	d.96	NIL	48	12/31	d.41	d 51		3/31	NIL	NIL	3
1855 Halliburton Co	HAL	31	3	3	1.20		45- 65	(45-185%)	30.7	3.5%	1.01	1.10	38	12/31	.11	32		3/31	.25	.25	3 CBO
239 2060 Hallwood Grdup	HWG	14	3	5	1.15		20- 40	(45-185%)	18.2	NIL	.77	NIL	69	1/31	d.06	1 27		6/30	▼NIL	.28	4
411 Hamilton Oil (OTC)	HAML	30	4	3	.65		30- 45	(0- 50%)	61.2	0.3%	.49	.10	46	12/31	d.06	20		6/30	.025	.025	3
1690 Hancock Fabrics	HKF	23	–	3	NMF		30- 40	(30- 75%)	12.5	2.1%	1.84	.48	29	1/31	.52	43		6/30	▲.12	.10	–
982 Hancock (John) Invs. Tr.	JHI	20	3	1	.60		25- 30	(25- 50%)	NMF	10.0%	NMF	2.00	56	9/30	20.74(q)	20 40(q)		3/31	.46	.46	3
1762 Handleman Co.	HDL	31	1	3	1.40		30- 40	(N- 30%)	14.6	1.9%	2.12	.58	26	1/31	.62	48		6/30	.14	.12	1
593 Handy & Harman	HNH	21	3	3	.80		25- 40	(20- 90%)	21.2	3.3%	.99	.70	65	12/31	.19	d.03		3/31	.165	.165	3
510 Hanna (M A.) Co.	MAH	26	▲1	3	.95		35- 55	(35-110%)	10.0	1.5%	2.61	.40	51	12/31	.47	21		3/31	.10	.067	2
1510 Hannaford Brothers	HRD	27	1	3	1.05		35- 50	(30- 85%)	15.4	1.4%	1.75	.37	36	12/31	.36	.29		3/31	▲.045	.08	2
1140 826 Hanson PLC (ADR)	HAN	16	1	2	.90		25- 35	(55-120%)	8.0	5.1%	2.00	.81	10	12/31	.39	32		3/31	.58	.362	2 CBO
1797 Harcourt Brace Jov	HBJ	9⅝	–	5	NMF		25- 35	(55-160%)	NMF	NIL	d1.79	NIL	83	12/31	d1.04	d1.00		3/31	NIL	NIL	– ASE
1798 Harland (John H.)	JH	20	2	1	1.05		30- 45	(50-125%)	12.7	3.5%	1.57	.70	83	3/31	♦.37	.34		3/31	▲.17	.145	4
1355 Harnischfeger Inds.	HPH	17	3	3	1.25		25- 40	(45-135%)	12.1	1.4%	1.40	.23	30	1/31	.28	.12		6/30	.05	.05	4 PHL
1043 Harris Corp.	HRS	29	3	3	1.20		40- 60	(40-105%)	10.3	3.0%	2.82	.88	52	12/31	.65	.60		3/31	.22	.22	3 CBO
1439 594 Harsco Corp.	HSC	25	5	1	.95		40- 50	(60-100%)	22.9	4.8%	1.09	1.20	65	12/31	d.87	67		6/30	.30	28	5
★★ 631 Hartford Steam Boiler (OTC)	HBOL	42	1	3	.85		45- 65	(5- 55%)	11.8	3.3%	3.56	1.40	23	3/31	♦.97	79		6/30	.35	.30	2
1605 Hartmarx Corp.	HMX	27	3	3	1.15		35- 55	(30-105%)	12.6	4.4%	2.14	1.20	32	2/28	.50	47		6/30	▲.30	275	3
1553 Hasbro Inc. (ASE)	HAS	31	3	3	1.25		25- 45	(N- 30%)	13.5	0.8%	1.41	.16	18	12/31	.36	.11		6/30	▲.04	.03	3 PAC
1691 Haverty Furniture (OTC)	HAVT	12	3	3	1.00		15- 25	(25-110%)	8.5	3.0%	1.41	.36	29	12/31	.41	.39		3/31	.09	.087	3
1719 Hawaiian Elec.	HE	30	4	1	.65		35- 45	(15- 50%)	10.0	7.0%	2.99	2.10	91	3/31	♦.83	.76		6/30	♦ .51	.48	3
221 Healthdyne Inc. (OTC)	HDYN	4⅝	–	5	1.20		7- 15	(50-225%)	NMF	NIL	d.28	NIL	14	12/31	d.18	d.09		3/31	NIL	NIL	–
894 Hechinger Co. 'A' (OTC)	HECHA	18	2	3	1.05		40- 60	(120-235%)	12.9	0.9%	1.39	.16	5	1/31	.34	.29		3/31	.04	.04	3
1233 Hecla Mining	HL	13	3	3	.95		20- 30	(55-130%)	20.3	0.4%	.64	.05	70	12/31	.14	.17		12/31	.05	.05	4 ASE
1577 Heekin Can (OTC)	HEKN	30	3	4	1.00		35- 60	(15-100%)	8.8	NIL	3.41	NIL	–	3/31	.56	.51		3/31	NIL	NIL	2
2061 Hees Int'l Bancorp. (TSE)	HIL.TO	31 (b)	1	2	.70		45- 65	(45-110%)	11.7	2.7%	2.68	.85	80	12/31	.65(b)	.54(b)		6/30	▲.41 (b)	.35 (b)	2 TSE
1692 Heilig Meyers	HMY	19	3	3	1.10		25- 40	(30-110%)	10.4	2.1%	1.82	.40	29	2/28	.24	.21		6/30	▲.10	.09	3
1470 Heinz (H.J.)	HNZ	51	3	1	1.00		75- 90	(45- 75%)	14.4	3.0%	3.53	1.54	40	1/31	.78	.69		3/31	.36	.31	3 CBO
811 Helene Curtis	HC	54	2	3	1.20		60- 90	(10- 65%)	14.4	1.2%	3.75	.65	31	2/28	.89	2 27		3/31	.15	.15	2
1856 Helmerich & Payne	HP	27	3	3	.90		35- 55	(30-105%)	28.4	1.6%	.95	.43	38	12/31	.21	.20		6/30	.105	.10	3 NYS
367 Helvetia Fund	SWZ	9¾	–	3	NMF		20- 30	(115-220%)	NMF	0.5%	NMF	.05	–	12/31	10.99(q)	12.34(q)		3/31	NIL	NIL	–
1378 Henley Group 'A' (OTC)	HENG	71	–	3	NMF		100- 120	(40- 70%)	NMF	NIL	d6.69	NIL	77	9/30	d.71	.40		3/31	NIL	NIL	– CBO
1289 511 Hercules Inc.	HPC	47	▲4	3	1.05		70- 100	(50-115%)	13.4	4.8%	3.50	2.24	51	3/31	♦.90	.82		3/31	.56	.48	3 ASE
1471 Hershey Foods	HSY	28	3	2	1.05		35- 45	(25- 80%)	14.7	2.5%	1.91	.70	40	12/31	.51	.45		3/31	.175	.155	3 ASE
839 1096 Hewlett-Packard	HWP	57	2	2	1.20		100- 140	(75-145%)	14.3	0.6%	4.00	.34	71	1/31	.83	.71		3/31	.085	.065	3 CBO
240 565 Hexcel Corp.	HXL	30	4	3	1.10		35- 55	(15- 85%)	13.8	1.5%	2.17	.44	78	3/31	♦.22	48		3/31	.11	.10	4
1693 Highland Superstores (OTC)	HIGH	6½	4	4	1.05		20- 30	(210-360%)	14.4	NIL	.45	NIL	29	1/31	.24	.20		3/31	NIL	NIL	4
1578 Hillenbrand Ind	HB	31	4	2	.85		40- 50	(30- 60%)	16.8	1.6%	1.87	.50	50	2/28	.44	.37		6/30	.125	.10	4
691 1777 Hilton Hotels	HLI	59	4	1	.95		65- 85	(10- 45%)	19.5	1.7%	3.02	1.05	80	3/31	♦.27	.58		3/31	.25	.225	2 PAC
HMT Inc.	HMT	43	–	3	NMF		45- 70	(5- 65%)	7.6	3.7%	5.64	1.60	4	10/31	1.55	.91		6/30	▲.40	.30	–
...Inds.	HSI	37	4	3	.90		15- 25	(N- 45%)	42.5	2.8%	.40	.44	78	2/28	.06	.26		3/31	.11	.11	4
...(ADR)	HIT	116	3	3	.90		175- 260	(50-125%)	24.5	0.7%	4.74	.77	43	9/30	2.06(p)	1.46(p)		3/31	NIL	NIL	3 CBO
...rp.	HIA	37	–	4	NMF		40- 70	(10- 90%)	NMF	NIL	NMF	NIL	60	12/31	d.59	d.48		3/31	NIL	NIL	– CBO
...	HFF	61	–	3	.90		40- 70	(N- 15%)	15.8	2.3%	3.85	1.40	40	2/28	.89	.07		3/31	.33	.33	– CBQ
...ot	HD	39	1	3	1.25		55- 80	(40-105%)	22.0	0.3%	1.77	.12	5	1/31	.37	.32		3/31	.03	.02	2 PHL
... Corp.	HFD	37	2	3	1.10		45- 65	(20- 75%)	6.4	0.5%	5.81	.20	84	12/31	1.51	89		6/30	.05	.05	2 CBO
...Group	HME	13	2	3	1.00		20- 35	(55-170%)	6.5	1.5%	2.00	.20	23	12/31	.45	23		6/30	.05	.05	3
1... ...rnestake Mining	HM	13	▼4	3	.65		35- 55	(90-170%)	19.1	1.5%	.68	.20	70	12/31	.16	17		3/31	.05	.05	3 CBO
106 Honda Motor (ADR)(•)	HMC	29	3	3	1.00		40- 60	(40-105%)	16.2	0.7%	1.79	.20	12	12/31	.38	36		3/31	NIL	.11	3 PHL
1016 Honeywell, Inc.	HON	73	▲3	3	1.15		80- 120	(10- 65%)	NMF	2.9%	d7.00	2.13	62	3/31	♦1.46	1.36		6/30	♦.525	.525	3 CBO
1289 912 HON INDUSTRIES (OTC)	HONI	23	▲2	2	.65		40- 55	(10- 75%)	11.1	2.1%	▲2.07	.48	82	3/31	♦.54	25		3/31	▲.12	.10	3
239 670 Horizon Corp.	HZN	2⅛	4	5	1.15		3- 5	(45-140%)	NMF	NIL	d3.69	NIL	81	12/31	d3.49	d.09		3/31	NIL	NIL	3
1473 Hormel (Geo. A.) (ASE)	HRL	22	3	1	1.00		30- 50	(35-125%)	12.0	2.0%	1.70	.45	40	1/31	.36	32		6/30	.11	.09	3
1694 Horn & Hardart (ASE)	HOR	7¼	4	5	1.30		12- 20	(65-175%)	22.8	NIL	.32	NIL	29	12/31	.08	.19		3/31	NIL	NIL	5
238 1282 Hospital Corp. of Amer.								SEE FINAL SUPPLEMENT													
1799 Houghton Mifflin	HTN	45	–	3	1.10		35- 55	(N- 20%)	22.5	1.5%	2.00	.66	83	12/31	d.20	d 23		3/31	.165	.155	– PAC
840 2062 Household Int'l	HI	54	–	3	NMF		85- 115	(55-115%)	9.3	4.1%	5.79	2.19	69	12/31	1.29	1.35		6/30	.535	.50	– ASE
1695 House of Fabrics	HF	24	3	3	.90		25- 40	(5- 65%)	12.9	2.0%	1.86	.48	29	1/31	.70	64		9/30	.12	.12	2
715 Houston Inds.	HOU	29	5	3	.80		35- 50	(20- 70%)	10.2	10.2%	2.85	2.96	90	12/31	.40	.63		6/30	.74	.74	4 NYS
882 Hovnanian Enterpr. (ASE)	HOV	9¼	2	4	1.40		15- 25	(60-170%)	6.2	NIL	1.50	NIL	35	11/30	.34	.24		3/31	NIL	NIL	3
1017 Hubbell Inc. 'B' (ASE)	HUBB	35	3	2	.95		45- 65	(45- 85%)	12.5	3.3%	2.81	1.17	62	3/31	♦.70	62		6/30	28	238	3
1642 Hudson's Bay Co. (TSE)	HBC.TO	26 (b)	2	4	.65		25- 40	(N- 55%)	36.1	2.3%	.72	.60	21	1/31	2.29(b)	1.72(b)		6/30	.15 (b)	.15 (b)	2
1474 Hudson Foods 'A' (ASE)	HFI	11	3	4	.70		15- 20	(35- 80%)	10.1	1.1%	1.09	.12	40	12/31	.12	d 43		6/30	.03	.03	3
1763 Huffy Corp.	HUF	17	3	3	1.10		13- 19	(N- 10%)	13.0	2.1%	1.31	.35	26	3/31	♦.50	46		6/30	.08	.073	2
896 Hughes Supply	HUG	19	3	3	.95		25- 40	(30-110%)	8.9	1.7%	2.13	.32	5	1/31	.53	52		6/30	♦.08	.073	3
1283 Humana Inc.	HUM	31	2	3	1.15		40- 60	(30- 95%)	12.4	3.2%	2.50	.98	25	2/28	.63	56		6/30	.23	.20	3 CBO
654 Huntington Bancshs. (OTC)	HBAN	20	3	2	.75		25- 40	(25-100%)	8.2	4.0%	2.44	.79	58	3/31	♦.61	55		6/30	.185	.168	3
1905 273 Hunt (J.B.) (OTC)	JBHT	20	3	3	1.20		45- 65	(125-225%)	13.2	1.2%	1.51	.24	27	3/31	.21	25		6/30	♦.06	.05	3
1126 Hunt Mfg	HUN	30	2	3	.90		35- 55	(15- 85%)	17.8	1.3%	1.69	.40	59	2/28	.36	30		3/31	▲.10	.085	3
1427 Hydraulic Co.	THC	28	5	3	.80		35- 50	(25- 80%)	12.0	5.6%	2.33	1.58	–	12/31	.63	.74		6/30	▲.395	38	3

(Page / Industry Rank annotations and arrows appear in the left margin near HMT Inc. and the following rows)

(c) Dividends estimated partly exempt from ordinary income tax.
d Deficit.
(e) Includes distribution of assets.
(f) The estimate may reflect a probable increase or decrease. If a dividend boost or cut is possible but not probable, two figures are shown, the first is the most likely.

(g) Dividends subject to foreign withholding tax for U.S. residents.
(h) Est'd Earnings & Est'd Dividends after conversion to U.S. Dollars at Value Line estimated translation rate.
(j) Trading suspended.

(k) 12 months   (m) 9 months   (p) 6 months
(q) Asset value.   (r) Estimates
('s) Rank removed due to outstanding exchange offer.
(u) Excludes distribution of assets.

N Negative figure   NA Not available.
NC Not comparable   NMF No meaningful figure

Factual material is obtained from sources believed to be reliable, but the publisher is not responsible for any errors or omissions contained herein.

Figure 9.5: "Part 1: Summary of Advices and Index" from *Value Line Investment Survey*, 28 April 1989.

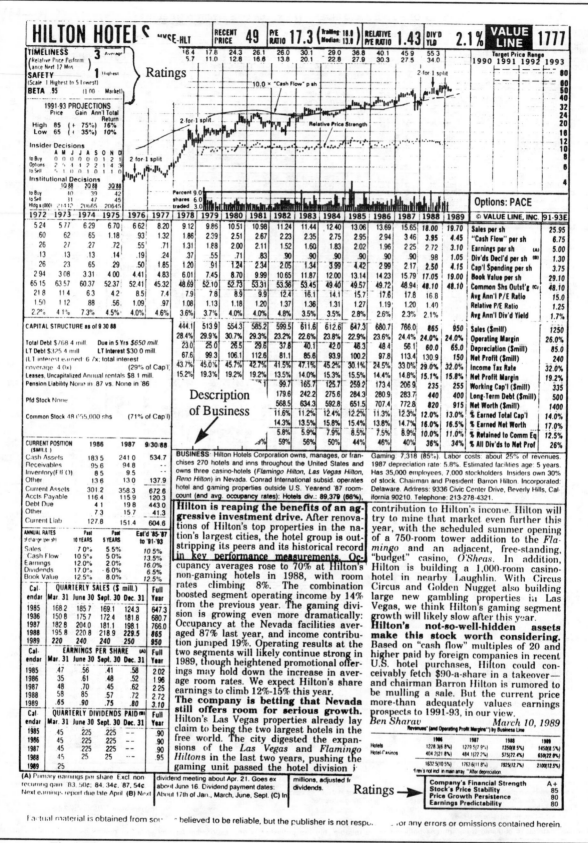

Figure 9.6: "Hilton Hotels" Entry from *Value Line Investment Survey*, 3 March 1989.

116

business. Three *Value Line Investment Survey* ratings are given, including timeliness, safety, and the beta coefficient, which represents Hilton's price fluctuation relative to other stocks. Other ratings include Hilton's financial strength, price stability, price growth persistence, and earnings predictability. For more instruction on how to read and interpret *Value Line Investment Survey*, see the paperback booklet *How To Use the Value Line Investment Survey: A Subscriber's Guide* (New York: Value Line, Inc., 1985).

If more information is needed on your company, or if your library does not subscribe to *Value Line Investment Survey*, the next step is to look in *Moody's Manuals* (New York: Moody's Investors Service, 1954-) and/or Standard & Poor's *Standard Corporation Descriptions* (New York: Standard & Poor's Corporation, 1915-).

Moody's Manuals

Moody's Manuals are eight hard-bound sets of volumes that are issued annually:

Moody's Transportation Manual,
Moody's Public Utilities Manual,
Moody's Bank & Finance Manual,
Moody's Industrial Manual,
Moody's OTC Manual,
Moody's Municipal & Government Manual,
Moody's International Manual, and
Moody's OTC Unlisted Manual.

There is an alphabetical name index to all eight volumes called *Moody's Complete Corporate Index*, which lists the specific *Manual*, volume, and page number for each company (figure 9.7). Here you determine that Hilton Hotels Corporation can be found in the *Moody's Industrial Manual* on page 429 in volume 1.

Over 22,000 companies that are listed on the major stock exchanges are included in *Moody's Manuals*, although the amount of information on each company varies according to its size and importance. Figure 9.8 illustrates the first page of the Hilton report from *Moody's Industrial Manual*. Each report includes a brief company history, a description of business, a list of properties and subsidiaries, detailed financial data, and a reprint of the letter to stockholders (figure 9.9). Note the section in the letter to stockholders where Barron Hilton addresses directly the problem of overbuilding and how Hilton plans to expand cautiously.

Each *Moody's Manual* is kept up-to-date by a loose-leaf volume called "News Reports." Changes in management, recent financial reports, and other information from news releases are published in these "News Reports," which have weekly and cumulative indexes.

		Vol	Page
Hewden Stuart PLC (United Kingdom)	INTL	2	3972
Hewitt Memorial Hospital	B&F	2	5085
◆ Hewlett-Packard Co.	IND	1	3033
Hewlett-Packard Ltd. (United Kingdom)	INTL	2	3972
Hexagon (Sweden)	INTL	2	3512
Hexcel Corp.	IND	1	3034
Hi-Port Industries, Inc.	OTC		2050
Hi-Shear Industries, Inc.	IND	1	3035
Hi-Tech Robotics Ltd.	UOTC		584
Hi, Tiger International, Inc.	UOTC		585
Hia, Inc.	OTC		1635
HIA, Inc.	UOTC		585
Hibernia Corp.	B&F	1	2048
Hibernia National Bank In New Orleans (La.)	B&F	1	2048
Hibernia Savings Bank (The) (Mass.)	B&F	1	2048
Hickam (Dow B.) Inc.	OTC		1635
Hickok Electrical Instrument Co.	UOTC		586
Hickory Furniture Co.	UOTC		586
Hicksville Bank (Ohio)	B&F	1	2618
Hickson International PLC (United Kingdom)	INTL	2	3973
Hidalgo County Bank & Trust Co. (Mercedes, Tex.)	B&F	1	2618
Hidroelectrica De Cataluna, S.A. (Spain)	INTL	2	3430
Hidroelectrica Del Cantabrico, S.A. (Spain)	INTL	2	3430
Hidroelectrica Espanola, S.A. (Spain)	INTL	2	3430
Hiex Development USA Inc.	UOTC		587
Higate Limited (South Africa)	INTL	2	3340
◆ Higbee Co.	UOTC		587
Higby (J.), Inc.	OTC		2051
Higgs & Hill PLC (United Kingdom)	INTL	2	3973
High Country Ventures, Inc.	OTC		543
High Country Ventures, Inc.	UOTC		54
High Income Advantage Trust	B&F	2	4529
High Income Advantage Trust III	B&F	2	4530
High Point Bank & Trust Co. (High Point, N.C.)	B&F	1	2049
High Point Financial Corp.	B&F	1	2049
High Point, Thomasville & Denton R.R. Co.	TRANS		379
High Yield Income Fund, Inc.	B&F	2	4530
High Yield Plus Fund, Inc.	B&F	2	4531
Highcroft Investment Trust PLC (United Kingdom)	INTL	2	3974
Highland Distilleries Co. PLC (United Kingdom)	INTL	2	3974
Highland Community Bank (Chicago, Ill.)	B&F	1	2618
Highland Electronics Group PLC (United Kingdom)	INTL	2	3974
Highlander International Corp.	UOTC		588
Highland Lakes National Bank (Kingsland, Tex.)	B&F	1	2049
Highland Park Bank & Trust (Topeka, Kan.)	B&F	1	2049
Highland Superstores, Inc.	OTC		2051
Highlands & Lowlands Berhad (Malaysia)	INTL	2	2901
Highline Industries, Inc.	UOTC		588
Highveld Steel And Vanadium Corp. Ltd. (South Africa)	INTL	2	3340
Highwood Resources Ltd. (Canada)	INTL	1	974
Hilb, Rogal and Hamilton Co.	B&F	2	5721
Hill 50 Gold Mine N.L. (Australia)	INTL	1	129
Hill Minerals N.L. (Australia)	INTL	1	129
Hill Samuel & Co., Ltd. (United Kingdom)	INTL	2	3975
Hill Samuel Group PLC (United Kingdom)	INTL	2	3975
Hillenbrand Industries, Inc.	IND	1	3036
Hills Bank & Trust Co. (Hills, Ia.)	B&F	1	2050
◆ Hills Department Stores, Inc.	IND	1	3036
Hills Industries Ltd. (Australia)	INTL	1	130
Hillsdale County National Bank (Hillsdale, Mich.)	B&F	1	2050
Hillsdown Holdings PLC (United Kingdom)	INTL	2	3976
Hillside Gold & Minerals	UOTC		549
◆ *Hilton Hotels Corp.*	IND	1	4291
Himedics, Inc.			
Himedics, Inc.			
Himont Inc.			
Hinderliter Industries, Inc.			
Hindustan Motors Ltd. (India)			
Hinesville Bank (Hinesville, Ga.)			
Hingham Institution for Savings			
Hino Motors, Ltd. (Japan)			
Hipotronics, Inc.			
Hiroshima Sogo Bank, Ltd. (The) (Japan)			
Hitachi Cable, Ltd. (Japan)			
Hitachi Credit Corporation (Japan)			
Hitachi Koki Co., Ltd. (Japan)			
Hitachi, Ltd. (Japan)	INTL	2	2616
Hitachi Maxell, Ltd. (Japan)	INTL	2	2618
Hitachi Metals, Ltd. (Japan)	INTL	2	2617
Hitachi Sales Corp. (Japan)	INTL	2	2619
Hitachi Zosen Corp. (Japan)	INTL	2	2620
Hitech Engineering Co.	UOTC		589
Hiteck International Products, Inc.	UOTC		589
HITK Corp.	B&F	2	4531
Hitox Corporation of America	OTC		1635
HK-TVB Ltd. (Hong Kong)	INTL	1	1850
HMG/Courtland Properties, Inc.	B&F	2	5086
HMO America, Inc.	OTC		2052
H.M.S.S., Inc.	OTC		2052
Hocking Valley Bank (Athens, Oh.)	B&F	1	2050
Hodgson Holdings PLC (United Kingdom)	INTL	2	3976
Hodgson Houses, Inc.	UOTC		590
Hoechst A.G.	IND		438
◆ *Hoechst A.G. (Germany, Fed. Rep.)*	INTL	1	1713
Hoesch AG (Germany, Fed. Rep.)	INTL	1	1763
Hoechst Celanese Corp.	IND		444
◆ *Hoechst Celanese Corp.*	INTL	1	1719
Hoechst Holland N.V. (Netherlands)	INTL	2	2988
F. Hoffmann-La Roche & Co. A.G. (Switzerland)	INTL	2	3673
Hofmann Industries, Inc.	IND	1	3040
Hogan Systems, Inc.	OTC		2053
HOH Water Technology Corp.	UOTC		590
Hoisington (Kans.) National Bank	B&F	1	2618
Hojgaard & Schultz A/S (Denmark)	INTL	1	1452
Hokkaido Electric Power Co. Inc. (Japan)	INTL	2	2620
Hokkaido Takushoku Bank, Ltd. (Japan)	INTL	2	2620
Hokuetsu Bank, Ltd. (Japan)	INTL	2	2621
Hokuriku Electric Power Co., Ind. (Japan)	INTL	2	2622
Holco Mortgage Acceptance Corp. I	B&F	2	5479
Holden-Day Inc.	UOTC		591
'Holderbank' Financiere Glaris Ltd. (Switzerland)	INTL	2	3674
Holec N.V. (Netherlands)	INTL	2	2989
◆ *Holiday Corp.*	IND	1	1305

		Vol	Page
◆ Holiday Inns, Inc.	IND	1	3040
Holiday Rambler Corp.	UOTC		592
Holiday Services, Inc.	UOTC		592
John Holland Holdings Ltd. (Australia)	INTL	1	130
Holland Industries, Inc.	TRANS		1179
Hollandsche Beton Groep NV (Netherlands)	INTL	2	2989
Hollas Group (The) (United Kingdom)	INTL	2	3977
Hollidaysburg Trust Co (Pa.)	B&F	1	2618
Hollinger Inc. (Canada)	INTL	1	974
Hollis, PLC (United Kingdom)	INTL	2	3977
Hollming OY (Finland)	INTL	1	1514
Holly Corp.	IND	1	3041
◆ Holly Farms Corp.	IND	1	3042
Hollywood Park Realty Enterprises, Inc. and Hollywood Park Operating Co.	UOTC		592
Holmen Bruk AB (Sweden)	INTL	2	3513
Holmes County Bank & Trust Co. (Lexington, Miss.)	B&F	1	2618
Holometrix, Inc.	UOTC		593
Holston Land Company, Inc.	TRANS		267
Holt (John) Group Ltd. (United Kingdom)	INTL	2	3978
Holton Inter-Urban Ry. Co.	TRANS		342
Holyoke Water Power Company	UTIL	2	2939
Holyoke & Westfield R.R. Co.	TRANS		391
Holzstoff Holding AG (Switzerland)	INTL	2	3675
Homasote Co.	IND	1	3043
The Home Avenue Railroad Company	TRANS		261
Home Bank of Guntersville (Al)	B&F	1	2618
Home Beneficial Corp.	B&F	2	5721
Home Beneficial Life Insurance Co., Inc. (Richmond, Va.)	B&F	2	5721
Home Building Society (Australia)	INTL	1	130
Home & City Savings Bank (Albany, N.Y.)	B&F	1	2050
◆ Home Depot, Inc.	IND	1	3044
Home Federal Corp.	B&F	1	2762
Home Federal Savings Bank of Georgia	B&F	1	2051
Home Federal Savings Bank, Northern Ohio (Lakewood)	B&F	1	2051
Home Federal Savings Bank (Salisbury, NC)	B&F	1	2051
Home Federal Savings Bank (S.C.)	B&F	1	2052
Home Federal Savings Bank (Xenia, Oh.)	B&F	1	2052
Home Federal Savings and Loan Association of the Rockies	B&F	1	2762
Home Federal Savings and Loan Association of Upper East Tennessee (Johnson City, Tenn.)	B&F	1	2762
Home Insurance Co. (The)	B&F	2	5722
Home Intensive Care, Inc	OTC		1636
Home Interstate Bancorp	B&F	1	2053
Home National Bank of Arkansas City (KS)	B&F	1	2618
Home National Bank of Sutton (W.V.)	B&F	1	2618
Home Office Reference Laboratory, Inc.	OTC		1636
◆ Home Owners Savings Bank F.S.B.	B&F	1	2763
Home Port Bancorp., Inc.	B&F	1	2053
Home Savings of America, A Federal Savings & Loan Assn.	B&F	1	2765
Home Savings Association of Pennsylvania	B&F	1	2766
Home Savings Bank (Brooklyn, N.Y.)	B&F	1	2053
Home Savings and Loan Association (Durham, NC)	B&F	1	2766
◆ Home Shopping Network Inc.	IND	1	3044
Home State Bank (Crystal Lake, Ill.)	B&F	1	2054
Home State Bank (Erie, Ks)	B&F	1	2618
Home State Bank (Hobart, Ok)	B&F	1	2618
Home State Bank (Jefferson, Iowa)	B&F	1	2618
Home State Bank of Kansas City (Kansas)	B&F	1	2054
Home State Bank (Lewis, Ks)	B&F	1	2618
Home State Bank (Loveland, Co)	B&F	1	2618
Home State Bank & Trust Co. (Humboldt, Neb)	B&F	1	2618
Home Trust & Savings Bank (Osage, Ia)	B&F	1	2618
Home Unity Savings and Loan Association	B&F	1	2767
...mecare Management, Inc.	OTC		1637
...ed Corp.	B&F	1	2767
...ee Village Resorts, Inc./Homefree Investors L.P.	B&F	2	5086
...National Bank (Homer, La)	B&F	1	2618
...ake Mining Co.	IND	1	3046
...ead Financial Corp.	B&F	1	2768
...ead Savings, A Federal Savings & Loan Assoc. (Burgame, CA.)	B&F	1	2769
...ead Industries, Inc.	UOTC		594
...ead Minerals Corp.	UOTC		594
...own BanCorporation, Inc.	B&F	1	2054
...ndustries, Inc.	OTC		2053
...Motor Co., Ltd.(Honda Giken Kogyo Kabushiki Kaisha) (Japan)	INTL	2	2622
Honduras (Republic of)	INTL	1	1833
◆ HonFed Bank, A Federal Savings Bank	B&F	1	2769
Honesdale National Bank (Honesdale, Pa.)	B&F	1	2054
◆ Honeywell Finance Inc.	B&F	2	5479
◆ Honeywell Inc.	IND	1	3047
Honeywell Ltd. (Canada)	INTL	1	975
Hong Kong	INTL	1	1837
Hong Kong Aircraft Engineering Co. Ltd. (Hong Kong)	INTL	1	1851
Hong Kong Carpet Holdings Ltd.	INTL	1	1851
Hong Kong & China Gas Co., Ltd. (Hong Kong)	INTL	1	1851
Hongkong Electric Holdings Ltd.	INTL	1	1852
Hong Leong Industries Berhad (Malaysia)	INTL	2	2901
Hongkew Holdings Ltd. (Hong Kong)	INTL	1	1852
Hongkong Land Co. Ltd.	INTL	1	1852
Hongkong Realty & Trust Co., Ltd.	INTL	1	1853
Hongkong and Shanghai Banking Corp.	INTL	1	1853
Hongkong and Shanghai Hotels, Ltd.	INTL	1	1854
Hongkong Telecommunications Ltd.	INTL	1	1854
Honshu Paper Co., Ltd. (Japan)	INTL	2	2624
Hooker Corp. Ltd. (Australia)	INTL	1	131
Hooker Enterprises, Inc.	UOTC		595
Hooper Holmes, Inc.	IND	1	2402
Hopewell Holdings Ltd. (Hong Kong)	INTL	1	1855
Hopkinson Holdings PLC (United Kingdom)	INTL	2	3978
Hopper Soliday Corp.	B&F	2	5480
Horace Cory PLC (United Kingdom)	INTL	2	3979
Horace Mann Growth Fund, Inc.	B&F	2	4531
Horizon Bank N.A. (Waterloo, NY)	B&F	1	2618
Horizon Corp.	B&F	2	5086
Horizon Financial Services, Inc.	B&F	2	2770
Horizon Gold Shares, Inc.	UOTC		595
Horizon Healthcare Corp.	IND	1	3050
Horizon Industries, Inc.	OTC		1637
Horizon Village Corp., Canada	IND	1	3051
Horizon Village Corporation, Canada	INTL	1	976
Horizon Enterprises, Inc.	UOTC		595

↑ ↑ ↑
Page
Volume
Manual Name

Figure 9.7: Entry for Hilton Hotels from *Moody's Complete Corporate Index*, 1988.

MOODY'S INDUSTRIAL MANUAL 429

HILTON HOTELS CORPORATION

CAPITAL STRUCTURE

LONG TERM DEBT

Issue	Rating	Amount Outstanding	[5]Times Charges Earned 1988	1987	Interest Dates	Call Price	Price Range 1988	1987
1. Int'l Leisure Corp. Coll. trust 8s, 1993	A1	$7,800,000			J&D1	[1]101.33	......	93 - 56½
2. Hilton New Jersey Corp. senior deb. 11⅜s, 1992	A2	74,800,000	4.78	8.28	J&D1	[3]	104 -101½	109 -100
3. Hilton New Jersey Corp. senior deb. 10⅝s, 1994	A2	75,000,000			J&J15	[3]	103⅛-100¾	105 -101⅛
4. 9¼% Notes, due 1998	A2	199,200,000			J&D1	[3]	100 - 97	
5. Other long term debt	......	214,700,000			......	......	......	......

CAPITAL STOCK

Issue	Par Value	Rating	Shares Outstanding	Earned per Sh. 1988	1987	Divs. per Sh. 1988	1987	Call Price	Price Range 1988	1987
1. Common	$2.50	......	[2]48,100,000	[2]$2.72	[2][4]$2.80	[4]$0.95	[4]$0.90	......	[4]55¼- 34	[4]45⅞- 27½

[1]Subject to change; see text. [2]Based on average common and common equivalent shs; adj. for 2-for-1 split 6/88. [3]Callable in future, see text. [4]Restated to reflect 2 for-1 stock split in 1988. [5]Including finance subsidiaries.

HISTORY

Incorporated ... 46, pursuant to ... der which Co. acq ... Co., Palmer House ... ay- ton Biltmore ... red assets of Lubb ... ex- ico Hilton Hot ... on June 1, 1946.

Hilton Hot ... ly- owned subsidi ... ... over the invest ... for the operation ... tal United States.

In 1949-50, Co. purchased a majority interest in Hotel Waldorf-Astoria Corp., which leased and operated the Hotel Waldorf-Astoria. Hotel Waldorf-Astoria Corp. was merged into Hilton Hotels Corp. Dec. 31, 1953.

In Oct., 1954, Co. acquired the furniture, fixtures, operating equipment and other assets of Hotels Statler Co., Inc. except for land, buildings and leasehold estates. The land, buildings and leasehold estates of Hotels Statler Co. was acquired by Statler Hotels Delaware Corp., which was merged into Hilton Hotels Corp. in 1962.

In Oct., 1958, Hilton Credit Corp. was organized as an affiliate to operate a credit card service under the name of "Carte Blanche". Co. transferred its credit card list, credit files, etc. to the new company in exchange for 1,000,000 shares. Hilton Credit Corp. was merged into Carte Blanche Corp. as of Dec. 31, 1965, and in 1970 Hilton completed a tax-free exchange of all its Carte Blanche shares for Avco Corp. preferred stock.

In a series of transactions in 1961, Co. acquired a 50% interest in Hilton-Burns Hotels Co., owner of the Hilton Hawaiian Village complex of land and buildings. Also, in 1961, Hilton acquired interests in the companies building the New York Hilton and Washington Hilton Hotels. Hilton owns a 50% interest in each of these three hotels.

On Dec. 1, 1964, stock of Hilton Hotels International, Inc. was distributed to Co.'s stockholders on the basis of one share of Hilton International Co. for each two shares of Co. stock held. Hilton International Co. merged into Trans World Airlines, Inc. in 1967. Acquired by Allegis Corp. early in 1987, Hilton International was purchased by Ladbroke PLC later that year.

In 1966, Co. initiated a franchise program under the Statler Hilton name. Beginning in 1969, the franchise program was conducted under the Hilton name rather than the Statler Hilton identification.

On Feb. 29, 1972, Co. merged International Leisure Corp. into Co. on the basis of 0.35 Co. common shares for each Leisure share. Leisure's principal assets were the Las Vegas Hilton and Flamingo Hilton hotel-casinos. Co. had acquired a 44% interest in Leisure in 1970, an additional 6% interest plus one share in Mar., 1971, and an additional 35.8% interest in Aug., 1971.

In Feb., 1975, Co. sold a 50% interest in six hotels to Prudential Insurance Co. of America for $83,400,000 ($66 million in cash and $17.4 million in existing mortgage indebtedness). The six hotels involved in the transaction were the San Francisco Hilton, Los Angeles Hilton, Beverly Hilton, Dallas Statler Hilton, Washington Statler Hilton and Tarrytown Hilton Inn.

In 1976, Co. sold the New Yorker Hotel and the Boston Statler Hilton.

In 1977, Co. purchased the lessor's interest in the Waldorf-Astoria for $35,800,000.

In 1979, Co. sold the New York Statler Hilton and a small parcel of vacant land for $24,000,000.

On Dec. 29, 1981, acquired the Sahara Reno, in Reno, Nev., for $34,500,000 cash.

In 1983, Co. sold the wholly-owned Terrace Hilton and the 50%-owned Los Angeles Hilton.

In 1984, Co. sold its wholly-owned Denver Hilton and 50% owned Kona Hilton. Co. also sold 660,000 shares of Avco common stock. Net proceeds from these transactions were $33,265,000.

In 1984, the wholly-owned Conrad Hilton was transferred to a joint venture for redevelopment. Co. has a 33% interest in the joint venture. The property opened in 1985 as the Chicago Hilton and Towers.

In 1985, Co. sold its wholly-owned Shamrock Hilton in Houston, Texas and its completed but unopened Atlantic City Hilton Hotel-Casino.

In late 1986, Co. closed the Atlanta Airport and New Orleans Airport Hiltons for redevelopment.

In 1987, Co. sold its interest in the 50% owned Beverly Hilton and Dallas Hilton properties, as well as its interest in land adjacent to other joint ventures. The after-tax gains from all property transactions was $27,188,000.

In 1988, Co. acquired from the Equitable Life Assurance Society its 65% equity interest in the Logan Airport Hilton. This property is now wholly-owned.

Acquisition Development: In June 1988, Co. announced that its board of directors has authorized the acquisiton of a 19.5 acred undeveloped parcel of land on the Colorado river in Laughlin, Nev. Co. contemplates developing a hotel/casino on the site which is currently owned by Horeshoe Club Operating Co.

BUSINESS

Hilton Hotels Corp. is primarily engaged in ownership and management of hotels and hotel-casinos. All of these properties are located in the United States, with the exception of the Gold Coast Conrad International Hotel & Jupiters Casino located in Queensland, Australia and the La Belle Creole Resort Hotel on the French side of St. Martin in the West Indies. On Feb. 1, 1989, Hilton owned or leased and operated 14 hotels and managed 34 hotels partly or wholly-owned by others. In addition, 222 hotels were operated under the "Hilton" name by others pursuant to franchises granted by a subsidiary of Hilton.

Four of the hotels have substantial gaming operatiosn, three of which are wholly-owned by the Co. and are located in Nevada and the fourth of which is partially-owned by the Co. and is located in Australia. The Co.'s hotel-casinos accounted for approximatley 51%, 52% and 53% of its total income contribution in 1986, 1987 and 1988, respectively.

The Co., through a wholly-owned subsidiary, is also engaged in the sale of furniture, furnishings, equipment and supplies to hotels, motels and inns throughout the United States and, through a 51% owned company, it is engaged in the operation of a computerized reservation system for use by Hilton and others.

Revenue & Income Contribution, by line of business, years ended Dec. 31 (in thousands of dollars):

Revenue:	1988	1987	1986
[1]Hotels	1,395,200	1,279,400	1,228,300
[1]Gaming	695,300	589,700	483,700
Total	2,090,500	1,869,100	1,712,000
[2]Income Contrib.:			
Hotels	115,100	100,700	83,600
Gaming	128,600	107,700	88,100
Total	243,700	208,400	171,700

[1]Includes properties owned or managed. [2]Includes Hilton's proportionate share of unconsolidated affiliated.

Number of Facilities, years ended Dec. 31:

	1988	1987	1986
Owned 100% (excl. Las Vegas)	9	8	8
Partially owned & managed	12	13	14
Other hotels managed	21	22	22
Gaming	4	4	4
Other hotels franchised	225	224	223

Number of Guest Rooms, years ended Dec. 31:

	1988	1987	1986
Owned 100% (excl. Las Vegas)	6,494	6,027	6,085
Partially owned & managed	13,409	13,528	14,350
Other hotels managed	13,383	14,183	13,425
Gaming	7,326	7,318	7,318
Other hotels franchised	54,876	55,641	55,602

Occupancy Ratio, years ended Dec. 31:

	1988	1987	1986
Hotels Owned or Managed:			
Occupancy ratio	70%	68%	65%
Gaming:			
Occupancy ratio	87%	84%	84%

Management & Franchise Fees, years ended Dec. 31:

Fees ($000):	1988	1987	1986
Management	33,300	31,300	28,800
Franchise	33,500	31,900	30,700
Total	66,800	63,200	59,000
Number of Rooms Open:			
Management	26,792	27,711	27,775
Franchise	54,876	55,641	55,602
Total	81,668	83,352	83,377

PROPERTIES

Following is a list of the 14 hotels as of Feb. 1, 1989 which Hilton leases or fully owns and the number of rooms in each:

[2]Logan Airport Hilton, Boston, Mass.	542
[1]Atlanta airport Hilton, Atlanta, Ga.	500
[1]New Orleans Airport Hilton, New Orleans, La.	315
[1]Flamingo Hilton, Las Vegas, Nev.	2,927
[1]Las Vegas Hilton, Las Vegas, Nev.	3,174
[2]Oakland Airport Hilton, Oakland, Cal.	362
[1]Palmer House, Chicago, Ill.	1,694
[2]Pittsburgh Hilton, Pittsburgh, Pa.	717
[1]Portland Hilton, Portland, Ore.	455
[2]San Diego Hilton, San Diego, Cal.	353
[2]San Francisco Airport Hilton, San Francisco, Cal.	527
[2]Seattle Airport Hilton, Seattle, Wash.	173
[1]Waldorf-Astoria, New York, N.Y.	1,692
[1]Reno Hilton, Reno, Nev.	603

[1]Owned in fee. [2]Leased.

Following is a list of managed hotels (some of which Hilton partially owns) and the number of rooms in each:

Anaheim Hilton, Anaheim, California	1,577
Anchorage-Westward Hilton Anchorage, Alaska	591
Atlanta Hilton Atlanta, Georgia	1,224
The Beverly Hilton, Beverly Hills, California	579
[1]Chicago Hilton & Towers, Chicago, Illinois	1,543
O'Hare Hilton, Chicago, Illinois	885
[1]Hilton Hawaiian Village, Honolulu, Hawaii	2,523
Hilton at Walt Disney World, Orlando, Florida	813
Kona Hilton, Kailua-Kona, Hawaii	444
Los Angeles Airport Hilton, Los Angeles, Cal.	1,279
Los Angeles Hilton & Towers Los Angeles, California	900
Brown Hotel, Louisville, Kentucky	294
[2]Fontainebleau Hilton, Miami, Florida	1,206
[1]Miami Airport Hilton, Miami, Florida	500
[1]New Orleans Hilton, New Orleans, Louisiana	1,602
[1]New York Hilton, New York, New York	2,036
Novi Hilton, Novi, Michigan	236
Pasadena Hilton, Pasadena, California	250
[1]Parsippany Hilton, Parsippany, New Jersey	508
[1]Rye Town Hilton, Rye, New York	438
Hilton Palacio del Rio, San Antonio, Texas	482
[1]San Francisco Hilton & Tower, San Francisco, California	1,491
Meadowlands Hilton, Secaucus, New Jersey	295
Terrace Hilton, Cincinnati, Ohio	329
[1]Tarrytown Hilton, Tarrytown, New York	242
Turtle Bay Hilton & Country Club, Oahu, Hawaii	486
[1]Washington Hilton, Washington, D.C.	1,122
[1]Capital Hilton, Washington, D.C.	539
Short Hills Hilton, Short Hill, N.J.	300
Irvine Hilton, Irvine, Calif.	536
Kauai Hilton & Beach Villas, Kauai, Hawaii	485
McLean Hilton, McLean, Virginia	457
[1]Gold Coast Conrad International Hotel & Jupiters Casinos, Queensland, Australia	622
LaBelle Creole Hotel, St. Martin, French West Indies	156

[1]Hilton has up to 50% interests in joint ventures which own each of the properties referenced to this footnote.

[2]The Company, subject to certain exceptions, has a right of first refusal to purchase an interest in the Fontainebleau Hilton.

SUBSIDIARIES

The following are subsidiaries of the Co. as of Dec. 31, 1988, other than name-holding and wholly inactive subsidiaries, and their State or Country of Incorporation or Organization. All are wholly-owned, except as noted.

BAC 1-11 Corp. (Nev.)
Benco, Inc. (Nev.)
Lebanco, Inc. (Nev.)
Hapeville Investors, Inc.
Hilton Hawaii Corp. (Del.)
Hilton Casinos, Inc. (Nev.)
Hilton Hotels U.S.A. (Cal.)
Conrad International Hotels Corp. (Nev.)
Conrad International Investment Corp. (Nev.)
Hilton Inns, Inc. (Del.)
Hilton New Jersey Corp. (N.J.)
Hilton Hotel Partners I, Inc. (Del.)
Hilton Hotel Partners II, Inc. (Del.)
Hilton Pennsylvania Hotel Corp. (Del.)
Hilton Products, Inc. (Ill.)
Hilton Quebec, Inc. (Canada)
Hilton Washington Corp. (N.Y.)
Hilton Tours, Inc. (Cal.)
Hilton Equipment Corp. (Del.)
Hotel Waldorf-Astoria Corp. (N.Y.)
Hotels Statler Co., Inc. (Del.)
Hilton Systems, Inc. (Nev.)

Figure 9.8: First Page from "Hilton Hotels Corporation" Report from *Moody's Industrial Manual*, 1989.

Palmer House Co. (Ill.)
Hilton Gaming Corporation (Nev.)
Hilton Nevada Corporation (Nev.)
Hilton Nevada Casinos, Inc. (Nev.)
Kenner Investors, Inc. (Del.)
Stevens Hotel Corp. (Ill.)
The Beverly Hilton Corp. (Calif.)
The New York Hotel Corp. (N.Y.)

Partially-owned Subsidiaries:
Compass Computer Services, Inc. (Del.) (50%)
Hilton Service Corp. (Del.) (51%)
Main & Holcombe Corp. (Tex.) (40%)
Statler Dallas Corp. (Tex.) (49%)

AFFILIATES

The following are special purpose corporations formed in connection with the operation of beverage service at particular hotels. Hilton Hotels Corporation does not directly own the shares of these corporations.
Hilton Beverage Corp. (La.)
New Orleans Hilton Beverage Corp. (La.)
Statler Hilton Package Store, Inc. (Tex.)

LETTER TO STOCKHOLDERS

The following is the letter to stockholders of Barron Hilton, Chairman and President of Hilton Hotels Corporation as it appeared in the Company's 1988 Annual Report:

To Our Stockholders:

We are pleased to report that your Company achieved record revenues and earnings from operations for the second consecutive year, continuing its positive momentum both financially and operationally. Both lodging and gaming made significantly improved contributions to earnings.

Net income for the year totaled $130.9 million, or $2.72 per share, compared with $112.7 million, or $2.25 per share from operations for 1987. Inclusive of property transactions, your Company earned $139.9 million, or $2.80 per share in 1987. There were no property transactions in 1988.

The Company also continued to achieve significant cash flow from operations (income before interest, depreciation and income taxes), reaching $312 million in 1988 as compared to $271 million in 1987 and $225 million in 1986. This allows us to continue the growth of our businesses and to capitalize more readily on opportunities while continuing our policy of distributing significant annual dividends to our stockholders.

Other highlights for 1988 include an increase in the quarterly cash dividend rate and a 2-for-1 stock split in the form of a 100% stock distribution. The balance of this message is devoted to the factors which contributed to the most successful operating year in the history of Hilton Hotels Corporation.

Reputation and Industry Leadership

The Hilton name is one of the most highly respected in the world. According to a recent independent survey, Hilton is the ninth most esteemed of American brand names, and one of the top 25 global brand names. Our role as an official sponsor of both the 1988 Winter and Summer Olympics furthered this favorable name recognition, while helping finance our athletes' participation in the Games. I am proud to report our sponsorship of the Olympics will continue with the 1992 Games.

Name recognition is one aspect of our heritage; recognition of Hilton as an industry leader and innovator is another. Commencing with the first hotel started by my father, Conrad Hilton, in Cisco, Texas in 1919, the objective of establishing a system of hotels of predictable high quality catering to the diverse needs of our guests from city to city around the world has continued. Over the years Hilton pioneered the "towers" concept, so popular today. Hilton was instrumental in developing the hotel convention business. Ours was the first hotel company to offer direct-dial telephones in guestrooms. We were in the forefront of other major moves in the lodging industry, contracting our management services to owners and developers, joint venturing hotel ownership, establishing full service hotels at airports and serving smaller cities through our Hilton Inns franchise system. And, Hilton was the first national hotel company to enter the gaming market by purchasing in 1970 what are now the Flamingo Hilton and the Las Vegas Hilton.

That background provides the context for our current expansion. Today the market segments being served by Hilton are being diversified with the introduction of Hilton Suites, our moderately-priced CrestHil by Hilton program and the expansion of our worldwide operations through Conrad International Hotels. With a strategic domestic and international expansion program built on a solid foundation of 269 hotels in the U.S., we will continue to maintain our preeminent position in the lodging industry.

In a related development, Hilton will acquire a 32.5% interest in CONFIRM, a joint venture developing an integrated travel reservations system using state of the art computer technology. The design and development of this system is expected to take several years. Upon completion, CONFIRM will be used by Hilton and its partners, American Airlines, Marriott and Budget Rent-A-Car, and will be marketed to others in the airline, car rental and lodging industries.

Dividend Increased

In recognition of the earnings progress of the Company, the Board of Directors in June increased the annual cash dividend rate by 11 percent to $1.00 per share from $.90 per share. Our stated dividend policy is to pay out as cash dividends to stockholders approximately 40 percent of our operating earnings and the Directors' action is in keeping with that policy.

Also in June the Board authorized a 2-for-1 stock split in the form of a 100% stock distribution. The stock split serves the purpose of making your Company's stock more accessible to a broader market.

Growth Factors

Our 1988 performance is directly attributable to our investment in our product, our heightened commitment to service through a creative new employee training program, and an extensive quality assurance program. It reflects as well the results of an insightful, innovative marketing strategy.

Outstanding performances were achieved in 1988 by many of our most recently renovated or expanded hotels, including the Waldorf-Astoria in New York, the Capital Hilton in Washington, D.C., the Chicago Hilton & Towers, the San Francisco Hilton on Hilton Square, the Hilton Hawaiian Village in Honolulu, and the Las Vegas Hilton and Flamingo Hilton in Las Vegas. Our expansion and renovation program gave us first-class facilities at a fraction of the cost that would have been required to build comparable properties today.

Our renovation and expansion efforts have been rewarded by increases in our occupancy and average room rates. Our system-wide growth in average rate has been nearly double that of inflation in the past three years, while at the same time hotel occupancy grew from 65 percent in 1986 to 70 percent this year. Hotel income contribution in 1988 increased by 14 percent over 1987 and 38 percent over the 1986 level.

Focused marketing programs have complemented our improved facilities by targeting key market segments. Special efforts targeted at the leisure market through our "Golden Summer of $59" program and to the business/leisure traveler in our spring and fall "WeekEnder" programs were highly successful.

Our HHonors frequent traveler program was introduced in mid-1987. By the end of 1988 the program membership and room night activity were advancing strongly, and enhancements for 1989 promise to make HHonors even more attractive to its targeted member base.

Our gaming operations continue to be a major source of earnings growth. In 1988, gaming income contribution increased 19 percent and accounted for 53 percent of operating income. The Las Vegas Hilton and Flamingo Hilton recorded sharp gains for the year, while the Reno Hilton reversed a loss in 1987 and produced a profit for 1988. Income from the Gold Coast Conrad International Hotel & Jupiters Casino in Queensland, Australia, also improved significantly in 1988.

In 1989-90 we will spend more than $300 million expanding and refurbishing our Nevada operations, including the construction of a new hotel-casino, the Flamingo Hilton-Laughlin, in Laughlin, Nevada. These and other hotel, gaming and international expansion programs for 1989 and 1990 are discussed in detail later in this report. Following their completion these projects are expected to significantly enhance our future earnings.

Asset Value

The fundamental job of management is to build stockholder value. We believe that the way to accomplish this is to invest in properties with above average earning potential and to provide quality service to our guests. Over four decades we have patiently built a portfolio of assets that has produced a large, secure and growing stream of income and cash flow. Consequently, the value of our Company has sharply increased.

There are several ways to define value. We provide three measures in this report. The first, "stockholders' equity per share," gives the book or historical accounting basis of our assets. At the end of 1988 our stockholders' equity per share was $17.03, which represented an eight percent increase from the equity per share of $15.80 in 1987.

The deficiencies of stockholders' equity per share are apparent. For a hotel such as the Waldorf-Astoria that was acquired many years ago, the historical accounting basis bears little relationship to its value today. Therefore, since 1976 we also have presented supplementary information on the current value of our assets and liabilities. Under this approach, real estate values, for example, are based on independent appraisals using the estimated present values of future income streams. Using this second approach the current value of Hilton's stockholders' equity was about $62 per share at the end of 1988, up 17 percent from $53 per share in 1987.

A third measure of value is reflected in the public securities markets, the collective wisdom of investors determining the price they will pay or the price for which they will sell a share of stock. These investors make their own determinations about future earnings, future dividends and future residual values. During 1988, the price of Hilton's stock traded on the New York Stock Exchange between a range of $34 and $55 per share. The stock closed the year at $53⅝ per share, up from $35½ per share at the end of 1987.

The distortion of historical cost has never been more evident than today. In recent years there have been a number of significant purchases of classic or "trophy" hotels as well as hotel groups at premium prices. For example, in 1982 the Bel-Air Hotel in Los Angeles was sold for $348,000 per room. In 1988 Maxim's de paris Hotel in Manhattan sold for $500,000 per room. In 1987 and 1988 Hilton International and Intercontinental Hotels were sold for $1.1 billion and $2.1 billion, respectively, reflecting substantial premiums over the historical cost of their respective assets. Such prices paid for these hotels are considerably higher than the valuations assigned to our hotels as reflected in the supplementary current value information included in this report.

Each sale of a hotel property or group is a special situation with each transaction having unique attributes, both positive and negative. Nonetheless, I believe it is valuable to review these transactions because they tend to affirm the wisdom of our basic strategy of investing in quality properties that offer superior location, service and facilities and the support of a loyal clientele. Such properties have the ability to raise room rates beyond those of the average hotel in both normal and inflationary times, and also have strong underlying real estate values that tend to appreciate over time because they are unique and irreplaceable.

Without doubt, real asset values are being created by Hilton, but, more importantly, there is a solid basis of earnings performance and growth that underlies these values.

Accord With Conrad N. Hilton Foundation

On November 25, 1988, I advised Hilton Hotels Corporation that I reached a tentative accord with the Conrad N. Hilton Foundation resolving the issue of my right to acquire shares of Hilton Hotels Corporation stock under the terms of an option granted in my father's will.

Under this agreement in principle, which must be approved by the courts and the Internal Revenue Service, the 13.6 million shares of stock held in my father's estate would be divided so that, following the distribution, I will have sole voting power over approximately 25% of the outstanding common stock. The Foundation will vote an additional 9% of the stock.

When the California Court of Appeals ruled in March, 1988 that I had a valid option to acquire all of my father's stock, it gave me the opportunity to structure an arrangement whereby my father's two objectives, retaining control of the stock in family hands and benefiting charity through the Conrad N. Hilton Foundation, could both be achieved. I am confident this accord reflects my father's intentions, and I am delighted that this cloud of uncertainty has finally been dispelled.

Strategy For Success

We take great pride in our history of providing lodging excellence. Hilton is a company built on service. Service is what the Hilton name promises. The financial success described above is the result of our delivering on that promise — providing quality lodging and hospitality to our guests. The record earnings we have achieved this year and the solid financial base that we have built — the strongest in our industry — have made possible an unprecedented capital investment program. We are on the move, building a company of new dimensions and excitement, but, ultimately, a company that will provide increasingly greater value for our stockholders.

This report begins graphically by showing you our product, representative hotels of the Hilton family. We are proud of all of our 271 properties representing 95,000 rooms and the 38,000 Hilton employees who bring them to life and greatness. The report also describes how we "deliver" for our customers, identifying significant service programs, marketing strategies and expansion plans that enhance value for our guests and our Company. And, with a note of deepest appreciation to the individuals photographed, we present a selection of our guests, the people on the receiving end of Hilton service. They are drawn from among the 40 million guests from some 53 countries on 5 continents of the world who stayed in Hilton hotels during 1988.

Changes in the Board of Directors

We were deeply saddened by the death in November, 1988 of a member of our Board of Directors, James R. Shepley. Jim had a long and distinguished business career and had been a member of Hilton's Board since 1984. His contributions to the Company were many and invaluable. His insightful perspective and wise counsel will be sorely missed.

In January 1989 the Board of Directors elected Donald R. Knab, former President of The Prudential Realty Group and current Chairman and Chief Executive Officer of BPT Properties, L.P., as a Director of Hilton Hotels Corporation.

Outlook For 1989

Our economy has enjoyed one of the longest and strongest expansion periods in American history. Certainly no student of history or economics would predict that it will continue forever. While the outlook for 1989 is still reasonably favorable, the overzealous building that took place in many markets in the United States in the first half of this decade has created a serious supply-demand imbalance. Cheap debt, tax-driven syndications, and other factors promoting artificial growth have produced an unprecedented number of undercapitalized and troubled hotels.

Hilton studiously avoided being part of this syndrome. Instead, we carefully targeted our expansion primarily in underdeveloped markets with a variety of lodging and gaming products. Furthermore, our highly secure financial position — we have the lowest debt/equity ratio and the strongest cash position in the industry — will aid us in taking advantage of new opportunities and weathering any economic storms that may arise.

I want to express my thanks to our dedicated directors and officers for their noteworthy contributions and, on behalf of them, express our sincere

Figure 9.9: Excerpts from "Hilton Hotels Corporation" Report from *Moody's Industrial Manual*, 1989.

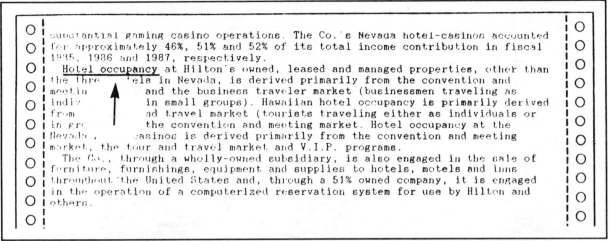

substantial gaming casino operations. The Co.'s Nevada hotel-casinos accounted for approximately 46%, 51% and 52% of its total income contribution in fiscal 1985, 1986 and 1987, respectively.

Hotel occupancy at Hilton's owned, leased and managed properties, other than the thre els in Nevada, is derived primarily from the convention and meetin   and the business traveler market (businessmen traveling as indiv   in small groups). Hawaiian hotel occupancy is primarily derived from   nd travel market (tourists traveling either as individuals or in gr   the convention and meeting market. Hotel occupancy at the Nevada .   asinos is derived primarily from the convention and meeting market, the tour and travel market and V.I.P. programs.

The Co., through a wholly-owned subsidiary, is also engaged in the sale of furniture, furnishings, equipment and supplies to hotels, motels and inns throughout the United States and, through a 51% owned company, it is engaged in the operation of a computerized reservation system for use by Hilton and others.

Figure 9.10: Excerpts from Search on Hilton Hotels Corp. from *Moody's 5000 Plus*.

The reports of the top 5,000 companies in *Moody's Manuals* are searchable on *Moody's 5000* (New York: Moody's Investors Service), a CD-ROM database (figure 9.10). Searches can be done by company name or by specific words. For example, the whole file could be searched for the phrase "occupancy rates." The information is identical to that published in the *Moody's Manuals*. Ask a reference librarian if you have *Moody's 5000* available in your library.

Standard and Poor's *Standard Corporation Descriptions*

Standard & Poor's *Standard Corporation Descriptions* is another investment service that includes much of the same information as *Moody's Manuals*. *Standard Corporation Descriptions* is arranged in six loose-leaf volumes, with each volume covering a section of the alphabet. However, within each volume, companies are not arranged alphabetically. In order to find the report on Hilton, look in the yellow company index section in the front of volume F-K (figure 9.11). The main report on Hilton is on page 3932. This index, in addition to listing the main report, also lists other pages that update the main report. The most current information, however, on Hilton Hotels will be found in a separate volume of *Standard Corporation Descriptions* labeled "Daily News," which has its own index in the front of the volume.

There is a CD-ROM database called *Standard & Poor's Corporations*, which includes information from *Standard Corporation Descriptions* and other Standard & Poor's products. The file includes information on over 9,000 publicly owned and 40,000 privately owned companies. In addition there is extensive personal and professional data on nearly 70,000 business executives affiliated with the companies covered. Ask a reference librarian if this CD-ROM service is available in your library.

121

HETRA COMPUTER & COMMUNICATIONS INDUSTRIES, INC. 3246
Acquisition by JWP Inc. Effected 2707
Agrees to be Acquired by JWP Inc. 3610
HEWLETT-PACKARD CO. 4381
Interim Consol. Earns.: Jan. '89 2707
Annual Report 2707
Acquires Eon Systems Inc.; Agrees to Acquire Minority Interest in Hilco Technologies Inc 2707
Details of Agreement to Form Alliance With 3Com Corp 2707
Annual Earns 3131
Interim Consol. Earns. July '88 3610
Current Position: Apr. 30 '88 3610
Higher Quarterly Dividend 3610
Agrees to Acquire Interest in Octel Communications Corp 3610
Unit Forms Joint Venture With Telecom Australia 3610
Repurchase of Additional Common Authorized 3610
Interim Consol. Earns. Apr. '88 4159
New Facilities Planned 4159
Interim Consol. Earns. Jan. '88 4635
HEXCEL CORP. 2390
Interim Consol. Earns. Sept. '88 3131
Interim Consol. Earns. June '88 3610
Interim Consol. Earns. Mar. '88 4159
HI-PORT INDUSTRIES, INC. 3729
Annual Earns 2707
Interim Consol. Earns.. Sept. '88 3131
Ending Some Packaging Operations 3131
Interim Consol. Earns. June '88 3610
Interim Consol. Earns. Mar. '88 4159
Forecasts 1988 Net Sales 4159
HI SHEAR INDUSTRIES INC. 2365
Interim Consol. Earns. Nov. '88 2708
Interim Consol. Earns. Aug. '88 3131
Interim Consol. Earns. Feb. '88 4635
HI TECH ROBOTICS LTD.• 4074
Interim Consol. Earns. Sept. '88 3131
HIBERNIA BANK (SAN FRANCISCO)
Purchased by Security Pacific Corp 3610
HIBERNIA CORP. 4509
Annual Earns 2708
Unit Acquires Deposits and Certain Assets of Natl Bank of Bossier City (La.) 2708
Interim Consol. Earns. Sept. '88 3131
Insured Deposits and Secured Liabilities of First Natl. Bank, Covington, Transferred to Unit 3131
Interim Consol. Earns.: June '88 3610
Unit Assumes Deposits of Natl. Fidelity Bank of Shreveport 3610
Class A Common Offered 3610
Interim Consol. Earns. Mar. '88 4159
Stock Distribution and Higher Quarterly 4159
No Longer Directors 4159
HIBERNIA SAVINGS BANK• 4382
Annual Earns 2708
Interim Consol. Earns. Sept. '88 3132
Interim Consol. Earns. June '88 3610
Higher Quarterly Dividend 3610
Interim Consol. Earns. Mar. '88 4159
New Chairman 4159
HICKAM (DOW B.) INC. 3230
Annual Earns. 2708
Interim Consol. Earns. Sept. '88 3132
Interim Consol. Earns. Mar. '88 4159
HICKOK ELECTRICAL INSTRUMENT CO. 2619
Interim Consol. Earns. Dec. '88 2708
Interim Consol. Earns. June '88 3611
Interim Consol. Earns. Mar. '88 4159
HICKORY FURNITURE CO. 2878
Interim Consol. Earns. Sept. '88 2708
Interim Consol. Earns. June '88 3611
Interim Consol. Earns. Sept. '87 4635
HIGBY'S (J.) INC.♦ 2954
Management Changes 2708
Estimates 1988 Net Loss, Gross Operating Revenues 2708
Units in Operation and Planned 2708
HIGH CALIBER MANUFACTURING INC.• 3911
HIGH HOPES INC.• 2969
HIGH INCOME ADVANTAGE TRUST 2529
HIGH INCOME ADVANTAGE TRUST II 3505
NYSE Symbol 3132
Initial Dividend 3132
HIGH INCOME ADVANTAGE TRUST III 2454
HIGH LEVEL RESOURCES LTD.• 2998
HIGH PLAINS CORP. 3771
Interim Earns. Sept. '88 2708
Annual Report 2708
Withdraws Registration Statement Covering Proposed Offering of Common 3132
Annual Earns 3611
HIGH POINT FNCL. CORP.★ 4086
HIGH RESOLUTION SCIENCES INC.♦ 2939
HIGH RIVER GOLD MINES LTD.• 2553
HIGH VOLTAGE ENGINEERING CORP.
Control Acquired By Unit Of Hyde Park Partners L.P. 4159
HIGH YIELD INCOME FUND INC. 2879
HIGH YIELD PLUS FUND INC. 3740
Interim Earns. Sept. '88 3132
Quarterly Dividend 3611
HIGHGRADE VENTURES LTD.• 3196
HIGHLAND CAPITAL INC.• 2420
Interim Earns. Dec. '88 2708
HIGHLAND FUNDING CORP.
Initial Public Offering of Common and Warrants 4636
Address 4636
HIGHLAND PARK NATL. BANK (Dallas, Tex.)
Closed 3611
HIGHLAND SUPERSTORES INC. 2847
Dec. '88 Sales 2708
Interim Consol. Earns.: Oct. '88 3132
Interim Consol. Earns. July '88 3611
Interim Consol. Earns.: Apr. '88 4160
HIGHLINE INDUSTRIES INC. (NEV.) 4434
Annual Report 2708
HIGHWOOD RESOURCES LTD.♦ 2430
HILB, ROGAL & HAMILTON CO. 2957
Annual Earns. 2709
Acquires Three Florida and One Pennsylvania Concern; Agrees in Principle to Acquire Evans & Drumm Inc. 2709
Completes Acquisition of Evans & Drum Inc. 2709
Higher Quarterly Dividend 2709
Agrees in Principle to Acquire Turner, Wood & Smith Insurance Agency Inc. 2709
Interim Consol. Earns.: Sept. '88 3132
Acquires Two Concerns 3132
Acquires Foss, Cates, Hudson, & Sims Agency Inc. 3132
Interim Consol. Earns.: June '88 3611
Interim Consol. Earns.: Mar. '88 4160
Acquires Florida Insurance Agency 4160
Acquires Two Texas Concerns 4160
HILDON MINING EXPLORATIONS LTD.• 3047
Interim Earns.: Dec. '88 2709
HILLCRAFT CORP.• 2782
HILLENBRAND INDUSTRIES INC. 2391
Interim Consol. Earns.: Aug. '88 3132
Interim Consol. Earns.: May '88 3611
Interim Consol. Earns.: Feb. '88 4160
HILLHAVEN CORP.
Natl. Medical Enterprises Inc. Plans Spin-Off-See that Co., L-O Page 3674
HILLS DEPARTMENT STORES INC. 3510
Dec. '88 Sales 2709
Annual Earns 2709
Interim Consol. Earns.: Oct. '88 3132
Interim Consol. Earns.: July '88 3611
Agrees to Acquire Certain Gold Circle Stores After Being Sold by Campeau Corp.-See that Co., C-E Page 6772
Interim Consol. Earns.: Apr. '88 4160
HILLSDOWN HOLDINGS plc
Unit Purchases Hencu Beheers By 4160
HILLTOP PRODUCTS INC.• 3272
HILTON HOTELS CORP. 3932
Annual Earns. 2709
Interim Consol. Earns.: Sept. '88 3132
Portion of Medium-Term Notes, Series A, Priced 3132
Transferring Management of Kuwaiti Hotel to Government Group 3132
Files Shelf Registration Covering Debt Securities to Be Offered Under SEC Rule 415 3132
Interim Consol. Earns.: June '88 3612
Directors Declare Distribution of Preferred Purchase Rights 3612
Quarterly Dividend 3612
Interim Consol. Earns.: Mar. '88 4160
HILTON NEW JERSEY CORP.
Debs. Described Under Hilton Hotels Corp.
HIMEDICS INC.• 2553
HIMONT INC. 4416
Annual Report 2709
Acquires Poliresine S.p.A. 2709
Acquires Italplastica S.p.A. 2709
Higher Quarterly Dividend 2709
Three-Year Capital Investment Plans; Related Long-Term Sales Goal 2709
Directorate: Mar. 16 '89 2709
Annual Earns. 3133
Changes from Fiscal to Calendar Year 3133
Higher Quarterly and Special Dividends 3133
Date for 1989 Annual Meeting of Shareholder 3133
Plans Belgian Facility 3133
Agrees to Acquire Minority Interest in Indelpro S.A. 3133
Interim Consol. Earns.: July '88 3612
Current Position: Apr. 30 '88 3612
Interim Consol. Earns.: Apr. '88 4160
Plans New Factory in Italy 4160
Interim Consol. Earns.: Jan. '88 4637
Signs Letter of Intent to Purchase Plastic Compounding Plant 4637
HINDERLITER INDUSTRIES INC. 2420
Interim Consol. Earns.: Dec. '88 2709
Interim Consol. Earns.: Sept. '88 3133
Interim Consol. Earns.: Mar. '88 4160
Interim Consol. Earns.: Dec. '87 4637
HINES (EDWARD) LUMBER CO.
Fifth Liquidating Distribution 4160
HINGHAM INSTITUTION FOR SAVINGS (MASS.)★ 3050
Annual Earns 2709
HIPOTRONICS, INC. 3484
Annual Earns. 2709
Backlog: Dec. '88 2709
Interim Consol. Earns.: Aug. '88 3133
Interim Consol. Earns.: May '88 3612
Interim Consol. Earns.: Feb. '88 4160
Forecasts Fiscal 1988 Results 4160
HIRAM WALKER-GOODERHAM & WORTS LTD.
Interest Sold by GW Utilities Ltd. to Allied-Lyons PLC 4161
HISWAY RESOURCES CORP.★ 2636
HITACHI LTD. 2478
HITECH ENGINEERING CO. (d/b/a/ T.H.E. Co.)• 3935
Interim Consol. Earns.: Sept. '88 3133
Date for 1988 Annual Meeting of Stockholders 3133
Acquires Marketing Business 3133
Directorate: Oct. 17 '88 3133
Interim Earns.: Mar. '88 3612
Current Position: Mar. 31 '88 3612
Principal Stockholder 3612
HITOX CORP. OF AMERICA 2352
HOBART CORP.
Notes described under Premark Intl. Inc.
HODGSON HOUSES, INC. 3348
Interim Consol. Earns.: June '88 3612
HOECHST AG 3873
Hoechst Celanese Corp. Plans to Sell Rigid Polyvinyl Chloride Film Division and Certain Related Assets 2710
Unit Sells Baton Rouge, La., Plant and Related Businesses 2710
Unit's Offer to Purchase Remaining Common of Celanese Canada Inc. Expires with No Shares Being Purchased-See that Co., C-E Page 5938
Cape Industries Inc. Acquires Terate Resin Business of Hercules Inc.-See Amer. Petrofina Inc., A-B Page 4658
Unit Opens New Jersey Facility 3612
Hoechst Celanese Corp. Files Shelf Registration Covering Medium-Term Notes to Be Offered Under SEC Rule 415 3612
HOECHST CELANESE CORP.
Files Shelf Registration Covering Medium-Term Notes to Be Offered Under SEC Rule 415 3612
HOFMANN INDUSTRIES INC. 3375
Interim Consol. Earns.: Jan. '89 2710
Interim Consol. Earns.: Oct. '88 3134
Interim Consol. Earns.: July '88 3612
Interim Consol. Earns.: Jan. '88 4637
HOGAN SYSTEMS INC. 2320
Interim Consol. Earns.: Dec. '88 2710
Interim Consol. Earns.: Sept. '88 3134
Interim Consol. Earns.: June '88 3612
Interim Consol. Earns.: Dec. '87 4638
HOKURIKU BANK LTD.★ 3050
HOLCO MORTGAGE ACCEPTANCE CORP.-1 2998
Receives Final Payment on Defaulted Mortgage 2710
Higher Quarterly and Special Dividends 2710
Interim Consol. Earns.: Sept. '88 3134
Interim Consol. Earns.: June '88 3612
HOLDEN-DAY, INC.♦ 2949
HOLIDAY CORP. 2546
Sells Five Hotels to Limited Partnership 2710
Interim Consol. Earns.: Sept. '88 3134
Interim Consol. Earns.: July '88 3612
Interim Consol. Earns.: Apr. '88 4161
8.625% Notes 1993 and 9% Notes 1995 of Holiday Inns Inc. Offered 4638
HOLIDAY-GULF HOMES INC.♦ 2949
HOLIDAY INNS INC.
Debs. described under Holiday Corp.
HOLIDAY RV SUPERSTORES INC. 2348
Interim Consol. Earns.: July '88 3134
Interim Consol. Earns.: Jan '88 4161
Interim Consol. Earns.: Apr. '88 4161
HOLLY CORP. 2912
Interim Consol. Earns.: Jan. '89 2710
Evaluating Possibility of Being Acquired 2710
Completes Acquisition of Two Units from Southern Union Co. 2710
Interim Consol. Earns.: Oct. '88 3134
Agrees to Acquire Certain Units From Southern Union Co. 3134
Interim Consol. Earns.: Apr. '88 4161
Interim Consol. Earns.: Jan. '88 4638
HOLLY FARMS CORP. 3484
Date Set for Stockholder Votes on Proposed Acquisition by ConAgra Inc. 2710
Board Rejects "Sweetened" Tender Offer by Tyson Foods Inc 2710
Interim Consol. Earns.: Aug. '88 3134
Interim Consol. Earns.: Nov. '88 3134
Board Rejects "Sweetened" Offer from Tyson Foods Inc.-See ConAgra Inc., C-E Page 6370
Reaches Definitive Agreement to be Acquired by ConAgra Inc.-See that Co., C-E Page 6370
Interim Consol. Earns.: Feb. '88 4161
Interim Consol. Earns.: Nov. '87 4638
HOLLY SUGAR CORP.
Merged 4161
Interim Consol. Earns.: Dec. '87 4638
HOLLYWOOD INVSTMT. CORP.
Common Listed on Vancouver SE; Symbol 3134
Address 3134
HOLLYWOOD PARK REALTY ENTERPRISES INC. 4075
Interim Comb. Earns.: Sept. '88 3134
Interim Comb. Earns.: June '88 3613
Primary Lender to Reduce Interest Charge; "Tentatively" Agrees to Extend Maturity of Borrowings 3613
Agrees With Associated Concern to Sell Los Alamitos Race Course and Adjoining Property 3613
HOLMES (D.H.) CO., LTD. 3836
Certain Conditions of Agreement to be Acquired by Dillard Dept. Stores Inc. Satisfied 2710
Interim Consol. Earns.: Oct. '88 3134
Discussing Being Acquired by Dillard Dept. Stores Inc.-See that Co., C-E Page 6407
Current Position: Apr. '88 3613
Interim Consol. Earns.: July '88 3613
Retains Financial Advisor to Explore Possibility of Being Acquired 3613
Interim Consol. Earns.: Apr. '88 4161

Figure 9.11: "General Index" from Standard & Poor's *Standard Corporation Descriptions.*

PERIODICAL ARTICLES

All of the sources looked at thus far were prepared by or based on information supplied by the publicly owned company itself. Hilton Hotels Corporation provided all the information that went into the ARS and 10-K Report. And the investment services use the data from the ARS and 10-K Report as the basis for their calculations and observations. Where can you find information that may be more critical of the company? What are people outside the company saying about Hilton Hotels? Have any trade secrets or rumors of management shifts leaked lately? Where can you find this sort of information?

The best way to find this type of information is to look for newspaper and periodical articles about Hilton Hotels Corporation. Articles are good sources of information on marketing strategies, involvement in legal actions, buyouts, takeovers, and management actions. Searching for periodical articles on Hilton Hotels is an easy task. Use the same periodical indexes that you used for industry research: *Business Periodicals Index, Business Index/INFOTRAC™, Predicasts F&S Index: United States*, or *The Wall Street Journal Index*.

Business Periodicals Index and *Business Index/INFOTRAC™* file the articles about companies in one alphabetical sequence with all other subjects. Use the company name as the subject. Figure 9.12 illustrates an entry from *Business Periodicals Index* on Hilton Hotels Corporation.

Predicasts F&S Index: United States and *The Wall Street Journal Index* both have separate sections for company names. Figure 9.13 illustrates a citation from *Predicasts F&S Index: United States* on Hilton Hotels Corporation.

Since periodical indexes were illustrated in detail in chapter 4, you may want to review that section.

High technology industries—*cont.*

Securities

Goodbye, Steve Jobs! In the high-tech world, innovators are out, standards in. J. Scholl. pors tab *Barrons* 69:13+ F 13 '89

Remaindered stocks: beware authors offering investment advice [three early eighties books on high-tech stocks] D. R. Eidelman. tab *Barrons* 69:26-7+ F 13 '89

Still in the saddle [S. Robertson's Robertson, Colman & Stephens' IPOs] por *Venture* 10:65-6 O '88

Strategic planning

Strategies for stimulating home-grown technology-based economic development. G. G. Udell. *Bus Horiz* 31:60-4 N-D '88

Suppliers

Technology partnerships can pay off for banks. J. Bienkowski. *Bankers Mon* 105:54 N '88

Japan

Japan even with U.S. in high-tech indicators. W. Lepkowski. tab *Chem Eng News* 66:20-1 D 12 '88

Southern Europe

Development: sun, sea and high-tech. J. Heard. il *Int Manage* 43:31+ O '88

Western Europe

See also

Eureka (Program)

European Strategic Programme of Research and Development in Information Technology

High temperature reactors *See* Nuclear reactors—High temperature reactors

Highbeam Business Systems

Riding trends onto the B.E. 100s [CEO H. F. Davis] por *Black Enterp* 19:70 N '88

Higher education

Can higher education foster higher morals? D. Bok. *Bus Soc Rev* no66:4-12 Summ '88

CFOs: early signs of a business career. L. E. Boone and others. graphs tabs *Bus Horiz* 31:20-4 S-O '88

School and beyond. D. Furth. il *OECD Obs* no154:12-14 O-N '88

Highway construction *See* Road construction

Highway departments

State trims highway budget [Colorado] *ENR* 221:19-20 S 22 '88

Highway engineering

See also

Highway departments

Road construction

Highway finance *See* Roads—Federal aid; Roads—Finance

Highway research

Asphalt research starts [Auburn U. and U. of California, Berkeley] *ENR* 221:16 D 15 '88

Highway traffic noise *See* Traffic noise

Highway trust fund *See* Roads—Federal aid

Highways *See* Roads

Hijacking *See* Theft from motor vehicles

Hill, Holliday, Connors, Cosmopulos Inc.

HHCC—thriving in the shade. V. Free. *Mark Commun* 13:51-4 N-D '88

Hill Samuel Group plc, London

Financing: foreign merchant banks. *Pensions Investm Age* 16:29-32 N 14 '88

Hillebrand (J. F.) GmbH *See* J. F. Hillebrand GmbH

Hills, Carla Anderson, 1934-

Why Bush picked a rookie to carry the ball on trade. P. Magnusson and R. Fly. por *Bus Week* p32 D 19 '88

Hilton Hotels Corp.

Hilton announces sites for CrestHil. R. Selwitz. *Hotel Motel Manage* 203:3+ S 25 '88

Hilton pushes unity for strength: renovations help put company earnings at record level. M. DeLuca. *Hotel Motel Manage* 203:1+ S 25 '88

McGavren Guild's prize: Hilton's radio budget. *Telev/Radio Age* 36:34 S 19 '88

Himont Inc.

Himont and Statoil pushing ahead D. Hunter. *Chem*

Business, amigo? No! ¿Amigo business? ¡Si! [marketers should enhance community and cultural relations] E. Loza. *Public Relat J* 44:8-10 Je '88

Coors courts Hispanics [Adolph Coors Co. agrees to contribute a share of its profit to Hispanic communities] R. Hamel and T. Schreiner. *Am Demogr* 10:54 N '88

A craving for coupons [coupon usage] R. Fannin. graph *Mark Media Decis* 23:14 O '88

Cultural calculations [Hispanic Monitor, joint venture of Yankelovich Clancy Shulman and Market Development] W. Wood. il *Mark Media Decis* 23:137-8 Ag '88

Hispanic hot spot [New York City] J. Schlosberg. *Am Demogr* 10:49+ Ag '88

Hispanics lag as U.S. TV stars. *Telev/Radio Age* 36:72 Ag 8 '88

Marketers map Hispanic plans. E. Fitch. *Advert Age* 59:62 O 3 '88

Marketing to Hispanics. *Advert Age* 59:42-4 Ag 29 '88

Perspectives: marketing to Hispanics. *Advert Age* 59:32 O 31 '88

Special report: marketing to Hispanics. *Advert Age* 59:S1-S26 S 26 '88

Telemundo novela to Anglo market? J. Forkan. *Telev/Radio Age* 36:50-2 Ag 22 '88

U.S. Hispanics drawn to network family sitcoms [BBDO study] *Telev/Radio Age* 36:11 S 5 '88

U.S. Spanish TV networks team up for national people-meter service; Nielsen, Arbitron bid on $25-mil. plan [Telemundo Group and Univision Holdings] il *Telev/Radio Age* 36:12 O 31 '88

An underserved market [Hispanic middle class' newspaper readership demands] D. Gersh. *Ed Publ Fourth Estate* 121:16-17+ S 17 '88

Hispanic periodicals *See* Spanish periodicals

Hispanics in the United States

See also

Hispanic market

A common language, a diverse people. R. J. Crimmins. *Stat Bull (Metrop Life Insur Co)* 69:13 O-D '88

Hispanic Americans: an emerging group [magnitude, ethnicity and geographic location] graph tabs *Stat Bull (Metrop Life Insur Co)* 69:2-7 O-D '88

Hispanic Americans: an emerging group [profile of diverse characteristics] tabs *Stat Bull (Metrop Life Insur Co)* 69:8-12 O-D '88

Education

Can business throw a net under Hispanic dropouts? T. Mason and S. D. Atchison. il *Bus Week* p151+ F 20 '89

Employment

Hispanic immigration and labor market segmentation. G. DeFreitas. bibl graph tabs *Ind Relat* 27:195-214 Spr '88

Hispanic men: divergent paths in the U.S. labor market. B. R. Chiswick. tab *Mon Labor Rev* 111:32-6 N '88

How the Hispanic population boom will hit the work force. G. Koretz. graph *Bus Week* p21 F 20 '89

Historic houses, etc.

Conservation and restoration

See also

Building rehabilitation tax credits

Eyesores into showplaces—even without a tax break. J. Weber, Jr. graph il *Bus Week* p36 Ja 16 '89

Making Miami nice [G. Sanchez's Polonia Restoration tries to save Miami Beach's Art Deco district] J. Ralston. por *Venture* 10:29-30 O '88

A surprise-filled renovation [Underground Atlanta restoration project] il *ENR* 221:14 N 17 '88

Historical cost accounting

See also

Current value accounting

Histories, Medical *See* Medical records

History

See also

Business history

Economic history

Figure 9.12: Sample Citation on Hilton Hotels Corporation from *Business Periodicals Index*, April 1989.

Hiawatha Oil & Gas 110 **COMPANIES**

To sell gas reserves, leases & pipelines to Castle Energy, PA — O&G Jour 09/21/87 p26

Hibbitt Karlsson

Modifies nonlinear analysis software for Digital Equipment VAX units — Computrwld 09/21/87 p32

Hibernia Bank

Uses kangaroo symbol to promote 2-in-one financial svc — Bank MktgM 10/00/87 p58

Hickman (Dow B)

To buy up to 100,000 shrs of current 2.19mil shrs of common stock — D&C Ind 12/00/87 p70

Hicks & Haas

To acquire Sybron for about $390mil in cash & stock — WSJ (NJ) 10/01/87 p10

HIEX Development USA

Will market its new technology for extracting precious metals from ore — SkilMining 10/24/87 p22

Higbee

Legal action by city of Cleveland may prevent sale to May Co, OH — HFD 11/30/87 p8

High Country

Is on steady course toward goal of becoming No 1 US lodging mgmt firm — H&M Mgmt 10/12/87 p3

High Point Chemical

Is acquired by Kao Corp America — Am Dyestuf 08/00/87 p14

Kao Corp of America buys for undisclosed sum — S&C Spec 09/00/87 p94

This fiber processing chem mfr has been acquired by Kao Corp America — Japan Chem 09/03/87 p8

Kao buys — J Amer Oil 11/00/87 p1555

High Tech Paging

US West Paging will acquire this paging products & svcs vendor — Telephone 09/15/87 p34

High Vacuum Equipment

Coors orders vacuum web coating sys for PE film at pkg plant, TN — PFF Convrt 09/00/87 p167

High Voltage Engineering

Financial analysis — Value Line 11/06/87 p1017

Highland Pump

EVI acquires this oil & gas industry downhole production pumps maker — MetalwNews 11/30/87 p2

Has been 100% acquired by EVI (Houston, TX) — O&G Jour 11/30/87 p17

Highland Superstores

Names E Mondry to post of chief exec — WSJ (NJ) 11/12/87 p44

Top 10 major appliance retailers' 1986 sales, table — HFD 08/10/87 p105

Financial ranking data, 1986 — OTC Review 09/00/87 p34

Hilevel Technology

Will be 25% acquired by Fluke for $6mil — Elec News 09/21/87 p30

Sold 25% stake to John Fluke Mfg for $6 mil — Elec News 11/09/87 p52

Hilfiger (Tommy)

Expanded to 6 freestanding designer apparel shops from 1 since 1985 — Women Wear 10/26/87 pS86

Hill & Griffith

Gets patent for oil coating that protects foundry molds from pitting — Mod Paint 11/00/87 p90

Hill & Knowlton

Signs creative & cost effective PA management agreement with Monsanto — Bus Intnl 10/19/87 p329

Hill Bros Chemical

Sells Swim Chem div to Bio-Lab — S&C Spec 10/00/87 p81

Hillenbrand Industries

Financial analysis — Value Line 11/27/87 p1575

Financial forecast, 1988 — Fin World 01/05/88 p33

Hills Dept Stores

Decision to go public presented — Mergers 12/00/87 p56

Hillsborough Bank & Trust

To be acquired by Merrimack Bancorp for $6.7 mil — Am Bank 11/20/87 p20

Hilltemp

Introduces noncontact, small production system to bend plastic sheet — Mod Plast 11/00/87 p133

Hilton Hotels

May sell Beverly Hilton Hotel to Japanese investors over $100mil, CA — WSJ (NJ) 10/15/87 p5

May sell its Beverly Hilton Hotel to Griffin — NY Times N 11/17/87 p33

To sell jtly-owned 592 room Beverly Hilton Hotel to Merv Griffin, CA — WSJ (NJ) 11/17/87 p10

Has designed the prototype of a courtyard-style hotel, CrestHil — H&M Mgmt 09/07/87 p1

Consumer ratings of hotel and motel chains — Consmr BG 12/00/87 p301

To buy back 3.9mil shrs, about 16%, on 25mil common outstanding — WSJ (NJ) 10/20/87 p59

Investment rating data, 1987 — Forbes 10/26/87 p386

Financial analysis — Value Line 12/11/87 p1778

Court invalidates 2 IRS rulings preventing B Hilton from buying 27.4% — WSJ (NJ) 11/23/87 p15

Hilton Intnl

May be sold by United Air Lines, possible bidders listed — Economist 09/11/87 p63

Will be acquired by Ladbroke Group from Allegis for $1.07bil — Ad Age 09/21/87 p34

Ladbroke Group to acquire from Allegis for $1.07 bil — Acq Month 10/00/87 p64

Ladbroke Group to acquire — AGEFI 10/07/87 p10

Will be sold by Allegis, parent of United Airlines — WSJ (NJ) 11/25/87 p4

Is acquired by Ladbroke Group from Allegis for $1.07bil — H&M Mgmt 10/12/87 p1

Ladbroke Group buys for $1.07bil from Allegis — NY Times N 10/15/87 p47

Himont

Montedison to hold 80% by buying Hercules' 38.7% shr & another 3% — Chem Ind 09/21/87 p630

Montedison to buy Hercules' 38.7% & addtl stock for final 80% hldg — Pckgng Wek 09/23/87 p3

Montedison to acquire 38.7% for 88.7% hldg for $1.49 bil — Acq Month 10/00/87 p67

To be over 80% held by Montedison, which bought Hercules' 38.5% stake — Plast Tech 10/00/87 p99

To have 38.5% shr purchased by Montedison for 77% hldg from Hercules — Daily News 09/14/87 p15

To form jt vtr to mfr 300,000 m tpy of PP homo- & copolymer, Norway — PlasIndEur no/19/87 p1

Montedison to acquire 38.5% for 77-80% hldg — Plast Mod 09/00/87 pS7

Montedison to acquire 38.5% from Hercules for 77% hldg — RevIndChim 09/16/87 p11

To have stake owned by Montedison rise to 80%, vs 38.7%, for $1.6bil — Plas Rubr 09/19/87 p1

To be acquired by Montedison, which will buy Hercules' 38.5% stake — C&E News 09/21/87 p7

Montedison to acquire 38.7% from Hercules for 77.4% hldg — Chimie Act 09/21/87 p6

Montedison to acquire 38.7% from Hercules for 77.4% hldg — Eur Chem N 09/21/87 p4

Montedison to buy 38.5% stake from Hercules for 77% hldg — CISChemRpt 09/28/87 p1

Montedison to acquire 38.5% for 77% hldg — Mondo Econ 09/28/87 p80

Montedison to buy 38.5% stake from Hercules for 77% hldg — O&G Jour 09/28/87 p47

To have majority acquired by Montedison — ManufChem 10/00/87 p8

To have 38.5% shr acquired by Montedison from Hercules for 77% hldg — Mod Plast 10/00/87 p18

Hercules sells to Montedison for $1.49bil — Chem Week 09/23/87 p9

Acquisition by Montedison fits strategy to diversify geographically — Chem Mkt R 09/28/87 p3

Is now 77% owned by Montedison, which bought Hercules' 38.5% stake — C&E News 10/05/87 p12

To be 38.5%-sold by Hercules to Montedison for $1.49bil — WSJ (NJ) 09/14/87 p4

Has 38.5% stake acquired by Montedison for $1.5bil — Economist 09/25/87 p71

This mfr of polypropylene is 38.5% acquired by Montedison for $1.49bil — WSJ (NJ) 09/28/87 p54

Montedison buys 38.5% shr from partner Hercules for nearly $1.5bil — Plast Wrld 10/00/87 p12

Hercules sells 37.5% to Montedison; discusses Hercules' policy — C&E News 10/12/87 p9

Montedison to buy 38.5% share from Hercules for 77% hldg — Hydrocarbn 11/00/87 p31

Thailand to use polypropylene process at 100,000 m tpy plant — Sole 24ore 10/02/87 p11

HMC Polymers to use technology at new 100,000 m tpy PP plant — Aushandel 10/05/87 p1

HMC Polymers to use process at 100,000 m tpy polypropylene plant — Chemische 11/00/87 p44

China to use Spheripol process at new 60,000 m tpy polypropylene plant — Aushandel 11/11/87 p3

To supply polypropylene technology to Alcudia and Tarragona Quimica — InfoChimie 09/00/87 p116

To supply technology for polypropylene mfr to HMC Polymers — Chimie Act 09/21/87 p5

Licenses PP technology for Chemokomplex's new 110mil lb/yr PP unit — C&E News 09/28/87 p8

New polypropylene plant in Hungary to use Spheripol process — Eur Chem N 09/28/87 p23

Jtly licenses polypropylene process to Nippon Petrochemicals — Chemfasern 10/00/87 p960

Licenses China to use polypropylene process technology — Eur Chem N 10/12/87 p36

Licenses Yukong for polypropylene process — Chem Eng 11/09/87 p25

Tisza Vegyi Kombinat to use polypropylene technology under licence — Europ Chem 11/13/87 p545

Hungary to build 60,000 m tpy PP plant using this co's technology — ModPlstInt 12/00/87 p10

Planned & current PP capacity (table) — Plast Wrld 11/00/87 p52

To expand US polypropylene capacity by 300mil lb/yr by mid-1988 — Chem Mkt R 11/30/87 p3

Polypropylene capacity, 1987 (table) — Chem Mkt R 11/30/87 p26

To build 50 mil lb polypropylene composites compounding plant, TN — Jrl Comm 12/10/87 p9B

Will build a plastics compounding plant in Jackson, TN — Chem Mkt R 12/14/87 p4

Will build 50 mil lb/yr PP composites & alloys plant, TN — Chem Week 12/16/87 p5

Reports net income of $226.906 mil for FY ending 10/31/87 — WSJ (NJ) 12/03/87 p36

Net income was $226.9 mil in FY ended 10/87, up 133% vs previous FY — Chem Week 12/09/87 p5

Financial forecast, 1988 — Fin World 01/05/88 p20

Hinderliter Industries

May boost 15.8% in Vortec to controlling stake if it does not merge — WSJ (NJ) 10/09/87 p15

Vortec (US), home health-care equip firm, rejects merger proposal — WSJ (NJ) 10/29/87 p19

Reports $4.043 mil net income or $1.15/shr for FY ending 6/30/87 — WSJ (NJ) 12/01/87 p30

Hino Diesel Trucks

Will begin selling Class 3 diesel trucks in model year 1989 — Auto News 11/02/87 p12

Hiro Real Estate

Bought leasehold interest in Mobil's NYC headquarters bldg, US — WSJ (NJ) 12/02/87 p57

History Book Club

Buyer found for this Harcourt Brace Jovanovich subsid — Globe & Ml 10/09/87 pB18

May be sold by Harcourt Brace Jovanovich to unnamed buyer — WSJ (NJ) 10/09/87 p10

Hitachi

Consumer ratings of home video cameras — Consmr Rpt 11/00/87 p656

US color television market share data for 1986 tabulated by firm — Appliance 09/00/87 p60

US video cassette recorder market share data for 1986 (table) — Appliance 09/00/87 p60

Hitachi America

Is sampline a new line of 4-bit microcontrollers — Elec News 10/05/87 p34

New CD ROM device provides data, audio playback — Info Wld 10/26/87 p42

Offers Winchester disc drive with average seek time of 12-ms — Computrwld 12/07/87 p71

Hitachi Metals

Has formed a wholly owned subsid to produce aluminum wheels in the US — Am Mtl Mkt 10/12/87 p2

Jtly formed Sintering Technologies to build powdered metals plant, US — Auto News 11/23/87 pE34

Hitachi Metals Intnl

To jtly form Sintering Technologies — Am Mtl Mkt 10/09/87 p2

Jtly forms Sintering Technologies to build powdered metals plant — Asian WSJ 10/12/87 p14

To jtly form Sintering Technologies with 2 other firms — MetalwNews 10/12/87 p4

Jtly forms Sintering Technologies to build powdered metals plt, US — Auto News 11/23/87 pE34

Hitachi Powdered Metals

To jtly form Sintering Technologies — Am Mtl Mkt 10/09/87 p2

Jtly forms Sintering Technologies to build powdered metals plant, IN — Asian WSJ 10/12/87 p14

To jtly form Sintering Technologies with 2 other firms — MetalwNews 10/12/87 p4

Hitachi Sales America

Will introduce 2 portable cellular phones in 1/88 — Mobil Ph N 11/26/87 p10

Hitachi Zosen

Wins contract for construction of 2 crude carriers from Overseas Ship — Am Mtl Mkt 09/23/87 p7

HITK

Address to New York Society of Security Analysts — Wall St T 11/16/87 p8/4/8

HLS Hldg

Is medical mgmt svcs co formed by merger of Health Learning Systems — SCRIP 10/16/87 p12

HM Consultants

This mgmt consultant expands svcs to insurance-related consulting — BInsurance 10/12/87 p14

HMK Group Companies

Acquires Monson Chemicals — Chem Mkt R 11/30/87 p4

HMO/Alliance

Will be acquired by fellow HMO Keystone Health Plan West — Mod Health 11/06/87 p38

HNG Cortez Pipeline

Has been acquired by Cortez Vickers from Enron for $21mil — O&G Jour 09/07/87 p24

Hobart

To jtly develop welding equipment with Oerlikon-Buehrle Konzern — LSA 10/08/87 p20

Dishwasher market share data for 1986 (table) — Appliance 09/00/87 p59

Disposer market share data for 1986 (table) — Appliance 09/00/87 p59

Compactor market share data for 1986 (table) — Appliance 09/00/87 p59

Jtly develops plasma arc welder for shuttle tank with Martin Marietta — MetalwNews 11/23/87 p8

Hobart Bros

To buy Wollard Airport Equipment, airport passenger bridges mfr — DieselProg 09/00/87 p108

To exchange welding technology with that of Oerlikon Buehrle — Am Mac&Man 10/00/87 p33

Hobart McIntosh

Amer-Yhtyma acquires paper whlslr — Aushandel 11/13/87 p3

Hobbs Gas

Financial results, 1986 — P&G Jour 08/00/87 p24

Hoechst

Wins FDA approval to market intravenous streptokinase preparation — SCRIP 11/13/87 p22

Gets US patent for support film & pressure sensitive adhesive tape — Adhesives 10/00/87 p61

Hoechst Celanese

Life Technologies may acquire Calbiochem Behring — SCRIP 10/28/87 p9

Figure 9.13: Sample Citation on Hilton Hotels from *Predicasts F&S Index: United States*, December 1987.

SUMMARY

1) Publicly owned companies disclose their financial situation in an annual report to shareholders and in a 10-K Report. The two reports together constitute detailed information on the company's finances and future plans. Your library may have the reports in either print or microfiche formats.

2) Investment firms publish reports on publicly owned companies that provide a condensation of the information in the ARS and 10-K Reports as well as advice to investors. Three such investment reports are *Value Line Investment Survey, Moody's Manuals*, and Standard & Poor's *Standard Corporation Descriptions*.

3) Periodical articles are also valuable sources of information on publicly owned companies. Use *Business Periodicals Index, Business Index/INFOTRAC*tm, *Predicasts F&S Index: United States*, and *The Wall Street Journal Index*.

CHAPTER 10

SUBSIDIARY COMPANIES

In addition to being privately or publicly owned, a company can also be a subsidiary or a division of another company. A subsidiary company is one that is more than 50 percent owned by another company—called the parent company. It may or may not be incorporated as a separate company. This is true even though it may conduct a business totally different from that of the parent company, or at a different location. A division, on the other hand, is a separate operating unit of a company. Although it may have a different name from the company, it does not have its own stock, and it is not incorporated.

Subsidiaries and divisions do not issue annual reports or 10-K Reports. Instead their financial data are part of their parent company's data, often buried in such a way that it is difficult, or even impossible, to determine how the subsidiary or division is doing financially.

Both publicly owned companies, such as Hilton Hotels Corporation, and privately owned companies, such as Red Roof Inns, can be parents, subsidiaries, or divisions. Tracing the family trees of large corporations can often be very complex. In this chapter these subsidiary and parent roles will become clearer as you examine such a relationship for Hilton Hotels Corporation.

Hilton Hotels Corporation is a very large publicly owned company, which usually implies that it is a parent as well. Where can you find out if Hilton Hotels is, indeed, a parent company with subsidiaries or is itself a subsidiary? Where can you find a list of its divisions? As more and more large companies merge with one another or acquire each other, the tangle of "who-owns-whom" becomes increasingly complex. Is there a reference source that will untangle all of these company relationships?

Although there are several reference sources (see Appendix B for a listing) that supply parent-subsidiary-division hierarchies, one of the most well-known is *Directory of Corporate Affiliations* (Skokie, IL: National Register Publishing Co., 1967-). This source provides a "who-owns-whom" directory for all companies listed on the New York and American Stock Exchanges as well as over-the-counter stock companies and privately owned companies. This two-volume tool provides an alphabetical, geographical, and SIC approach to over 40,000 parent companies, subsidiaries, and divisions.

"Section 1—Alphabetical Cross Reference Index" in the front of volume I of *Directory of Corporate Affiliations* (figure 10.1) provides one alphabetical listing for all parents, subsidiaries, and divisions in the entire directory. Hilton Hotels Corporation's boldface listing indicates that it is a parent company, and that its entry is on page 537.

Turning to page 537, you locate the information contained in figure 10.2. First of all, *Directory of Corporate Affiliations* supplies basic information about the company, including address, telephone number, ticker symbol, listed stock exchanges, assets, earnings, liabilities, net worth, number of employees, number of hotels, and SIC numbers. After this, it provides a listing of corporate officers and directors. The asterisk above the company name shows that the information has been obtained from the company being listed, while the "DE" to the right of the telephone number indicates that the company is incorporated in the state of Delaware.

Finally, it lists the name, address, telephone number, SIC numbers, and officers of Hilton Hotels Corporation's divisions and subsidiaries. Three divisions and five subsidiaries are listed (figure 10.2).

As indicated in figure 10.2, one of the subsidiaries is Hilton Service Corporation. The "(1)" after the name indicates that Hilton Service Corporation is a subsidiary of the parent company, Hilton Hotels Corporation. The number to the right of that, 7748-006, is for internal use of the publisher and has no other significance.

As with most subsidiaries and divisions, you will not find a separate ARS or 10-K Report for Hilton Service Corporation. Its financial, operational, and managerial data are buried in the parent company's—Hilton Hotels Corporation—reports. Hilton Service Corporation is mentioned once in Hilton's 1988 10-K Report (figure 10.3). This information adds only slightly to the information found in the *Directory of Corporate Affiliations*. The financial charts do not separate the divisions and subsidiaries from the parent companies' data.

Since the information on a subsidiary or division is buried in the annual report and the 10-K Report, usually the most successful method for finding information on a subsidiary or division is to look for periodical articles. However, a thorough check for Hilton Service Corporation in the last few years of *Predicasts F&S Index: United States*, *INFOTRAC*tm, and *The Wall Street Journal Index* did not reveal one entry. Although there may have been articles that mentioned or discussed Hilton Service Corporation, they evidently are buried under the parent company's name—much like the information in the ARS and 10-K Report. This is not an unusual situation. It is very difficult to locate information on subsidiaries and divisions.

AL HEALTH DIV.—See Friona

DIV.—See Friona Industries, L. P.
RP.—See Hi Shear Industries Inc.
DUSTRIES INC.
CHNOLOGY CORP.—See Hi-Shear

ERIALS, INC.—See Chemical
ration
ONITE COMPANY—See Great
Ore Properties
RPORATION
ESTMENT SECURITIES, INC.—See

IN NEW

tion

—See Archer

elephone And

Corporation

ment Stores,

e Dillard

of Resources &

INC.—See Johnson

ACHINES CO.—See

RATION
RPORATION—See Adobe
on
MICAL DIV.—See Kao
merica
ANDLEMAN, ASHEBORO AND
RAILROAD CO.—See Norfolk
oration
RAINEY HOSPITAL—See Hospital
America
AL COMPANY—See The Pittston

GY PUBLISHING CORP.—See

GINEERING CORPORATION
ASSISTANCE
he Heal Group
OAN PROGRAM OF
Group
N PROGRAM OF
al Group
PROGRAM OF
e Heal Group
ROGRAM OF
Group
O.—See

co Energy

Medical

orporation

e

ee

—See National

Rouse

ll Industries, Inc.
ee Capital Cities/

—See American

3, INC.
CO—See Rochester Tel

—See Texfi Industries,

---

506 HIGHLANDS INSURANCE CO.—See Halliburton Company
1155 HIGHLINE FINANCIAL SERVICES, INC.—See Xerox Corporation
178 HIGHWAY 36 LAND DEVELOPMENT COMPANY—See Browning-Ferris Industries, Inc.
414 HILCO, INC.—See First NH Banks, Inc.
547 HILL COUNTRY HOSPITAL—See Hospital Corporation of America
599 HILL REFRIGERATION CORPORATION—See Jepson Corp.
537 HILL-ROM COMPANY, INC.—See Hillenbrand Industries, Inc.
234 HILL STEPHENS COFFEE CO.—See Chock Full O' Nuts Corporation
536 **HILLENBRAND INDUSTRIES, INC.**
758 HILLHAVEN CONVALESCENT CENTER ADRIAN—See National Medical Enterprises, Inc.
LHAVEN CONVALESCENT CENTER See National Medical Enterprises, Inc.
ALESCENT CENTER al Medical Enter

MF
758 HILLHAVEN CONV... MEMPHIS—See National Medical Enterprises, Inc.
758 HILLHAVEN CONVALESCENT CENTER MOBILE—See National Medical Enterprises, Inc.
758 HILLHAVEN CONVALESCENT CENTER RALEIGH—See National Medical Enterprises, Inc.
758 HILLHAVEN CONVALESCENT CENTER SALT LAKE CITY—See National Medical Enterprises, Inc.
758 HILLHAVEN CONVALESCENT CENT SARASOTA—See National Medical Inc.
758 HILLHAVEN CONVALESCENT C SAVANNAH—See National Medic Inc.
758 HILLHAVEN CONVALESCENT CEN VANCOUVER—See National Medical Enterprises, Inc.
758 HILLHAVEN CONVALESCENT CENTER WILMINGTON—See National Medical Enterprises, Inc.
758 HILLHAVEN CONVALESCENT HOSPITAL ANAHEIM—See National Medical Enterprises, Inc.
758 HILLHAVEN CONVALESCENT HOSPITAL BURLINGAME—See National Medical Enterprises, Inc.
758 HILLHAVEN CONVALESCENT HOSPITAL CLAREMONT—See National Medical Enterprises, Inc
758 HILLHAVEN CONVALESCENT HOSPITAL MENLO PARK—See National Medical Enterprises, Inc.
758 HILLHAVEN CONVALESCENT HOSPITAL OAKLAND—See National Medical Enterprises, Inc.
758 HILLHAVEN CONVALESCENT HOSPITAL ORANGE—See National Medical Enterprises, Inc.
758 HILLHAVEN CONVALESCENT HOSPITAL PALO ALTO—See National Medical Enterprises, Inc.
758 HILLHAVEN CONVALESCENT HOSPITAL SACRAMENTO—See National Medical Enterprises, Inc.
758 HILLHAVEN CONVALESCENT HOSPITAL SAN RAFAEL—See National Medical Enterprises, Inc.
758 HILLHAVEN CONVALESCENT HOSPITAL SANTA ANA—See National Medical Enterprises, Inc.
758 HILLHAVEN EXTENDED CARE—See National Medical Enterprises, Inc.
758 HILLHAVEN HEALTHCARE, PHOENIX—See National Medical Enterprises, Inc.
758 HILLHAVEN HIGHLAND HOUSE—See National Medical Enterprises, Inc.
758 HILLHAVEN, LITTLE ROCK—See National Medical Enterprises, Inc.
758 HILLHAVEN NURSING HOME—See National Medical Enterprises, Inc.
758 HILLHAVEN OMAHA—See National Medical Enterprises, Inc.
759 HILLHAVEN REHABILITATION CONVALESCENT—See National Medical Enterprises, Inc.
759 HILLHAVEN REHABILITATION & CONVALESCENT CENTER—See National Medical Enterprises, Inc.
758 HILLHAVEN REHABILITATION CONVALESCENT CENTER, ASHEVILLE—See National Medical Enterprises, Inc.

---

758 HILLHAVEN REHABILITATION CONVALESCENT CENTER, DURHAM—See National Medical Enterprises, Inc
758 HILLHAVEN REHABILITATION & CONVALESCENT HOSPITAL—See National Medical Enterprises, Inc.
759 HILLHAVEN TOPEKA—See National Medical Enterprises, Inc.
759 HILLHAVEN WEST—See National Medical Enterprises, Inc.
759 HILLHAVEN WICHITA—See National Medical Enterprises, Inc.
758 HILLHAVEN-LASALLE NURSING CENTER—See National Medical Enterprises, Inc.
758 HILLHAVEN-LAWTON C CENT HOSPITAL—See N erprises, Inc.
758 HILLHAVEN C n—See Nation
759 H

s, INC.
S, INC.—See Colgate-
ompany
e HILLSBORO SUN BANK—See SunTrust Banks, Inc.
232 HILLSBOROUGH PROPANE GAS COMPANY—See Chesapeake Utilities Corporation
992 HILLSDALE DAILY NEWS—See Stauffer Communications, Inc
354 HILLSDALE TOOL & MFG. CO.—See Eagle-Picher Industries, Inc.
936 HILLSHIRE FARM COMPANY—See Sara Lee Corporation
759 HILLSIDE MANOR CONVALESCENT HOSPITAL—See National Medical Enterprises, Inc.
537 HILTON EQUIPMENT CORP.—See Hilton Hotels Corporation
537 **HILTON HOTELS CORPORATION**
537 HILTON HOTELS DIV.—See Hilton Hotels Corporation
537 HILTON HOTELS, NEVADA DIV.—See Hilton Hotels Corporation
289 HILTON INDUSTRIES, INC.—See Core Industries Inc
537 **HILTON INTERNATIONAL CO.**
537 HILTON NEVADA CORP.—See Hilton Hotels Corporation
537 HILTON SERVICE CORPORATION—See Hilton Hotels Corporation
537 HILTON SUITES—See Hilton Hotels Corporation
537 HILTON TOURS, INC.—See Hilton Hotels Corporation
83 HINCKLEY & SCHMITT, INC.—See Anjou International Company
538 HINDERLITER HEAT TREATING, INC.—See Hinderliter Industries, Inc.
537 **HINDERLITER INDUSTRIES, INC.**
870 HINES-PARK FOODS, INC.—See The Procter & Gamble Company
203 HINGHAM MARINER—See Capital Cities/ABC, Inc.
71 HINGHAM WATER CO.—See American Water Works Company, Inc.
312 HINKLE EASTER PRODUCTS—See Darda Inc. (USA)
538 **HIPOTRONICS, INC.**
538 HIPOTRONICS INTERNATIONAL, INC.—See Hipotronics, Inc.
538 **HIRAM WALKER-ALLIED VINTNERS**
538 HIRAM WALKER, INC.—See Hiram Walker-Allied Vintners
511 HISTACOUNT GROUP—See Hanson Industries Inc.
1048 HISTORY BOOK CLUB, INC—See Time Warner Inc.
1157 HIT OR MISS, INC—See Zayre Corporation
203 HITCHCOCK PUBLISHING COMPANY—See Capital Cities/ABC, Inc.
112 HITCO MATERIALS—See BP America Inc.
576 HI-TEK POLYMERS INC.—See Interchem Inc.
374 HITTMAN EBASCO ASSOCIATES INC.—See Enserch Corporation
692 HI-VOL PRODUCTS—See Masco Industries, Inc.
1121 HMF, INC.—See Washington Gas Light Co.
928 HMG SPORTS, EVENTS & LICENSING—See Saatchi & Saatchi Advertising, Inc.
538 **HOBART BROTHERS CO.**
864 HOBART CORPORATION-USA—See Premark International, Inc.
995 HOBBS DIV.—See Stewart-Warner Corporation

---

995 HOBBS DIV., Stewart Warn
1032 HOBBS TRAII
676 HOBIE CAT (Forbes Holdin
381 HOBSON BRC MOULD WOR
803 BERNARD HC Group, Inc.
291 G. L. HODSOI Black Corpora
538 HOECHST CE Hoechst Celar
538 HOECHST CE
538 HOECHST CE INTERMEDIAT Celanese Cor
539 HOECHST CE See Hoechst (
539 HOECHST CE PRODUCTS G Corporation
CHST CE —See
577 r. E Corp
1010 HOFER A Cheese Asso
250 HOFFMAN AIF Clarkson Indus
839 HOFFMAN EN Pentair, Inc
865 HOFFMAN PR Corporation
692 HOFFMAN PR Industries, Inc.
928 HOFFMAN YO Saatchi Advert
539 **HOFFMANN-L**
539 **HOFMANN IN**
539 **HOGAN SYST**
698 HOGAN TRAN CORPORATIC
811 HOLBROOK S Inc.
203 HOLBROOK S
865 J. L. HOLCOMI Corporation
1041 HOLCROFT/L Corporation
1143 HOLD EVERY Inc.
834 HOLDEN ENE Penn Central (
676 HOLDER DIVI Holdings Inc.
239 L. S. HOLDIN(Corporation
540 HOLIDAY CAS
540 HOLIDAY CLU Holiday Corpor
539 **HOLIDAY COI**
540 HOLIDAY DEV Corporation
540 HOLIDAY EQU CORPORATIO
540 HOLIDAY INN Corporation
540 HOLIDAY INN- Corporation
540 HOLIDAY INNS Corporation
539 HOLIDAY INNS
540 HOLIDAY INNS Holiday Corpor
540 HOLIDAY INNS Corporation
540 HOLIDAY INNS Holiday Corpor
540 HOLIDAY INNS Holiday Corpor
540 HOLIDAY PACI Holiday Corpor
540 HOLIDAY PACI CORPORATIOI
541 **HOLIDAY RV !**
515 HOLIDAY RAM Harley-Davidso
541 HOLIDAY RV F Holiday RV Sup

Boldface Indicates Parent Company

Figure 10.1: Section 1: "Alphabetical Cross Reference Index" from *Directory of Corporate Affiliations*, 1990.

Mfr. Air Fluidized Support Beds Hospital
Beds; Wound Care Therapy
S.I.C.: 2599
Walter Rosebrough *(Pres.)*

7747-000
HILLER AVIATION
(Acquired By Rogerson Aircraft
Corporation)

20886-230
HILLS BROS. COFFEE, INC.
(Acquired by Nestle Holdings, Inc.)

•
9067-000
**HILLS DEPARTMENT STORES,
INC.**
15 D** **d
Ca
Te
Y
H
A
E
Li
N
A
Er
Fisca.
Discount Department Stores
S.I.C.: 5311
Stephen A. Goldberger *(Chm. Bd.,
Pres. & Chief Exec. Officer)*
George R. Friese *(Vice Chm. Bd.)*
Raymond Brinkman *(Sr. V.P.-Opers.)*
John C. Brouillard *(Sr. V.P.-Fin. &
Admin.)*
Andrew J. Samuto *(Sr. V.P.-Real Estate
Devel. & Human Resources)*
Eugene O'Donnell *(Sr. V.P. & Gen.
Mdse. Mgr.)*
Stephen A. Feldman *(V.P. & Treas.)*
William K. Friend *(V.P., Sec. & Corp.
Counsel)*
Paul T. Gannon *(V.P.-MIS)*
John G. Reen *(V.P. & Controller)*
R. Wesley McDonough *(V.P.-Adv. &
Mktg.)*
Lawrence H. Miller *(V.P.-Personnel)*
Larry Voelker *(V.P.)*
Michael Fahey *(Dir.-Pur.)*
Board of Directors:
Stephen A. Goldberger
Robert D. Buzzell
George R. Friese
Dean C. Kehler
Thomas H. Lee
James L. Moody, Jr.

4488-000
Foley, Hoag & Eliot *(Transfer Agent)*
Ten Post Office Sq.
Boston, MA 02210
Tel.: 617-482-1390

4681-000
Porter, Wright, Morris & Arthur *(Legal
Firm)*
Columbus, OH

3665-008
Manufacturers Hanover Trust
Co. *(Transfer Agent)*
450 W. 33rd St., 8th Floor
New York, NY 10001
Tel.: 212-613-7192

Divisions:
9067-001
C.R.H International, Inc. **(1)**
35 N. 4th
Columbus, OH 43215   (OH)
Tel.: 614-460-8700   **(100%)**
S.I.C.: 5199
Herbert H. Schiff *(Chief Oper. Officer)*

9067-002
Gallenkamp **(1)**
35 N. 4th
Columbus, OH 43215
Tel.: 614-460-8700   **(100%)**
Well-Known Brands of Dress Shoes, Casuals,
Boots, Tennis & Athletic Footwear for the
Entire Family
S.I.C.: 5661
Dennis Tishkoff *(Chief Oper. Officer)*

9067-003
Leased Conventional Dept. Stores Div.
(1)
35 N. 4th
Columbus, OH 43215
Tel.: 614-460-**   (100%)**
Dennis Tish**   *Officer)*

9067-007
Leased Discount Dept. Stores Div. **(1)**
35 N. 4th
Columbus, OH 43215
Tel.: 614-460-8700   **(100%)**
Dennis Tishkoff *(Chief Opr. Officer)*

9067-010
Retail Footwear Div. **(1)**
33 North High St.
Columbus, OH 43215
Tel.: 614-460-8700
Footwear
S.I.C.: 5661
Dennis B. Tishkoff *(Pres.)*

9067-008
Rudnick Company **(1)**
2901 State St.
Hamden, CT 06507   (CT)
Tel.: 203-288-5651   **(100%)**
Leased Domestics Depts.
S.I.C.: 5714; 5719
David Rudnick *(Chief Oper. Officer)*

7748-000
**HILTON HOTELS
CORPORATION**
9336 Civic Center Dr.
Beverly Hills, CA 90209
Mailing Address: P.O. Box 5567
Beverly Hills, CA 90210
Tel.: 213-278-4321   DE
Telefax: 213-205-4599
Year Founded: 1946
HLT—(NYSE PS Bo MW)
Assets: $1,892,500,000
Earnings: $130,900,000
Liabilities: $1,078,400,000
Net Worth: $814,100,000
Approx. Rev.: $953,600,000
Emp: 35,000
Fiscal Year-end: 12/31/88
272 Hotels: Owned, Leased or
Franchised
S.I.C.: 7011; 7999; 6794
Barron Hilton *(Chm. Bd., Pres. & Chief
Exec. Officer)*
John V. Giovenco *(Exec. V.P.-NV
Gaming Opers. & Pres.,NV Div.)*
Gregory R. Dillon *(Exec. V.P.-Intl.)*
Carl T. Mottek *(Exec. V.P.-Opers. &
Pres.-Hilton Hotels Div.)*
William C. Lebo, Jr. *(Sr. V.P. & Gen.
Counsel)*
Maurice J. Scanlon *(Sr. V.P.-Fin.)*
Robert F. Eiseman *(Sr. V.P.-Pur.)*
Cheryl L. Marsh *(Corp. Sec.)*
Molly McKenzie *(Personnel Dir.)*
Board of Directors:
Barron Hilton
Raymond C. Avansino, Jr.
Gregory R. Dillon
Donald W. Douglas, Jr.
John V. Giovenco
Eric Hilton
Donald R. Knab
Benjamin V. Lambert
Carl T. Mottek
Thomas R. Wilcox
Sam D. Young, Jr.

22660-000
First National Bank of Chicago *(Transfer
Agent)*
(Formerly First Chicago Corporation)
One First National Plaza, Ste. 0123
Chicago, IL 60670
Tel.: 312-407-4660

21870-004
Arthur Andersen & Co. *(Auditors)*
911 Wilshire Blvd.
Los Angeles, CA 90017

Divisions:
7748-001
Hilton Hotels Div. **(1)**
9336 Santa Monica Blvd
Beverly Hills, CA 90210
Tel.: 213-278-4321
Telefax: 213-205-4599
Emp: 38,000
Hotels
S.I.C.: 7011
Carl T. Mottek *(Pres.)*
Robert F. Eiseman *(Sr. V.P.-Pur.)*
Joseph F. Frederick, Jr. *(Sr. V.P.-Central
Region)*
Peter Kleiser *(Sr. V.P.-Food & Beverage)*
Jorgen H. Hansen *(Sr. V.P.-Southern Reg.)*
William R. McDonald *(Sr. V.P.-Human
Resources)*
Dieter H. Huckestein *(Sr. V.P.-Hawaiian Reg.)*
Hilmar A. Rosenast *(Sr. V.P.-Western Reg.)*

Robert C. Moore *(Sr. V.P.-Sls.)*
Arthur A. Surin *(Sr. V.P.-Eastern Reg.)*
Robley T. Barber *(Sr. V.P.-Properties)*
Donald L. Harrill *(Sr. V.P.-Franchising &
Devel.)*
James L. Philon *(Sr. V.P.-Real Estate &
Construction)*
Michael A. Ribero *(Sr. V.P.-Mktg Services)*
James M. Anderson *(V.P.-Labor Rels &
Personnel Admin.)*
David S. Conway *(V.P.-Real Estate Devel.,
Southwest Region)*
Stephen L. Dietrich *(V.P.-Real Estate Devel.,
Central Region)*
Gregory L. Francois *(V.P.-Real Estate Devel.,
Western Region)*
Terry A. Logsdon *(V.P.-Real Estate Devel.,
Southeastern Reg.)*
Thomas B. Parris *(V.P.-Real Estate Devel.,
Eastern Reg.)*
J. Michael Curran *(V.P.-Franchise Mktg.)*
Robert E. Dirks *(V.P.-Mktg Programs)*
Francis M.N. DuBeau *(V.P.-Project Admin.)*
Allen C. Hermansen *(V.P.-Franchise Opers.)*
Brian D. Stevens *(V.P.-Sls.)*
Dennis Koci *(V.P.-Staff Services)*
Donald L. Tobias *(V.P.-Project Admin.)*
Eva A. Walley *(V.P.-Front Office Opers. &
Systems)*
Yoshi Okomoto *(Asst. V.P.-Sales)*

7748-002
Hilton Nevada Corp. **(1)**
3000 Paradise Blvd.
Las Vegas, NV 89114

7748-009
S.I.C.: 7011
Barron Hilton *(Chm. & Chief Exec. Officer)*
John V. Giovenco *(Pres.)*
John T. Fitzgerald *(Sr. V.P. & Pres.-Las
Vegas Hilton)*
James Newman *(Sr. V.P.-Casino Opers.-Las
Vegas Hilton)*
Horst Dziura *(Sr. V.P. & Pres.-Flamingo
Hilton)*
David A. Hilton *(Sr V.P.-Casino Opers.-
Flamingo Hilton)*
Paul V. Houdayer *(V.P.-Food & Beverage)*
William J. Sherlock *(V.P. & G.M.-Flamingo
Hilton)*

Subsidiaries:
Conrad International Hotels
Corporation **(1)**
P.O. 5567, 9336 Civic Center Dr.
Beverly Hills, CA 90209
Tel.: 213-278-4321
Telefax: 213-205-4670
Emp: 40
Lodging & Gaming
S.I.C.: 7011
Barron Hilton *(Chm. Bd.)*
Gregory R. Dillon *(Pres.)*
Eric M. Hilton *(Exec. V.P.)*
William C. Lebo *(Sr. V.P. & Gen. Counsel)*

7748-006
Hilton Service Corporation **(1)**
2050 Chennault Dr.
Carrollton, TX 75006-5096
Tel.: 214-770-6000
Telefax: 214-991-0048
Emp: 400
Reservation Service
S.I.C.: 7389
Marvin Smith *(Exec. Dir.)*

7748-007
Hilton Tours, Inc. **(1)**
9876 Wilshire Blvd.
Beverly Hills, CA 90210
Tel.: 213-550-0520   **(100%)**
Emp: 12
Tour Bookings
S.I.C.: 4724
Barron Hilton *(Pres.)*
Carl T. Mottek *(Exec. V.P.)*
Michael A. Ribero *(Sr. V.P.)*
Maurice J. Scanlon *(Sr. V.P.)*
William C. Lebo, Jr. *(Sr. V.P. & Asst. Sec.)*
Marvin Smith *(V.P. & Gen. Mgr.)*
David C. Johnson *(V.P. & Counsel)*
Steve Krithis *(Treas. & Asst. Sec.)*
Cheryl L. Marsh *(Sec.)*
William B. Rees *(Asst. Sec.)*

7748-003
Hilton Equipment Corp. **(1)**
9336 Civic Center Dr.
Beverly Hills, CA 90209   (DE)
Tel.: 213-278-4321   **(100%)**
Telefax: 213-205-4305
Hotels
S.I.C.: 7011
Robert F. Eiseman *(Sr. V.P. & Gen. Mgr.)*

7748-010
Hilton Suites **(1)**
2050 Chenault Dr.
Carrollton, TX 75006   (DE)
Tel.: 214-991-5500   **(100%)**
Telefax: 214-991-0048
S.I.C.: 7011
Barron Hilton *(Pres.)*
Carl T. Mottek *(Exec. V.P.)*
Robley T. Barber *(Exec. V.P.)*
Maurice J. Scanlon *(Sr. V.P.)*
William C. Lebo, Jr. *(Sr. V.P.)*
John R. Weeman, Jr. *(V.P.-Devel.)*
Larry J. Mundy *(V.P.-Devel. & Asst. Sec.)*
Michael W. Fairchild *(V.P.-Design & Const.)*
Thomas W. Nelson *(V.P. & Comptroller)*
Steven A. Miller *(V.P. & Treas.)*
Cheryl L. Marsh *(Sec.)*
Steve Krithis *(Asst. Treas. & Asst. Sec.)*

•
28488-008
HILTON INTERNATIONAL CO.
(Sub. of Ladbroke Group Plc)
605 Third Ave.
New York, NY 10158
Tel.: 212-973-2200   DE
Telefax: 212-867-9863
Approx. Sls.: $1,807,000,000
Emp: 45,000
Fiscal Year-end: 12/31/88
International Hotel Management
S.I.C.: 7011
J. Jarvis *(Chm. Bd., Pres. & Chief
Exec. Officer)*
D. Michels *(Sr. V.P.-Sls. & Mktg.)*
David Hoffman *(Sr. V.P.-Human
Resources & Devel.)*
Ronald G. Drake *(V.P.-Sls. & Mktg.)*
Anthony Potter *(V.P.-U.S.A. Opers.)*
M. Hirst *(Deputy Chief Exec. Officer)*
Martin Gatto *(Chief Fin. Officer)*
Geoffrey Chester *(General Counsel &
Sec.)*
Mike Bugsgang *(U.K.) (Corp. Public
Rels. Exec.)*
Barry Harris *(Natl. Sls. & Mktg. Dir.-
U.S. Reg.)*
Robert C. Mackey *(Natl. Sls. & Mktg.
Dir.-Vista Intl. Hotels)*
Geri Webb Holton *(Adv. Dir.)*

**   on:**
28488-009
**   **ternational Hotels **(1)**
**   **1 Ave.
**   **k, NY 10158
**   **2-973-2200
**   **x: 212-367-9863
**   **national Hotel Mngmt.
**   **I.C.: 7011
Robert C. Mackey *(Dir.-Mktg.)*

41967-000
**HINDERLITER INDUSTRIES,
INC.**
7134 South Yale Ave., Ste. 600
Tulsa, OK 74136
Mailing Address: P.O. Box 35505
Tulsa, OK 74153
Tel.: 918-494-0992
Assets: $12,933,000
Earnings: ($3,266,000)
Liabilities: $8,589,000
Net Worth: $4,344,000
Approx. Sls.: $27,926,000
Fiscal Year-end: 6/30/88
Mfr. of Precision & Specialty Parts &
Equipment for the Gas Transfer
Industry & A Major Force in the Heat
Treating Industry
S.I.C.: 3398; 4922
John L. Robertson *(Chm. Bd. & Chief
Exec. Officer)*
Richard H. Hughes *(Pres. & Chief
Oper. Officer)*
Richard T. Maddox *(V.P. & Chief Fin.
Officer)*
Jimmy C. Strong *(V.P.-Personnel)*
Lesley W. Jaggers *(V.P. & Chief Acctg.
Officer)*
Gerald D. Haag *(V.P., Corp. Counsel &
Sec.)*
Robert C. Diffenderfer *(V.P. & Corp.
Devel.)*
Board of Directors:
John L. Robertson
Richard R. Hughes

(continued next page)

(handwritten/annotated) Notes information obtained from the Hilton directly

(handwritten/annotated) State of incorporation

(handwritten/annotated) [arrow pointing to Subsidiaries]

537

Figure 10.2: Section 2: "Parent Companies" from *Directory of Corporate Affiliations*, 1990.

ADDITIONAL INFORMATION

Designing and Furnishings Services

Hilton, through its wholly-owned subsidiary, Hilton Equipment Corporation, organized in 1967, and through its Corporate Properties Division has provided designing and furnishings services and has distributed furniture, furnishings, equipment and supplies primarily to hotels owned, leased or managed by Hilton, and, to a lesser extent, to hotels franchised by Hilton or owned and operated by others. The revenues of this operation depend primarily on the number of new hotels under construction which will be operated by Hilton and, in addition, on refurbishing and remodeling of existing Hilton hotels.

Computer Systems

Compass Computer Services, Inc. ("Compass"), 50% of which is owned by Hilton and the balance by Budget Rent-A-Car, Inc. ("Budget"), operates a computerized reservation system for, among other things, hotel reservations. This system also provides Hilton with certain statistical data and registration packets. Compass is being managed by a subsidiary of AMR Corporation. For information relative to the Company's investment in Compass, see "Investments" in the Notes to Consolidated Financial Statements on pages 36 and 37 in the 1988 Stockholders Report, which information is incorporated herein by reference.

In addition, the Company has entered into a joint venture with AMR, Budget and Marriott Corporation to develop CONFIRM, an integrated travel reservation system using state of the art computer technology. The design and development of this system is expected to take several years and, upon completion, CONFIRM will be used by its partners and will be marketed to others in the airline, car rental and lodging industries.

Reservation System

The Compass computerized reservation system is presently utilized by Hilton Service Corporation, the operator of a worldwide system of reservation offices for hotels operated by Hilton, Hilton International Co., their affiliates and others. Hilton Service Corporation is owned 51% by Hilton and 49% by Hilton International Co.

Marketing

Hotel occupancy at Hilton's owned, leased or managed properties, other than the four hotel-casinos in Nevada and Australia, the four hotels in Hawaii and the hotel in St. Martin, is derived primarily from the convention and meeting market and the business traveler market (businesspersons traveling as individuals or in small groups). Hawaiian and St. Martin hotel occupancy is primarily derived from the tour and travel market (tourists traveling either as individuals or in groups) and the convention and meeting market. Hotel occupancy at the Company's hotel-casinos is derived primarily from the convention and meeting market, the tour and travel market and junket and V.I.P. programs. As indicated under "Additional Information—Statistical Data" below, these sources of business are sensitive to general economic and other conditions.

Statistical Data

For information relative to Number of Properties, Number of Available Rooms, Occupancy Ratios and Management and Franchise Fees for the five fiscal years ended December 31, 1988, see the Ten Year Summary on pages 46 and 47 in the 1988 Stockholders Report, which information is incorporated herein by reference.

Hilton's occupancy ratios are affected by general economic conditions, as well as competition, work stoppages and other factors affecting particular properties. Hotel-casino occupancy in 1984 and

10

Figure 10.3: Excerpt about Hilton Service Corporation from Hilton Hotels Corporation 10-K Report, 1988.

Many times you may have the name of a company about which you know very little. If the company does not appear in the standard reference sources, such as *The Million Dollar Directory* or *Moody's Manuals*, that may be a clue that it is a subsidiary or a division. In these cases, consult *Directory of Corporate Affiliations'* "Alphabetical Cross Reference Index," as shown in figure 10.1.

Now you understand how to tell the difference among privately owned, publicly owned, and subsidiary companies. You also know where to look for basic information on all three types of companies. Since information on publicly owned companies is readily available, it is necessary to understand the basics of one other business concept—financial ratios. Chapter 11 will explain what financial ratios are, why they are important, and where to find them.

SUMMARY

1) A company may be a parent, subsidiary, or division. A *subsidiary* is a company that is more than 50 percent owned by another company. A *division* is a separate operating unit of a parent company. Both publicly and privately owned companies can have subsidiaries and divisions.

2) A company that does not appear in the standard corporate directories is probably a subsidiary or a division. Check in *Directory of Corporate Affiliations* for the "family trees," or "who owns whom" information.

3) Information on subsidiaries or divisions is usually very difficult to locate because it is generally contained within the parent company's reports and articles.

4) Periodical articles are your best source for locating more information on subsidiaries, but, here too, they may be difficult to find.

CHAPTER 11

FINANCIAL RATIOS

During your research thus far, you may have noticed several occurrences of financial ratios in tools such as *Moody's Manuals, Value Line Investment Survey*, and *Industry Surveys*. In this chapter you will discover what financial ratios are and why they are useful.

Financial ratios are numbers or percentages that are used to evaluate the "health" of a company. They are called ratios because they are attained by dividing one number by another. Ratio analysis compares one figure on the financial statement to another. Different kinds of ratios measure different strengths or weaknesses in a company. For example, the current ratio, which is one measure of a company's solvency, compares assets to liabilities. The current ratio is computed as follows:

$$\text{Current ratio} = \frac{\text{Total current assets}}{\text{Total current liabilities}}$$

A current ratio of 2:1 means the company has twice as many assets as it has liabilities. This is a useful figure for a banker or financial analyst who is considering a potential loan to the company. Some other commonly used financial ratios include:

$$\text{Quick ratio} = \frac{\text{Current assets minus inventory}}{\text{Current liabilities}}$$

$$\text{Debt to equity ratio} = \frac{\text{Total debt}}{\text{Total owner's equities}}$$

$$\text{Profit margin} = \frac{\text{Net profit after taxes}}{\text{Sales}}$$

$$\text{Inventory turnover} = \frac{\text{Sales}}{\text{Inventory}}$$

In order to calculate the above ratios for Hilton Hotels Corporation, you must find Hilton's current assets, total debt, inventory, and so on. These numbers are available in *Moody's Industrial Manual* (figure 11.1). You can easily compute the current ratio by locating the total current assets and the total current liabilities in the balance sheet. Likewise, all of the other ratios mentioned above could be computed from the figures available in *Moody's Industrial Manual* (figure 11.1). Other excellent sources for these numbers are the annual report to shareholders or 10-K Report for Hilton Hotels Corporation.

For example, Hilton Hotels Corporation's 1988 current ratio could be calculated from the consolidated balance sheet illustrated in figure 11.1. Total current assets for 1988 were $596.2 million, while the current liabilities were $306.7 million. When these two numbers are divided the calculation equals 1.9. (Total current assets were 1.9 times larger than current liabilities.)

Although you can calculate ratios from the financial figures in *Moody's Manuals* or the company's 10-K Report, there is an easier way to find them. Because of the demand for the more common financial ratios, several reference tools provide them, including *Moody's Manuals* (figure 11.2) and Standard & Poor's *Industry Surveys* (figure 11.3). The calculations have already been done for you!

Now that you have the financial ratios for Hilton Corporation, how can they be used to diagnose the "health" of the company? There are two methods to do this diagnosis. The first method compares the company's ratios against the same company's past ratios, which is called a time series analysis or intrafirm analysis. *Industry Surveys* (figure 11.3) provides five years of ratios for Hilton—in this illustration, from 1983 to 1987. As seen in this illustration, Hilton's current ratio has gone from 2.6 to 2.4 in the last 3 years, and, as already shown above, in 1988, the current ratio fell to 1.9.

The second method compares Hilton Corporation's ratios against the average or typical ratios of the lodging industry, which is called a cross-sectional analysis, interfirm analysis, or comparative analysis. In order to do a comparative analysis, you must find sources for industry ratios as well. Several standard ratio sources are listed in Appendix B. For illustrative purposes, we will concentrate on Dun & Bradstreet's *Industry Norms & Key Business Ratios* (Murray Hill, NJ: Dun & Bradstreet, Inc., 1982/83-).

BALANCE SHEETS

CONSOLIDATED BALANCE SHEET, AS OF DEC. 31

(in thousands of dollars)

	1988	[1]1987
ASSETS:		
Cash & equivalents	313,700	169,600
Temporary investments	120,600	71,400
Other current assets	151,900	117,300
Total current assets	586,200	358,300
Invest. in & notes from unconsol. affl.	216,200	203,200
Other investments	43,000	44,300
Restricted securities	16,900	69,900
[1]Property & equipment	1,112,400	948,900
[1]Less: Accum. depreciation	323,300	286,300
Construction in progress	212,700	66,900
Net property & equipment	1,001,800	729,500
Other assets	28,400	18,400
Total	1,892,500	1,423,600
LIABILITIES:		
Current liabilities	306,700	151,400
Long term debt	568,500	283,700
Deferred income taxes	179,100	173,800
Insurance revenues and other	24,100	41,900
Common stock ($2.50 par)	127,600	127,500
Additional capital	18,500	19,500
Retained earnings	855,400	770,900
Stkhldrs' equity	1,001,500	917,900
[2]Less com. stk. in treasury (at cost)	187,400	145,100
Total stockholders' equity	814,100	772,800
Total	1,892,500	1,423,600
Net current assets	279,500	206,900

[1]Restated to conform to 1988 presentation.

[2]1988 comprised of (in $000):

	Cost	Deprec.
Land	87,900	......
Bldgs., leaseholds & improv.	735,100	205,700
Furniture & equip.	283,000	117,600
Prop. for devel. or sale	6,400	......
Constr. in prog.	212,700	......
Total	1,325,100	323,300

[3]Number of shares: 1988, 3,200,000; 1987, 2,700,000.

NOTES TO CONSOLIDATED FINANCIAL STATEMENTS

(As Taken From Annual Report of Company)

Summary of Significant Accounting Policies

PRINCIPLES OF CONSOLIDATION — The consolidated financial statements include the accounts of Hilton Hotels Corporation and its majority and wholly-owned subsidiaries (the Company). All material inter-company transactions are eliminated. With the exception of entities with restricted securities, there are no significant restrictions on the transfer of funds from the Company's wholly owned subsidiaries to Hilton Hotels Corporation.

Investments in unconsolidated affiliates are stated at cost adjusted by equity in undistributed earnings.

CASINO REVENUES/PROMOTIONAL ALLOWANCES — Casino revenues are the aggregate of gaming wins and losses. Promotional allowances consist of complimentary food, beverage and accommodations.

PROPERTY, EQUIPMENT AND DEPRECIATION — Property and equipment are stated at cost. Interest incurred during construction of facilities is capitalized and amortized over the life of the asset.

Costs of improvements are capitalized; costs of normal repairs and maintenance are charged to expense as incurred. Upon the sale or retirement of property and equipment, the cost and related accumulated depreciation are removed from the respective accounts, and the resulting gain or loss, if any, is included in income.

Depreciation and amortization are computed using the straight line method over the estimated useful lives of the assets. Leasehold improvements are amortized over the shorter of the assets life or lease term.

PRE-OPENING COSTS — Operating costs and expenses associated with the opening of hotels or major additions to hotels are deferred and charged to income over a three year period after the opening date.

UNAMORTIZED LOAN COSTS — Debt discount and issuance costs incurred in connection with long-term debt are amortized by charges to expense principally on the bonds outstanding method.

SELF-INSURANCE — The Co. is self-insured for various levels of general liability, workers' compensation and employee medical coverage. Insurance reserves include the present values of projected settlements for claims.

INCOME TAXES — The provisions for deferred income taxes reflect the results of timing differences in recognizing income or deductions for financial reporting and income tax purposes.

Investment tax credits are accounted for on the flow-through method as a reduction of Federal income taxes.

STOCK OPTION PLANS — No charges or credits to income are made with regard to the options granted under the Co.'s stock option plans.

RESTRICTED SECURITIES — The proceeds from two issues of industrial development revenue bonds were restricted for the redevelopment of two hotel properties.

NET INCOME PER SHARE — Net income per share is based on the weighted average number of common shares outstanding plus the common stock equivalents which arise from the assumed exercise of stock options.

During 1988 the Co.'s Board of Directors authorized a 2-for-1 stock split in the form of a 100 percent stock distribution. All share and per share data in the consolidated financial statements and notes have been restated accordingly.

RECLASSIFICATIONS — The consolidated financial statements for prior years reflect certain reclassifications to conform with classifications adopted in 1988. These classifications have no effect on net income.

In 1988, the Co. has presented a statement of cash flows in accordance with Statement of Financial Accounting Standards No. 95 and has restated prior periods to be consistent witht he current year presentation.

Accounts and Notes Receivable

Included in other current assets at Dec. 31, 1988 and 1987 are accounts and notes receivable as follows ($000):

	1988	1987
Hotel accts. & notes receiv.	88,400	75,800
Less allow. for doubtful accts.	7,900	3,300
	80,500	72,500
Casino accts. receiv.	47,900	26,400
Less allow. for doubtful accts.	9,100	6,700
	38,800	19,700
Fed. tax refund receiv.	2,000	2,600
Total	121,300	94,800

Based primarily on historical trends, an allowance for estimated uncollectible casino receivables is provided to reduce casino accounts receivable to amounts anticipated to be collected within twelve months of the date credit was granted. Such allowanced are included in casino expenses in the amount of $11.9 million, $5.5 million and $5.4 million in 1988, 1987 and 1986, respectively.

Inventories

Included in other current assets at Dec. 31, 1988 and 1987 are inventories of $10,300,000 and $9,500,000, respectively, determined on a first-in, first-out basis.

Investments

The composition of the Company's total investments in and notes from unconsolidated affiliates at December 31, 1988 and 1987 is as follows (in $000):

	1988	1987
Equity investments		
50% owned unconsolidated affiliates		
Hotel partnership joint ventures (seven in 1988 and in 1987)	175,300	170,600
Other	10,200	10,200
Less than 50% owned unconsolidated affiliates		
Hotel partnership joint ventures (11 in 1988, ten in 1987)	24,900	18,300
Other	1,800	2,600
Total equity investments	212,200	199,100
Notes receivable (net of current maturities of $300 and $800)	4,000	4,100
Total	216,200	203,200

The changes in the Company's equity investments in such affiliates are as follows (in $000):

	1988	1987
Investments, Jan. 1	199,100	226,900
Earnings	16,400	12,600
Distributions received	(20,600)	(14,700)
Additional investments	21,900	38,100
Transfer of assets	(4,600)	(35,200)
Net proceeds from joint venture	......	(16,100)
Sales of interest in hotel partnership joint vent.	......	(12,500)
Investments, Dec. 31	212,200	199,100

Three unconsolidated affiliates have limitations on distributions of earnings under certain circumstances. At December 31, 1988 one property had a restriction on such distributions of $7,900,000.

Management fees totalling approximately $20,200,000, $17,200,000 and $16,000,000 were charged by the Company to its unconsolidated affiliates in 1988, 1987, and 1986, respectively. Other group services were provided to unconsolidated affiliates with no significant element of profit.

Summarized balance sheet information of the 50% owned affiliates at December 31, 1988 and 1987 is as follows (in $000):

	1988	1987
Current assets	90,000	93,600
Property and other assets, net	770,500	739,700
Current liabilities	56,700	60,000
Long-term debt and other	402,500	368,900
Equity	401,300	404,400

Summarized balance sheet information of the less than 50% owned affiliates at December 31, 1988 and 1987 is as follows (in $000):

	1988	1987
Current assets	58,000	39,800
Property and other assets, net	511,900	540,400
Current liabilities	175,900	47,500
Long-term debt and other	292,000	424,100
Equity	101,100	108,500

Of total long-term joint venture obligations of $694,500,000 at December 31, 1988, $663,300,000 is secured solely by venture assets or is guaranteed by other venture partners without recourse to the Company.

The Company's proportionate share of equity as reflected in the unconsolidated affiliates' financial statements is $22,200,000 and $23,800,000 in excess of its cost in 1988 and 1987, respectively, and is being amortized over the estimated useful lives of the underlying assets. Such amortization amounted to $1,600,000, $1,900,000 and $1,900,000 annually in 1988, 1987 and 1986.

The Company's proportionate shares of capital expenditures and depreciation expense of unconsolidated affiliates were $42,100,000 and $28,100,000, respectively, in 1988, $99,300,000 and $24,300,000, respectively, in 1987, and $92,200,000, and $22,900,000, respectively, in 1986.

Summarized results of operations of the 50% owned affiliates for the three years ended December 31, 1988 are as follows: (in $000):

	1988	1987	1986
Revenue	460,700	435,500	401,100
Expenses	425,500	401,500	373,700
Operating income	32,300	31,900	26,400

Summarized results of operations of the less than 50% owned affiliates for the three years ended December 31, 1988 are as follows (in $000):

	1988	1987	1986
Revenue	346,400	291,000	240,900
Expenses	344,600	312,200	262,100
Operating income	1,800	(21,200)	(21,200)

The proportionate taxable income or loss of all partnership joint ventures is included in the taxable income of their respective partners. Therefore, no provisions for income taxes on such entities, except for certain local taxes on income of partnership joint ventures in the District of Columbia and the Federal income tax of a corporate joint venture, are included in the above statements.

Other investments at December 31, 1988 and 1987 consist of (in $000):

	1988	1987
Safe harbor tax lease benefits	10,700	11,600
Other notes and investments	32,300	32,700
Total	43,000	44,300

Property and Equipment

Property and equipment at December 31, 1988 and 1987 are as follows (in $000):

	1988	1987
Land	87,900	55,100
Building and leasehold improvements	735,100	628,200
Furniture and equipment	283,000	258,300

Figure 11.1: "Consolidated Balance Sheet" for Hilton Hotels Corporation, *Moody's Industrial Manual*, 1988.

hotels. These additions w.
hotel system.

Gaming

The gaming segment enjoyed excellent growth in 1988, as revenue and income contribution increased

...ent and other tax credits in ... to credits of $2.4 million in 1987 ... million in 1986. In 1988, 1987 and 1986 the Company recognized $2.4 million, $3.9 million and $5.0 million, respectively, in tax benefits from transactions with Alaskan Native Corporations.

Dividends paid on co... and 1986, represent 35 perce... percent, respectively, of net incom... erty transactions. The Company's objec... pay dividends of approximately 40% of net opera... ing income.

FINANCIAL & OPERATING DATA

Statistical Record	1988	1987	1986
[1]Earned per share — common:			
On year-end shares	$2.73	$2.86	$1.96
On average shares	$2.72	$2.80	$1.96
[1]Dividends per share — common	$0.95	$0.90	$0.90
Price range — common	55¼-34	46-28	40-30
[1] — Common (adj.)	55.25-34.00	45.88-27.50	40.13-30.25
Net tangible assets per share — common	$18.25	$15.80	......
Price range — Int'l. Leis. collect. trust 8s, 1993	......	93-56½	78-78
— Hilton N.J. sr. deb. 11⅜s, 1992	104-101½	109-100	105¼-103
— Hilton N.J. sr. deb. 10⅝s, 1994	103¾-100¼	105-101⅛	101-101
Times charges earned:			
Before income taxes	4.78	8.28	4.81
After income taxes	3.68	5.81	3.88
Net tangible assets per $1,000 l.t. debt	$2,432	$3,724	......
Net current assets per $1,000 l.t. debt	$492	$1,190	......
Number of shares — common:			
[1]Year-end	47,800,000	48,900,000	49,700,000
[1]Average	48,100,000	50,000,000	49,900,000
Financial & Operating Ratios			
Current assets ÷ current liabilities	1.91	2.37	......
% cash & securities to current assets	53.51	47.33	......
% net current assets to net worth	34.33	26.77	......
% property depreciated	24.40	28.18	......
% annual deprec. to gross property	4.80	5.61	......
Capitalization:			
% long term debt	36.40	23.06	......
% Deferred inc. taxes	11.47	14.13	......
% common stock & surplus	52.13	62.81	......

FINANCIAL & OPERATING DATA (Cont'd):

	1988	1987	1986
% revenue to net property	95.19	115.67	......
% revenue to total assets	50.39	59.27	......
% net income to total assets	6.92	9.83	......
% net income to net worth	16.08	18.10	......
Analysis of Operations	%	%	%
Revenues	100.00	100.00	100.00
Operating costs & expenses	74.44	75.30	76.81
Operating expense	25.56	24.70	23.19
Gain (loss) from property transactions	......	5.19	(.34)
Operating income	25.56	29.89	22.85
Interest & dividend income	3.42	2.71	3.34
Interest expense, net	(5.13)	(3.45)	(4.59)
Interest, net, of unconsolidated affiliates	(2.29)	(1.87)	(1.73)
Corporate expense	(2.18)	(2,17)	(2.38)
Net before taxes	19.38	25.11	17.49
Provision for income taxes	5.65	8.53	4.28
Net income	13.73	16.58	13.21

[1]Restated to reflect 2-for-1 stock split in 1988.

LONG TERM DEBT

1. International Leisure Corp. collateral trust 8s, due 1993:

Rating — A1

AUTH. — $50,000,000; outstanding Dec. 31, 1988, $7,800,000.

DATED — Dec. 1, 1968. DUE — Dec. 1, 1993.

INTEREST — J&D1.

...USTEE — Morgan Guaranty Co., NYC.

...NATION — Fully registered, $1,000 and

... in part after Dec. 1

vided such debt is incurred and related security interests are created within 18 months of the acquisition of such subsidiary and such debt does not exceed the acquisition cost of such subsidiary; (5) security interests to secure debt incurred to construct additions or to make capital improvements to properties of the Guarantor or any subsidiary, provided such debt i... ...red and related security interests are ... ...months of completion of ... ...ove-ments ar... con...

SECURITY — GUARANTEE — SALE & LEASE-BACK — Same as senior debenture 11⅜s, above.

OFFERED — ($75,000,000) at 100 (proceeds to Co. 99.30) on May 6, 1983 thru Lehman Brothers Kuhn Loeb Inc. and associates.

4. Hilton Hotels Corporation, 9¾% notes due 1998:

Rating — A2

AUTH — $100,000,000; outstg. Dec. 31, 1988, $199,200,000.

...TED — Oct. 11, 1988. DUE — June 1, 1998

...ST — J&D 1 to holders regis...

Figure 11.2: "Financial & Operating Data" for Hilton Hotels Corporation, *Moody's Industrial Manual*, 1988.

Company	Yr. End	Current Ratio					Debt / Capital Ratio (%)					Debt as % of Net Working Capital				
		1983	1984	1985	1986	1987	1983	1984	1985	1986	1987	1983	1984	1985	1986	1987
DIVERSIFIED																
• BRUNSWICK CORP	DEC	1.9	1.9	1.9	1.5	1.3	22.9	18.2	14.6	46.5	29.3	54.6	41.7	35.2	307.0	247.4
• GENERAL CINEMA CORP	OCT	0.8	1.2	0.6	0.9	1.8	33.9	51.9	41.4	37.1	53.9	NM	1229.8	NM	NM	248.8
• GULF & WESTERN INC	OCT	1.9	1.9	1.9	1.6	1.8	34.2	31.7	33.2	39.7	38.6	94.1	89.6	105.2	256.3	172.0
• NEWS CORP LTD -ADR	JUN	NA	NA	NA	1.1	0.9	NA	NA	NA	39.1	52.8	NA	NA	NA	2022.5	NM
• PEPSICO INC	DEC	1.3	1.4	1.5	1.1	1.1	27.0	21.7	30.5	48.1	43.8	184.6	103.2	121.3	937.9	1189.7
PILLSBURY CO	†MAY	1.2	1.2	1.0	1.0	1.0	29.6	32.3	39.1	37.1	36.7	271.4	365.1	4122.5	3070.3	12080.0
SONY CORP -AMER SHARES	†MAR	1.4	1.4	1.5	1.6	1.1	16.7	13.8	17.7	18.6	22.5	40.7	32.6	42.2	41.6	147.8
ENTERTAINMENT																
AMC ENTERTAINMENT INC	†MAR	0.5	NA	NA	NA	NA	35.3	43.6	57.5	73.4	83.2	NM	NA	NA	NA	NA
CINEPLEX ODEON	DEC	NA	NA	1.0	1.0	0.9	NA	NA	49.8	58.3	56.9	NA	NA	NA	NM	NM
COLUMBIA PICTURES ENTMNT INC	†FEB	NA	NA	NA	NA	1.1	NA	NA	NA	NA	45.7	NA	NA	NA	41731.8	664.5
• DISNEY (WALT) COMPANY	SEP	1.4	NA	NA	NA	NA	17.0	37.5	34.3	22.0	17.8	364.9	10.7	7.6	NA	NA
• HANDLEMAN CO	†APR	1.9	1.7	1.9	2.1	2.1	5.7	7.0	5.1	7.6	6.0	8.0	10.7	7.6	11.4	8.7
• KING WORLD PRODUCTIONS INC	AUG	NA	1.1	1.4	1.9	1.9	NA	31.0	7.3	0.0	31.1	NA	207.8	10.6	0.0	36.0
• LORIMAR TELEPICTURES	†MAR	1.4	1.3	1.8	1.9	2.5	33.6	22.8	46.6	50.4	64.3	82.5	90.5	138.6	138.5	174.4
MCA INC	DEC	1.9	2.1	1.8	2.0	2.2	0.0	7.9	5.1	13.3	37.7	0.0	24.0	16.9	44.5	126.4
MGM/UA COMMUNICATIONS INC	AUG	NA	NA	NA	NA	NA	NA	NA	29.3	32.4	62.8	NA	NA	645.5	NA	NA
ORION PICTURES CORP	†FEB	NA	NA	NA	NA	NA	55.2	47.8	59.3	64.0	69.9	NA	NA	NA	NA	NA
UNITED ARTISTS COMMUN	DEC	0.8	0.4	0.5	0.5	NA	66.6	64.0	58.9	79.1	83.5	NM	NM	NM	NM	NA
VIACOM INC	DEC	0.8	0.9	1.4	1.3	0.7	56.6	55.6	46.9	70.6	70.5	NM	NM	537.3	1426.6	NM
• WARNER COMMUNICATIONS INC	DEC	1.6	0.9	1.0	1.3	1.2	39.1	59.7	44.7	29.7	21.2	96.9	NM	NM	170.0	182.5
GAMING-HOTELS																
• BALLY MFG CORP	DEC	1.6	1.1	1.3	1.1	1.1	47.8	58.8	57.9	65.9	68.3	383.8	2296.7	879.9	5140.6	3941.6
• CAESARS WORLD	JUL	0.6	1.1	0.8	1.8	1.1	56.0	54.2	48.5	51.9	16.6	NM	2970.3	NM	326.1	694.9
CIRCUS CIRCUS ENTERPR INC	JAN	2.9	4.8	2.8	1.3	2.3	53.9	58.9	51.5	39.4	34.7	301.7	169.4	290.0	1216.2	302.8
• GOLDEN NUGGET INC	DEC	6.0	2.3	6.3	3.0	3.6	56.7	54.8	68.6	65.2	43.6	120.2	178.3	152.3	278.1	153.3
• HILTON HOTELS CORP	DEC	2.6	1.9	3.3	2.4	2.4	24.7	27.5	26.1	24.5	23.1	146.2	219.2	109.7	162.0	137.1
• HOLIDAY CORP	DEC	0.7	0.8	0.7	0.7	1.0	30.0	40.6	57.6	56.6	136.3	NM	NM	NM	NM	NM
• RAMADA INC	DEC	0.7	0.7	0.9	0.8	0.8	60.6	54.7	49.5	53.8	58.5	NM	NM	NM	NM	NM
RESORTS INTERNATIONAL -CL A	DEC	2.1	2.8	1.5	1.5	0.4	54.6	74.4	76.9	82.0	80.5	181.4	154.0	481.9	733.	NM
SHOWBOAT INC	DEC	2.4	2.4	1.2	1.4	1.9	0.0	0.0	47.0	66.2	76.2	0.0	0.0	1819.1	3114.9	712.7
HOTELS / MOTELS																
CARNIVAL CRUISE LINES	NOV	NA	NA	NA	0.6	1.7	NA	NA	NA	47.1	12.4	NA	NA	NA	NM	56.3
(cont'd)																

Data by ⟨S&P⟩ Standard & Poor's Compustat Services, Inc.

Figure 11.3: Financial Ratios for Hilton Hotels Corporation from *Industry Surveys*, 16 March 1989.

137

Industry Norms & Key Business Ratios (figure 11.4) is arranged in columns according to SIC numbers. Notice that SIC 7011 (Hotels/Inns/Tourist C) is arranged between SIC 6799 (Investing Inst NEC) and SIC 7021 (Rooming/Boarding Hses). In addition to the SIC number and short title at the top of each column, you also find that the reporting year is 1987 and the averages (norms) are the result of surveys from 2051 establishments or companies.

Along the left hand column of figure 11.4 are the balance sheet and income statement items. "Cash" is the first item in the balance sheet figures, and the reporting establishments had an average of $99,063 accounting for 9.4 percent of total assets. "Net sales" begins the income statement figures.

Below the balance sheet and income statement items you see "Ratios." These fourteen ratios are the ones that Dun & Bradstreet considers to be standard. The first six ratios relate to solvency; the next five ratios relate to efficiency; and the last three ratios relate to profitability. The method of calculation for each of these ratios can be found in the front of the book.

Notice that some ratios are given in "times." For example, the median quartile of the quick ratio for SIC code 7011 is 0.7—or, total assets are 0.7 times total liabilities. Many ratios are given in percentages, and the collection period is given in number of days.

The abbreviations "UQ," "MED," and "LQ" stand for upper quartile, median quartile, and lower quartile. Since the median quartile is the midpoint of all companies in the sample, this is probably the best number to select for your comparative analysis unless you've been instructed otherwise by your professor. Upper quartile and lower quartile are mid-points of the upper and lower halves.

Now that you have an introductory view of financial ratios and how to use *Industry Norms & Key Business Ratios*, try comparing several financial ratios for Hilton Hotels Corporation against the same industry ratios. Is Hilton's quick ratio higher or lower than the 0.7 times median for the industry? Is Hilton Corporation's return on sales ratio higher or lower than the 5.2 percent median for the industry? Based on these two ratios only, does Hilton appear to be in better or worse condition than the industry norms?

The last chapter in this book will provide suggestions for utilizing other resources in the library.

	SIC 6799 INVESTING INST NEC (NO BREAKDOWN) 1987 (333 ESTAB)		SIC 7011 HOTELS/INNS/TOURIST C (NO BREAKDOWN) 1987 (2051 ESTAB)		OARDING HSES (DOWN) 1987 (24 ESTAB)		SIC 7032 SPORTS/AMUSEMENT CAMP (NO BREAKDOWN) 1987 (113 ESTAB)	
	$	%	$	%	$	%	$	%
CASH	322,846	16.1	99,063	9.4	53,550	10.6	101,142	13.5
ACCOUNTS RECEIVABLE	176,462	8.8	42,155	4.0	14,145	2.8	25,473	3.4
NOTES RECEIVABLE	102,268	5.1	9,485	0.9	505	0.1	4,495	0.6
INVENTORY	56,147	2.8	14,754	1.4	3,031	0.6	14,235	1.9
OTHER CURRENT	380,998	19.0	47,424	4.5	26,270	5.2	42,704	5.7
TOTAL CURRENT	1,038,722	51.8	212,881	20.2	97,501	19.3	188,049	25.1
FIXED ASSETS	332,872	16.6	428,924	40.7	167,721	33.2	265,966	35.5
OTHER NON-CURRENT	633,661	31.6	412,062	39.1	239,963	47.5	295,185	39.4
TOTAL ASSETS	2,005,255	100.0	1,053,867	100.0	505,185	100.0	749,200	100.0
ACCOUNTS PAYABLE	56,147	2.8	36,885	3.5	18,692	3.7	11,987	1.6
BANK LOANS	24,063	1.2	3,162	0.3	---	---	2,248	0.3
NOTES PAYABLE	86,226	4.3	24,239	2.3	15,156	3.0	18,730	2.5
OTHER CURRENT	214,562	10.7	103,279	9.8	28,290	5.6	71,174	9.5
TOTAL CURRENT	380,998	19.0	167,565	15.9	62,138	12.3	104,139	13.9
OTHER LONG TERM	306,804	15.3	485,833	46.1	225,313	44.6	118,374	15.8
DEFERRED CREDITS	24,063	1.2	3,162	0.3	3,536	0.7	2,248	0.3
NET WORTH	1,293,389	64.5	397,308	37.7	214,198	42.4	524,440	70.0
TOTAL LIAB & NET WORTH	2,005,255	100.0	1,053,867	100.0	505,185	100.0	749,200	100.0
NET SALES	879,842	100.0	672,284	100.0	442,550	100.0	500,000	100.0
GROSS PROFIT	311,464	35.4	432,951	64.4	231,011	52.2	272,500	54.5
NET PROFIT AFTER TAX	101,182	11.5	33,614	5.0	30,093	6.8	39,000	7.8
WORKING CAPITAL	657,724	---	45,316	---	35,363	---	83,910	---

RATIOS	6799 UQ	MED	LQ	7011 UQ	MED	LQ	OARDING UQ	MED	LQ	7032 UQ	MED	LQ
SOLVENCY												
QUICK RATIO (TIMES)	4.9	1.1	0.4	1.9	0.7	0.3				3.0	1.0	0.3
CURRENT RATIO (TIMES)	14.6	3.1	1.2	3.1	1.2	0.5				4.7	1.7	0.8
CURR LIAB TO NW (%)	2.8	12.9	59.3	8.4	27.2	71.5				3.6	12.6	31.6
CURR LIAB TO INV (%)	54.5	136.6	203.0	83.9	282.6	599.3				95.6	231.0	492.3
TOTAL LIAB TO NW (%)	6.2	31.4	118.4	42.6	134.1	335.8				8.0	23.9	73.1
FIXED ASSETS TO NW (%)	3.4	19.8	94.9	80.6	141.0	302.1	128.1	171.7	263.1	72.7	103.6	176.6
EFFICIENCY												
COLL PERIOD (DAYS)	15.3	31.8	111.7	4.4	10.2	19.4	4.2	11.9		1.7	4.0	9.5
SALES TO INV (TIMES)	37.6	7.7	3.4	134.4	74.4	33.3	201.2	75.8	40.2	48.6	30.3	19.8
ASSETS TO SALES (%)	84.7	234.4	490.1	81.8	154.1	276.9	75.3	116.3	159.3	58.8	107.4	156.9
SALES TO NWC (TIMES)	7.3	1.4	0.5	20.2	8.4	3.7	206.4	5.2	3.5	16.6	10.8	4.2
ACCT PAY TO SALES (%)	1.2	3.8	11.1	1.6	3.1	6.0	3.0			0.9	1.9	4.2
PROFITABILITY												
RETURN ON SALES (%)	36.9	16.2	0.8	14.0	5.2	(1.6)	16.3	8.2	2.1	15.0	5.1	0.2
RETURN ON ASSETS (%)	8.2	2.1	0.1	8.2	2.5	(1.4)	33.7	24.6	12.0	11.5	1.9	(0.8)
RETURN ON NW (%)	14.6	3.5	(0.1)	26.3	8.7	(2.0)	92.8	81.9	65.9	17.1	4.0	(1.6)

UQ = upper quartile
MED = medium quartile
LQ = lower quartile

Figure 11.4: Ratios from *Industry Norms & Key Business Ratios*, 1989.

139

SUMMARY

1) Financial ratios are percentages used to evaluate the financial "health" of a company.

2) There are many types of financial ratios, such as current, quick, debt to equity, profit margin, and inventory turnover.

3) A company's ratios may be compared with its own past ratios (intrafirm analysis) or with industry averages (interfirm analysis).

4) A company's ratios may be calculated from raw financial data reported in such sources as *Moody's Industrial Manual* or the 10-K Report. Frequently these sources have precalculated company ratios, so you do not need to do the related calculations.

5) Pre-calculated industry ratios can be located in such sources as Dun & Bradstreet's *Industry Norms & Key Business Ratios*.

CHAPTER 12

OTHER RESOURCES

As you followed the search strategy in this book, you found industry and company information in both computerized and printed formats. These information resources included:

- computer databases and other technology,
- industry overviews,
- periodical and newspaper indexes,
- statistics,
- associations and directories,
- private company information,
- public company information,
- subsidiary company information, and
- financial ratios.

You were introduced to the most important and widely available reference tools in each of these areas. But these are only part of the resources available. By making use of other resources, you can strengthen your grasp of information access and management. This chapter will introduce several resources that will provide additional materials for industry and company research. These include:

- business guides and bibliographies,
- specialized indexes,
- interlibrary loan,
- card catalogs, and
- local resources.

HOSPITALS
See: HOSPITAL ADMINISTRATION

HOTEL AND MOTEL INDUSTRY
See also: TRAVEL INDUSTRY

GENERAL WORKS

Effective Front Office Operations. Michael L. Kasavana. Van Nostrand Reinhold Co., Inc., 115 Fifth Ave., New York, NY 10003. (212) 254-3232. 1981. $21.95.

Hotel Accounting. John D. Lesure. John Wiley and Sons, Inc., 605 Third Ave., New York, NY 10158. (800) 526-5368 or (212) 850-6418. 1978. $68.50. Fourth edition.

Hotel and Motel Security Management. Walter J. Buzby and David Paine. Butterworth's, 80 Montvale Ave., Stoneham, MA 02180. (800) 544-1013 or (617) 438-8464. 1976. $26.95.

Introduction to Hotel and Restaurant Management: A Book of Readings. Robert A. Brymer. Kendall/Hunt Publishing Co., 2460 Kerper Blvd., Dubuque, IA 52001. (319) 589-2923. 1981. $15.95. Fifth edition.

The Lodging and Food Service Industry. Gerald W. Lattin. Educational Institute of the American Hotel & Motel Association, P.O. Box 1240, East Lansing, MI 48823. (517) 353-5500. 1985. $34.95. General survey of the hospitality industry.

Management of Hotel and Motel Security. Harvey Burstein. Marcel Dekker, Inc., 270 Madison Ave., New York, NY 10016. (212) 696-9000. 1981. $33.00.

Principles and Practice of Management in the Hospitality Industry. James R. Keiser. Van Nostrand Reinhold Co., Inc., 115 Fifth Ave., New York, NY 10003. (212) 254-3232. 1980. $24.95.

Purchasing: Selection and Procurement for the Hospitality Industry. John M. Stefanelli. John Wiley and Sons, Inc., 605 Third Ave., New York, NY 10158. (800) 526-5368 or (212) 850-6418. 1988. Price not set. Third edition.

Work, Analysis and Design for Hotels, Restaurants and Institutions. Edward Kazarian. AVI Publishing Co., 115 Fifth Ave., New York, NY 10003. (212) 254-3232. 1979. $24.50. Second edition.

The World of the Restaurant. H. Berberoglu. Kendall/Hunt Publishing Co., 2460 Kerper Blvd., Dubuque, IA 52001. (319) 589-2923. 1981. $16.50.

ABSTRACTING AND INDEXING SERVICES

Hotel and Travel Index. Jerry Preece. Ziff-Davis Publishing Co., One Park Avenue, Rm. 1011, New York, NY 10016. (212) 725-8322. Quarterly. $60.00 per issue.

DIRECTORIES

Directory of Hotel and Motel Systems. American Hotel Association Directory Corp., 888 Seventh Ave., New York, NY 10019. (212) 265-4506. Annual. $17.50 per year.

Hotel and Motel Red Book. American Hotel Association Directory Corp., 888 Seventh Ave., New York, NY 10019. (212) 265-4506. Annual. $35.00.

Official Hotel and Resort Guide. Ziff-Davis Publishing Co., One Park Ave., New York, NY 10016. (212) 725-3837. Annual. $225.00 for three volumes in looseleaf binder, including one year's updates.

Travel Weekly's World Travel Directory. Murdoch Magazines, One Park Ave., New York, NY 10016. (212) 503-3600. Annual. $85.00.

U.S. and International Directory of Hotel, Restaurant, and Institutional Schools. Council on Hotel, Restaurant and Institutional Education, Human Development Building, Rm. 118, University Park, PA 16802. (814) 863-0586. Irregular. $5.00.

ENCYCLOPEDIAS AND DICTIONARIES

Uniform System of Accounts and Expense Dictionary for Small Hotels, Motels, and Motor Hotels. Educational Institute of the American Hotel & Motel Association, P.O. Box 1240, East Lansing, MI 48823. (800) 752-4567 or (517) 353-5500. 1987. $24.95. Defines account classifications.

FINANCIAL RATIOS

Expenses in Retail Business. NCR Corporate Education--Learning Systems, Dayton, OH 45479. Annual. $1.25.

HANDBOOKS AND MANUALS

Check In--Check Out. Principles of Effective Front Office Management. Jerome J. Vallen. William C. Brown Co., 2460 Kerper Blvd., Dubuque, IA 52001. (319) 588-1451. 1985. Price on application. Third edition.

The Collective Bargaining Handbook for Hotels, Restaurants, and Institutions. Arch Stokes. Van Nostrand Reinhold Co., Inc., 115 Fifth Ave., New York, NY 10003. (212) 254-3232. 1981. $57.95.

Hospitality Industry Managerial Accounting. Raymond S. Schmidgall. Educational Institute of the American Hotel & Motel Association, P.O. Box 1240, East Lansing, MI 48823. (517) 353-5500. 1986. $34.95.

Management of People in Hotels, Restaurants, and Clubs. Donald E. Lundberg and James P. Armatas. William C. Brown Co., 2460 Kerper Blvd., Dubuque, IA 52001. (319) 588-1451. 1980. Price on application. Fourth edition.

Managing Front Office Operations. Charles E. Steadmon. Educational Institute of the American Hotel & Motel Association, P.O. Box 1240, East Lansing, MI 48823. (517) 353-5500. 1985. $34.95. Covers reservation, registration, and check-out procedures.

Multinational Executive Travel Companion. Guides to Multinational Business, Inc., Harvard Square, Box 92, Cambridge, MA 02138. (617) 868-2288. Annual. $60.00.

Professional Management of Housekeeping Operations. R.J. Martin. John Wiley & Sons, Inc., 605 Third Ave., New York, NY 10158. (800) 526-5368 or (212) 850-6465. 1986. $33.95. For hotels and motels.

Strategic Hotel-Motel Marketing. David A. Troy and Christopher W. L. Hart. Educational Institute of the American Hotel & Motel Association, P.O. Box 1240, East Lansing, MI 48823. (517) 353-5500. 1986. $34.95. Second edition.

Supervision in the Hospitality Industry. John P. Daschler and Jack D. Ninemeier. Educational Institute of the American

Figure 12.1: Entry on "Hotel and Motel Industry" from *Encyclopedia of Business Information Sources*, 7th ed., 1988.

Business Guides and Bibliographies

There are literally hundreds of other business indexes, databases, handbooks, and manuals available for business research. Several business bibliographies that will lead you to these other resources are illustrated below. Other bibliographies and guides are listed in Appendix B. You can always ask a reference librarian to recommend one.

The *Encyclopedia of Business Information Sources*, edited by James Woy, 7th edition (Detroit, MI: Gale Research, 1988) is a good starting place for almost any business research topic. Here you can find the most important indexes, almanacs, directories, handbooks, manuals, online databases, statistics sources, and associations on one thousand different subjects ranging from the cattle industry to nursing homes to direct marketing. The alphabetical arrangement of the subjects makes this an easy bibliography to use. Of course, the "hotel and motel industry" subject has not been overlooked (figure 12.1).

Handbook of Business Information: A Guide for Librarians, Students, and Researchers, by Diane Wheeler Strauss (Englewood, CO: Libraries Unlimited, Inc., 1988), is an annotated and illustrated guide to business research basics. If you are having trouble understanding how to conduct library research in accounting, finance, investments, marketing, and other business areas, this is an excellent place to begin. Besides introducing the basic resources, the handbook provides definitions and explanations of business fundamentals such as how to read a newspaper stock table as well as what stock exchanges are and how they operate (figure 12.2).

If you are lucky, an author may have compiled a bibliography on just the topic you're researching. If so, this is an excellent place to begin your search strategy. A good example of a specialized bibliography is *Hotel and Restaurant Industries: An Information Sourcebook*, by Judith M. Nixon (Phoenix, AZ: Oryx, 1988), which provides annotations to over one thousand books and periodicals. These titles cover over twenty different areas related to hotels and restaurants, including accounting, career planning, food purchasing, franchising, and management (figure 12.3).

If you familiarize yourself with the basic layout and potential applications of these business research guides, your library tasks will be more productive and fulfilling. They will lead you to information that otherwise would be undiscovered.

Price-Earnings Ratio

The price-earnings ratio, also known as the price-earnings multiple, multiple, p/e ratio, or p/e, is one of the most commonly used measures of stock value, particularly in comparison with other stocks in the same industry. The price-earnings ratio of a stock is simply the price of the stock divided by its earnings, normally its earnings for the past 12 months. The formula for this is:

$$P/E = \frac{\text{Price of a share of stock}}{\text{Earnings per share of the stock for the most recent 12-month period}}$$

Thus, a share of Alberta Electronics, selling for $35, with an earnings of $7 per share in the past 12 months will have a p/e ratio of 5. In other words, the market is willing to buy a share of Alberta Electronics at a price five times greater than its current earnings.

Generally speaking, stocks in a given industry tend to have similar price-earnings ratios, and growth industries tend to have higher p/e ratios than more established industries. The p/e ratio is but one measure of stock value, but it is one of the most widely used. Price-earnings ratios are included in the newspaper stock tables for the New York and American Stock Exchanges.

Warrants

Warrants exist in a sort of financial netherworld. They are neither stock nor bond, have no book value, and pay no dividends. A warrant is a purchasable right that allows investors to buy corporate securities (usually common stock) for an extended time at a fixed price. When the designation *wt.* follows a corporate name (or abbreviation) in a newspaper stock table, it indicates that the security in question is a warrant.

STOCK EXCHANGES

A stock exchange is a central marketplace where shares of stock and other securities are bought and sold, using the auction system. There are two national exchanges in this country as well as several regional exchanges (see figure 13.1). Each exchange is a private organization that sets its own standards for the securities it will list (or trade); only securities that have been admitted to a specific exchange can be traded there, and then only by exchange members or their representatives. The two largest exchanges are the national exchanges, the New York Stock Exchange and the American Stock Exchange.

New York Stock Exchange

The New York Stock Exchange traces its origins back to 1792, when a group of 24 brokers gathered under a buttonwood tree on Wall Street to devise rules of conduct for the trade of stock—hitherto unregulated—and to take buy and sell orders for those who wanted to trade. From these modest beginnings, the New York Stock Exchange has become the world's leading securities exchange, with more than 141 million shares of stock traded daily.

The standards for the stocks that it lists are also the most stringent. The NYSE requires that a company earn at least $2.5 million annually, that it have net tangible assets of at least $18 million, and that it have at least 1,100,000 shares of publicly held common stock. It is on this exchange that "blue-chip" stocks are traded—companies like Exxon and General Motors, IBM and AT&T. Although the companies that list shares on the exchange constitute

EXCHANGES

National:
- New York Stock Exchange (NYSE: "Big Board")
- American Stock Exchange (Amex)

Regional:
- Boston
- Cincinnati
- Inter-Mountain (Salt Lake City)
- Midwest
- Pacific
- Philadelphia
- Spokane

Dually traded stocks: traded on national AND regional exchanges.

OVER-THE-COUNTER MARKET (OTC)
Decentralized. Informal. Any stock can be traded OTC. No strict listing standards.
These stocks sometimes called "unlisted" stocks.
NASDAQ an automated information network, provides current price quote on securities.

Fig. 13.1. Buying and selling stocks.

less than 1/10th of 1 percent of all U.S. corporations, they earn some 80 percent of the country's total corporate income.

Membership on the exchange, which has been described as an exclusive club, is costly and hard won. The number of "seats" or memberships on the exchange is limited to 1,366, most representing brokerage firms. The price of a seat on the exchange fluctuates; in recent years, it has ranged from $200,000 to more than half a million dollars. In addition, prospective members must be sponsored by two current members in good standing, and must be approved by the Board of Directors.

The New York Stock Exchange offers a wide range of informational and educational services. It sponsors, for example, the Investors Information Program, a countrywide offering of courses on investing through member brokerage firms. It also distributes free and inexpensive publications describing different types of investments. Some of these publications are available locally through member brokerage firms; others, such as the "Investors' Information Kit," a collection of four of the NYSE's most popular pamphlets, can be ordered directly from the exchange.[2] Another useful publication is listed below.

New York Stock Exchange. **Fact Book.** New York: The Exchange, 1956- . Annual.

The *Fact Book* is an annual compilation of current and historical statistics, with a summary of the previous year's activity and a description of the NYSE's organization and administration. It is an ideal quick reference source for people seeking answers to questions on the volume of shares traded, lists of stocks with largest market value, and the exchange's history.

American Stock Exchange

The American Stock Exchange, also known as Amex, is the second largest exchange in the country. Requirements for listing a stock on the Amex are not as stringent as on the New York Stock Exchange. As a result, it serves as the market for smaller, younger companies that grow, it has been said, from "new chips to blue chips."

Figure 12.2: Entry on "Stock Exchanges" from *Handbook of Business Information*, 1988.

Management

636. Albrecht, Karl, and Zemke, Ron. *Service America!: Doing Business in the New Economy.* Homewood, IL: Dow Jones-Irwin, 1985. 203 p.

Based on the premise that service is becoming ever more important in the American economy, the authors discuss key factors that govern service quality. Customer service is seen as a strategic business tool. Management personnel are told to think of their jobs as service positions too. Presents a new model for service management based on the authors' theories.

637. Axler, Bruce H. *Management of Hospitality Operations.* Hotel-Motel Management Series. Indianapolis, IN: Bobbs-Merrill, 1976. 351 p.

This is a management text for the operational manager. This type of manager is defined as having primary responsibility but not complete authority. In contrast to administrators and executive managers who formulate policy, the operational managers are concerned with implementation of policy directly and on a daily basis. Chapters include operational management, techniques and concepts of management, management of work and material, controls and profits, management of business activity, and guest relations.

638. Brymer, Robert A., ed. *Introduction to Hotel and Restaurant Management: A Book of Readings.* 4th ed. Dubuque, IA: Kendall/Hunt Publishing Co., 1984. 305 p.

A book of readings containing articles by various experts. In this edition, the majority of articles are written by hospitality educators rather than by executives out in the industry. The articles are grouped under the following headings: "Hospitality Industry," "Hospitality Corporations," "Hospitality Operations" (which includes management, marketing, cost control, property management, and service), and "Allied Fields" (which looks at tourism, clubs, theme parks, hospitals, and casinos). Taken as a whole, these forty-four articles cover most subjects found in the hospitality curricula.

639. Bullaro, John J., and Edginton, Christopher R. *Commercial Leisure Services: Managing for Profit, Service, and Personal Satisfaction.* New York: Macmillan, 1986. 364 p.

This is a text on the basic skills and knowledge necessary for the successful management of a commercial leisure service organization. It deals with marketing and managing as well as with theoretical and practical aspects. Chapters appear on starting a leisure service, financial management, accounting, organizing, marketing, commercial leisure service and the law, and the application of the computer.

640. Cassee, Ewout, ed., and Reuland, Rudolf, ed. *The Management of Hospitality.* International Series in Hospitality Management. Oxford: Pergamon Press, 1983. 219 p.

This is a collection of ten papers presented at the International Jubilee Conference on Management of Hospitality in October 1979, at the Hague, Netherlands. Titles include "External Influences on the Hospitality Industry," "Marketing in the Hospitality Indus-

Figure 12.3: Sample Page from "Management" Section of *Hotel and Restaurant Industries*, 1988.

SPECIALIZED INDEXES

These business guides may lead you to a specialized index, such as *Lodging and Restaurant Index*, edited by Judith M. Nixon (West Lafayette, IN: The Restaurant, Hotel, and Institutional Management Institute, Purdue University, 1985-). A specialized index will provide you with citations to trade journals that are not covered by the primary indexes illustrated in chapter 4. Figure 12.4 shows several citations from the 1988 *Lodging and Restaurant Index* for "HILTON."

Notice that many of the citations are from journals that are not indexed in *Business Periodicals Index, Business Index/INFOTRAC^{tm}*, and *Predicasts F&S Index: United States. Lodging and Restaurant Index* is leading you to specialized scholarly and trade journals. An extract from a specialized journal—*FIU Hospitality Review*—is illustrated in figure 12.5.

Although your library may not subscribe to the *FIU Hospitality Review* or many of the other journals covered by the *Lodging and Restaurant Index*, you can probably obtain photocopies of the articles through interlibrary loan.

INTERLIBRARY LOAN

As with most search strategies, the one you followed in this book may have led to a typical problem. Your library did not have the periodical article, 10-K Report, statistical publication, or other resource that you especially needed! No library has every source, so this problem can occur at even the largest research libraries. When you encounter this problem, however, most libraries offer a service called "interlibrary loan."

Interlibrary loan will help you identify other libraries that own a particular source, and then help you obtain that source from one of them. In the case of a book or government publication, the original publication is usually borrowed. In the case of a periodical or newspaper article, however, the lending library usually sends a photocopy of the article. Some interlibrary loan operations also have the capability of sending telefacsimiles. In most cases, reference resources, such as periodical indexes and manuals, cannot be borrowed through interlibrary loan.

Although this service can be extremely valuable, there are several drawbacks:

1) There may be a charge for borrowing the items or a charge for the cost of the photocopies.

2) There is usually at least a two- to three-week lag between the time you request the item and the time you receive it. You may be able to shorten this time by paying an extra charge for priority mail, overnight delivery, or telefacsimile delivery.

HEALTH FOODS

Off-Premise Catering: Gene Singletary: Catering To The Gold Coast. Klein, Roberta. RESTAURANT BUSINESS v87/3 p157-160 Feb 10 1988.

From The Restaurant Business Test Kitchen: Menu Ideas; Produce Primer: Apples To Zucchini. Allmendinger, Scott. RESTAURANT BUSINESS v87/13 p167-173 Sep 1 1988.

Insights: Reports On Markets, Trends And Ideas: Good Earth Restaurants: Beyond The Age Of Aquarius. RESTAURANT BUSINESS v877/16 p20 Nov 1 1988.

The Way The Rookie Crumbles. Soeder, John. RESTAURANT HOSPITALITY v72/9 p150 Sep 1988.

Restaurant Management: Food Trends: Lighten It Up. Haverstock, Donna. RESTAURANT MANAGEMENT v2/10 p58-59 Oct 1988.

R&I Exclusive: Nutrition Report: Selling Wellness. Backas, Nancy. RESTAURANTS & INSTITUTIONS v98/25 p46-48+ Oct 14 1988.

Institutions: Health Care: Exciting Times For Dietetic Profession. Stephenson, Susie. RESTAURANTS & INSTITUTIONS v 98/24 p99-100 Sep 30 1988.

HEARTTHROB ENTERPRISES, CHICAGO, IL

Spatz's Goal Is To Have Heartthrobs All Over The World: Entertainment Clubs Fight Boredom With Diversity. Walkup, Carolyn. NATION'S RESTAURANT NEWS v22/49 p4 Dec 5 1988.

HEARTWOOD, TACOMA, WA

*The Heartwood, Tacoma, Washington: Natural Cheer. Birney, Dion. RESTAURANT/HOTEL DESIGN INTL v10/11 p72-77 Nov 1988.

HEATING AND COOLING

Beyond The Range: Gas Cooling Research Portends The Future. FOODSERVICE EQUIP & SUPPLIES SPEC v41/2 p92-93 Jun

Energy Update: New Gas Chiller Gives Industry An Edge In Electric-Dominated Cooling Market. FOODSERVICE EQUIP & SUPPLIES SPEC v41/6 p64-65 Oct 25 1988.

Think Comfort, And Savings, In Energy Control. LODGING HOSPITALITY v44/12 p71-72 Nov 1988.

Beyond The Range: Gas Cooking Research Portends The Future. RESTAURANTS & INSTITUTIONS v98/14 p136-137 Jun 10 1988.

HEIDI'S FROZEN YOGURT

Heidi's Expects Image To Improve In Wake Of Johnston Merger. Alva, Marilyn. NATION'S RESTAURANT NEWS v22/41 p3 Oct 10 1988.

HEMMETER CORP.

Chris Hemmeter: Re-Creating Paradise. Bekcy, Michelle. MEETINGS & CONVENTIONS v23/6 p181-184 Jun 1988.

HEPATITIS

*Food Safety: The Cutting Edge. Zuckerman, David; Gindin, Rona. FOOD MANAGEMENT v23/12 p90-94+ Dec 1988.

Hotel's Massive Effort Contains Hepatitis Scare. HOTEL/MOTEL SECURITY & SAFETY MGNT v6/8 p1-2 Jul 1988.

HERBIE K

Food & Beverage Report: Herbie K's Offers Diner-Style Menu, 1950's Nostalgia. Selwitz, Robert. HOTEL & MOTEL MANAGEMENT v 203/11 p68-70 Jul 25 1988.

Insights: Reports On Markets, Trends And Ideas. RESTAURANT BUSINESS v87/10 p20-28 Jul 1 1988.

HERBS AND SPICES

A Slice Of Slomon: Herbs And Spices: The Sure Cure For Blah Pizza. Slomon, Evelyne. PIZZA TODAY v6/11 p16-18 Nov 1988.

Pro's Pantry: Garlic In All Its Glory. Jones, Roberta. RESTAURANT BUSINESS v87/1 p147-148 Jan 1 1988.

Pro's Pantry: Add A Little Spice. Jones, Roberta. RESTAURANT BUSINESS v87/3 p274-276 Feb 10 1988.

Behind The Scenes: How Does His Garden Grow?: A Milwaukee Restaurant's "Kitchen Of The Market" Depends On Fresh Herbs. Bregar, Bill. RESTAURANT MANAGEMENT v2/2 p84-85 Feb 1988.

*Menu Ideas: Seasoned Showstoppers. Rowe, Megan. RESTAURANT MANAGEMENT v2/12 p58-64+ Dec 1988.

Food Facts: When You Want Spicy Hot, Capsicums Deliver. Backas, Nancy. RESTAURANTS & INSTITUTIONS v98/28 p184 Nov 11 1988.

HERSHEY POCONO RESORT, WHITE HAVEN, PA

Strategies: What, No More Chocolate? Hershey To Sell Pocono Resort. Lima, Tony. LODGING HOSPITALITY v44/3 p46 Mar 1988.

HEWLETT-PACKARD

Business & Industry: Hewlett-Packard Introduces Authentic Southwest Cuisine. Stephenson, Susie. RESTAURANTS & INSTITUTIONS v98/28 p134 Nov 11 1988.

HICKAM AIR FORCE BASE, HAWAII

Sea Breezes Into Fifth Year. Murphy, Wm. B. MILITARY CLUBS & RECREATION v10/4 p12-13 Apr 1988.

HILLTOP STEAK HOUSE, SAUGUS, MA

HillTop: Hilltop Steak House Keeps Packing 'Em In. Carlino, Bill. NATION'S RESTAURANT NEWS v22/40 pF86-F91 Oct 3 1988.

HILTON

*An Analysis Of Stock Market Performance: The Dow Jones Industrial Average And The Three Top Performing Lodging Firms 1982–1988. Ringstrom, N. H.; Moncarz, Elisa S. FIU HOSPITALITY REVIEW v6/2 p28-54 Fall 1988.

Test Your Knowledge: Falling Through The Cracks: No-Competition Agreements. HOSPITALITY LAW v3/12 p5-6 Dec 1988.

Hilton Invests In Las Vegas. Lalli, Sergio. HOTEL & MOTEL MANAGEMENT v203/8 p3+ May 30 1988.

Hilton International Relies On Hybrid Global Network. HOTEL & MOTEL MANAGEMENT v203/1 p76-77 Jan 11 1988.

Hilton Pushes Unity For Strength: Renovations Help Put Company Earnings At Record Level. DeLuca, Michael. HOTEL & MOTEL MANAGEMENT v203/14 p1+ Sep 25 1988.

Hilton Announces Sites For CrestHil. Selwitz, Robert. HOTEL & MOTEL MANAGEMENT v203/14 p3+ Sep 25 1988.

An Interview With: Thomas G. Daly. HOTEL/MOTEL SECURITY & SAFETY MGNT v6/9 p13-15 Aug 1988.

Conference '88: In San Francisco--'Hilton Faces The Future'. O'Connor, Stefani C. HOTEL & RESORT INDUSTRY v11/10 p80-84 Oct 1988.

H&RISpecial Report: All-Suites: Competitors Get Tough Market Share Grows to 4%. Martin, Frances. HOTELS & RESTAURANTS INTL. v22/3 p50-52 Mar 1988.

A Step By Step Approach To Hotel Development: XII: Atlanta's Airport Hilton: Testimonial To Feasibility. LODGING v14/4 p 47-52 Dec 1988.

158

Figure 12.4: Sample Page on Hilton from *Lodging and Restaurant Index*, 1988.

An Analysis of Stock Market Performance:
The Dow Jones Industrial Average and the
Three Top Performing Lodging Firms
1982 – 1988

by
N. H. Ringstrom, Professor
and

Elisa S. Moncarz, Associate Professor
School of Hospitality Management
Florida International University

An interesting comparison can be made between the Dow Jones Industrial Average and the three top performing, publicly held lodging firms which had $100 million or more in annual lodging revenues. The authors provide that analytical comparison with Prime Motor Inns, Inc., the Marriott Corporation, and Hilton Hotels Corporation.

In an attempt to determine how selected hospitality stocks had fared since the beginning of the Bull Market until more recent times, a study was undertaken. Obviously a detailed examination of all hospitality firms was not feasible for the period in question. The field was thus narrowed down to only selected hotel companies. Based on a criterion of size, only those with $100 million in annual lodging revenues or more resulted in the inclusion of the following six major hotel firms: Prime Motor Inns, Inc., Marriott Corporation, Hilton Hotels Corporation, Ramada Inc., Holiday Corporation and La Quinta Motor Inns, Inc.

The study was commenced by collecting data on the closing stock prices for each company on the last day of each month for the period July 1982–January 1988 (all amounts were rounded to the nearest dollar). Preliminary analysis indicated that of these six firms, the three best performers were Prime Motor Inns, Marriott, and Hilton. More detailed study was thus limited to these last named companies.

The detailed performance of each firm's stock prices can be observed in the appropriate chart for that company. Short-term trend movements during selected time periods were observed both upward and downward. Then appropriate percentage changes, increases, or decreases were obtained for each period.

These percentage changes for each company were then matched against comparable percentage changes in the Dow Jones Industrial Average (DJIA) period-for-period. Observations could thus be made as to whether the firm outperformed the Dow during a given period

Figure 12.5: Article by N. H. Ringstrom and Elisa S. Moncarz from
F.I.U. Hospitality Review 6:2 (Fall 1988).

3) Some libraries restrict the service to certain types of users.

Interlibrary loan policies will differ among libraries. Check with your library's interlibrary loan office to see if you are eligible for the service, and, if so, what the costs are.

CARD CATALOGS

Although the card catalog is extremely important to most search strategies, it usually plays a less important role for industry and company information. This is true for two reasons:

1) Even though a book may have been published in the last year, the lead time for book publishing typically is one to five years. Therefore, the information is not recent enough for a current overview, survey, or forecast.

2) Very few books are written on companies. Some of the very large and older companies do have books written about them, but be careful to determine if such a work is a self-commissioned history. These are usually complimentary and descriptive in nature, and they do not provide a critical analysis of the company. Also, you will want to be alert to the publication date of the book, as mentioned above.

Whether your library has an online catalog or a traditional card catalog, you should check for books on your industry and company. You may be fortunate and find a very recent work on your industry or company. Figure 12.6 illustrates two cards found in a card catalog—one on the lodging industry and one on Hilton Hotels Corporation.

LOCAL RESOURCES

Many libraries actively collect information on local industries and companies. Some libraries may index the local newspaper or local and state periodicals. If so, that index may lead to valuable information on local industry trends and small companies not available elsewhere. Since libraries arrange this information in various formats, it is wise to ask a reference librarian for leads to these resources.

If you were to ask a reference librarian in Tucson for information about the local hotel industry, they would probably show you the *Index to Arizona News in the Arizona Daily Star* (Tucson: University of Arizona Library, 1953-). Many large academic and public libraries index their local newpaper(s). Ask a reference librarian if your library has such an index.

149

```
                 HOTELS, TAVERNS, ETC.---UNITED STATES
                      --STATISTICS.
338.476479473
G585h        Gomes, Albert J.
                 Hospitality in transition : a
             retrospective and prospective look at
             the U.S. lodging industry / Albert J.
             Gomes. -- Houston, Tx. : Pannell Kerr
             Forster, Houston Administrative Office,
             c1985.
                 viii, 166 p. : ill. ; 23 cm.
                 Bibliography: p. 161-165.




                 1. Hotels, taverns, etc.--United
             States--Statistics.  2. Motels--United
             States--Statistics.  I. Title


     InLP     10 APR 36     13148708   IPLHst        85-72663
```

```
                 HILTON, CONRAD NICHOLSON, L887-

926.4794
H563a        Hilton, Conrad Nicholson, 1887-
                 Be my guest. Englewood Cliffs, N.J.,
             Prentice-Hall [c1957]
                 238 p. illus. 18 cm.
                 Autobiography.






                 1. Hilton, Conrad Nicholson, L887-
             I. Title

     InLP     17 JAN 83     37- .53   IPLHst
```

Figure 12.6: Catalog Cards for *Hospitality in Transition* by Albert J. Gomes
and *Be My Guest* by Conrad Hilton.

Looking at figure 12.7, the heading "HOTELS AND MOTELS" in the January-March 1989 issue of the *Index to Arizona News in the Arizona Daily Star* reveals over twenty references. In addition to references about local companies and business dealings, note that one reference, marked with the arrow, talks about "occupancy." That article is reproduced in figure 12.8.

In addition to local resources found in the library, there may be local organizations such as the Chamber of Commerce or economic development office that can assist you. Always remember that a reference librarian is a valuable resource for locating information on questions you may have.

```
at 4 Carondelet heal'      `ters in So Ariz   Je 6 1/3

HOTELS AND MOTELS ◄──Subject
(see also DUDE RANC           PALOMA)
(for items on the se      .otels, motels, resorts, see REAL ESTATE)
owners of Holiday Inn ∟ıoadway want the city to help them expand instead of
building a new hotel at TCC  F 8 B 1/1
Holiday Inn-Broadway Partners wants control of the Convention Center, but th∢
Arts District opposes their scheduling arts events  F 10 B 1/1
Culture Shock, ed against control of the Convention Center by the Hilton Inn
Broadway Partners  F 17 14/1
TCC is being pressured by convention officials and Holiday Inn to provide mo:
hotel rooms for the expanded TCC  F 17 C 5/1
survey of 9 local resorts indicate many are nearly full;  the big 3 resorts
Loew's Ventana Canyon, Westin La Paloma and Sheraton Tucson El Conquistador
say there is room for one more  F 27 Outlook 8/1
Hotel Congress, established in 1919, has been redesigned, is makinc      ⌐me-
back, illus (artist L Boyce)  Mr 11 B 14/2
hotel market is holding its own, graph of occupancy  Mr 14 D 1/2 ◄──────
Kroeger family was taken with dream of El Presidio Hotel (1928),
B Henry feature  Mr 15 B 6/1
hostelry business is booming;  with LPGA Open and basketball tournam⌐⌐, the
"No Vacancy" signs are up  Mr 17 C 9/4
Ramada Inn to sell its 825 hotels and motels to Hong Kong development firm,
to concentrate on its 3 gambling casinos  Ap 16 B 10/2
Sierra Club objects to plans for expanding Grand Canyon Nat'l Park's North
Rim hotel and restaurant, map  My 4 B 1/1
Howard and Frances Schonwit buy 85-yr-old Copper Queen Hotel of Old Bisbee
My 24 B 11/4
profile of Gary Lind, exec asst mgr of Westin La Paloma, biog info, port
My 28 F Moneyplus 2/1
city's lodging industry is brighter, but analyst says city has enough, graph,
breakdown of visitor type  Je 9 C 9/1
Sierra Club obtains court order to bar construction of new hotel on North Rin
of the Grand Canyon  Je 11 B 4/5

HOUSING
(see also HOMELESS)
10 families win chance to buy bargain homes, in city-sponsored lottery, in
Demonstration Homeownership Program  F 3 B 4/1
"Smart House" is a computerized home to help cerebral palsy victim P Suedkamı
to be a "living laboratory" for housing for the handicapped, illus F 19 C 1/]
Primavera Foundation to build apts for single parents and their children, on
the southside, despite protests  Ap 18 B 1/5:  plan killed  Ap 20 B 1/5

HOYUNGOWA, CRAIG (HOPI INDIAN)
Hopi man pleads guilty to charges of 2nd degree murder in '88 killing of Hopi
tribal police officer  My 3 B 2/5

HUGHES AIRCRAFT
(for items on the TCE contamination, see WATER POLLUTION)
PHH Homequity, relocation firm in Calif, works to ease the qualms of Hughes

                            70
```

Figure 12.7: Entry under "Hotels and Motels" in
Index to Arizona News in the Arizona Daily Star, January-June 1989.

Hotel market in Tucson holds its own

Average occupancy reached 60% in '88

By Bob Christman
The Arizona Daily Star

Tucson had a 60 percent average occupancy rate for its major hotels and resorts in 1988, enough to beat out the statewide 59 percent average and Phoenix's 57 percent average.

However, Daniel B. Oaks, manager of Pannell Kerr Forster public accountants in Phoenix, said his company's survey indicates Tucson's success resulted more from a lack of additional supply than an increase in demand.

In 1988, new room supply was up only 3.4 percent in Tucson over the previous year, he said. Between 1986 and 1987, supply jumped 16.2 percent.

Because additional rooms will increase by only 111 for a total 8,602 this year, demand in Tucson is expected to outstrip supply. The overall average occupancy rate will creep up to 61 percent in 1989, Oaks predicted. The rate was 58 percent in 1987.

Average room rates for what's called a "major lodging facility" in Tucson increased to $60 last year, up $2 from the previous year. The demand-supply pinch is expected to push room rates up another $2 average this year.

A major lodging facility is defined in the survey as one that has an average room rate of at least $23, has "a well-recognized and reputable position in its respective market, is open throughout the year, and is operated exclusively as a hotel."

Oaks said the higher demand vs. supply in 1989 also likely will lessen the

Tucson's hotels		1986	1987	1988	1989*
Northwest	No. of rooms	1,554	1,864	1,864	1,864
	Occupancy rate	55%	60%	63%	66%
	Avg. room rate	$76	$83	$87	$92
Northeast	No. of rooms	1,013	1,239	1,241	1,241
	Occupancy rate	58%	57%	58%	61%
	Avg. room rate	$74	$74	$78	$83
Downtown	No. of rooms	2,125	2,124	2,090	2,089
	Occupancy rate	53%	51%	51%	51%
	Avg. room rate	$39	$39	$42	$43
Central	No. of rooms	1,406	1,622	1,620	1,620
	Occupancy rate	56%	63%	67%	71%
	Avg. room rate	$56	$55	$54	$55
Airport	No. of rooms	1,325	1,597	1,676	1,788
	Occupancy rate	65%	60%	60%	60%
	Avg. room rate	$41	$40	$40	$41

*Projections.   Source: Pannell Kerr Forster

Jon Hassen, The Arizona Daily Star

need to heavily discount rates to get business in Tucson.

And, "providing demand growth continues at a level close to current levels, the Tucson metropolitan lodging market should become a strong market over the next few years," he said.

The Tucson lodging market is divided into five sectors in the survey. Four of the sectors averaged 62 percent occupancy last year. But the downtown sector had a 51 percent average occupancy last year, and room use this year is expected to be unchanged from 1988, the survey says.

In contrast, hotels in the central Tucson market had the highest average occupancy rate in Tucson with 67 percent, and occupancy is projected at 71 percent this year.

Oaks said downtown Tucson is faced with competition from other sectors, and he supported the contention of Tucson officials that the expanding Tucson Convention Center needs an adjoining hotel.

"If you have a convention center, you need to have a strong, quality, nationally affiliated hotel to entice meeting planners," he said.

Oaks said the average occupancy rate in Phoenix is down because of the addition of new rooms there. But he said the demand in Phoenix should begin to catch supply this year, resulting in better occupancy rates.

Concerning resorts, Oaks said Tucson's three major resort hotels are doing well, "and Tucson is getting above its fair share of demand, compared with Phoenix."

"Tucson competes directly with Phoenix in terms of resorts. Tucson can be mentioned in the same breath as Phoenix and Palm Springs in terms of resorts," he said.

"It's important for people in Tucson to realize they have a viable resort community. It is doing a little better than Phoenix, and certainly it is holding its own against the state."

U.S. banks earned record profit last year, says FDIC

WASHINGTON (AP) — U.S. banks earned a record $25.3 billion last ... the gov...

the third quarter.

... is the first time we have ever ...

commercial banks earned ... up from $3.7 b... the ...

Figure 12.8: Article on Hotel Market in Tucson from *Arizona Daily Star*, 14 March 1989.

153

SUMMARY

1) Business research guides can lead you to hundreds of other valuable and specialized resources not mentioned in this book.

2) Specialized indexes can lead you to periodical and journal articles not indexed in the major business indexes.

3) The library's interlibrary loan service can borrow items for you from other libraries.

4) The card catalog plays a minor role in industry and company research, but it might yield a valuable resource.

5) Local resources and organizations may lead you to unique information.

6) A reference librarian should always be consulted to make sure you have not overlooked a valuable or unique resource.

LIBRARY SKILLS TEST

A: The Catalog Card

Directions: Use the catalog card pictured below to answer the following questions.

Questions:

1) Would this card be filed under "The," "Lundberg," or "hotel?"
2) Is this item part of a series?
3) How many pages are in the book?
4) Where else would cards be filed in the catalog for this book? (Mark all that pertain.)
   a) Hotels, taverns, etc.
   b) Lundberg, Donald E.
   c) Bibliography
   d) CBI Pub. Co.
   e) Restaurants, lunch rooms, etc.

```
                  The hotel and restaurant business

  TX
  911       Lundberg, Donald E.
  L785          The hotel and restaurant business /
  1979       Donald E. Lundberg. -- 3d ed. -- Boston
             : CBI Pub. Co., c1979.
                378 p. : ill. ; 28 cm.
                Bibliography: p. [367]-368.
                Includes index.




                1. Hotels, taverns, etc.
                2. Restaurants, lunch rooms, etc.
                I. Title

  AzU      25 JUN 80      4591341   AZUAat         79-207
```

**Catalog Card for *The Hotel and Restaurant Business*,
3d ed. by Donald E. Lundberg.**

B: A Periodical Index

Directions: Use the sections from *Business Periodicals Index* pictured on the right to answer the following questions.

Questions:

1) How would you find the full title of the periodical that has an article entitled, "Hoteliers must address the employee-shortage problem?"

2) What is the complete date of this article?

3) On what page(s) is the article printed?

4) What volume is it in?

5) Under what subject heading is the article listed?

6) What other subject headings could you use to locate additional articles on this subject?

Hotels and motels —Design and construction—*cont.*
New Golden Nugget shows Wynn's confidence in Vegas [casino resort, Las Vegas, Nev.] S. Lalli. *Hotel Motel Manage* 202:2+ N 2 '87
Olympics visitors should rest easy; Canadian hotel beefs up footings around flowing water [on Lake Louise near Calgary] M. P. Sponseller and S. Browne. il *ENR* 220:50-1 Ja 21 '88
Patent obtained for environmentally controlled buildings [James A. Rhodes & Assoc.] P. M. LaHue. il *Hotel Motel Manage* 203:3+ Ja 11 '88
Poor management, overbuilding are main hotel woes. D. Ciandella. *Natl Real Estate Investor* 29:30+ D '87
Quality Inns and Benchmark open courtyard hotel. M. J. Hess. *Natl Real Estate Investor* 29:32+ Je '87
Quality's McSleep Inn is the awaited better mousetrap [editor] M. DeLuca. *Hotel Motel Manage* 202:6 O 12 '87
Quality's newest entry: McSleep. M. DeLuca. *Hotel Motel Manage* 202:1+ S 28 '87
Radisson will add 40 all-suites. T. Breen. il *Hotel Motel Manage* 202:1+ Je 8 '87
Referendum approval dooms historic Huntington Sheraton [Pasadena. Calif.] K. Seal. il *Hotel Motel Manage* 202:2+ Je 29 '87
Staggered-truss system saves on building costs. il *Hotel Motel Manage* 202:56 Ap 27 '87
Travelers in wheelchairs deserve proper accommodations. M. Joyce. *Hotel Motel Manage* 202:92-3 N 2 '87
Directories
Franchise company scorecard. *Hotel Motel Manage* 202:72 S 7 '87
Guide to 10 top hotels in six major business cities [Atlanta, Chicago, Dallas, Los Angeles, New York and Washington, D.C.] *Bus Mon* 129:66+ Ap '87
Luxurious living away from home [GuestPlus nationwide club] *Sales Mark Manage* 139:53 Ag '87
Technology show yellow pages [directory of manufacturers of hotel products and services] *Hotel Motel Manage* 202:72+ Ap 13 '87
Employees
See also
Collective bargaining—Hotels and motels
Concierges
Hotels and motels—Personnel management
Women in the hotel and motel industry
Compassion, communication are keys to dealing with AIDS. B. Gatty. *Hotel Motel Manage* 202:3+ N 23 '87
Copley maids fight orders, retain mops [Boston's Copley Plaza Hotel] M. Fisher. *Hotel Motel Manage* 203:2+ F 1 '88
Employee drug use: just say no [hotels, restaurants] R. A. Palmer. *Cornell Hotel Restaur Adm Q* 28:20-2 My '87
Ergonomics can be key to boosting reservation sales [hotel reservation agents] E. Garely. *Hotel Motel Manage* 202:40-1 O 12 '87
Hair style tests appearance policy [cornrow hairstyle] C. Blalock. *Hotel Motel Manage* 203:3+ F 22 '88
Hotel near Washington first to be fined under new law [immigration law and other issues] B. Gatty. *Hotel Motel Manage* 202:18+ D 14 '87
Hoteliers must address the employee-shortage problem. A. Marshall. *Hotel Motel Manage* 203:17+ F 22 '88
Housekeepers gaining deserved respect. M. Fisher. *Hotel Motel Manage* 202:26+ N 23 '87
Image-boosting effort can help attract career-seekers. B. Thomas. *Hotel Motel Manage* 202:50 Je 8 '87

Sample Citation on "Hotels and Motels" from *Business Periodicals Index*, 1987/88.

ANSWERS TO THE LIBRARY SKILLS TEST

A: The Catalog Card

1) "hotel." This is a replica of the "title card" that would be filed in the catalog under title. When the initial word is "a," "an," or "the," it is ignored.

2) This volume is not part of a series. If it were, the series title would appear at the end of the "collation line." This is the line on which the number of pages and size of the volume are given. In this case, a series title would come after "378 p. : ill. ; 28 cm."

3) 378 pages.

4) a) Yes. This is one of two subject headings for this book, which are listed at the bottom of the card. The fact that the heading is preceded by an Arabic numeral is the clue that it is a subject heading.

   b) Yes. He is the author of this book, and the author always has an author card in the catalog.

   c) No. "Bibliography" is a note about the existence and location of a bibliography in the book. This will not appear as a heading in the catalog.

   d) No. "CBI Pub. Co." is the publisher. Sometimes a publisher will be listed in the catalog if it had something to do with the authorship of the volume. This frequently happens for government bodies and organizations who both sponsor research and study and then publish the results. An example is the American Hotel and Motel Association. If the publisher is to be given an entry, there will be a numbered item at the bottom of the card, such as "II. CBI Pub. Co."

   e) Yes. This is the other subject heading, as listed at the bottom of the card.

ANSWERS TO THE LIBRARY USE QUIZ (CONTINUED)

B: A Periodical Index

1) Look in the list of periodicals at the front of *Business Periodicals Index.* Here you will find a section called "Abbreviations of Periodicals Indexed." Most periodical indexes have such a list, which decodes the abbreviated titles. In this case the full title of the periodical with the abbreviation "Hotel Motel Manage" is *Hotel & Motel Management.*

2) February 22, 1988.

3) It begins on page 17. The + indicates that the article is continued on another page.

4) Volume 203.

5) The main subject heading is "Hotels and motels," as indicated at the top left of the page. However, because of the large number of articles under this heading, this article appears under the subheading "Employees." The subject heading for this article is:

   "Hotels and motels—Employees"

6) Looking back at the "See also" references listed at the beginning of the "Employees" subheading, you will locate these cross-references:

   "Collective bargaining—Hotels and motels,"
   "Concierges,"
   "Hotels and motels—Personnel management," and
   "Women in the hotel and motel industry."

APPENDIX B

ADDITIONAL RESOURCE MATERIALS: A BIBLIOGRAPHY

This bibliography is intended to list materials that are similar to the works illustrated in each chapter, and, therefore, is arranged in the same order as the chapters in the book. In the main body of the book we have tried to choose the most well-known and widely available reference materials to illustrate, but in many cases there are several similar titles that could have been substituted. Not all libraries will have all the titles we have chosen. If the title illustrated is not available, check in this bibliography for other choices or ask your reference librarian to show you additional similar sources.

CHAPTER 2 — ONLINE SEARCH MANUALS AND DIRECTORIES

Batt, Fred. *Online Searching for End Users: An Information Sourcebook.* Phoenix, AZ: Oryx Press, 1988. 116 p.

Directory of Online Databases. New York: Cuadra/Elsevier, 1979— . Quarterly.

Fenichel, Carol H., and Thomas H. Hogan. *Online Searching: A Primer.* Marlton, NJ: Learned Information, 1981. 152 p.

Hoover, Ryan E. *Executive's Guide to Online Information Services.* White Plains, NY: Knowledge Industry Publications, 1984. 296 p.

Howitt, Doran, and, Marvin I. Weinberger. *Inc. Magazine's Databasics: Your Guide to Online Business Information.* New York: Garland, 1984. 614 p.

Lucas, Amy F. *Encyclopedia of Information Systems and Services.* 10th ed. Detroit, MI: Gale Research, 1989. 2 vols.

Mayros, Van, and D. Michael Werner. *Data Bases for Business: Profiles and Applications.* Radnor, PA: Chilton Book Co., 1982. 178 p.

The North American Online Directory: A Directory of Online Information Products & Services with Names & Numbers. New York: R.R. Bowker Co., 1987. 379 p.

Popvich, Charles J. *Business and Economics Databases Online: Environmental Scanning with a Personal Computer*. Littleton, CO: Libraries Unlimited, 1987. 276 p.

Scanlon, Jean M., Ulla de Stricker, and Anne Conway Fernald. *Business Online: The Professionals Guide to Electronic Information Sources*. New York: John Wiley and Sons, 1989. 368 p.

CHAPTER 2 — ONLINE DATABASES

ABI/INFORM. Louisville, KY: UMI/Data Courier, 1971— . Weekly.
    Provides citations and abstracts of articles from over 800 business journals. No print counterpart.

Business Dateline. Louisville, KY: UMI/Data Courier, 1985— . Weekly.
    Provides full text of major articles from U.S. and Canadian regional business publications.

Business NewsBank. New Canaan, CT: NewsBank, Inc., 1986— . Monthly.
    Provides references from the newspapers and regional business publications of over 450 U.S. cities. Emphasis is on companies, especially small and privately held ones. Full text of the articles is available on microfiche. Corresponds to the printed publication of the same name.

Business Periodicals Index. Bronx, NY: H. W. Wilson, 1982— . Twice a week.
    Provides citations to journal articles from over 300 business journals; it is the online version of the index with the same name.

Corporate Affiliations. Wilmette, IL: National Register Publishing Company. Quarterly.
    Corresponds to the printed *Directory of Corporate Affiliations*. It lists corporate family structures (i.e., "who owns whom" information). In addition, it includes address, telephone number, ticker symbol, stock exchange, SIC codes and descriptions, number of employees, total assets, sales, net worth, and names of executives and directors.

Corporate and Industry Research Reports (CIRR). Eastchester, NY: JA Micropublishing. Monthly.
    Provides indexes and abstracts of analytical research reports prepared by leading analysts and economists from regional, national, and international securities and investment firms. Corresponds to the printed publication with the same name.

D&B—Canadian Dun's Market Identifiers. Parsippany, NJ: Dun's Marketing Services. Quarterly.

Includes addresses with financial and marketing data for more than 350,000 Canadian companies. No printed counterpart.

D&B—Dun's Electronic Business Directory. Parsippany, NJ: Dun's Marketing Services. Quarterly.

Provides directory information for over eight and one-half million businesses and professionals in the United States. Includes addresses, telephone numbers, SIC codes and descriptions, and employee size ranges. Covers private and public companies. Despite its name, this file is not intended to reflect the information contained in printed yellow pages.

D&B—Dun's Financial Records Plus. Murray Hill, NJ: Dun & Bradstreet Credit Services. Quarterly.

Contains financial information, complete spreadsheet analysis, industry comparisons, and company history and operations information on over 750,000 U.S. businesses. An additional 750,000 private companies are included with history and operations information only. This file has the most complete data available online for private company research. However, it is very expensive to search; be sure to ask for a cost estimate.

D&B—Dun's Market Identifiers. Parsippany, NJ: Dun's Marketing Services. Quarterly.

Contains current addresses with brief financial and marketing information on nearly 2.3 million U.S. businesses. No printed counterpart.

D&B—International Dun's Market Identifiers. Parsippany, NJ: Dun's Marketing Services. Quarterly.

Contains directory listings, sales volume, and marketing data for over 475,000 leading companies around the world. Corresponds in part to the *Principal International Businesses Directory*.

D&B—Million Dollar Directory. Parsippany, NJ: Dun's Marketing Services. Annual.

Provides directory information for over 160,000 companies with a net worth over one-half million dollars. Includes both public and privately owned companies. Equivalent to the five-volume printed *Million Dollar Directory*.

Disclosure and *Compact Disclosure*. Bethesda, MD: Disclosure Information Group.

Provides business and financial information extracted from the annual reports and financial reports of over 1,200 publicly owned companies. *Disclosure* is the online version; *Compact Disclosure* is the CD-ROM version.

FINDex. Gaithersburg, MD: National Standards Associations, Inc., 1977— . Quarterly.
   Indexes and abstracts commercially available industry and marketing research reports produced by research firms. Corresponds to the printed *FINDex: The Directory of Market Research Reports, Studies, and Surveys*.

HBR/Online (Harvard Business Review). New York: Wiley, 1971— . Bimonthly.
   Contains the full text of the articles appearing in the *Harvard Business Review* since 1976 plus abstracts of articles in the journal from 1971 to 1975.

Management Contents. Belmont, CA: Information Access Company, 1974— . Monthly.
   Indexes and abstracts journal articles from over 700 U.S. and international journals on all aspects of business and management. Printed counterpart is *Business Publications Index and Abstracts*.

Media General Plus. Richmond, VA: Media General Financial Services, Inc. Weekly.
   Provides detailed financial and stock price information on public companies listed on the New York Stock Exchange and the American Stock Exchange, plus all NASDAQ National Market Systems companies and selected over-the-counter (OTC) companies.

Moody's Corporate News—U.S. New York: Moody's Investor Services, Inc., 1983— . Weekly.
   Has current business news and financial information on 13,000 publicly held U.S. companies. Information is in text and tabular format and includes earnings reports and balance sheets. A corresponding file on international companies is called *Moody's Corporate News—International*.

Moody's Corporate Profiles. New York: Moody's Investor Services, Inc. Weekly.
   Provides descriptive and financial information on publicly held U.S. companies listed on the New York Stock Exchange, the American Stock Exchange, and over 1,000 of the most active emerging over-the-counter (OTC) companies.

PAIS International. New York: Public Affairs Information Service, Inc., 1972— . Monthly.
   Indexes public policy literature of business, economics, finance, law, international relations, government, political science, and other social sciences.

PTS Annual Reports Abstracts. Cleveland, OH: Predicasts. Monthly.
   Abstracts information from the annual reports issued by over 3,000 publicly held U.S. corporations and selected international companies.

PTS F&S Index. Cleveland, OH: Predicasts, 1972— . Weekly.
   Indexes U.S. and international company, product, and industry information from a wide range of business publications. Excellent source for merger & acquisition information as well as new product information. Corresponds to *Predicasts F&S Index United States, Predicasts F&S Index Europe, and Predicasts F&S Index International*.

PTS PROMT. Cleveland, OH: Predicasts, 1972— . Daily.

Abstracts the significant information appearing in thousands of newspapers, business magazines, government reports, trade journals, and special reports throughout the world. Corresponds to the printed publication with the same name.

PTS U.S. Forecasts. Cleveland, OH: Predicasts, 1971— . Monthly.

Contains abstracts of market, product, industry, and economic forecasts for the United States published in trade journals, business and financial publications, newspapers, government reports, and special studies. Corresponds to the printed product *Predicasts Forecasts*.

Standard & Poor's Corporate Descriptions Online. New York: Standard & Poor's/McGraw-Hill. Biweekly.

Provides detailed descriptions of over 9,000 publicly held companies including background information, income and balance sheet figures, and stock and bond data. Corresponds to *Standard Corporation Descriptions*.

Standard & Poor's News. New York: Standard & Poor's/McGraw-Hill 1979—. Daily.

Provides general and financial information on publicly owned U.S. companies. Equivalent to the printed *Standard & Poor's Corporation Records Daily News* and *Cumulative News*.

Standard & Poor's Register—Corporate. New York: Standard & Poor's/McGraw-Hill. Quarterly.

Provides basic facts on 45,000 leading public and private U.S. companies. Records include address, listing of officers and directors with positions, and brief financial information. Corresponds to the printed publication *Standard & Poor's Register of Corporations*, volume one.

Trinet Company Database and *Trinet U.S. Businesses*. Parsippany, NJ: Trinet, Inc. Quarterly.

Provides directory, financial, and marketing information on U.S. single and multi-establishment companies. Covers private and public companies. Printed equivalents are *Trinet Top 1,500 Companies, Trinet Second 1,500 Companies*, and *Trinet Top 1,500 Private Companies*.

CHAPTER 3 — INDUSTRY OVERVIEWS

Darnay, Arsen J., ed. *Manufacturing USA: Industry Analyses, Statistics, and Leading Companies*. Detroit, MI: Gale Research Inc., 1991. 1755 p.

The Dow Jones-Irwin Business and Investment Almanac. Homewood, IL: Dow Jones-Irwin, 1982— . Annual.

Moody's Investors Service. *Moody's Industry Review*. New York: Moody's Investors Service, 1978— . Loose-leaf service with weekly updates.

Rukeyser, L., editor-in-chief. *Louis Rukeyser's Business Almanac*. New York: Simon and Schuster, 1988. 704 p.

U. S. Department of Commerce. International Trade Administration. *U.S. Industrial Outlook*. Washington, DC: U.S. Government Printing Office, 1984— . Annual.

CHAPTER 4 — PERIODICAL AND NEWSPAPER INDEXES

Business NewsBank. New Canaan, CT: Newsbank, Inc., 1985— . Quarterly.

Business Publications Index and Abstracts. Detroit, MI: Gale Research, 1983— . Monthly.

The New York Times Index. New York: New York Times Co., 1913— . Semimonthly.

Predicasts F & S Index Europe. Cleveland, OH: Predicasts, 1979— . Monthly.

Predicasts F & S Index International. Cleveland, OH: Predicasts, 1979— . Monthly.

PROMT, Predicasts Overview of Markets and Technology. Cleveland, OH: Predicasts, 1977— . Monthly.

Public Affairs Information Service Bulletin. New York: Public Affairs Information Service, 1915— . Bimonthly.

CHAPTER 4 — PERIODICAL DIRECTORIES

Editor & Publisher International Year Book. New York: Editor & Publisher Co., 1959— . Annual.

Gale Directory of Publications and Broadcast Media. Detroit, MI: Gale Research, 1990— . Annual.

Geahigan, Priscilla C., and Robert F. Rose. *Business Serials of the U.S. Government*, 2d ed. Chicago: American Library Association, 1988. 86 p.

Newsletters in Print. Detroit, MI: Gale Research, 1988— . Annual.

Oxbridge Directory of Newsletters. New York: Oxbridge Communications, Inc., 1979—. Annual.

The Serials Directory: An International Reference Book. Birmingham, AL: EBSCO Publishing, 1986— . Annual (with quarterly updates).

The Standard Periodical Directory. New York, Oxbridge Pub. Co., 1964/65— . Biennial.

Working Press of the Nation. Burlington, IA: National Research Bureau, 1945— . Annual.

CHAPTER 5 — STATISTICS

Economic Statistics Bureau of Washington, DC. *The Handbook of Basic Economic Statistics.* Washington, DC: Economic Statistics Bureau, 1947— . Monthly.

Predicasts Basebook. Cleveland, OH: Predicasts, 1974— . Annual.

Predicasts Forecasts. Cleveland, OH: Predicasts, 1980— . Quarterly (with annual cumulations).

Sears, Jean L., and Marilyn K. Moody. *Using Government Publications.* Volume 2: *Finding Statistics and Using Special Techniques.* Phoenix, AZ: Oryx Press, 1986.

Standard & Poor's Statistical Service. New York: Standard & Poor's Corporation, 1977— . Loose-leaf service for updating.

Statistical Services Directory. Detroit, MI: Gale Research, 1982— . Annual.

United States. Bureau of Economic Analysis; and United States. Bureau of Foreign and Domestic Commerce. *Survey of Current Business.* Washington, DC: U.S. Government Printing Office, 1921— . Monthly.

United States. Bureau of Economic Analysis. *Business Statistics.* [Statistical supplement to the *Survey of Current Business*]. Washington, DC: U.S. Government Printing Office, 1973— . Biennial.

United States. Bureau of the Census. *County and City Data Book.* Washington, DC: U.S. Government Printing Office, 1949— . Irregular.

United States. Bureau of the Census. *Historical Statistics of the United States, Colonial Times to 1970.* Bicentennial ed. Washington, DC: U.S. Government Printing Office, 1975. 2 vols.

United States. Bureau of the Census. *State and Metropolitan Area Data Book*. Washington, DC: U.S. Government Printing Office, 1979— . Annual.

Wasserman, Paul. *Statistics Sources*. Detroit, MI: Gale Research, 1962— . Irregular.

CHAPTER 6 — ASSOCIATIONS

Allard, Denise M., ed. *Organizations Master Index*. Detroit, MI: Gale Research, 1987. 1120 p.

Encyclopedia of Associations. Regional, State, and Local Organizations. Detroit, MI: Gale Research, 1987— . Biennial.

Kruzas, Anthony, Robert C. Thomas, and Kay Gill, eds. *Business Organizations and Agencies Directory: A Guide to Trade, Business, and Commercial Organizations, Government Agencies, Stock Exchanges, Labor Unions, Chambers of Commerce, Diplomatic Representation, Trade and Convention Centers, Trade Fairs, Publishers, Data Banks and Computerized Services, Educational Institutions, Research Centers, and Libraries and Information Centers*. 4th ed. Detroit, MI: Gale Research, 1988. 2101 p.

Research Centers Directory. Detroit, MI: Gale Research, 1962— . Irregular.

Russell, John J. *National Trade and Professional Associations of the United States*. Washington, DC: Columbia Books, 1982— . Annual.

CHAPTER 6 — DIRECTORIES

FINDex: The Directory of Market Research Reports, Studies and Surveys. New York: FIND/SVP Information Clearinghouse, 1979— . Annual (with updates).

International Directories in Print. Detroit, MI: Gale Research, 1988— . Biennial.

Klein, Bernard. *Guide to American Directories*. Coral Springs, FL: B. Klein Publications, 1960— . Irregular.

Piccirelli, Annette, ed. *Government Research Directory: A Descriptive Guide to Approximately 3,000 U.S. Government Research and Development Centers, Institutes, Laboratories, Bureaus, Test Facilities, Experiment Stations, Data Collection and Analysis Centers, and Grants Management and Research Coordinating Offices in Agriculture, Business, Education, Energy, Engineering, Environment, the Humanities, Medicine, Military Science, and Basic and Applied Sciences*. 6th ed. Detroit, MI: Gale Research, 1991. 1200 p.

Trade Directories of the World. Queens Village, NY: Croner Publications, 1953— . Irregular.

World Chamber of Commerce Directory. Loveland, CO: Worldwide Chamber of Commerce Directory, Inc., 1961— . Annual.

CHAPTER 7 — PRIVATE, PUBLIC, OR SUBSIDIARY COMPANIES?

Predicasts F&S Index of Corporate Change. Cleveland, OH: Predicasts, 1981— . Quarterly.

Principal International Businesses. London: Dun & Bradstreet International, Ltd., 1974— . Annual.

Standard & Poor's Register of Corporations, Directors and Executives. New York: Standard & Poor's Corporation, 1928— . Annual.

Wood, Donna, ed. *Brands and Their Companies*. Detroit, MI: Gale Research, 1990—. Irregular.

Wood, Donna, ed. *Companies and their Brands*. Detroit, MI: Gale Research, 1990— . Irregular.

CHAPTER 8 — PRIVATE COMPANY DIRECTORIES

Contacts Influential. [available for major cities in the United States] Arvada, CO: Contacts Influential. Annual.

Dun's Directory of Service Companies. Parsippany, NJ: Dun's Marketing Services, 1989— . Annual.

Local city directories.

Local telephone directories.

Macmillan Directory of Leading Private Companies. Wilmette, IL: National Register Publishing Co., 1986— . Annual.

Microcosm. [available for major cities in the United States] Mountain Lakes, NJ: Dun's Marketing Services. Semi-annual.

Predicasts Company Thesaurus. Cleveland, OH: Predicasts, 1985— . Annual.

Standard Directory of Advertisers. Skokie, IL: National Register Publishing Co., 1964— . Annual.

State industrial directories.

Thomas Register of American Manufacturers and *Thomas Register Catalog File*. New York: Thomas Publishing Co., 1905/1906— . Annual.

CHAPTER 8 — BUSINESS RANKINGS

Business Rankings Annual 1990, comp. by the Brooklyn Public Library Business Library. Detroit, MI: Gale Research, 1990. 612 p.

Dun's Business Rankings. Parsippany, NJ: Dun's Marketing Services, 1982— . Annual.

Fortune 500 Directory. New York: Time, Inc., 1955— . Annual.

Trinet Directory of Leading U.S. Companies: Top 1,500, Trinet Directory of Leading U.S. Companies: Second 1,500, and *Trinet Directory of Leading U.S. Companies: Private*. Parsippany, NJ: Trinet, Inc., 1984— . Annual.

CHAPTER 9 — PUBLIC COMPANY DIRECTORIES AND INFORMATION

Corporate and Industry Research Reports (CIRR). Eastchester, NY: JA Micropublishing, 1982— . Quarterly.

Moody's Handbook of Common Stocks. New York: Moody's Investors Service, 1965— . Quarterly.

The Outlook. New York: Standard & Poor's Corporation, 1937— . Weekly.

SEC Filing Companies. Washington, DC: Disclosure, Inc., 1981— . Annual.

Standard & Poor's Stock Market Encyclopedia. New York: Standard and Poor's Corporation, 1962— . Semiannual.

Standard & Poor's Stock Reports. New York: Standard & Poor's Corporation, 1973— . Quarterly.

CHAPTER 10 — SUBSIDIARY INFORMATION AND CORPORATE FAMILY STRUCTURES

America's Corporate Families and International Affiliates. Parsippany, NJ: Dun's Marketing Services, 1982— . Annual.

International Directory of Corporate Affiliations. Wilmette, IL: National Register Publishing Co., 1981— . Annual.

Who Owns Whom North America. London: Dun & Bradstreet Ltd., 1969— . Annual.

CHAPTER 11 — FINANCIAL RATIOS

Annual Statement Studies. Philadelphia, PA: Robert Morris Associates, 1964— . Annual.

Financial Studies of the Small Business. Orlando, FL: Financial Research Associates, 1976— . Annual.

IRS Corporate Financial Ratios. 4th ed. Lincolnshire, IL: Schonfeld & Associates, 1990. 239 p.

Troy, Leo. *Almanac of Business and Industrial Financial Ratios.* Englewood Cliffs, NJ: Prentice-Hall, 1971— . Annual.

Troy, Leo. *The Partnership Almanac: A Sourcebook of Financial Data, Trends, and Performance Ratios.* Englewood Cliffs, NJ: Prentice Hall, 1989. 293 p.

CHAPTER 12 — OTHER RESOURCES

Business and Economics Books and Serials in Print. New York: R. R. Bowker Co. 1981— . Irregular.

Daniells, Lorna M. *Business Information Sources.* Rev. ed. Berkeley, CA: University of California Press, 1985. 673 p.

Daniells, Lorna M. *Business Reference Sources: An Annotated Guide for Harvard Business School Students.* Rev. ed. Boston, MA: Baker Library, Graduate School of Business Administration, Harvard University, 1987. 131 p.

Directory of Business and Financial Services. Washington, DC: Special Libraries Association, 1963— . Irregular.

Lavin, Michael R. *Business Information: How to Find It, How to Use It.* Phoenix, AZ: Oryx Press, 1987. 299 p.

Lucas, Amy F. *Encyclopedia of Information Systems and Services*. 10th ed. Detroit, MI: Gale Research, 1989. 2 vols.

Piele, Linda J., John C. Tyson, and Michael B. Sheffey. *Materials & Methods for Business Research*. New York: Libraryworks, 1980. 209 p.

Schlessinger, Bernard S., Rashelle S. Karp, and Virginia S. Vocelli, eds. *The Basic Business Library: Core Resources*. 2d ed. Phoenix, AZ: Oryx Press, 1989. 278 p.

Sears, Jean L., and Marilyn K. Moody. *Using Government Publications*. Phoenix, AZ: Oryx Press, 1985-1986. 2 vols.

Uhlan, Miriam, ed. *Guide to Special Issues and Indexes of Periodicals*. 3d ed. Washington, DC: Special Libraries Association, 1985. 160 p.

Washington Researchers Publishing Staff. *How to Find Information about Companies: The Corporate Intelligence Source Book*. 7th ed. Washington, DC: The Researchers, 1988. 610 p.

INDEX OF TITLES

This index includes only the titles of reference sources covered in the twelve chapters. It excludes sources mentioned but not illustrated, and it also excludes sources listed only in "Appendix B: Additional Resource Materials: A Bibliography."

ABI/INFORM 14-15, 17, 21

Advertising Age 102

American Statistics Index 65, 72

Annals of Tourism Research 44-45

Arizona Daily Star 153

Arizona Lodging Forecast 1989 . . . . 76, 78-79

Business Index 47, 50-51, 53, 59, 99, 101, 106, 123, 126, 128, 146

Business Periodicals Index 17, 47-51, 53, 59, 123-124, 126, 146, 155, 158

Compact Disclosure 113-114

D&B Dun's Financial Record Plus 99

D&B—Dun's Market Identifiers 99-100, 106

D-U-N-S Account Identification Service 98-99, 106

Directories in Print 74, 81-84, 86

Directory of Corporate Affiliations 127-130, 132

Directory of Hotel Systems 103

Encyclopedia of Associations 73-77, 80-81, 86

Encyclopedia of Business Information Sources 142-143

F.I.U. Hospitality Review 146, 148

Guide to SEC Corporate Filings 112

Handbook of Business Information 143-144

Hilton Hotels Corporation's Annual Report 108-110, 113-114, 134

Hilton Hotels Corporation's 10-K Report 111, 113, 128, 131, 134

Hotel & Motel Management 46-47, 105

Hotel and Restaurant Industries 143, 145

Hotel & Travel Index 81, 85

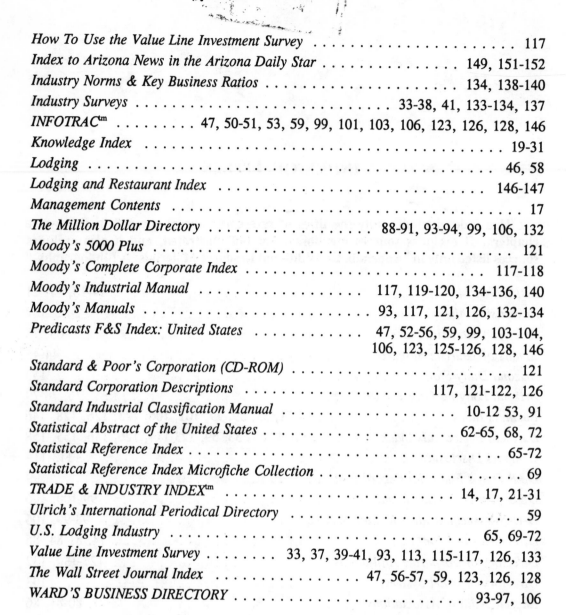

How To Use the Value Line Investment Survey 117

Index to Arizona News in the Arizona Daily Star 149, 151-152

Industry Norms & Key Business Ratios 134, 138-140

Industry Surveys 33-38, 41, 133-134, 137

*INFOTRAC*tm 47, 50-51, 53, 59, 99, 101, 103, 106, 123, 126, 128, 146

Knowledge Index 19-31

Lodging 46, 58

Lodging and Restaurant Index 146-147

Management Contents 17

The Million Dollar Directory 88-91, 93-94, 99, 106, 132

Moody's 5000 Plus 121

Moody's Complete Corporate Index 117-118

Moody's Industrial Manual 117, 119-120, 134-136, 140

Moody's Manuals 93, 117, 121, 126, 132-134

Predicasts F&S Index: United States 47, 52-56, 59, 99, 103-104,
106, 123, 125-126, 128, 146

Standard & Poor's Corporation (CD-ROM) 121

Standard Corporation Descriptions 117, 121-122, 126

Standard Industrial Classification Manual 10-12 53, 91

Statistical Abstract of the United States 62-65, 68, 72

Statistical Reference Index 65-72

Statistical Reference Index Microfiche Collection 69

*TRADE & INDUSTRY INDEX*tm 14, 17, 21-31

Ulrich's International Periodical Directory 59

U.S. Lodging Industry 65, 69-72

Value Line Investment Survey 33, 37, 39-41, 93, 113, 115-117, 126, 133

The Wall Street Journal Index 47, 56-57, 59, 123, 126, 128

WARD'S BUSINESS DIRECTORY 93-97, 106